INTRODUCTION TO WATER RESOURCES

INTRODUCTION TO WATER RESOURCES

John C. Clausen
University of Connecticut

Long Grove, Illinois

For information about this book, contact:
Waveland Press, Inc.
4180 IL Route 83, Suite 101
Long Grove, IL 60047-9580
(847) 634-0081
info@waveland.com
www.waveland.com

Copyright © 2018 by Waveland Press, Inc.

10-digit ISBN 1-4786-2800-6
13-digit ISBN 978-1-4786-2800-2

All rights reserved. No part of this book may be reproduced, stored in a retrieval system, or transmitted in any form or by any means without permission in writing from the publisher.

Printed in the United States of America

7 6 5 4 3 2 1

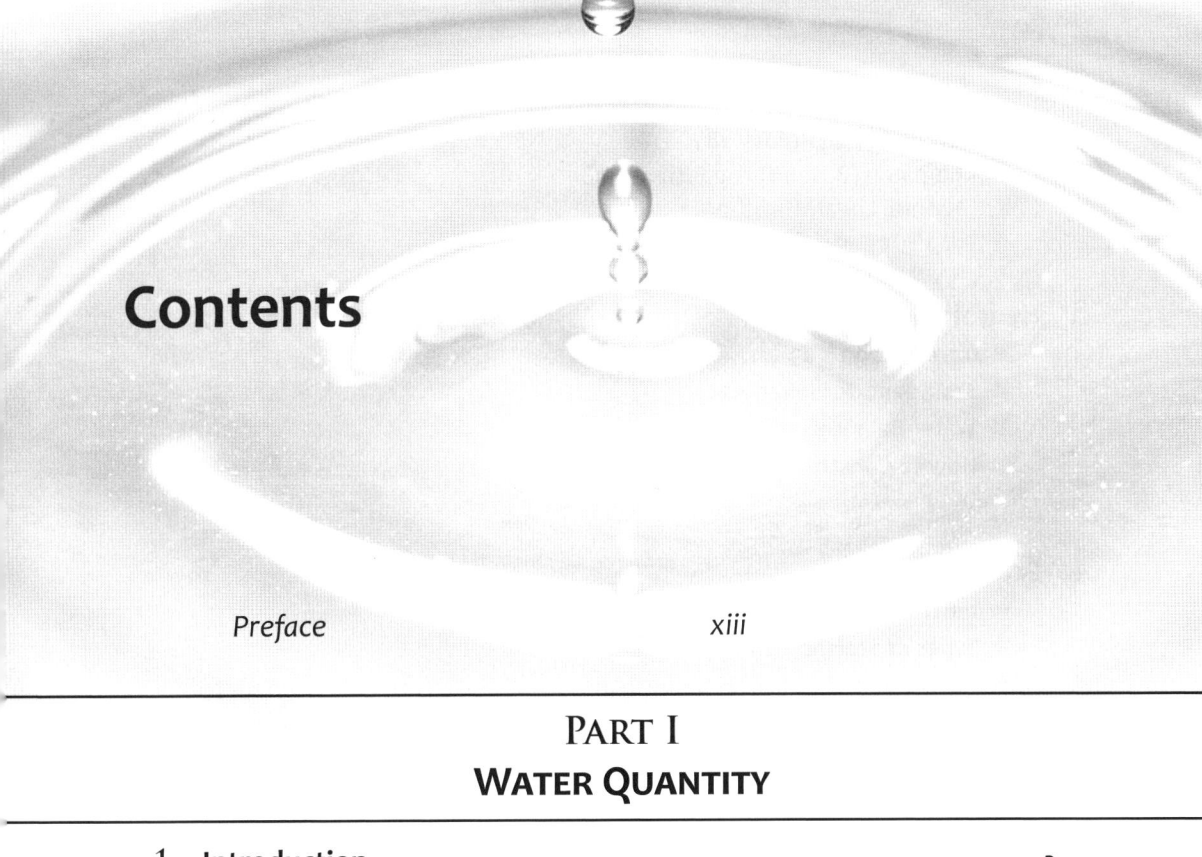

Contents

Preface　　　　　　　　　　xiii

PART I
WATER QUANTITY

1 Introduction　　　3
- Purpose of This Book　4
- What Is Water?　4
- Water Resources Problems　5
- Properties of Water and Their Ecological Implications　7
- Top Ten Concepts in Water Resources　8
  - REFERENCES　10

2 Water Resources Units　　　11
- Introduction　11
- Unit Conversions　13
- Significant Digits　14
  - Rounding Off　15
- Water Quantity Units　15
- Water Quality Units　15
  - Event Mean Concentration (EMC)　15
  - Equivalence Units　16
  - Moles/Liter　17
  - Censored Values　17
  - Mass Export and Loading　17

- **Review of Log Rules** 18
  - Common (Base 10) Logarithms 18
  - Natural Logarithms 20
    - PROBLEMS 20
    - REFERENCES 21

3 Hydrologic Cycle 23
- **Introduction** 23
- **Storages and Fluxes** 25
- **Water Balance** 26
- **How to Construct an Annual Water Budget** 27
  - PROBLEMS 28
  - REFERENCES 28

4 Precipitation 29
- **Introduction** 29
- **Types of Storms** 29
- **Measurement of Precipitation** 30
- **Average Precipitation Methods** 32
  - Arithmetic 32
  - Thiessen Polygons 32
  - Isohyetal 33
  - Watershed Boundary/Mapping 33
- **Precipitation Frequency Analysis** 35
  - Exceedance Probability 35
  - Recurrence Interval 35
- **Errors in Precipitation Measurements** 36
  - PROBLEMS 37
  - REFERENCES 38

5 Interception 39
- **Introduction** 39
- **Measurement of Interception** 40
- **Factors Affecting Interception Loss** 42
  - PROBLEMS 45
  - REFERENCES 45

6 Evapotranspiration 47
- **Introduction** 47
- **Importance** 47
- **Factors Affecting ET** 47
- **Measurement of ET** 48
  - Direct Methods 49
  - Indirect Methods 52
  - Estimates of ET 52

- PET vs. ET   56
    - PROBLEMS   57
    - REFERENCES   58

7 Infiltration and Soil Water   61
- Introduction   61
- Infiltration   61
    - Forces Involved in Infiltration   62
    - Factors Affecting Infiltration   64
    - Measurement of Infiltration   65
    - Infiltration Equations   66
- Soil Water   67
    - Amount of Water   68
    - Energy Status of Water   69
    - Soil Water Terms   71
        - PROBLEMS   73
        - REFERENCES   73

8 Ground Water   75
- Introduction   75
- Ground Water Flow   78
- Effect of a Well   80
- Flow Nets   81
    - PROBLEM   82
    - REFERENCES   82

9 Streamflow   83
- Introduction   83
- Components of Streamflow   84
- Time of Concentration   84
- Basin Lag   85
- Hydrograph Separation   87
- Streamflow Measurement   88
    - Velocity Measurements   90
    - Choosing the Stream Gaging Site   93
- Flood Frequency Analysis   93
- Uncertainties in Estimating Discharge   94
    - PROBLEMS   94
    - REFERENCES   96

10 Watershed Management   99
- Introduction   99
- Water Yield   100
- Streamflow Pattern   102
- Forest (Vegetation) Management   103

- Snowpack Management 103
- Urban Watershed Management 104
- Reservoir Watershed Management 104
    - PROBLEM 105
    - REFERENCES 105

PART II
WATER QUALITY

11 Introduction to Water Quality   109
- Introduction 109
- Water Quality Definitions 110
- Sources of Pollution 110
- Magnitude of the Water Quality Problem 111
    - Surface Water 111
    - Sources of Surface Water Pollutants 111
    - Ground Water 113
    - Pharmaceuticals, Hormones, Steroids 113
- Soil Quality 113
    - PROBLEMS 114
    - REFERENCES 115

12 Physical Characteristics of Water   117
- Introduction 117
- Turbidity 117
- Solids (Residue) 119
- Odor 123
- Temperature 124
- Color 125
- Conductivity 126
    - PROBLEMS 126
    - REFERENCES 127

13 Chemical Characteristics of Water   129
- Introduction 129
- Common Chemical Characteristics of Water 130
- Classification of Chemicals in Water 131
    - Human Influences 132
- Important Chemical Constituents of Water 132
    - pH and Carbonates 132
    - Alkalinity 134
    - Acidity 136

Dissolved Oxygen   136
Biochemical Oxygen Demand   136
Nitrogen   136
Phosphorus   139
- **Methods of Analysis**   142
    - PROBLEM   143
    - REFERENCES   143

14 Biological Characteristics of Water   145
- **Introduction**   145
- **Plankton**   145
    - Phytoplankton   145
    - Zooplankton   151
- **Macroinvertebrates**   154
- **Macrophytes**   156
- **Pathogens in Water**   160
    - Bacteria   160
    - Protozoans   161
    - Viruses   161
- **Bioassay**   161
    - PROBLEM   161
    - REFERENCES   164

15 River Water Quality   167
- **Introduction**   167
- **Physical Processes in Rivers**   167
    - Mixing   168
    - Longitudinal Dispersion Coefficient   168
- **Other River Processes**   170
- **Biological Characteristics of Rivers**   171
    - Water Quality Zones   171
- **Chemical Characteristics of Rivers**   172
    - Reaction Kinetics   172
    - Zero-Order Reactions   173
    - First-Order Reactions   174
    - Reactors   175
    - Reactor Response to Different Inputs   176
- **Dissolved Oxygen**   178
    - Deoxygenation   179
    - Reoxygenation   180
    - Streeter-Phelps Oxygen Sag Equation   180
        - PROBLEMS   184
        - REFERENCES   185

16 Lakes and Reservoir Water Quality — 187

- **Introduction** 187
- **Physical Limnology** 187
  - Physical Origin of Lakes 187
  - Physical Characteristics of Lakes 188
  - Light 189
  - Thermal Stratification 190
  - Seiche 192
- **Biological Characteristics of Lakes** 192
- **Chemical Characteristics of Lakes** 194
  - Oxygen 194
  - Productivity 195
  - Eutrophication 196
  - Carlson Trophic State Index (TSI) 197
  - Prediction Model 197
- **Lake Restoration** 201
  - Algae Techniques 201
  - Macrophyte Techniques 202
    - PROBLEMS 202
    - REFERENCES 204

17 Soil and Ground Water Quality — 205

- **Introduction** 205
- **Soil Water** 205
  - Particulate Pollutant Transport 205
  - Adsorption of Pollutants on Soil Particles 206
  - Phosphorus Soil Index 208
  - Soil Mass Balance 208
  - Toxic Metals in Soils 209
- **Ground Water** 210
  - Contaminant Transport 210
  - Contaminant Remediation 214
    - PROBLEMS 214
    - REFERENCES 215

18 Best Management Practices — 217

- **Introduction** 217
- **Urban Stormwater BMPs** 217
  - Planning and Construction Period 220
  - Post-Construction Period 221
  - Road and Highway BMPs 224
- **Agricultural Practices** 226
  - Erosion and Sediment Control 226

Confined Animal Facility Management   228
Nutrient Management   228
Pesticide Management   229
Grazing Management   230
Irrigation Water Management   231
- **Silvicultural Practices**   232
  - PROBLEM   236
  - REFERENCES   236

PART III
WATER AND SOCIETY

19 Water Laws, Regulations, and Standards   241
- **Introduction**   241
- **Water Quality**   242
- **Federal Regulations and Rules**   246
  - Water Quality Standards   247
  - Stormwater Regulations   247
  - Total Maximum Daily Loads (TMDL)   247
- **Water Quantity**   248
  - Water Rights (Law)   248
  - Basin Transfers   250
  - Drainage Law   251
  - Floodplain Management   251
  - Instream Flows   252
    - REFERENCES   252

20 Water Policy   255
- **Introduction**   255
- **Policy Formulation**   256
- **Water Availability and Use**   257
- **International Water Policy**   260
- **Water and Environmental Justice**   260
- **Sustainable Water Management**   261
  - PROBLEMS   262
  - REFERENCES   262

21 Water Economics   265
- **Introduction**   265
- **The Water Market**   266
- **Demand for Water**   266
  - Shifts in the Demand Curve   267

- **Supply of Water** 268
  - Shifts in the Supply Curve 269
- **Supply and Demand** 269
  - Shifts in Supply and Demand 269
- **Elasticity** 269
  - Estimating Demand 270
- **Water Externalities** 271
  - Water Pollution Trading 272
- **Costs of Production** 272
  - Production Function 272
  - Measures of Cost 272
  - Supply Analysis 273
- **More on Efficiency** 274
- **Economic Policy Analysis** 274
- **Water Pricing** 276
- **Cost–Benefit Analysis** 277
- **Direct and Indirect Economic Effects** 278
  - PROBLEMS 279
  - REFERENCES 279

Appendix A: Conversion Factors 281

Index: 287

Preface

Hydrology is a relatively young science, and the study of water quality is even younger. These fields are still evolving yet are predicated on some fundamental principles. This book was written to introduce college students to the foundations of the broader field of water resources. There are other references that synthesize the literature in greater detail than this one; it was not written to be a treatise or a handbook. Rather, this book was written because most water resources texts contain either an extensive treatment of hydrological concepts with only a chapter or two on water quality, or a focus on water quality with only a chapter or two on basic hydrologic concepts. A text such as this one is needed at this time because greater integration of water quantity and water quality is required to solve many of the real-world water resources problems.

Introduction to Water Resources emphasizes the fundamentals. Many current texts contain abundant case studies and examples. While there is benefit in such examples, there seems to be too much focus on the details of the case studies and less on the fundamentals of the science. Examples provided here are for numerical calculations. If students master the fundamentals, they can apply them to almost any situation. Hand in hand with this notion is that many texts are too long to be adequately covered in even a semester-long course. This book is intentionally brief. Hydrology is a quantitative science and students will be more successful with a knowledge of algebra. An understanding of water quality will be enhanced with a knowledge of chemistry.

The text is structured into three sections: Part I, Water Quantity; Part II, Water Quality; and Part III, Water and Society. Water quantity fundamentals explain important drivers of water quality and therefore should be studied first. Water and society introduces the social science aspect of water resources, which is an increasingly important topic. Students can enhance their understanding of chapter content by working through the Problems that are provided at the end of most chapters. The book's online resources include an Answer Key for instructors, as well as discovery learning exercises for some of the chapters.

These activities have been found to be successful in fostering learning in the classroom, especially in team settings. The website also contains copies of original legislation on various U.S. laws related to water resources. I prefer the originals to someone's interpretations.

I thank Laurie Prossnitz and Debi Underwood at Waveland Press for their editing, direction, and graphic skills. I also am indebted to my parents who introduced me to water in the "Land of Sky-Blue Waters," Arnett C. Mace, Jr. who introduced me to the science of water, and Sandy who made it meaningful.

John C. Clausen
Storrs, Connecticut

PART I

WATER QUANTITY

1

Introduction

There is a certain fascination with water. It is generally pleasant to view, touch, consume, and hear. Water expressions are used commonly throughout our society. A list of examples appears below.

Washed up	Up the creek without a paddle
Soaked to the bone	High water pants
A wet blanket	Drop in a bucket
Making waves	All wet
Icy stare	Waterlogged
Wet behind the ears	In a fog
Wet noodle	On cloud 9
Getting your feet wet	Water under the bridge
Snowed under	In hot water
Flooded with ideas	Watered-down version
A watertight alibi	Water, water everywhere and not a
Water over the dam	drop to drink
Flood of awareness	Like water off a duck's back
Swamped	

Water is a resource; that is, it has utility. But water has limited availability. We rely on water for various uses such as "the protection and propagation of fish and aquatic life and wildlife, recreational purposes, and the withdrawal of such waters for public water supply, agricultural, industrial, and other purposes" (United States Code [U.S.C.], 1972). Perhaps most importantly, water is necessary to sustain life. A comprehensive introduction to water, including its amount, quality, and numerous roles in society, is important for professionals working in multidisciplinary settings who are dealing with the many water problems confronting society.

Purpose of This Book

This text is intended to introduce students to the water resources discipline. It is short enough to be completed in a one-semester term. The text is divided into three sections—water quantity, water quality, and water and society. The chapters provide equal balance to the coverage of water quantity and water quality. But because water quality processes are so dependent on water quantity, a thorough understanding of water quantity is recommended before we study water quality. No subject is explored in great depth; rather, a wide variety of subjects are introduced with an emphasis on basic concepts. This book will prepare you for more advanced courses in water resources. It is suitable for a wide range of disciplines or majors. Hydrology focuses mainly on quantitative analysis, and interested students should be adept at algebra. Some calculus is used here, but it is not emphasized. Problems, most often quantitative, are found at the end of most chapters. Your understanding of water quality will also be enhanced by a basic knowledge of chemistry.

Before the discussion of water quantity begins, we will review some basic definitions, present an overview of water resources issues, and discuss the properties of water. **Hydrology** is the most basic term and is defined as

> [T]he science concerned with the waters of the earth in all their states—their occurrence, distribution, and circulation through the unending hydrologic cycle of precipitation, consequent runoff, streamflow, infiltration, and storage, eventual evaporation, and reprecipitation . . . including the physical, chemical, and physiological reactions of water with the rest of the earth and its relation to the life of the earth (American Public Health Association et al., 1969).

This common definition of hydrology is very broad and includes both water quantity and water quality.

What Is Water?

Water is defined as a molecule formed by two hydrogen atoms and one oxygen atom with the chemical formula H_2O (Figure 1.1). Water has many unique properties that will be discussed later in this book.

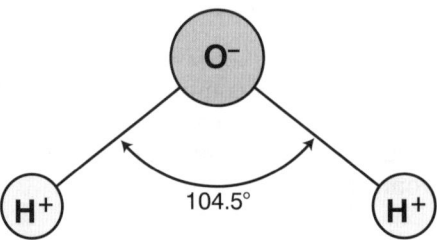

Figure 1.1 Structure of the water molecule.

The word *water* has Indo-European roots and can be found in the Old English *wæter*, Old High German *wassar*, Germanic *watar*, Greek *hudor*, Russian *voda*, Latin *unda*, and Sanskrit *ud-* which also means *wod-*, *wed-*, and *wend-* (American Heritage Dictionary, 2006).

Water Resources Problems

The earth is faced with ever expanding water resources problems. **Water quantity** problems are those dealing with the amount, timing, and distribution of water. The world's population has increased rapidly since around 1850, although the annual growth rate peaked in 1962 (Figure 1.2). Increases in the world's population have led to increasing demands on water for domestic consumption, animal consumption, irrigation for crops, hydropower, transportation, recreation, and industrial uses (Figure 1.3). Additionally, the growing need for land to be developed for either agriculture or urban living results in water resource consequences. Channel modifications have a further negative impact on water resources.

The negative consequences of all these demands and uses are mined ground water supplies, flooding, land subsidence, channel changes, and potential modifications in our climate that further affect the hydrologic cycle. Over one billion people lack access to safe drinking water. Sea level rise is one consequence of climate change that will displace human populations. Flood control involves levees and dams that have their own additional consequences.

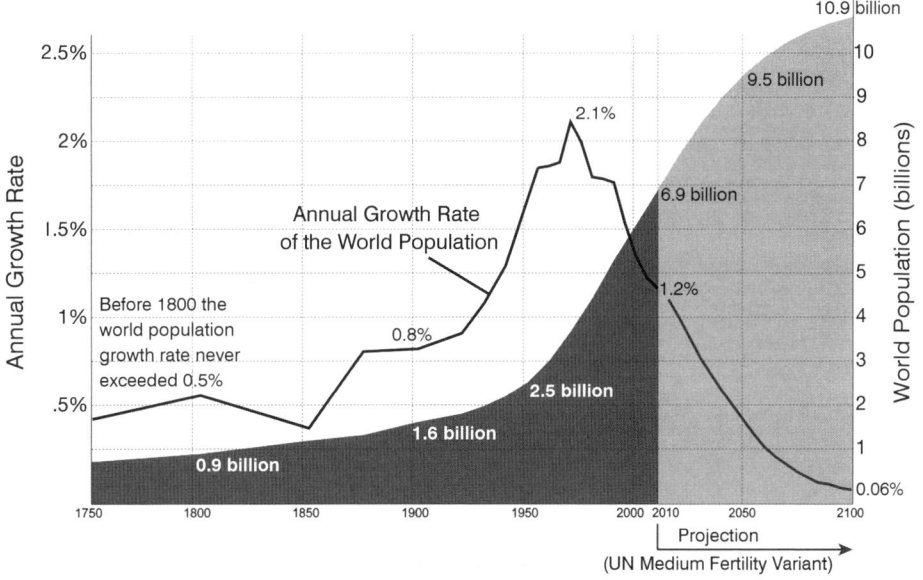

Figure 1.2 World population curve 1750–2100. (Adapted from Ortiz-Ospina and Roser, 2016, https://ourworldindata.org/world-population-growth/)

Figure 1.3 Common water uses.

Water quality problems are often linked to water quantity problems, but they also include contamination of ground water with hydrocarbons, salt, industrial wastes, nutrients, and even bacteria. Many lakes, streams, and estuaries have impaired water quality associated with pollutants from both point source and nonpoint (diffuse) sources. Point sources—well-defined locations like pipes or conduits—include municipal and industrial wastewater treatment facilities. Nonpoint sources include agricultural runoff, acidic deposition, mining, and urban stormwater. Together these sources adversely threaten or impact 71% of lake acres and 55% of river miles in the United States (U.S. Environmental Protection Agency [EPA], 2016).

▪ Properties of Water and Their Ecological Implications

Water exists in three states: solid, liquid, and gas at temperatures commonly found on earth. Water has an unusually high melting point, boiling point, heats of fusion and vaporization, specific heat, dielectric constant, viscosity, and surface tension. The unique properties of water are the result of the structure of the molecules forming water (Figure 1.1). This structure creates a dipolar character; one end of the molecule has a positive charge while the other end has a negative charge. One result of the dipolar nature of water is that it has high solvent prop-

Figure 1.4 An algal bloom is evidence of poor water quality.

erties, meaning that it readily dissolves or disperses many compounds. Definitions of the main properties of water and their ecological significance follow:

- **Surface tension** (lb/ft or N/cm) is the net inward force at the surface of liquid water due to hydrogen bonding (H atom attracted to O atom of another molecule) with other molecules of water. This property makes a water drop form a domed shape as viewed from the side. Surface tension also gives rise to capillarity and the rise of water in small pores in soils. It also enables organisms, such as the water strider, to utilize its surface.

- **Density** (lb/ft^3 or g/cm^3) is the mass per unit volume. Water has the greatest density at 4 °C and is less dense at colder and warmer temperatures. Ice floats because the density of water is less at 0 °C than at 4 °C. Density differences at different lake depths result in the stratification of waters into layers and the lack of mixing between layers. This lack of mixing means that chemicals, such as phosphorus, can build up in one layer but not in others. It also means that oxygen will not mix between layers.

- **Latent heat** (BTU/lb or kJ/kg) is the heat released or absorbed by melting (latent heat of fusion) or boiling (latent heat of vaporization) water. Water's high latent heat of vaporization means that it takes a great deal of energy to vaporize water.

- **Heat capacity** (kg-Cal or J/K) is the amount of heat required to change the temperature of a substance by a certain amount. The high thermal or heat capacity of water allows it to regulate or moderate changes in temperature, which influences both organisms and regional climates.

- **Viscosity** (Pa-s or centipoise) is the resistance to deforming by shear stress related to velocity. The low viscosity of water allows organisms of all sizes to easily move through it and allows water to rise within trees.

- **Dielectric constant** (permittivity—expressed as a ratio) is the tendency of a solvent to oppose the electrostatic attraction between ions of opposite charge. Most substances are soluble in water, which results in the dissolution of minerals with subsequent transport in rivers, ultimately to the oceans. Water carries essential nutrients and can transport wastes away because of this property.

■ Top Ten Concepts in Water Resources

Students of water resources should understand the following fundamental concepts upon completion of their studies (Box 1.1):

1. **Mass balance and the equation of continuity (the hydrologic cycle/water balance)**
   Water movements follow the law of conservation of mass as expressed through the equation of continuity, whereby any change in the storage of a system must equal inputs minus outputs.

CHAPTER 1 Introduction

> **BOX 1.1**
>
> **Top 10 Concepts in Water Resources**
>
> 1. Mass balance/equation of continuity (hydrologic cycle/water balance) (Chapters 3, 15)
> 2. Properties of water (Chapter 1)
> 3. The stochastic nature of hydrology (Chapter 4)
> 4. Flow equations—Darcy, Manning (Chapters 8, 9)
> 5. Potential (head) (Chapters 7, 8)
> 6. The watershed (Chapters 4, 10)
> 7. Advection and diffusion (Chapters 8, 15)
> 8. Nutrient cycling (Chapter 13)
> 9. Equilibrium theory (Chapter 13)
> 10. Energy balance (Chapter 6)

2. Properties of water
The unique properties of water influence the densities of water bodies, solubility of materials, thermal regulation, and capillarity.

3. The stochastic nature of hydrology
The occurrence and amount of precipitation, and therefore runoff, have random elements that follow probability theory.

4. Flow equations (Darcy's and Manning's)
The velocity of water is predictable in open channels and porous media following Manning's equation and Darcy's law.

5. Potential (head)
Water located in the ground moves from a position of high head (potential) to a position of low head.

6. The watershed
The watershed is the basic unit of management and is the area draining to a single point.

7. Advection and diffusion
Transport of the mass of a substance in water occurs due to advection, diffusion, and any reactions that may occur along the way.

8. Nutrient cycling
Nutrients cycle among geophysical, biological, and hydrologic systems at rates controlled by abiotic and biotic factors.

9. Equilibrium theory
Chemical and biological reactions proceed to achieve equilibrium (steady state) over time and distance.

10. Energy balance
Energy follows the laws of conservation of mass.

REFERENCES

American Heritage Dictionary. 2006. *The American heritage dictionary of the English language*, 4th ed. New York: Houghton Mifflin Harcourt.

American Public Health Association, American Society of Civil Engineers, American Water Works Association, and Water Pollution Control Federation. 1969. *Glossary: Water and wastewater control engineering*. New York: American Society of Civil Engineers.

Ortiz-Ospina, E., and M. Roser. 2016. World population growth. https://ourworldindata.org/world-population-growth/

U.S.C. (United States Code). 1972. *An act to amend the Federal Water Pollution Control Act*. PL 92-500. 86 Stat. Washington, DC: U.S. Government Printing Office. https://www.govinfo.gov/content/pkg/STATUTE-86/pdf/STATUTE-86-Pg816.pdf

U.S. Environmental Protection Agency (EPA). 2016. *Water Quality Assessment and TDML Information: National Summary of State Information*. Assessment and Total Maximum Daily Load Tracking and Implementation System (ATTAINS). https://ofmpub.epa.gov/waters10/attains_index.home. Accessed February 28, 2017.

2

Water Resources Units

■ Introduction

The use of units and unit conversions is fundamental to water resource management. Before proceeding with an explanation of water resources units and their conversions, a review of the fundamental units will serve as a starting point. The definition of a physical **quantity** is that it has a dimension (numerical magnitude) and a unit of measure. For example, the velocity of a stream could be 3.1 (dimension) cubic feet per second (unit). Historically, units have had some interesting beginnings. The foot, inch, and yard were all related to the size of parts of the human body. The foot was the length of Charlemagne's foot. The inch was the width of King Edgar's thumb across the knuckle. The yard was the reach of King Henry I's nose to his fingertips. A cubit was the length of the arm from the fingertips to the elbow. A fathom is the width of a seaman's outstretched arms. Other measures of length were based on how far someone could travel. The mile was 1,000 double steps of a Roman legionnaire. A furlong was the length of a furrow plowed by a team of oxen in one day. And an acre was the area of land a team of oxen could plow in one day (e.g., Cardarelli, 2003). Today we use both the English system of units and the modern form of the metric system, or S.I. (le Système International d'Unites) units. Since both systems are used commonly in the United States, the examples and problems in this book will use both English and S.I. units.

Any physical quantity can be expressed based on measures of length (L), mass (M), and time (T) using the format $L^a M^b T^c$ where a ranges from 0 to ±3, b is 0 or 1, and c ranges from 0 to −3 (Figure 2.1). Length is based on the distance from the pole to the equator (10^9 cm), which is a geophysical unit. Mass is based on water, where 1 g = 1 cm^3 of water at 4 °C. Time is based on the rate of earth's rotation. One day = 86,400 s = $2\pi/\omega$, where ω = the angular velocity of the earth's rotation. Geometric properties are those when mass is not involved (M^0). Static properties are those when time is not involved (T^0). Kinematic properties are those when time but not mass is involved, and dynamic properties are those when time and mass are involved. In Figure 2.1, "taking the moment" is an expression that means multiplying a physical quantity by distance (L). "Taking the rate" generally means dividing one quantity by another related quantity; in this case, by time. Several water resources terms have been added to the original diagram by Maxwell (1871), including area (L^2), volume (L^3), velocity (LT^{-1}), concentration (ML^{-3}), and discharge (L^3T^{-1}). Examples of how these terms are used in water resources are the **length** of a stream, the **area** of a watershed, the **volume** of a lake, the **velocity** of a stream, or the **discharge** of water from a watershed. When performing unit conversions, it is often useful to use these fundamental units first.

Some unit conventions in water resources are somewhat unique. For example, water balance components are sometimes expressed as a depth, rather than a volume. To illustrate, precipitation is often expressed as mm of depth, but it is really a depth over an area, which is a volume. Likewise, discharge from a

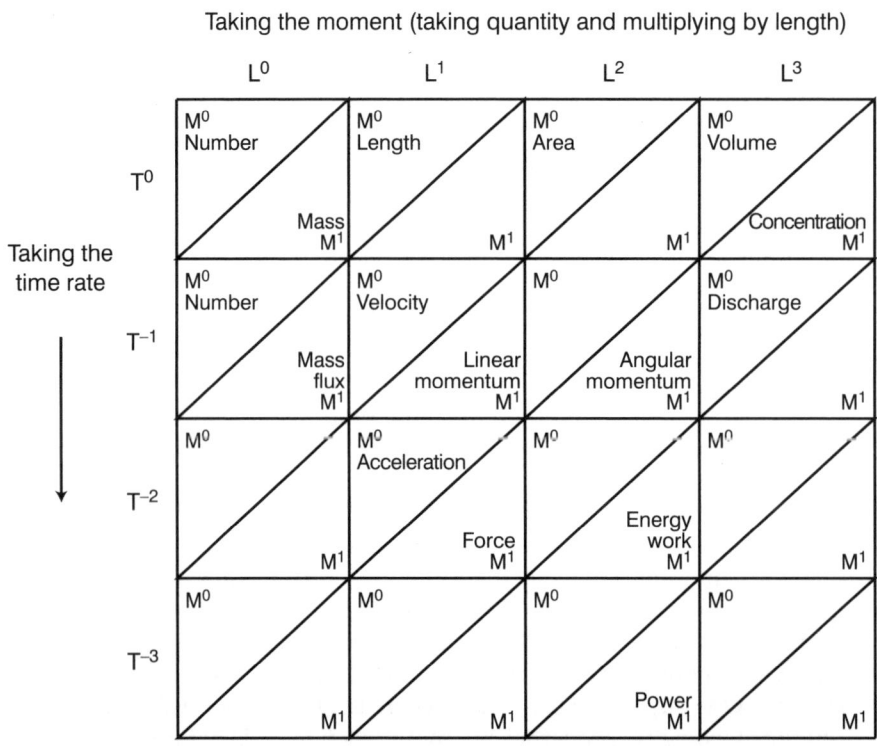

Figure 2.1 Fundamental units of length, mass, and time (after Maxwell, 1871).

watershed is often expressed as a rate, such as m³/s, but it may be expressed as mm over a watershed area for a given time period.

This chapter will enable you to achieve a basic understanding of the use of units and a format for making unit conversions. Standards for determining the number of significant digits to use as well as log rules will be reviewed. Units specific to water quantity and water quality are described in greater detail.

■ Unit Conversions

An important skill in water resources is the ability to convert units from one to another. This process is largely an exercise in algebra. Students of water resources commonly have difficulty converting units. Contributing to this issue is the lack of a strategy to convert units that applies to all situations. To convert from one unit to another, some general guidelines are useful:

1. For addition and subtraction use only the same units.

2. To convert units, use the following standard formula:

$$(X \text{ old units}) \times \left(Y \frac{\text{new units}}{\text{old units}} \right) = XY \text{ new units} \qquad [2.1]$$

where Y is a conversion factor as found in Appendix A.

3. Conduct the unit conversion in one continuous equation, rather than as a series of steps with different equations. It is useful to write down what units are desired first, and then add conversion factors and cancel units to achieve the desired units at the end. Cancelling is the process whereby the same units in the numerator and denominator can be crossed out, leaving just the numerical magnitude. Example 2.1 illustrates a conversion with only one conversion factor.

EXAMPLE 2.1 Converting Units

How many hectares are there in a 10 km² watershed? Conversion factors are given in Appendix A.

$$\text{ha} = 10 \text{ km}^2 \times \frac{100 \text{ ha}}{\text{km}^2} = 1{,}000 \text{ ha}$$

More complex conversions, such as m/s to ft/hr, follow the form:

$$\left(X \frac{\text{old units}_1}{\text{old units}_2} \right) \times \left(Y \frac{\text{new units}_1}{\text{old units}_1} \right) \times \left(Z \frac{\text{old units}_2}{\text{new units}_2} \right) = XYZ \frac{\text{new units}_1}{\text{new units}_2}$$

where Y and Z are conversion factors, such as m/ft and s/hr, respectively.

Significant Digits

Dimensions (numbers) should use the appropriate number of significant digits when reported. The number of significant digits denotes the true size of the unit. Portable calculators and computer programs often arbitrarily provide many more digits than are typically appropriate. The number of significant digits to report can be based on either the measurement taken or the mathematical operation used. When based on the measurement, the significant digits are the same as the observation (e.g., 7.6 ft is reported to 0.1 ft). When based on the mathematical operation, the number of **significant digits** is the number of digits beginning with the left-most nonzero digit and extending to the right to include all digits warranted by measurement precision, which may be a zero. Zeros within a number always are significant (e.g., 4308 and 43.08 both have four significant digits). Zeros that just set the decimal are not significant (e.g., 430,000 has two significant digits). However, zeros after the decimal are significant (e.g., 4.00 has three significant digits). There are two rules governing the number of significant digits.

- **Rule No. 1:**

    When multiplying and dividing, the factor with the fewest significant digits applies in the answer. For example:

    $$895.65 \times 35.9 = 32,200 \text{ or } 3.22 \times 10^4$$
    $$(5) \quad\quad (3) \quad\quad (3) \quad\quad = \text{Number of significant digits}$$

- **Rule No. 2:**

    For addition and subtraction, the decimal point determines the number of significant digits. For example:

    $$\begin{array}{r} 134.023 \\ + 1.5 \\ \hline 135.5 \end{array}$$

    Because the number with the fewest significant digits after the decimal point is 1.5, the answer is only reported to one decimal point.

    Some examples of the number of significant digits are given here:

25 = 2	25.0 = 3
2.5 = 2	0.250 = 3
0.25 = 2	0.0250 = 3
0.025 = 2	

The number 2500 could have two, three, or four significant digits, depending on whether the zeros are an actual measurement or are rounded. One way to solve this problem is through the use of **E notation**. For example, 2.5×10^3 (or 2.5E3) has two significant digits, whereas 2.50×10^3 (or 2.50E3) has three. The value for π or e should use the same number of significant digits as used in the other measurements. General practice is to round off to the correct number of significant figures at the end of the mathematic operation rather than for each conversion. Portable calculators and computer programs automatically do not round during mathematical operations except to some truncated number following the decimal point. This point is most often well beyond the number of significant digits that are appropriate.

Rounding Off

There are various conventions for rounding numbers. One such convention is to always round up. Another is the military round-off rule, which always rounds to the nearest even number. For example 31.45 would be rounded to 31.4, while 31.55 would be rounded to 31.6. In this book, the military round-off rule will be used.

Water Quantity Units

There are several unique conventions in expressing water quantity measurements. One example of a unique water quantity unit is a csm, which represents the discharge of a cubic foot per second per square mile of watershed area. Most measurements are expressed using S.I. units, but there are exceptions. For example, an ac-ft is one foot of water spread over an acre. It is really a unit of volume and is commonly used to describe the amount of water stored in reservoirs. Units such as cfs (ft^3/s), gpd (gallons per day), gpm (gallons per minute) are still commonplace conventions. Water quantity units will be discussed further in each chapter of water balance components later in this book. Conversion factors are summarized in Appendix A, and problems at the end of this chapter are designed to encourage practice in unit conversions.

Water Quality Units

There are several water quality units that are unique as compared to water quantity units. Several of these units are those learned in chemistry courses, such as moles/L, meq/L, mg/L. These units are essentially the **concentration** of a substance or mass per unit volume (Figure 2.1). Some of these unique conventions described next include event mean concentrations, equivalence units, moles per liter, and dealing with so-called censored values.

Event Mean Concentration (EMC)

Some years ago the U.S. Environmental Protection Agency (EPA) supported the Nationwide Urban Runoff Program (NURP), which involved the monitoring of 28 urban locations throughout the United States (EPA, 1983). Water quality data generated in that study were presented as event mean concentrations (EMC). The EMC is a flow-weighted concentration obtained for an individual stormflow period (Novotny, 2003) using the formula:

$$EMC = \frac{\sum Q_i C_i}{\sum Q_i} \qquad [2.2]$$

where Q_i = discharge representing the collected sample from the hydrograph
 C_i = concentration corresponding to that discharge

Equivalence Units

Equivalent weight units reflect the chemical formula of water quality species and therefore their chemical weight and ionic charge (Hem, 1985). These units are useful to construct the balance of cations and anions in water. To determine meq/L (milliequivalents/liter), use the following formula:

$$\text{meq/L} = \text{mg/L} \times \frac{1}{\text{combining weight}} \qquad [2.3]$$

where combining weight = $\dfrac{\text{formula weight}}{\text{charge}}$

Table 2.1 lists several combining weight inverses for common elements that are useful for this type of conversion. An example is also provided.

Table 2.1 Factors to convert mg/L to meq/L and molecular weights for common elements.

Element & species	$\dfrac{1}{\text{combining weight}}$	MW (g/mol)
Al^{3+}	0.11119	26.9815
Ca^{2+}	0.04990	40.0780
H^+	0.99209	1.0079
HCO_3^-	0.01639	61.0168
K^+	0.02557	39.0983
Mg^{2+}	0.08226	24.3050
NH_4^-	0.05544	18.0385
NO_3^-	0.01613	62.0049
PO_4^{3-}	0.03159	94.9714

EXAMPLE 2.2 Computing meq/L

What is the meq/L of 1.13 mg/L of phosphate (PO_4)? From Table 2.1, the 1/combining weight for PO_4 is 0.03159. Therefore, the appropriate calculation is:

$$\text{meq/L} = 1.13 \text{ mg/L} \times 0.03159 = 0.036 \text{ meq/L}$$

Moles/Liter

A mole of a substance is its atomic or molecular weight, usually expressed in grams. A solution with 1 mole per liter is called a molar solution. To obtain moles/L, divide mg/L by the atomic or formula weight (g/mol) of a substance.

EXAMPLE 2.3   **Computing moles/L**

How many moles per liter are there in 2 mg/L PO_4? From Table 2.1, the molecular weight of PO_4 is 94.9714 g/mol. Therefore the appropriate calculation is:

$$\text{mol}/\text{L} = \frac{2 \text{ mg/L}}{94.9714 \text{ g/mol}} \times \frac{1 \text{ g}}{1,000 \text{ mg}} = 0.000021 \text{ moles } PO_4/L$$

Censored Values

The chemical analyses of a number of substances that occur in trace concentrations sometimes result in reporting a value that is less than a certain limit of detection or is reported as not detected. The actual value is not known; it is only known that the value lies somewhere below that limit of detection. The term **censored** is applied to a set of data containing such values. In the case of data below a detection limit, the data would be left censored. The presence of such values prevents the calculation of statistics such as the mean and standard deviation of the data without modifications in how the data is reported. The U.S. Environmental Protection Agency (2000) has provided guidance on how to calculate statistics using data that include censored values or values below detection limits. These methods include replacing the non-detected value with half the detection limit or the detection limit, using adjusted means and standard deviations, or testing for proportions. The method used depends on the percentage of values below detection.

Mass Export and Loading

There are several terms applied to the mass flux of a water quality substance. In Figure 2.1, mass flux has the units of MT^{-1}. Estimating loads or mass exports for tributaries involves accurate flow and concentration data. The term *load* is applied when considering the mass transported **to** a location. The term *export* is applied when considering the mass transported **from** a location. Tributary load can be estimated from:

$$M = \sum \left[C_j \right] \times Q_j \times \Delta t \qquad [2.4]$$

where M = load (mass/time)
  C = concentration (mass/volume)
  Q = flow (volume/time)
  t = time

Flow is usually measured nearly continuously, while concentration usually is obtained from a number of discrete samples. There is considerable evidence that discrete concentration samples may not represent the distribution of water quality concentrations (e.g., Whitfield, 1982). Loads are influenced by whether there is systematic sampling or event-based approaches. Therefore, various techniques have been developed to modify the simple arithmetic approach provided in Eqn. 2.4. These methods include averaging, regression approaches, and ratio estimators (Endreny et al., 2005; Preston et al., 1989). A hydrograph separation technique has also been used (Raymond et al., 2013). The Beale ratio estimator has been recommended to improve estimates of tributary loads, but the actual method probably varies with the sampling approach (Richards, 1989; Preston et al., 1989).

Review of Log Rules

Logarithms are commonly used in water resources mathematics and for plotting water resource data. For example, stage-discharge relationships are often plotted on lognormal paper. Being able to determine the first-order reaction coefficient k also requires the use of logarithms. Also, the concentrations of many water quality constituents approximate exponential or lognormal distributions. Therefore, a review of basic log rules has been provided.

$$\text{By definition, if } X = a^Y \text{ then } Y = \log_a X$$

The base of the logarithm is $= a$; Y equals log base a of X.

Common (Base 10) Logarithms

- For common logs or $\log_{10}$, where $a = 10$, if $X = 10^Y$ then $Y = \log_{10} X$
- The log of two products is the sum of the logs of each variable, such that:

$$\log_{10}(XY) = \log_{10} X + \log_{10} Y$$

- The log of the division of two variables is the difference between the logs of each variable, such that:

$$\log_{10}(X/Y) = \log_{10} X - \log_{10} Y$$

- The log of a value raised to the power (n) is equal to n times the log of the value, such that:

$$\log_{10}(X^n) = n \log_{10} X$$

The antilog of both sides of this equation would be performed using the equation $Y = 10^a X^b$, or the general form of $Y = aX^b$.

The following example shows the use of logs for a stage-discharge rating curve.

EXAMPLE 2.4 **Computing a Stage-Discharge Rating Curve**

The following stage (height of water) and discharge data were collected from a small stream in northern Minnesota. Determine the stage-discharge rating equation.

Microsoft Excel, a computer spreadsheet program, was used to generate the graphs shown in the figures below. A linear regression trendline was applied to the data without transformation, as shown in Figure (a). The resulting line does not appear to fit the field measurements very well. Taking the log of both discharge and stage and performing a linear regression results in: Log $y = b$ log x + log a, where a = intercept and b = slope. This log-log relationship in Figure (b) appears to better fit the data.

Stage discharge data from the Toivola River.

Stage (ft)	Discharge (cfs)	Stage (ft)	Discharge (cfs)
3.69	19.62	3.19	17.5
4.60	38.15	2.13	7.38
4.42	38.7	4.40	37.92
3.69	26.2	3.47	25.58
3.28	20.07	6.65	152.0
2.81	13.7	3.60	21.6

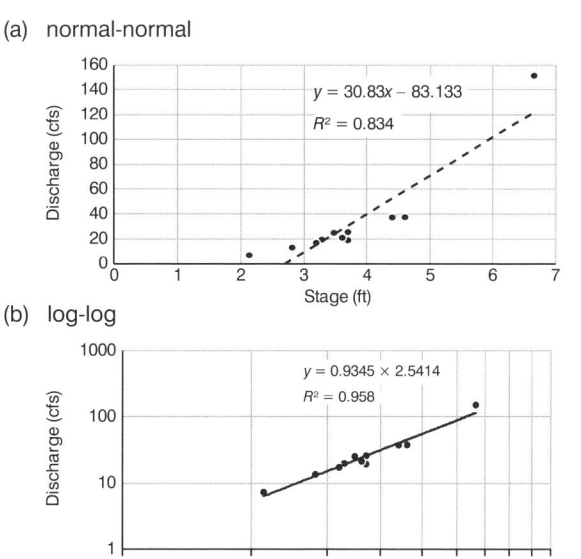

Toivola stage-discharge relationships.

Natural Logarithms

Natural logarithms use e as the base instead of 10, where e is approximately:

$$e = 1 + \frac{1}{1!} + \frac{1}{2!} + \frac{1}{3!} + \ldots + \frac{1}{n!} = 2.71828\ldots, \quad \text{and}$$

$$10 = 2.71828^{2.303}$$

For natural or Naperion logarithms and exponential calculations, by definition, if $e^X = Y$ then $\ln Y = X$. So the relationship between natural logs and log base 10 is:

$$\log_e X = 2.303 \log_{10} X \quad \text{and}$$

$$\log_{10} X = 0.434 \log_e X$$

Some examples will illustrate.

What is the $\log_{10}$ of 10?
$$\log_{10} 10 = 1$$

What is the $\log_e$ of 10?
$$\log_e 10 = 2.303$$

Solve the following equation for t (time, years):
$$0.01 = e^{-t/0.106}$$

$$\ln 0.01 = \ln e^{-t/0.106}$$

Since $\ln 0.01 = -4.60517$, therefore, the antilog is $-4.605 = -t/0.106$

$$t = 0.488 \text{ years}$$

■ Problems

2.1 A watershed is 640 acres in area. Assuming the watershed is a square, what is the length of the watershed in meters?

2.2 How many m^3/s are there in 25 ft^3/s?

2.3 How many cubic feet are there in 25 acre-feet?

2.4 If a 2-inch rain fell on the watershed in problem 2.1, how many gallons of water would that represent?

2.5 If the total phosphorus concentration is 0.05 ppm, what is the concentration in (a) µg/L, (b) % solution, (c) mg/L, (d) mg/m^3, and (e) ppb?

2.6 If the total phosphorus concentration in the soil is 300 mg/kg, what is the concentration in ppm?

2.7 Determine the EMC for stream nitrate given the following information:

Discharge (Q) (cfs)	Nitrate Concentration (mg/L)
5.3	1.15
8.2	1.30
1.7	0.85
4.0	1.05

2.8 What is the meq/L of 1.19 mg/L of nitrate (NO_3)? How many mol/L are there in 1.19 mg/L of nitrate?

2.9 If the concentration of total phosphorus in the Willimantic River at Merrow is 0.033 mg/L and the river flows at an average discharge of 66 cfs, what is the annual downstream loading of phosphorus in kg/yr and kg/ha/yr? The watershed area is 94 mi^2.

2.10 Determine the stage-discharge relationship for the stream draining the Corona Bog based on the following field measurements:

Stage (ft)	Discharge (cfs)
3.92	6.31
5.23	11.75
1.85	0.20
2.12	0.35
2.44	0.67
2.24	0.45
2.79	0.82

■ REFERENCES

Cardarelli, F. 2003. *Encyclopaedia of scientific units, weights and measures: Their SI equivalencies and origins.* London: Springer-Verlag.

Endreny, T. A., J. M. Hassett, and S. E. Wolosoff. 2005. Robustness of pollutant loading estimators for sample size reduction in a suburban watershed. *International Journal of River Basin Maangement* 3(1): 53–66.

Hem, J. D. 1985. *Study and interpretation of the chemical characteristics of natural water.* 3rd ed. Geological Survey Water-Supply paper 2254. Washington, DC: U.S. Government Printing Office. https://pubs.usgs.gov/wsp/wsp2254/pdf/wsp2254a.pdf

Maxwell, J. C. 1871. On the mathematical classification of physical quantities. *Proc. London Math. Soc.* III(34): 224.

Novotny, V. 2003. *Water quality: Diffuse pollution and watershed management*, 2nd ed. Hoboken, NJ: Wiley.

Preston, S. D., V. J. Bierman, Jr., and S. E. Silliman. 1989. *Evaluation of methods for the estimation of tributary mass loading rates.* Purdue University Water Resources Research Center. Technical Report No. 187. West Lafayette, IN: Purdue University.

Raymond, S., F. Moatar, M. Meybeck, and V. Bustillo. 2013. Choosing methods for estimating dissolved and particulate riverine fluxes from monthly sampling. *Hydrological Sciences Journal* 58(6): 1326–1339.

Richards, R. P. 1989. Evaluation of some approaches to estimating non-point pollutant loads for unmonitored areas. *Water Resources Bulletin* 25(4): 891–904.

U.S. Environmental Protection Agency (EPA). 1983. *Results of the nationwide urban runoff program.* Washington, DC: U.S. Environmental Protection Agency, Water Planning Division. https://www3.epa.gov/npdes/pubs/sw_nurp_vol_1_finalreport.pdf

U.S. Environmental Protection Agency (EPA). 2000. *Guidance for data quality assessment. Practical methods for data analysis,* EPA QA/G-9, QA00 Update. EPA/600/R-96/084. Washington, DC: Office of Environmental Information. https://www.epa.gov/sites/production/files/2015-06/documents/g9-final.pdf

Whitfield, P. H. 1982. Selecting a method for estimating substance loadings. *Water Resources Bulletin* 18(2): 203–210.

3

Hydrologic Cycle

■ Introduction

A thorough understanding of the hydrologic cycle is important as a precursor to understanding water quantity. Various components of the hydrologic cycle also influence water quality characteristics. For example, surface runoff picks up suspended and dissolved materials as it moves across the landscape. Greater amounts of surface runoff produce a greater export of materials. The current view of the hydrologic cycle is shown in Figure 3.1. The **hydrologic cycle** (water cycle) is the movement of water on earth from land to the oceans to the atmosphere and back to the land again. Water that is evaporated from oceans, lakes, and the land or transpired by plants becomes atmospheric moisture (Chapter 6). Condensation in the atmosphere results in precipitation, in its many forms, back to the surface of the earth (Chapter 4). Some of the precipitation is intercepted by vegetation and other surfaces and evaporates back to the atmosphere before reaching the ground (Chapter 5). Fallen precipitation that does reach the earth's surface is partitioned into runoff or infiltrates (Chapter 7) into the ground. These waters contribute to soil and ground waters (Chapter 8), which supply streams (Chapter 9). Streams eventually flow into the oceans, completing the cycle.

Our view of the hydrologic cycle is fairly modern. As recently as 1696, there were other views of the cycle of the earth's water. A commonly held view was called the **reverse hydrologic cycle** (Figure 3.2), in which water was believed to leave the oceans through passages in the earth and emerge in mountains as springs (Tuan, 1968). This belief was shared by Aristotle and Pliny, among other notables. This misconception was founded on the inability to describe where the ocean's water went after the rivers flowed into it, because the oceans never filled up. Though evaporation from the sea was recognized, it was believed to fall as rain directly back into the sea. John Ray (1722) believed that rain on the land came from evaporation from the land (Tuan, 1968).

24   PART I   Water Quantity

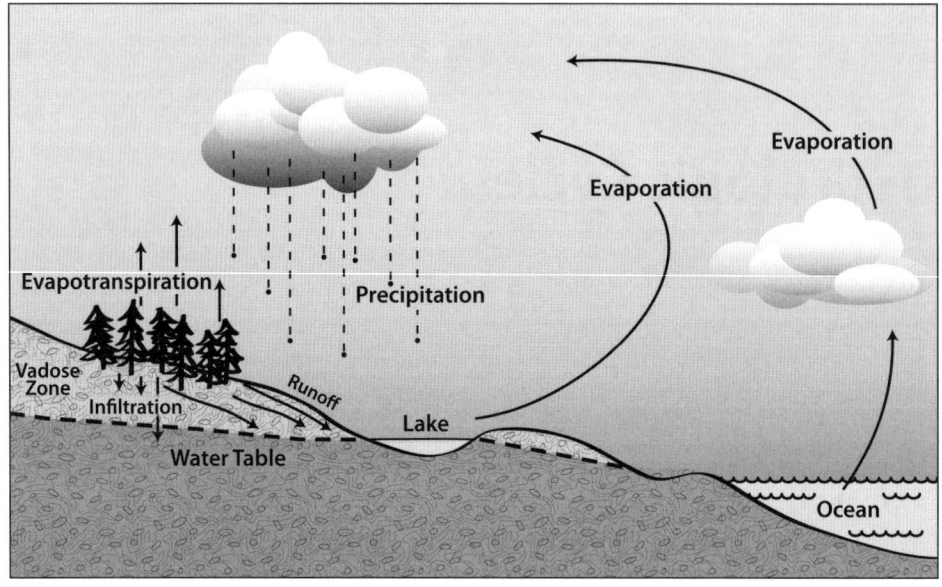

Figure 3.1   The hydrologic cycle.

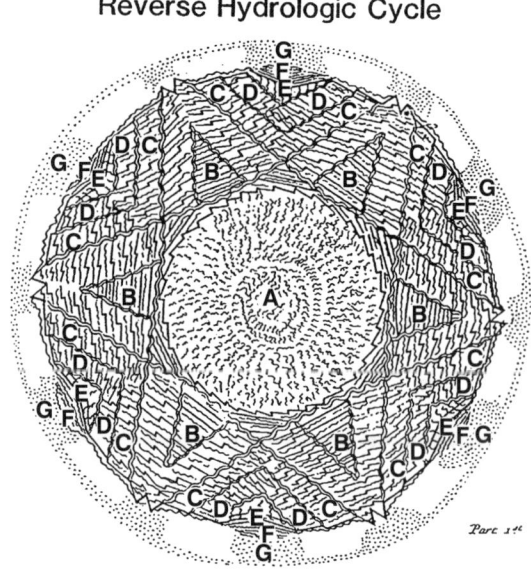

Figure 3.2   Reverse hydrologic cycle (adapted from Tuan, 1968, from Robinson, 1696). **A** is the central fire, **B** the mountains from the center to the surface, **C** heaths, **D** plains, **E** the channel of the sea, **F** the seas with the rivers flowing into them from the tops of the mountains, and **G** vapors arising from the seas. Jagged lines are strata, and double lines are the veins through which subterranean water circulates.

Storages and Fluxes

There have been many estimates of the amount of water stored in the various compartments on the earth and the major fluxes in the water budget, and most water texts contain such information. Ackermann et al. (1955) estimated that there were 80,000 cubic miles evaporated each year from oceans, 15,000 cubic miles evaporated from lakes and land surfaces of continents, while 24,000 cubic miles of precipitation fell on land surfaces. Hewlett (1982) reported that 97.1% of the earth's water is salt water in either the oceans or salt lakes and seas, 2.8% of the earth's water is fresh water, of which most is ice and snow (2.2%), and 0.6% is in ground water and soil. Fresh water in the atmosphere is a relatively small amount (0.001%). Trenberth et al. (2007) updated the storages and fluxes for the earth using a combination of newer measurements and modeling approaches (Tables 3.1 and 3.2; Figure 3.3). There also have been suggestions that some atmospheric moisture reaches terminal velocity and is lost to space and that tiny comets regularly contribute moisture to earth's atmosphere (Kerr, 1997).

Table 3.1 The volume of water stored in the major compartments of the earth.

Storages	Volume (km^3 × 10^3)	Percent of Total
Oceans	1,335,040	96.951
Ice	26,350	1.914
Ground water	15,300	1.111
Soil moisture	122	0.009
Permafrost	22	0.002
Atmosphere	12.7	0.001
Rivers/lakes	178	0.013
Total:	**1,377,024.7**	**100**

Source: Volume data from Trenberth et al., 2007.

Table 3.2 The earth's water balance.

Fluxes	Volume (km^3/yr × 10^3)	Percent of Total
Ocean evaporation	413	100
Ocean precipitation	373	90.3
Ocean to land water vapor transport	40	9.7
Land precipitation	113	100
Vegatation ET	73	64.6
Land runoff	40	35.4

Source: Volume data from Trenberth et al., 2007.

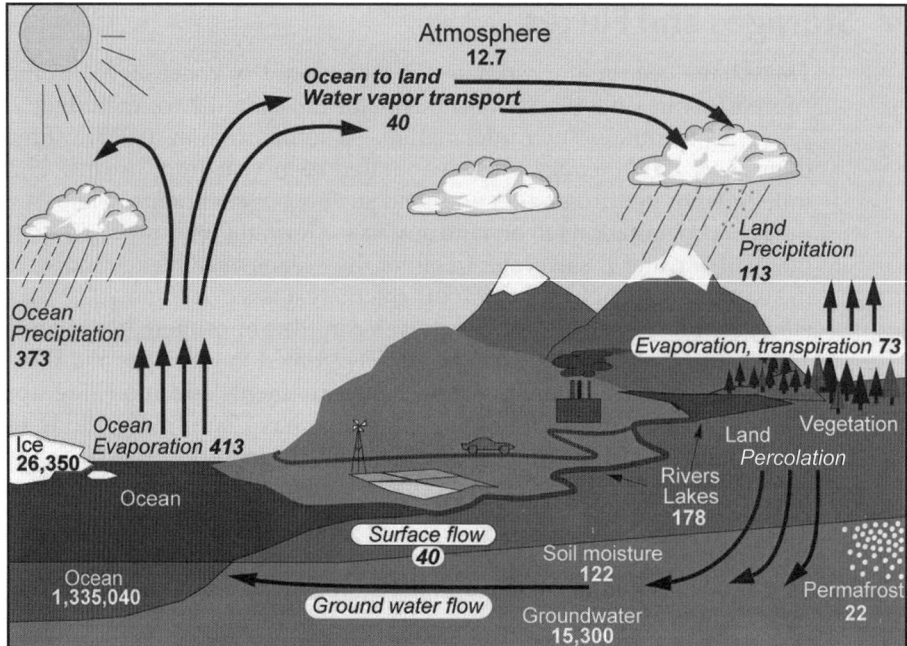

Units: Thousand cubic km for storage, and thousand cubic km/yr for exchanges.

Figure 3.3 The world water balance according to Trenberth et al. (2007). Used with permission of the American Meteorological Society.

■ Water Balance

The water balance (budget) equation is a specific case of the equation of continuity, where the change in storage is equal to inflow minus outflow:

$$\Delta S = i - q \qquad [3.1]$$

where S = storage
  i = inflow
  q = discharge

This equation is most easily shown as a vessel or container with inflow and outflow, somewhat like a lake or reservoir (Figure 3.4).

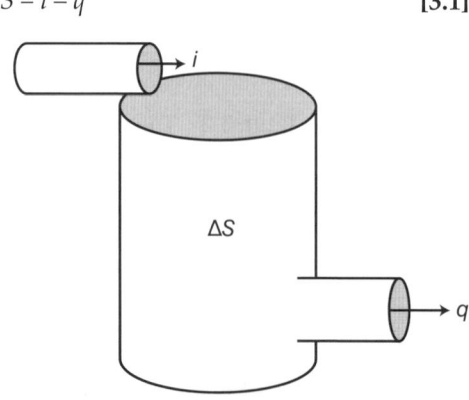

Figure 3.4 Storage volume with inflow, outflow, and a change in storage.

The water balance equation in its most simple form is shown as:

$$P = ET + Q \pm \Delta S \qquad [3.2]$$

where P = precipitation
ET = evapotranspiration
Q = streamflow (sometimes shown as RO for runoff)
ΔS = the change in storage

Components of the water balance equation are most often shown in units of depth, such as cm, but they may be expressed in units of volume (e.g., m³). The U.S. Geological Survey (1986), which monitors water resources throughout the United States, reported in its water summary that average annual precipitation ranges from less than 1 inch per year to 400 inches per year depending on location, and it averages 30 inches nationwide. Average annual discharge also has a high range, from less than 1 inch per year to over 60 inches per year. Thus, the relative proportions of water balance components vary greatly from location to location. Hewlett (1982) reported that for the lower 48 states, average annual precipitation is 76 cm, evapotranspiration is 53 cm, discharge is 23 cm, and change in storage is 0 cm. The change in storage is generally regarded to be zero over annual or longer periods of time, but there are frequent exceptions to this assumption.

The simplified water balance equation in Eqn. 3.2 does not include all components of the hydrologic cycle. De la Crétaz and Barten (2007) provide a more complete water balance equation that is simplified as follows:

$$P = I + E + T + Q_{OF} + Q_{SS} \pm GW \pm \Delta S \qquad [3.3]$$

where I = interception losses
E = evaporation from all surfaces
T = transpiration
Q_{OF} = overland flow
Q_{SS} = shallow subsurface flow
GW = ground water flow
 and the other terms were defined above

When ground water flow is negative, it is sometimes called leakage. However, that term may only apply to what is called deep leakage; that is, leakage out of a watershed. Each component of the water balance equation will be explored in subsequent chapters.

■ How to Construct an Annual Water Budget

A common hydrologic exercise is the construction of an annual water budget for a specific location. Therefore, it is useful to know where to locate readily obtainable sources of information for precipitation, evaporation, and runoff. Annual precipitation is easily available at numerous locations in the United States from the National Oceanic and Atmospheric Administration—National Weather Service (NOAA-NWS). Such data used to be published in "Local Climatological Data" for various states or several states together. More recently, such information is obtainable at the NOAA website (http://www.ncdc.noaa.gov/). Monthly normal (30-year) and annual precipitation is available by state. For example, the normal annual precipitation for the Ames, Iowa, 8 WSW gage located at 42.0208° N, −93.7741° W is 35.83 inches (National Oceanic and Atmospheric Administration, 2000). Runoff (discharge) data is also readily available in the United States from the U.S. Geological Survey. For example, the discharge at USGS gage #05471000 for the Southern Skunk River near Ames, Iowa, was 9.08 in. for the period 1953 to 2010 (U.S. Geological Survey, 2010). The watershed area for this gage is 556 mi^2 and it is noted that at low flow, the discharge is affected by pumping of water for Ames. Estimated evapotranspiration for Ames would then be calculated on a long-term basis as the difference between precipitation and discharge, in this case: 35.83 in. − 9.08 in. = 26.75 in.

■ Problems

3.1 If the annual precipitation of a 10 mi^2 watershed is 30 inches and the runoff averages 12 cfs, what is the annual average evapotranspiration (in.)?

3.2 Determine the estimated water balance of Mille Lacs Lake in central Minnesota.

3.3 For the Southern Skunk River described in this chapter, determine the average annual discharge in cfs.

■ References

Ackermann, W. C., E. A. Colman, and H. O. Ogrosky. 1955. Where we get our water. From ocean to sky to land to ocean. In *The yearbook of agriculture 1955* (pp. 41–51). Washington, DC: U.S. Department of Agriculture.

De la Crétaz, A. L., and P. K. Barten. 2007. *Land use effects on streamflow and water quality in the northeastern United States.* Boca Raton, FL: CRC Press.

Hewlett, J. D. 1982. *Principles of forest hydrology.* Athens: The University of Georgia Press.

Kerr, R. A. 1997. Spots confirmed, tiny comets spurned. *Science* 276: 1333–1334.

National Oceanic and Atmospheric Administration (NOAA). 2000. *Climatography of the United States.* No. 81. 1971–2000. 13 Iowa. Asheville, NC: National Environmental Satellite, Data, and Information Service, National Climate Data Center.

Robinson, T. 1696. *New observations of the natural history of the world of matter.* London.

Trenberth, K. E., L. Smith, T. Qian, A. Dai, and J. Fasullo. 2007. Estimates of the global water budget and its annual cycle using observational and model data. *J. Hydrometeorology* 8: 758–769.

Tuan, Y.-F. 1968. *The hydrologic cycle and the wisdom of God: A theme in geoteleology.* Toronto: University of Toronto Press.

U.S. Geological Survey (USGS). 1986. *National water summary 1985—Hydrologic events and surface-water resources.* U.S. Geological Survey Water-Supply Paper 2300. Washington, DC: U.S. Government Printing Office.

U.S. Geological Survey (USGS). 2010. *Annual water-data report.* http://waterdata.usgs.gov.

4
Precipitation

■ Introduction

Precipitation is the component of the hydrologic cycle that initiates many hydrologic and water quality processes. Precipitation occurrence and amount have a random (stochastic) component that follows probability theory. Precipitation occurs in many different forms including rain, snow, drizzle, sleet, hail, dew, and mist. Which forms occur vary with the particular climate region as well as with elevation differences. The characteristics of precipitation also vary with the type of storm producing the precipitation. This chapter discusses these storm types, how to measure precipitation, how to determine average precipitation over an area, and how to perform frequency analysis, including the probability of occurrence and return period. In addition, errors in precipitation measurements are also discussed in this chapter.

■ Types of Storms

Several types of storms produce precipitation (Table 4.1). Convectional precipitation, in the form of thunderstorms, occurs as the result of heating of the surface of the earth (Figure 4.1a). Heating of moist air will cause it to rise because it is less dense than cold air aloft. Convection storms can have high intensities (mm/hr), but usually they cover a relatively small area and are of short duration as compared to other storm types. Orographic storms are those that occur due to a barrier that forces the moist air to rise over the top, producing precipitation (Figure 4.1b). Such effects are common in mountainous areas, resulting in precipitation on the windward side of the mountains. The precipitation intensity and duration for orographic storms are more moderate than for convective storms. Frontal storms can be of two main types: warm fronts and cold fronts (Figure 4.1c). Warm fronts are characterized by lighter warm air replacing and pushing up over cold air. The slope of the line separating the warm from the cold air is gradual. As the warm air rises over the cold air, precipitation occurs, usually over a broad area. Cold fronts are characterized by heavier cold air replacing warm air by pushing under the warm air. This replacement results in a steep slope between the two air masses and the rapid rise of warm air aloft, producing precipitation. Fronts can cover large areas and move slowly.

Table 4.1 Types and characteristics of storms producing precipitation.

Type	Cause	Intensity	Duration	Area
Convectional	Surface heating	High	Short	Small
Orographic	Barrier/uplift	Medium	Medium	Small or large
Frontal—warm	Forcing up air	Low	Long	Large
Frontal—cold	Forcing up air	High	Medium	Medium

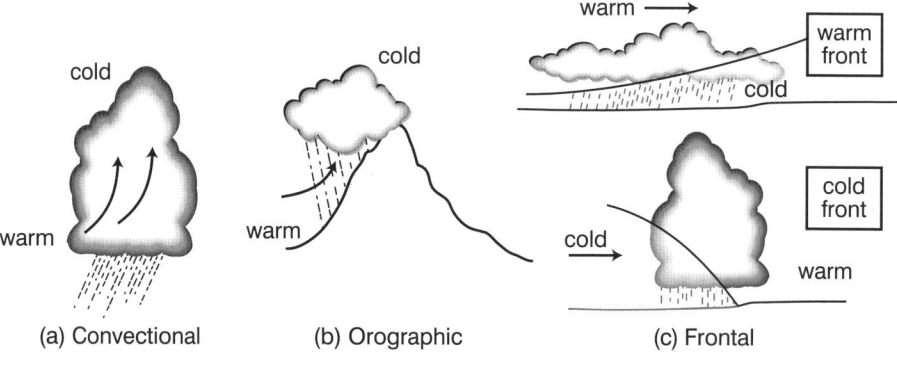

Figure 4.1 Diagram of precipitation storm types.

■ Measurement of Precipitation

Precipitation can be measured in as many ways as the volume of water can be measured. Past approaches have used weight, a calibrated volume with a measuring stick, and a tipping bucket (Figure 4.2). Precipitation in winter is problematic for measurement in cold regions, and heating may be required. The National Weather Service (1989) has provided guidance on establishing precipitation stations. Both standard and recording rain gages are recommended. The area around the rain gage opening should be free of obstructions (National Weather Service, 1989). For example, the tree height above the gage should be no greater than two times the distance from the gage, an angle of about 64°. In open areas, the height of objects should not exceed half their distance from the gage, or an angle of 27°. In areas where snow represents 20% or more of mean annual precipitation, the gage should be shielded to foster vertical fall into the gage. Alter shields are commonly used for this purpose (Figure 4.2b). The standard rain gage value is accepted as the correct value, and recording rain gage results should be adjusted to equal the standard value (Example 4.1).

(a) (b) (c)

Figure 4.2 Precipitation gages: (a) standard, (b) weighing bucket shielded, and (c) tipping bucket. Images (a) and (b) provided by author; image (c) courtesy of Sutron Corporation.

EXAMPLE 4.1 **Adjusting Precipitation Data**

The standard rain gage collected 35 mm of rain for a week's observation. The recording tipping bucket rain gage observed a lower amount of precipitation as shown in the table below. Determine the correct daily precipitation. The difference between the two gages is:

Difference = 35 − 30.48 = +4.52 mm

$$\text{Adjustment} = \frac{P_i}{\sum P}(\text{difference}) \qquad [4.1]$$

where P = precipitation depth (mm) for the ith interval.

Day	Unadjusted Depth (mm)	Weighted Adjustment (mm)	Adjusted Depth (mm)
1	0	0	0
2	12.7	+1.88	14.58
3	7.62	+1.13	8.75
4	0	0	0
5	0	0	0
6	10.16	+1.51	11.67
7	0	0	0
Total	30.48	+4.52	35.0

Average Precipitation Methods

Precipitation is rarely uniform across watersheds due to the inherent variability in the areal distribution of rainfall as well as elevational effects. Also, there are cases when there is no rain gage located within a watershed of interest. Several strategies have been developed to calculate average precipitation for a watershed for a water balance. These methods include the arithmetic, Thiessen polygon, and isohyetal approaches (Dunne and Leopold, 1978; USDA, 1993). Each of these methods will be discussed with examples.

Arithmetic

The arithmetic approach (Eqn. 4.2) uses the arithmetic average of all the rain gages in the watershed (Figure 4.3). The advantages of this approach are that it is simple, is good in level terrain if the gages are uniformly spaced, involves no interpretation, and is adaptable to automatic processing. Disadvantages of this approach are that results are poor if the gages are not uniformly spaced, it is not appropriate in mountainous terrain due to orographic effects, and it requires a dense network of gages. This method should not use gages outside the watershed unless they are very close to the boundary.

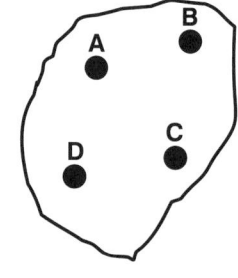

Figure 4.3 Watershed showing rain gage locations.

$$\overline{P} = \frac{P_1 + P_2 + \ldots + P_n}{n} \quad [4.2]$$

Thiessen Polygons

The Thiessen polygon approach assumes that the area closest to a gage within a watershed receives the same amount of precipitation. The watershed is divided into subareas, and average precipitation is determined from a summation of the individual precipitation amounts for that gage, weighted by subarea (Eqn. 4.3). Areas can be determined by a number of methods, including dot grids, planimeters, and digitized maps. To determine subareas, perpendiculars are drawn to the midpoint between gages and extended until they meet other bisectors and the watershed boundary (Figure 4.4).

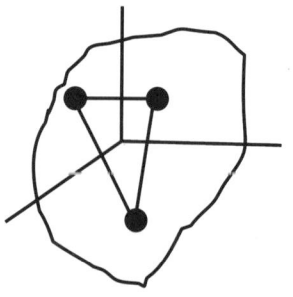

Figure 4.4 Watershed showing Thiessen polygons.

$$\overline{P} = \frac{P_1 A_1 + P_2 A_2 + \ldots + P_n A_n}{\sum (A_1 + A_2 \ldots + A_n)} \quad [4.3]$$

where A_n is the area closest to gage n.

Advantages of the Thiessen polygon approach are that gages outside the watershed can be used, the accuracy is greater than for the arithmetic approach, it can be used on unevenly spaced gages, the areas only need to be calculated once, and it is appropriate for computer use. Disadvantages of the approach include that no topographic effects are considered, it requires more work initially, and if the gages are changed, a new area calculation is needed.

Isohyetal

The isohyetal approach uses areas formed by contours between the gages, somewhat similar to the contours on a topographic map. These contours represent lines of equal precipitation. Several software programs are available for interpolating the data and producing contours on a map. This process is known as kriging. Contours also can be made by hand using a boxwood scale and determining points of precipitation along lines joining adjacent gages. These points of equal precipitation are then joined to form contours (Figure 4.5). The areas between contours and the associated precipitation can be used in Eqn. 4.3.

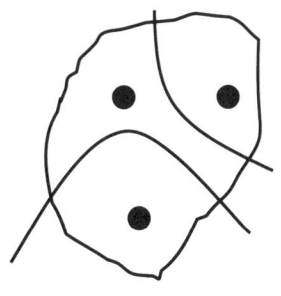

Figure 4.5 Watershed showing isohyetal contours.

Advantages of the isohyetal approach are that it considers topographic differences and orographic effects, gages can be spaced unevenly, outside gages can be used, and the process can be automated using GIS and kriging. Disadvantages of this approach are that the process has to be repeated for every storm, and the accuracy depends somewhat on the kriging algorithm used or the skill of the individual interpreting the work.

Watershed Boundary/Mapping

A **watershed** is defined as the area of land draining to a single point, usually a measuring gage in a stream. The term *drainage basin* or *catchment* is synonymous with watershed. In some parts of the world, watershed refers to the topographic divide rather than the contributing area. The area of a watershed is an important measurement, and the identification of the watershed boundary is needed to determine the area of a watershed as well as the proportion of land uses within a watershed that might influence water quality. An example of a watershed boundary is shown in Figure 4.6.

A useful skill is the ability to draw a watershed boundary. Automated methods are also available (e.g., StreamStats http://water.usgs.gov/osw/streamstats/). The following are guidelines for drawing watershed boundaries.

1. Start drawing the boundary at the bottom of the watershed.

2. Make marks on hilltops that separate the watershed of interest from adjacent watersheds.

3. The boundary must cross topographic contours perpendicularly.

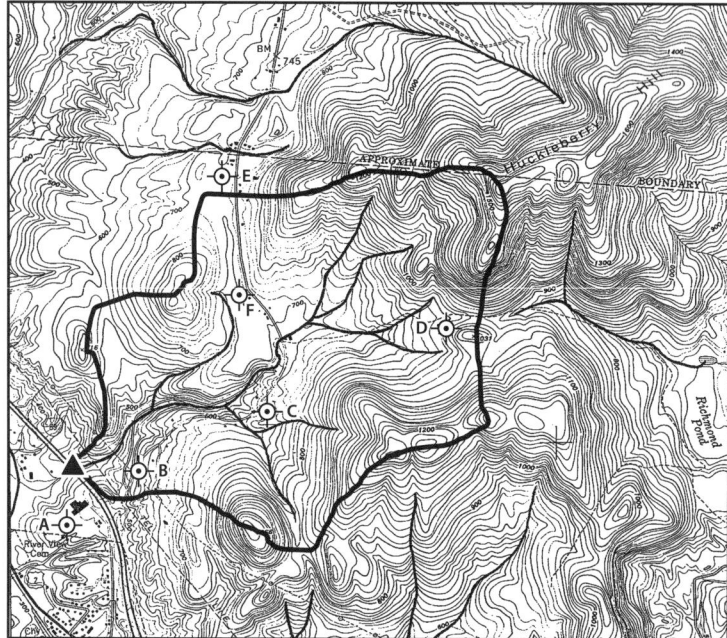

Figure 4.6 Watershed boundary drawn on topographic map. Letters refer to locations of precipitation gages.

4. The boundary cannot be parallel to topographic contours, except on hilltops.

5. Cross a saddle, which is a low area between two hills, in the middle.

6. Follow the ends of hills upward; do not follow valleys.

7. A final test is to pretend you are placing a drop of water in various parts of the watershed. Follow the drop downhill. If the drop ever crosses a boundary, a mistake has been made.

Overland flow in watersheds is often influenced by various features in watersheds that are difficult to distinguish on topographic maps. The main features modifying flow direction are roads, ditches, and culverts. Watershed divides in wetlands can be particularly challenging because there may be little elevation change. Watershed boundaries and areas may also change, depending on the flow conditions. During higher flow conditions, the watershed flow direction may be reversed from flow during lower flow conditions. This phenomenon occurs commonly in flat terrain. Field checking of overland flow is recommended to verify the watershed boundary.

Watershed boundaries for USGS 8-digit Hydrologic Unit Codes watersheds are readily available using geographic information system maps. However, watershed boundaries are generally not available for smaller watersheds, and they have to be prepared.

Precipitation Frequency Analysis

Precipitation occurs with a certain degree of randomness. The probability that it will rain is difficult to predict with certainty from time period to time period. The ability to predict the amount or intensity of precipitation is also difficult. In order to make such predictions, a statistical approach is used. The statistical analysis of precipitation is used to design the size of structures used to convey water, such as culverts and the height of bridges. Two terms are used with such analyses. The first is the probability of exceeding a certain precipitation amount. The second is the recurrence interval, or return period between precipitation amounts of a certain size.

Exceedance Probability

The **probability of exceedance** is determined from a list of precipitation amounts for the time period of interest, and is calculated using Eqn. 4.4.

$$P_i = \frac{m}{n+1} \times 100\% \qquad [4.4]$$

where P_i = the probability (chance) that precipitation will be equal to or exceed some value, and is also the cumulative % frequency
m = the rank of precipitation amounts with the highest value given the rank = 1
n = the total number of observations in the analysis

Since this analysis is most often conducted on annual data, n is often the number of years. These data are plotted on probability paper, as shown in Figure 4.7. The probability of a storm not occurring would be $1 - P$. The probability that a storm will occur within several (n) years can be determined from Eqn. 4.5:

$$q = 1 - (1 - P)^n \qquad [4.5]$$

where q = the probability that precipitation of some or greater value will occur in the next n years
P = the probability of exceedance

Recurrence Interval

The **recurrence interval (return period)** is the average interval (years) between events equaling or exceeding a given precipitation. Recurrence interval is determined from Eqn. 4.6:

$$T = \frac{1}{P_i} = \frac{n+1}{m} \qquad [4.6]$$

where T = the recurrence interval equal to the inverse of the probability of exceedance (P_i)
m = the rank of precipitation amounts, with the highest value given the rank = 1
n = the total number of observations in the analysis

Since this analysis is most often conducted on annual data, n is often the number of years. These data are plotted on probability paper, as shown in Figure 4.7. The duration of the precipitation event is also important. Data are typically summarized in 30-min to 24-hr durations (National Oceanic and Atmospheric Administration, 2013). For example, the 25-year, 24-hour storm might be 8 inches. That is to say, an 8-in storm over 24 hours is expected to occur once every 25 years. Examples 4.2 and 4.3 illustrate the use of these equations.

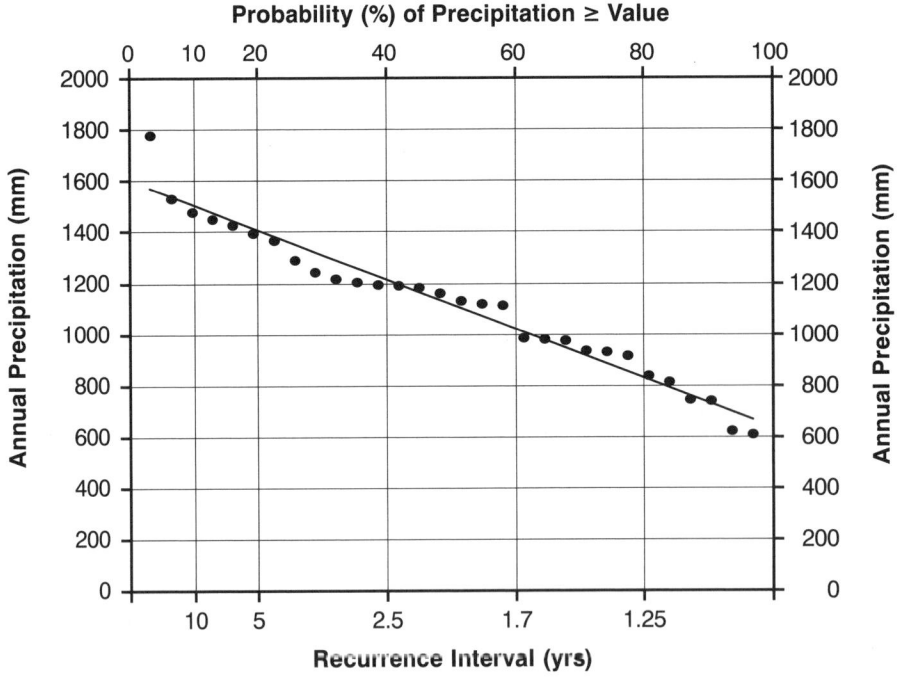

Figure 4.7 Precipitation frequency curve and recurrence interval for annual precipitation (mm) for the period 1961 through 1990.

■ Errors in Precipitation Measurements

There are several sources of errors that may occur in precipitation measurements. Errors in measurements from standard rain gages can be made on the dipstick and while recording the results on forms. Errors on all gages are influenced by calibration accuracy, the presence/absence of wind shields, the height above the ground, exposure angle, and the method used to determine the areal average (Winter, 1981). Also, the shorter the time period considered, the larger is the relative error. Errors increase with the precipitation amount but decrease with greater gage density, longer precipitation durations, and for larger areas. According to Winter (1981), instrument error is 1–5%, placement and height errors are 5–15%, and averaging errors over areas are 10–20% for monthly summaries and 60% for single storms.

EXAMPLE 4.2 Probability of Exceedance

Assume that the 25-year, 24-hour storm has been previously determined to be 142 mm in Mansfield, CT (Miller et al., 2002). What is the probability of this storm occurring in any given year?

$$P = \frac{1}{T} \times 100\% = \frac{1}{25} \times 100\% = 4\%$$

If we were to observe the 142 mm storm this year, what is the probability that the storm would occur next year? The answer is the same; there is a 4% chance that this storm will occur in any year.

EXAMPLE 4.3 Probability of Exceedance

What is the probability of the 100-year, 24-hour storm occurring in the next 25 years?

$$q = 1 - (1 - P)^n = 1 - (1 - 0.01)^{25} = 0.22 \times 100\% = 22\%$$

■ PROBLEMS

4.1 Determine the adjusted daily precipitation for the following rainfall collected for one week from a standard rain gage and a tipping bucket rain gage. The standard gage result was 1 in.

Day	Unadjusted Depth (mm)	Weighted Adjustment (mm)	Adjusted Depth (mm)
1	0		
2	11.27		
3	1.58		
4	0		
5	0		
6	9.55		
7	0		
Total	22.40		

4.2 Determine the average precipitation for the watershed in Figure 4.3 using (a) the arithmetic approach, (b) Thiessen polygons, and (c) the isohyetal method. Use the following data:

Gage	Precipitation (in.)
A	2.65
B	1.98
C	0.85
D	2.35

4.3 Determine the volume of water that occurred as precipitation for a 2.5-inch storm on a 40-acre watershed in (a) ac-ft, (b) m^3.

4.4 Determine the watershed boundary on a local topographic map in your area.

4.5 What is the return period in years for a storm that has a 1% chance of occurring this year?

4.6 What is the probability that the 50-year storm will occur this year?

4.7 For an in-depth exercise on precipitation and watershed mapping, see the "Structured Experiences" section of the online materials at waveland.com/Clausen.

■ REFERENCES

Dunne, T., and L. B. Leopold. 1978. *Water in environmental planning.* San Francisco: W.H. Freeman and Co.

Miller, D. R., G. S. Warner, F. L. Ogden, and A. T. DeGaetano. 2002. "Precipitation in Connecticut." Special Reports. Paper 36. Connecticut Institute of Water Resources. Storrs: University of Connecticut.
http://digitalcommons.uconn.edu/ctiwr_specreports/36

National Oceanic and Atmospheric Administration. 2013. *NOAA Atlas 14: Precipitation frequency atlas of the United States.*
http://www.nws.noaa.gov/oh/hdsc/PF_documents/Atlas14_Volume8.pdf

National Weather Service. 1989. *National Weather Service observing handbook no. 2: Cooperative station observations.*
http://www.nws.noaa.gov/os/coop/Publications/coophandbook2.pdf

U.S. Department of Agriculture. 1993. *National engineering handbook. Part 630—Hydrology.* National Resources Conservation Service, 210-VI-NEH. Chapter 4, Storm rainfall depth. http://www.nrcs.usda.gov/wps/portal/nrcs/detailfull/national/water/?cid=stelprdb1043063

Winter, T. C. 1981. Uncertainties in estimating the water balance of lakes. *Water Resources Bulletin* 17(1): 82–115.

5

Interception

■ Introduction

Interception is that part of precipitation that is caught and held by vegetation which evaporates before reaching the ground surface. Interception also occurs on some human-built features, such as rooftops. The process of interception has been well studied in the forest for a long period of time (e.g., Zinke, 1967). There is some debate as to what actually constitutes interception, and whether interception is part of evapotranspiration. Some argue that depression storage and the wetting of all surfaces is interception if it evaporates and does not infiltrate or run off the surface of the land. Water running down the stems of plants likely has important ecological implications as precipitation is funneled to the bases of tree trunks, especially in arid regions (Levia and Frost, 2003). In this chapter, the focus will be on interception by plants rather than by the built environment. Included in this chapter is a discussion of basic terms, how interception is measured, and the many factors that influence interception.

Both Zinke (1967) and Hewlett (1982) provided several useful definitions for interception terms. **Gross precipitation** is the precipitation measured in the open or above a canopy (Figure 5.1). **Net precipitation** is the precipitation that reaches the ground after passing through the vegetation and is composed of two components: throughfall and stemflow. **Total interception** is defined as the leaf storage capacity and evaporation during a storm. **Throughfall** is the portion of precipitation that reaches the ground by falling through openings and dripping from the canopy. **Stemflow** is the part of precipitation that reaches the ground by running down the stems or trunks of plants. **Storage capacity** is the depth of water on the intercepting surface area that can be stored. During

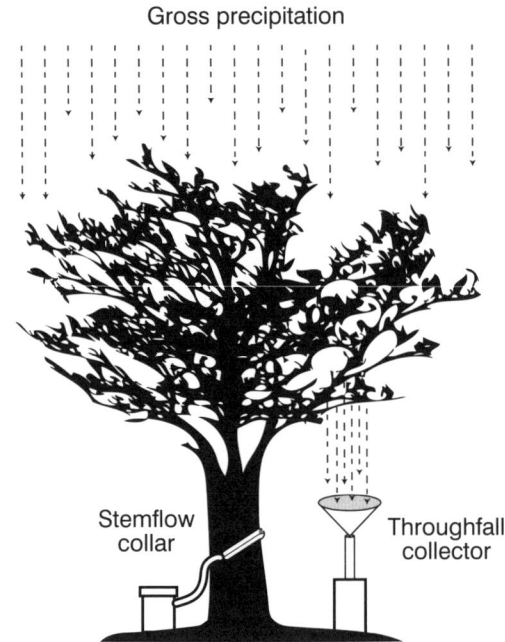

Figure 5.1 Interception terms used in a forest, showing a throughfall collector and stemflow collar.

rainfall, three phases of interception are recognized: wetting, saturation, and drainage after the storm has ceased (Li et al., 2016). Interception has been highest during the first minute of rainfall.

■ Measurement of Interception

Interception can be calculated as the difference between gross and net precipitation, or the difference between gross precipitation and throughfall plus stemflow:

$$I = P_g - (TF + SF) \qquad [5.1]$$

where I = interception
P_g = gross precipitation
TF = throughfall
SF = stemflow, all in the same units

Gross precipitation is typically measured using rain gages placed in the open near the study site. Gages mounted on towers above the canopy are also used to measure gross precipitation above forests. Errors in precipitation measurements will lead to errors in interception estimates (see Chapter 4), and can result in negative interception results.

Throughfall can be measured using troughs, funnels, plastic sheets, or rain gages (Eaton et al., 1973; Reynolds and Neal, 1991). A small roof with gutters has also been used (Andre et al., 2011). The number of gages to use is a function of the variability in observed throughfall, the confidence level, and the desired closeness to the true mean. Most statistical texts provide guidance on how to calculate the number of samples (gages) needed. For example, more gages are needed for smaller throughfall amounts and during the growing season than during seasons when throughfall is greater or during leaf off periods (Table 5.1).

Table 5.1 The number of throughfall gages needed to be within 5% of the standard error for hardwoods.

Throughfall (in)	No. of Gages for Season	
	Dormant	Growing
<0.19	24	46
0.20–0.39	6	18
0.40–0.59	6	14
>0.60	6	13

Source: Data from Zinke, 1967.

Stemflow is measured using stemflow collars, which can be constructed by applying expanding insulation foam around the tree. A trough cut into the foam directs stemflow to a sampling tube and bottle. Another method is to seal a length of split plastic hose to the tree (Crockford and Richardson, 2000; Levia and Frost, 2003). The calculation of stemflow depth over an area is not intuitive. In order to make an accurate calculation, the basal area of the sampled trees must be determined along with the basal area of the entire stand. **Basal area** is defined as the area of the cross section of tree stems per unit as measured at the diameter at breast height (1.3 m). Then the volume obtained in a stemflow collector can be extrapolated over an area (Example 5.1). This approach assumes that the storage capacity is proportional to the basal area of the stand.

Other methods for measuring interception include measuring the weight of a tree over time. This approach is only applicable to the use of a weighing lysimeter (see Chapter 6) or to weighing small trees in the greenhouse in a controlled experiment.

Interception, throughfall, and stemflow values are summarized for various locations and forest species around the world in Table 5.2. For these studies, interception has ranged from 5 to 35% of gross precipitation. Throughfall accounts for most of the water reaching the forest floor, ranging from 55 to 88%. Stemflow is much smaller, ranging from 0.2 to 13%. Both Gerrits et al. (2010) and Tsiko et al. (2012) have measured interception by the forest floor, indicating that it is a substantial portion of gross precipitation (18–22%).

Table 5.2 Summary of throughfall (TF), stemflow (SF), and interception (I) from various locations and species around the world.

Location	Species	TF (%)	SF (%)	I (%)	Period	Source
Belgium	Beech	55			Leafed	Andre et al., 2011
	Oak	65			Leafed	
		60			Leafless	
California	Oak	67	13	21	Leafed	Xiao et al., 2000
	Pear	66	10	24		
China	Spruce	65	0.2	35	Summer	He et al., 2014
England	Birch, oak	70	0.9	29	Leafed	Herbst et al., 2008
		77	3.5	20	Leafless	
Massachusetts	Birch, maple, oak	88			Summer	Guswa & Spence, 2012
	Hemlock	82				
Netherlands	Beech			18	Leafed	Gerrits et al., 2010
				5	Leafless	
	Forest floor			22		
New Hampshire	Maple, beech, birch	81	5	14	Leafed	Eaton et al., 1973
Wales	Spruce	66			1 year	Renolds & Neal, 1991
	Larch	64			Fall	
Zimbabwe	Msasa	75		25	Leafed	Tsiko et al., 2012
	Forest floor			18		

Factors Affecting Interception Loss

Several factors have been identified that influence interception losses, including vegetative type, ground cover, and climate (Crockford and Richardson, 2000). Throughfall plus stemflow in temperate forests has been reported to be 70–90% of gross precipitation (Levia and Frost, 2003). Stemflow, as a percentage of precipitation, has been found to vary from 0.3–13.1% (Crockford and Richardson, 2000). Interception in temperate regions has been reported to range from 15 to 50% (Gerrits et al., 2010).

Vegetation Type. Conifers generally have higher annual interception (17.1–21%) than deciduous trees (10.8–11.4%) (Crockford and Richardson, 2000). Stemflow in conifers (0.3–8.9%) is also higher than in hardwoods (1.7–4.1%). The primary reason for this difference is that conifers have greater surface areas than deciduous trees. Individual species characteristics also influence interception. Leaf characteristics, such as serration of leaf margins, the orientation of the leaf, its composition, whether rough or smooth, and its size all influence interception. Bark texture influences water-holding capacities, with smooth-barked trees storing less than rough-barked trees (Levia and Frost, 2003). Steeper branch inclination angles also

CHAPTER 5   Interception   43

EXAMPLE 5.1   **Stemflow Calculations**

Stemflow measurements were collected from a 24-inch dbh (diameter at breast height) white pine located in a stand shown in the figure below. Determine the depth of stemflow over the area. Individual stemflow measurements for July 2000, the diameters of the trees, and their basal areas in the stand were:

Date	Stemflow (L)
Jul 4	0.8
Jul 17	0.3
Jul 19	1.2
Total	2.3

Tree No.	Diameter (in)	Basal Area (in^2)	Basal Area (m^2)
1	8	50.3	0.03
2	12	113.1	0.07
3	24	452.4	0.29
4	36	1,017.9	0.65
Total			1.04

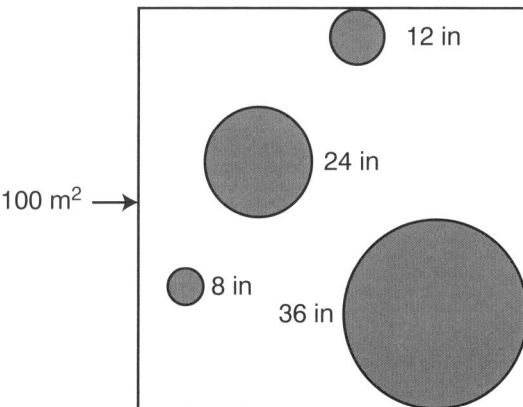

The calculations to determine the depth of stemflow are:

$$\text{mm} = 2.3\,\text{L} \times \frac{1000\,\text{cm}^3}{\text{L}} \times \frac{1}{1.04\,\text{m}^2} \times \frac{1\,\text{m}^2}{10{,}000\,\text{cm}^2} \times \frac{10\,\text{mm}}{1\,\text{cm}} = 2.21\,\text{mm}$$

increase stemflow. The structure of trees plays an important role in partitioning between stemflow and throughfall. Branches that focus interception toward the trunk increase stemflow. Branches more parallel with the ground decrease stemflow. By comparison, corn can have an interception of 40.7% and grass can intercept up to 32% of rainfall (Crockford and Richardson, 2000).

Ecoregion.   In a review, Levia and Frost (2003) report mean maximum stemflow as 3.5%, 11.3%, and 19.0% for tropical, temperate, and semiarid and arid regions, respectively. In tropical and subtropical rainforests, interception has varied greatly, from 8.9% (dryland shrubs) to 39% (humid subtropical forests) (Crockford and Richardson, 2000).

Seasons. Seasons also influence interception. Interception is greater in summer than in the winter (Gerrits et al., 2010; Herbst et al., 2008). Evaporation rates are higher in the summer and for some species, the surface area is greater prior to leaf fall. In deciduous forests, higher stemflow is observed in winter than in summer due to lower winter evaporation and leaf loss (Levia and Frost, 2003). Seasonal differences are not evident for conifers.

Forest Management. Thinning by reducing 50% of the basal area, and logging in general has been shown to reduce interception (Crockford and Richardson, 2000), which would allow more rainfall to reach the ground.

Canopy Structure. Canopy closure influences the amount of interception. For example, for *Quercus rubra* the amount of interception decreased with increasing distance from the tree, except at the dripline edge of the crown at 20 feet in the example shown in Table 5.3. Andre et al. (2011) also found greater throughfall closer to the tree than at the periphery, but only for small storms.

Table 5.3 Interception as a percent of gross precipitation at various distances from the tree.

Distance from tree (ft):	0	4	8	12	16	20
Interception (%):	57	30	29	22	21	36

Source: Data from Zinke, 1967.

Meteorological Characteristics. The intensity and amount of precipitation influences interception. Greater stemflow has been observed for larger rainfall amounts but lower rainfall intensities (Levia and Frost, 2003). But Gerrits et al. (2010) did not see an effect due to rainfall intensity. Andre et al. (2011) found higher throughfall proportions with greater rainfall amount in the leafed season but not during the leafless period, while Guswa and Spence (2012) measured a higher throughfall proportion with increasing precipitation amount. Increased wind speed increased stemflow for exposed trees (Levia and Frost, 2003), but not for throughfall in beech and oak forests in Belgium (Andre et al., 2011). For example, interception decreased as storm size increased for old growth *Pseudotsuga menziesii* in Oregon (Table 5.4).

Table 5.4 Interception as a function of storm size.

Precipitation (in)	Interception (% of precipitation)
<0.05	100
0.05–0.5	32
0.5–1.0	23
1.1–1.3	21
1.5–2.0	19

Source: Data from Zinke, 1967.

Problems

5.1 A funnel gage was used for throughfall measurements. For one rainfall event, a sample of 90 mL was collected using an 8-inch funnel. What is the depth of throughfall in mm?

5.2 Using a stemflow collar, a 50 mL sample was collected. If the tree diameter was 16 inches, what would be the depth of stemflow in mm?

5.3 If the precipitation over the canopy was 1.7 inches, stemflow was 0.2 inches, and throughfall was 1.2 inches, what was the interception as a percentage of gross precipitation?

5.4 For an in-depth exercise on measuring interception, see the "Structured Experiences" section of the online materials at waveland.com/Clausen.

References

Andre, F., M. Jonard, F. Jonard, and Q. Ponette. 2011. Spatial and temporal patterns of throughfall volume in a deciduous mixed-species stand. *J. Hydrology* 400: 244–254.

Crockford, R. H., and D. P. Richardson. 2000. Partitioning of rainfall into throughfall, stemflow and interception. *Hydrol. Processes* 14: 2903–2020.

Eaton, J. S., G. E. Likens, and F. H. Bormann. 1973. Throughfall and stemflow chemistry in a northern hardwood forest. *J. Ecol.* 61: 495–498.

Gerrits, A. M. J., L. Pfister, and H. H. G. Savenije. 2010. Spatial and temporal variability of canopy and forest floor interception in a beech forest. *Hydrol. Process* 24: 3011–3025.

Guswa, A. J., and C. M. Spence. 2012. Effect of throughfall variablity on recharge: Application to hemlock and deciduous forest in Massachusetts. *Ecohydrology* 5: 563–574.

He, Z-B., J-J. Yang, J. Du, W-Z. Zhao, H. Liu, and X-X. Chang. 2014. Spatial variability of canopy interception in a spruce forest of the semiarid mountain regions of China. *Agricultural and Forest Meteorology* 188: 58–63.

Herbst, M., P. T. W. Rosier, D. D. McNeil, and R. J. Harding. 2008. Seasonal variability of interception evaporation from the canopy of a mixed deciduous forest. *Agricultural and Forest Meteorology* 148: 1655–1667.

Hewlett, J. D. 1982. *Principles of forest hydrology*. Athens: University of Georgia Press.

Levia, D. F., and E. E. Frost. 2003. A review and evaluation of stemflow literature in the hydrologic and biogeochemical cycles of forested and agricultural ecosystems. *J. Hydrology* 274: 1–29.

Li, X., et al. 2016. Process based rainfall interception by small trees in Northern China. *Agricultural and Forest Meteorology* 218: 65–72.

Reynolds, B., and C. Neal. 1991. Trough versus funnel collectors for measuring throughfall volumes. *J. Env. Qual.* 20(3):518–521.

Tsiko, C. T., H. Makuirra, A. M. J. Gerrits, and H. H. G. Savenije. 2012. Measuring forest floor and canopy interception in a savannah ecosystem. *Physics and Chemistry of the Earth* 47–48: 122–127.

Xiao, Q., E. G. McPherson, S. L. Ustin, and M. E. Grismer. 2000. A new approach to modeling tree rainfall interception. *J. Geoph. Rsch.* 105(D23): 29,173–29,188.

Zinke, P. J. 1967. Forest interception studies in the U.S. In W. E. Sopper and H. W. Lull (eds.), *International Symposium on Hydrology*. Elmsford, NY: Pergamon Press.

Evapotranspiration

■ Introduction

Evaporation is the process by which water passes from liquid to the vapor state. **Transpiration** is the loss of water (evaporation) from the cuticle or the stomatal openings in the leaves of plants. Transpiration occurs as a by-product of photosynthesis. This reaction occurs by adding energy:

$$6CO_2 + 6H_2O \rightarrow C_6H_{12}O_6 + 6O_2 \qquad [6.1]$$

In the sunlight, chlorophyll plus a photon yields activated chlorophyll, which cleaves H_2O into $H^+ + OH^-$. Evapotranspiration (ET) is the combined processes of evaporation and transpiration. This chapter includes a discussion of the factors that influence ET and the techniques for either measuring or estimating ET.

■ Importance

Evapotranspiration is a process that dominates the water balance and controls such hydrologic phenomena as soil moisture content, ground water recharge, and streamflow. Evapotranspiration is responsible for returning 65% of precipitation falling on the land back to the atmosphere; in some parts of Africa, 90% is returned (Trenberth et al., 2007). Generally, evapotranspiration is viewed as a loss from the water budget in that it reduces the amount of streamflow, lake storage, and ground water available for direct human use.

■ Factors Affecting ET

Evapotranspiration is affected by a number of abiotic factors, such as barometric pressure, vapor pressure gradients, net radiation, wind, and type of vegetation.

These factors can be collectively shown graphically (Figure 6.1). When barometric pressure increases, evaporation or transpiration decreases. The increased density of gases in the atmosphere reduces the flux of vapor from plants, although this effect is considered relatively minor. As the vapor pressure gradient increases (steeper gradient) from the stomatal opening to the atmosphere, so does evapotranspiration (Figure 6.2). Vapor pressure is a function of temperature and relative humidity. **Relative humidity** is the ratio of actual water vapor density to saturated water vapor density. As the temperature increases, so does the saturated vapor pressure (Table 6.1). As relative humidity increases, the moisture in the air increases and evapotranspiration decreases. ET follows net radiation (R_n) during the day, increasing with higher net radiation. Higher wind speeds result in the removal of water vapor from the vicinity of the leaf, causing a steeper vapor pressure gradient and greater ET.

■ Measurement of ET

Actual measurement of evapotranspiration can only be accomplished at a relatively small scale. Both direct and indirect measures of evapotranspiration can be used.

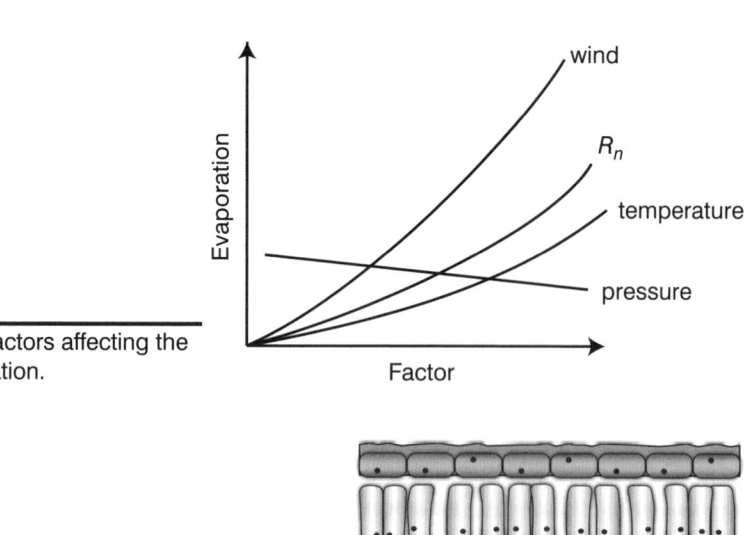

Figure 6.1 Factors affecting the rate of evaporation.

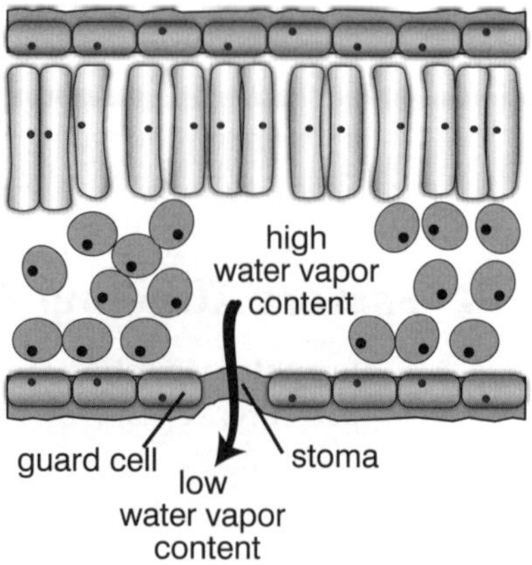

Figure 6.2 Diagram of a leaf showing stomata and vapor pressure gradient outward from saturated evaporation.

Table 6.1 Saturated vapor pressure and density for water.

Temperature (°C)	Saturated Vapor Pressure (mm Hg)	Saturated Vapor Density (gm/m^3)
−10	2.15	2.36
0	4.58	4.85
5	6.54	6.8
10	9.21	9.4
15	12.79	12.83
20	17.54	17.3
25	23.76	23
30	31.8	30.4
40	55.3	51.1

Source: Data from Weast, 1970.

Direct Methods

Potted Plants. By measuring the weight loss over time, ET can be directly measured as gms or cm^3 of water lost. If the surface cross-sectional area of the pot is known, ET can be expressed as a depth of water.

Cut-Shoot Method. A twig or stem will continue to transpire even when cut. The weight loss over time for the twig can be measured to estimate ET.

Weighing Lysimeter. A lysimeter is like a large potted plant that is installed in the field. These are expensive to construct but can hold whole trees. The lysimeter is used to determine the water balance for a block of soil (Figure 6.3). Another type of lysimeter is non-weighing and bottomless. A metal culvert (e.g., 36 in. diameter) is driven or dug to an impermeable layer, such as clay. Measurements of the water level in the cylinder can be used to estimate ET. Knowledge of the porosity of the soil is required. This approach assumes that there is no water movement through the open bottom of the lysimeter. This bottomless lysimeter has been used in peatland water balance studies (Kolka et al., 2011).

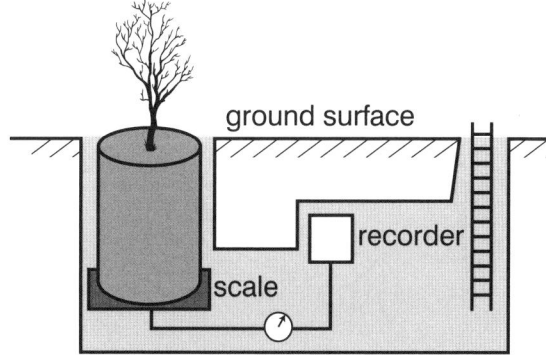

Figure 6.3 Schematic of a weighing lysimeter.

ET Tent. A tent or small chamber (Figure 6.4) can be used to measure evapotranspiration in the field. A fan blows air through the chamber and the moisture in the air is measured in the intake and exhaust from the tent (Brooks et al., 1991).

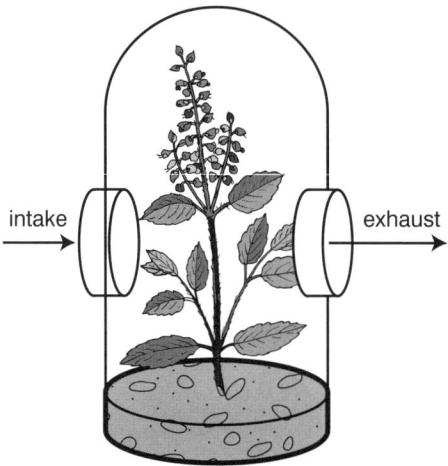

Figure 6.4 ET tent.

Eddy Covariance. The flux of moisture from an area can be measured using eddy covariance techniques. The basic approach assumes that within the boundary layer close to the earth's surfaces (50 – 100 m), the transport of moisture is governed by eddies that move air of higher moisture content upward and air of lower moisture content downward, resulting in the mass transfer of moisture (Figure 6.5a). These movements are called **fluxes,** which are the rate of transfer of quantities of wind and moisture across a unit area (Stull, 1989). These fluxes are divided into the three Cartesian directions typically noted as x, y, and z. Conventional notation for wind uses the components of u, v, and w (Figure 6.5b).

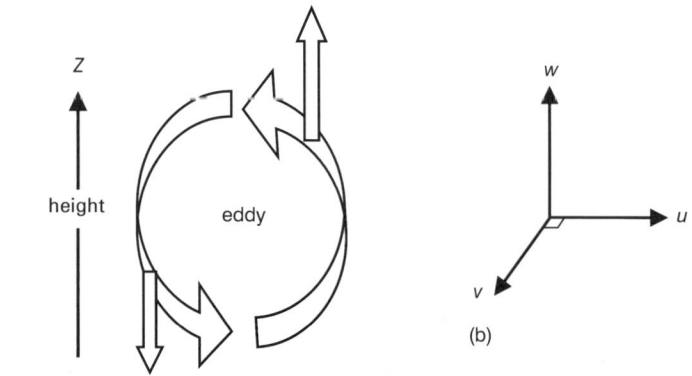

Figure 6.5 (a) Turbulent mixing eddy and (b) wind flux in the vertical (w), horizontal (u), and horizontal transverse (v) components.

The approach is based largely on statistics. Equations used assume a flat horizontal homogeneous surface and a neutral atmosphere (Kaimal and Finnigan, 1994). A neutral atmosphere is one that does not encourage vertical transport of air due to temperature differences. It changes with elevation at the same rate as the dry adiabatic lapse rate. Also, the wind profile from the surface upward is assumed to follow a logarithmic distribution.

The **covariance** of paired data is defined as the average value of the product of their individual deviations from their means. The flux of water vapor can be determined from:

$$LE = L_v\, \bar{\rho}'_v\, \bar{U}'_Z \qquad [6.2]$$

where LE = the latent heat flux
  ρ'_v = the instantaneous deviation of the water vapor density from the mean
  U'_Z = the instantaneous deviation of vertical wind speed from the mean
  L_v = the latent heat of vaporization of water (2.45×10^6 J/kg at 20°C)

The quantity $\rho'_v\, U'_Z$ is the covariance between the water vapor density and vertical wind speed. Example 6.1 illustrates eddy covariance calculations.

The technique requires very fast response instruments. A typical system would include a data logger, three-dimensional sonic anemometer, and temperature and humidity probes at a height of 1:100 (1 m height for 100 m fetch). The term **fetch** refers to the length over which the wind has blown. An averaging time must be selected, for example 30 minutes, and the sampling rate must be determined, such as 10 Hz or 10x observations per second (obs/s).

EXAMPLE 6.1 **Eddy Covariance Calculation**

On July 18, 2003, a data logger was used to record wind speed (w) and direction and the specific humidity (q) at a rate of 10 obs/s. While the testing went on for several days, only part of the data is shown. Determine the ET for this eddy covariance data.

Time (s)	w (m/s)	$\bar{w} - w = w'$ (m/s)	q (g/m³)	$\bar{q} - q = q'$ (g/m³)	w'q' (g/s/m²)
9:40:00.0	−0.05975	0.02273	15.1528	0.64345	0.014626
9:40:00.1	−0.10375	0.06673	15.1487	0.64755	0.043211
9:40:00.2	−0.162		0.12498	15.15	
9:40:00.3	−0.129		0.09198	15.1452	0.65105
9:40:00.4	−0.14275	0.10573	15.1471	0.64915	0.068635
9:40:00.5	−0.07275	0.03573	15.1497	0.64655	0.023101
9:40:00.6	−0.2215	0.18448	15.1479	0.64835	0.119608
9:40:00.7	−0.2805	0.24348	15.1509	0.64535	0.15713
9:40:00.8	−0.1545	0.11748	15.1412	0.65505	0.076955
9:40:00.9	−0.14925	0.11223	15.1506	0.64565	0.072461
9:41:59.9	−0.16825	0.13123	16.2993	−0.05305	-0.06602
Average	−0.03702		15.79625		0.049024

$$\text{ET} = \overline{w'q'} = 0.049024 \frac{\text{g}}{\text{s/m}^2} \times \frac{1 \text{ cm}^3}{\text{g}} \times \frac{1 \text{ m}^2}{10000 \text{ cm}^2}$$

$$\times \frac{10 \text{ mm}}{\text{cm}} \times \frac{3600 \text{ s}}{\text{hr}} = 0.176 \text{ mm/hr}$$

where w = the wind speed
 q = the specific humidity
 $\overline{w}$ and $\overline{q}$ = 30-minute average w and q
 w' and q' = deviations from average for each observation
 $\overline{w'q'}$ = the flux of moisture

Indirect Methods

Soil Moisture Loss.   A soil-moisture accounting procedure can be used to indirectly estimate ET. The volumetric soil water content (Chapter 7) is needed to determine the depth of water in the soil. For example:

July 12	6.50 in./ft of soil
July 19	6.35 in./ft of soil
difference:	0.15 in. = evapotranspiration

Evaporation Pan.   The U.S. Weather Bureau Class A weather stations use standardized evaporation pans (Figure 6.6). The installation usually includes a totalizing anemometer. A hook gage is used to accurately measure the depth of water in the pan. Records are widely available for stations across the United States. The pan must be kept clean, and a source of clean water is needed. They may absorb and conduct heat from the sides, and wind turbulence can cause flow over the edge. A coefficient relating pan evaporation to the rate of water use by a particular plant must be evaluated from some other direct measure of ET. The average pan coefficient is 0.7 to 0.8 (Haan et al., 1982). The pan coefficient varies seasonally and geographically.

Estimates of ET

Because ET is difficult to measure, several methods have been developed to estimate it. These approaches can be regarded as either water balance approaches or energy balance methods.

Water Balance.   A watershed water balance could be used to calculate ET if all other terms of the equation are known. Most often, this calculation is used for annual ET. Eqn. 3.2 can be solved for ET:

$$\text{ET} = P - (+Q \pm \Delta S) \qquad [6.3]$$

CHAPTER 6 Evapotranspiration   53

Figure 6.6 Evaporation pan.

Energy Balance. Several methods can be considered energy balance approaches. The first is the energy balance equation:

$$R_n = R_s(1-\alpha) + \Delta R_L \qquad [6.4]$$

where R_n = net radiation
R_s = shortwave radiation
α = the albedo
R_L = long-wave radiation

Shortwave radiation is solar radiation, most of which is at a wavelength between 0.3 and 3 μm. About half of this energy is in the visible spectrum between 0.4 and 0.7 μm. **Albedo** is the reflection coefficient of a surface for only shortwave radiation. Long-wave radiation is greater than 3 μm and is called terrestrial radiation. The relationship between net radiation and evaporation is shown by:

$$R_n = L_v + S + H \qquad [6.5]$$

where R_n = net radiation (sum of shortwave radiation received minus that reflected plus long-wave radiation received minus that absorbed)
L_v = latent heat of vaporization
S = storage in the ground
H = heat (sensible) in the air (Haan et al., 1982)

Thornthwaite PET. The Thornthwaite equation (Thornthwaite and Mather, 1957) for estimating potential evapotranspiration (*PET*) is a function of temperature and latitude:

$$PET = 1.6\left(\frac{10\,T}{I}\right)^a \quad [6.6]$$

where *PET* = the monthly potential evapotranspiration in cm/mo
T = mean monthly temperature (°C)
I = the annual heat index, determined from:

$$I = \sum_{i=1}^{12} i \quad [6.7]$$

where

$$i = \left(\frac{T}{5}\right)^{1.514} \quad [6.8]$$

$$a = 0.49239 + 0.01792\,I - 7.71 \times 10^{-5}\,I^2 + 6.75 \times 10^{-7}\,I^3 \quad [6.9]$$

If the temperature is less than 0°C, then there will be no *PET*. This formula does not account for a crop factor. Correction tables are used based on latitude that account for sunshine duration each month (Table 6.2).

Table 6.2. Correction factor for latitude and month.

Latitude	Jan.	Feb.	Mar.	Apr.	May	Jun.	Jul.	Aug.	Sep.	Oct.	Nov.	Dec.
60° N	0.54	0.67	0.97	1.19	1.33	1.56	1.55	1.33	1.07	0.84	0.58	0.48
50° N	0.71	0.84	0.98	1.14	1.28	1.36	1.33	1.21	1.06	0.90	0.76	0.68
40° N	0.80	0.89	0.99	1.10	1.20	1.25	1.23	1.15	1.04	0.93	0.83	0.78
30° N	0.87	0.93	1.00	1.07	1.14	1.17	1.16	1.11	1.03	0.96	0.89	0.85
20° N	0.92	0.96	1.00	1.05	1.09	1.11	1.10	1.07	1.02	0.98	0.93	0.91
10° N	0.97	0.98	1.00	1.03	1.05	1.06	1.05	1.04	1.02	0.99	0.97	0.96
0°	1.00	1.00	1.00	1.00	1.00	1.00	1.00	1.00	1.00	1.00	1.00	1.00
10° S	1.05	1.04	1.02	0.99	0.97	0.96	0.97	0.98	1.00	1.03	1.05	1.06
20° S	1.10	1.07	1.02	0.98	0.93	0.91	0.92	0.96	1.00	1.05	1.09	1.11
30° S	1.16	1.11	1.03	0.96	0.89	0.85	0.87	0.93	1.00	1.07	1.14	1.17
40° S	1.23	1.15	1.04	0.93	0.83	0.78	0.80	0.89	0.99	1.10	1.20	1.25
50° S	1.33	1.19	1.05	0.89	0.75	0.68	0.70	0.82	0.97	1.13	1.27	1.36

Source: Data from Dunne and Leopold, 1978.

Hamon's Method. Hamon's method (Hamon, 1963) uses humidity and possible sunshine hours to estimate potential evaporation, based on:

$$PET = kDP_t \quad [6.10]$$

where PET = the daily potential evaporation (inches)
  k = a constant (0.0065)
  D = the possible hours of sunshine in units of 12 hours
  P_t = saturated water vapor density in g/m³ at the daily mean temperature

Blaney-Criddle Method. The Blaney-Criddle method (1950) adds a crop factor in the equation:

$$PET = KF = KpT \quad [6.11]$$

where PET = potential evapotranspiration
  K = an annual, seasonal, or monthly crop use coefficient
  p = the proportion of daytime hours of the year occurring during the period
  T = mean monthly or daily temperature
  F = a climate coefficient (Dunne and Leopold, 1978; Haan et al., 1982)

Penman's Equation. One of the most widely used energy-based approaches to estimating evaporation is the Penman equation, or one of the modifications of this method. Penman (1948) developed an equation to determine evaporation from open water, bare soil, and grass:

$$E = \frac{(R_n \Delta + E_a \gamma)}{(\Delta + \gamma)} \quad [6.12]$$

where E = the evaporation rate from open water, bare soil, and turf (mm/d)
  R_n = the net radiant energy available at the surface (H in original publication)
  γ = a constant of wet and dry bulb hygrometer equation = 0.27 (°F) or 0.49 (°C)

and
$$\Delta = \frac{(e_s - e_a)}{(T_s - T_a)} \quad [6.13]$$

where Δ = the slope of the saturation vapor pressure curve (0.66 mb/°C)
  e_s, e_a = the saturated and actual vapor pressure, respectively
  T = the temperature

and
$$E_a = (e_a - e_d) f(u) \quad [6.14]$$

where E_a = the the vapor pressure deficit at 2 m
e_d = the saturated vapor pressure at the dew-point temperature
$f(u)$ = the wind velocity (Brooks et al., 1991)

Penman's equation has been modified for crop coefficients, slopes, and azimuths. Measurements are needed for net radiation, wet- and dry-bulb temperatures, and the wind speed at 2 m (Haan et al., 1982).

Lake Evaporation. Evaporation from lakes is estimated by using evaporation pans or through the Lake Mead equation:

$$E = Nu(e_w - e_a) \qquad [6.15]$$

where N = the mass-transfer coefficient
u = the mean wind velocity near the surface of the ground or water (knots)
e_w = the mean vapor pressure at the water surface temperature (mb)
e_a = the mean vapor pressure of saturated air at the dew point temperature (mb) (Harbeck, 1962)

■ PET vs. ET

Potential evapotranspiration occurs from a vegetated surface when the water loss to the atmosphere is unlimited by deficiencies in the supply of water. When water is limiting, evapotranspiration will be reduced. An evapotranspiration ratio can be calculated from:

$$ETR = \frac{ET}{PET} \qquad [6.16]$$

where ETR = the evapotranspiration ratio
ET = evapotranspiration
PET = potential evapotranspiration (Dunne and Leopold, 1978; Hann et al., 1982)

The model assumes that at the wilting point, the ETR is reduced to 50%; that is, ET is one-half of PET. The reduction in ETR begins somewhere between the wilting point and the field capacity. Although this value varies with soil type, an example would be that the reduction begins at 40% of the available water (Figure 6.7).

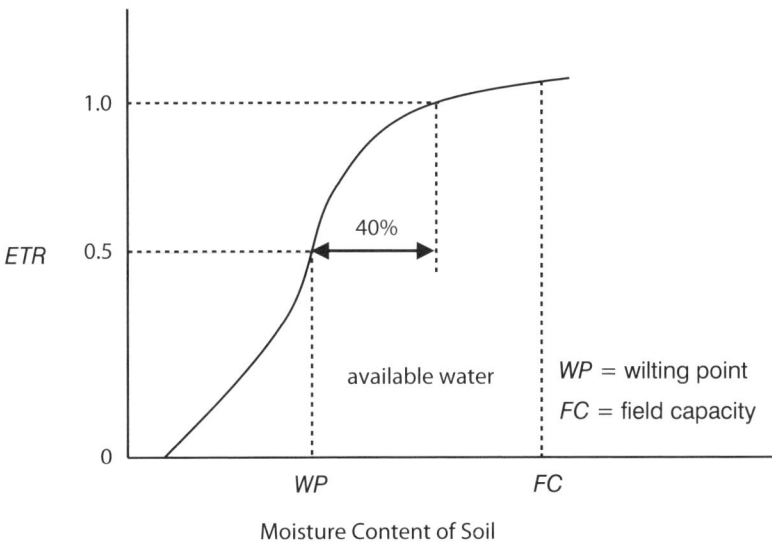

Figure 6.7 Evapotranspiration ratio (ETR) as a function of soil moisture content.

Problems

6.1 During a potted plant experiment, the weight of the pot at the beginning of the week was 1,045 g and at the end of the week was 907 g. What was the evapotranspiration in cm³/wk? If the pot has a diameter of eight inches, what is the evapotranspiration rate in cm/wk?

6.2 Estimate the average evapotranspiration (in./d) from the following data measured at a bottomless lysimeter. The porosity for this organic soil was 84%.

Date	Precipitation (in.)	Well Level (ft)
5/2	0.00	2.17
5/19	3.69	1.87
5/24	0.88	1.8
6/14	1.68	2.31
6/21	1.21	2.24
6/27	2.53	2.94
7/3	1.62	2.12
7/12	0.41	2.47

6.3 (a) Using the normal temperature data from an airport station in the following table, determine the monthly normal PET using Thornthwaite's method. Correct the PET for latitude. The station is located at 42°N. Show your calculations of a and I.

Month	Mean Temp (°F)	Mean Temp (°C)	i	PET (cm)	Latitude Correction Factor	Adj. PET (cm)	MC (%)	ET (cm)
Jan	26.0						40	
Feb	28.4						40	
Mar	36.9						40	
Apr	47.1						38	
May	57.8						32	
Jun	66.3						30	
Jul	71.5						27	
Aug	69.8						25	
Sep	61.7						30	
Oct	50.7						35	
Nov	41.4						40	
Dec	31.2						40	

(b) Given that the wilting point for the soil at the airport has a moisture content of 23% and at field capacity the moisture content is 36%, determine the monthly ET given the moisture contents in the preceding table and using the ETR model.

6.4 Using the answer from Problem 6.3, determine the pan coefficient for the Norfolk 2 SW Station in Connecticut based on the following temperature and pan evaporation data. This station is located at 42°N.

Month	Average Temperature (°F)	Pan Evaporation (in.)
May	58.0	3.88
Jun	62.0	4.32
Jul	66.8	3.84
Aug	66.4	3.70
Sep	60.4	2.23
Oct	46.7	1.12

REFERENCES

Blaney, H. F., and W. D Criddle. 1950. *Determining water requirements in irrigated areas from climatological and irrigation data*. USDA Soil Conservation Service, SCS-TP 96. https://archive.org/details/determiningwater96blan

Brooks, K. N., P. F. Folliott, H. M. Gregersen, and J. L. Thames. 1991. *Hydrology and the management of watersheds*. Ames: Iowa State University Press.

Dunne, T., and L. B. Leopold. 1978. *Water in environmental planning*. San Francisco: W. H. Freeman and Co.

Haan, C.T., H. P. Johnson, and D. L. Brakensiek. 1982. *Hydrologic modeling of small watersheds*. American Society of Agricultural Engineers. ASAE Monograph No. 5. St. Joseph, MI. http://www.tucson.ars.ag.gov/unit/publications/PDFfiles/277.pdf

Hamon, W. R. 1963. *Computation of direct runoff amounts from storm rainfall*. International Association of Scientific Hydrology Publication 63: 52–62.

Harbeck, Jr., G. E. 1962. *A practical field technique for measuring reservoir evaporation utilizing mass-transfer theory*. USDI-Geological Survey Professional Paper 272-E. http://pubs.usgs.gov/pp/0272e/report.pdf

Kaimal, J. C., and J. J. Finnigan. 1994. *Atmospheric boundary layer flows: Their structure and measurement*. New York: Oxford University Press.

Kolka, R. K., S. D. Sebestyen, E. S. Verry, and K. N. Brooks. 2011. *Peatland biogeochemistry and watershed hydrology at the Marcell Experimental Forest*. Boca Raton, FL: CRC Press.

Penman, H. L. 1948. Natural evaporation from open water, bare soil and grass. *Proceedings of the Royal Society of London*. Series A. 193(1032): 120–145.

Stull, R. B. 1989. *An introduction to boundary layer meteorology*. Boston, MA: Kluwer Academic Publishers.

Thornthwaite, C. W., and J. R. Mather. 1957. Instructions and tables for computing potential evapotranspiration and the water balance. Centerton, NJ: Drexel Institute of Technology, Laboratory of Climatology, *Publications in Climatology* 10(3): 185–311.

Trenberth, K. E., L. Smith, T. Qian, A. Dai, and J. Fasullo. 2007. Estimates of the global water budget and its annual cycle using observational and model data. *J. Hydrometeorology* 8: 758–769.

Weast, R. C. (ed.) 1970. *Handbook of chemistry and physics*. Cleveland, OH: The Chemical Rubber Co.

7

Infiltration and Soil Water

■ Introduction

Infiltration (f) is the process of water entering the surface of the soil (Horton, 1933). Infiltrating water is the supply for plant transpiration and ground water recharge. **Soil water** describes the amount of water contained within the soil as well as how tightly it is held in the soil matrix. Infiltration rates can easily be affected by land management practices, and a discussion of what affects infiltration rates is included in this chapter. Soil water is actually a storage volume that depends in part on infiltration rates. Therefore, these two components of water cycling are combined in this chapter. Also included is how we measure infiltration and soil water.

■ Infiltration

A number of terms used in the discussion of infiltration need to be defined. **Percolation** is the process of water movement through the soil, rather than the process of water entering the soil. **Infiltration rate** is the instantaneous rate at which water enters the soil (cm/hr). **Infiltration capacity** is the maximum rate that water can enter the soil (Horton, 1933) at any time or condition. The infiltration capacity is different from the actual infiltration rate because the actual infiltration rate is limited by the precipitation supply rate. For example, if the precipitation rate is less than the infiltration capacity, the actual infiltration rate would equal the precipitation rate. A typical infiltration curve is shown in Figure 7.1. At the beginning of precipitation, the initial infiltration rate (f_0) will often be high and remain constant until the point in time that the rainfall intensity (P) equals the infiltration rate. As the soil becomes saturated, the infiltration rate will decline (decay) to a final minimum infiltration capacity (f_c), which is approximately equal to the saturated hydraulic conductivity of the soil (k_s) (Skaggs and Khaleel, 1982).

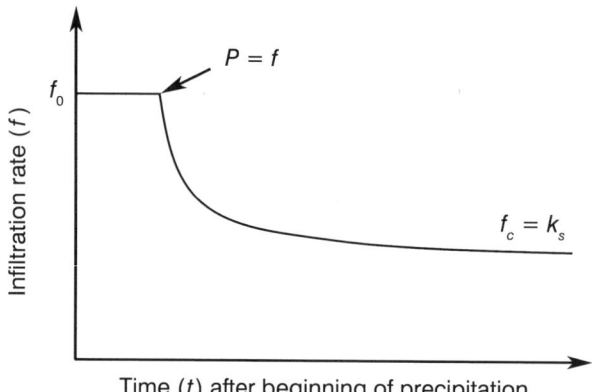

Figure 7.1 Idealized infiltration capacity curve.

Forces Involved in Infiltration

There are two forces involved in infiltration: *gravity* (Figure 7.2) and *capillary forces*. The following equations describe these two forces. Gravity or specific energy in the soil is:

$$\text{Gravity} = \pi r^2 h \rho g \qquad [7.1]$$

where r = radius of soil pores
h = head of water
ρ = density of water ≈ 1.0
g = gravitational constant

Force (F) equals:

$$F = ma = mg = \frac{m}{V} V = \rho g \qquad [7.2]$$

where m = mass
a = acceleration
V = volume

The other terms have been previously defined.

Capillary forces are described by:

$$2\pi r \gamma \cos \theta \qquad [7.3]$$

where γ = the surface tension
θ = the contact angle of the meniscus on glass

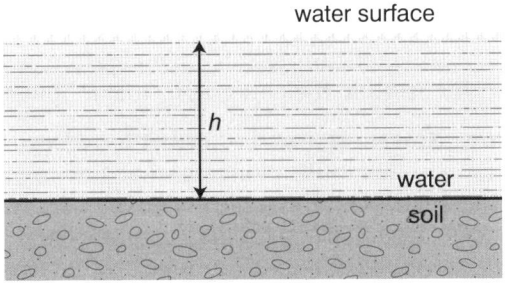

Figure 7.2 The effect of head on gravity from ponded water on top of the soil.

Capillarity is shown in Figure 7.3. Water rises up a capillary tube due to adhesion—the attraction between the water molecules and an unlike substance, in this case the glass tube—and cohesion, the attraction between dipolar water molecules that creates surface tension. The surface of the water forms a concave meniscus within the capillary tube because the water molecules are attracted to the sides of the glass tube. For the water to rise, gravity (g) must be less than the surface tension (γ).

To determine the height of rise (h), the following equation is used:

$$\pi r^2 h \rho g = 2\pi r \gamma \cos\theta \qquad [7.4]$$

and solved for h.

$$h = \frac{2\gamma \cos\theta}{r\rho g} \qquad [7.5]$$

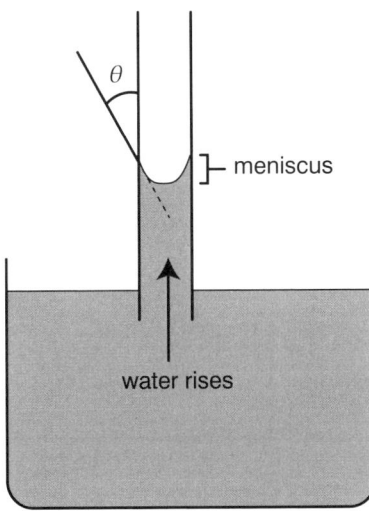

Figure 7.3 Capillary rise in a tube.

Factors Affecting Infiltration

The infiltration rate is influenced by several factors, including soil texture, land management, soil moisture, salinity, temperature, and frozen soil. These factors are further discussed in the paragraphs that follow.

Soil Texture.   Coarse-textured soils that have large pores, such as sandy loam or gravel, have higher infiltration rates than fine-textured soils (Figure 7.4) composed of clay or silt loam that have a larger number but smaller size of pores (Skaggs and Khaleel, 1982). Also, clay pans or compacted layers in the soil act to reduce infiltration. We can use hydraulic conductivity (Chapter 8) as an expression of these different textures.

Soil Structure.   Macropores, shrink/swell potential, and a restricting layer can all influence infiltration. Surface sealing can reduce infiltration rates during rainfall (Skaggs and Khaleel, 1982). Sealing can be caused by rainfall impact and colloidal swelling. Therefore, the surface cover of a soil can be important for infiltration.

Land Management.   Forest cover typically has greater infiltration rates than grasslands because forests have more organic matter that causes soil aggregates to form. Burning an area would reduce infiltration rates because it would remove soil organic matter and reduce aggregation of soil particles. In some cases burning results in clogged soil pores, and burned surfaces can be hydrophobic. Soil compaction in urban areas is another example of the effect of land management on infiltration. However, mulching the surface can increase infiltration. Agricultural cropping is also known to reduce infiltration because the soil is less protected from rainfall impact (Chow, 1964).

Soil Moisture.   The initial water content of the soil influences initial infiltration (Skaggs and Khaleel, 1982). As the moisture content increases in the soil, the infiltration rate decreases because the pores fill up. In very dry, sandy soils, the infiltration rate can actually increase over time with the release of trapped air, which initially impedes water infiltration.

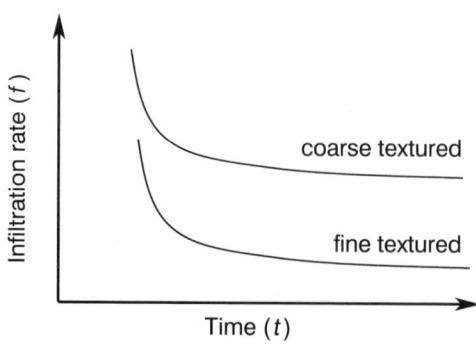

Figure 7.4   Effect of soil texture on infiltration rates.

Water Quality. Some of the chemical constituents in water can influence infiltration rates. For example, increased salinity of the water lowers the infiltration rate. Sodium in water breaks down aggregates and disperses the particles, resulting in clogged pores. Salt can be added to soil to lower the infiltration rate if desired, and road salt has this effect. Highly turbid surface water also reduces infiltration by clogging pores with sediment.

Temperature. The temperature of water influences the viscosity of water and therefore the infiltration rate. The infiltration rate would increase with temperature and decrease with increasing viscosity. A temperature increase from 40°F to 100°F could result in an increase in the infiltration rate by a factor of two.

Soil Freezing. Soil frost can affect infiltration rates, the effect depending on the type of frost present in the soil. There are four types of soil frost that can occur. *Concrete frost* occurs in saturated soils that have small particles, such as clays. This frozen structure is impervious to air and water (Chow, 1964). *Granular frost* occurs in unsaturated soils. In this case, crystals are formed that create aggregates of soil particles that allow greater infiltration rates than those in the original unfrozen soil. *Porous concrete frost* is another form of soil frost that is not completely frozen and breaks easily, allowing infiltration. *Honeycomb frost* is an open lattice of water crystals that can form in soils with high moisture content during fall and spring, and also allows infiltration. Frost heaving can occur with reduced infiltration rates, especially in saturated soils. Certain types of land management activities can influence the type of frost that forms. For example, clear-cutting favors concrete frost because less evapotranspiration may result in wetter soils in certain situations.

Measurement of Infiltration

Several types of infiltrometers have been used to measure infiltration rates. These include the single-ring infiltrometer, the double-ring infiltrometer, and a rainfall simulator/runoff plot (Bouwer, 1986; Chow, 1964). The single- and double-ring infiltrometers operate by flooding the surface of the soil to a shallow depth. A burlap bag can be used to protect the soil surface. A shallow head is constantly maintained in the infiltrometers. This depth can be maintained using a Mariotte column (Constanz and Murphy, 1987). The amount of water used to maintain the depth is recorded over time. The advantage of the double-ring infiltrometer (Figure 7.5) is that the outer ring is intended to aim the flow in the inner ring more directly downward. Rainfall simulators apply water to a plot through special nozzles to the point where ponding or runoff occurs (Grismer, 2012). Chow (1964) details methods for conducting rainfall simulations.

Infiltration can be estimated from a simplified water balance equation for the situation where the time interval is short, evapotranspiration is assumed not to occur, and overland flow, sometimes called surface runoff (SRO), can be measured: $P - SRO =$ Infiltration. This case would typically only be valid for the plot or field scale and applies to the use of a rainfall simulator.

Figure 7.5 Double-ring infiltrometer. (Photo courtesy of Larry Dingman.)

Infiltration Equations

Several infiltration equations have been developed. However, only the Horton (1940) and Green and Ampt (1911) equations will be included as examples in this chapter because they are the two equations most commonly used today.

Horton Equation. Horton (1940) described the infiltration capacity that will decrease with time (decay) as long as rainfall intensity is greater than the infiltration capacity as:

$$f_0 = f_c + (f_0 - f_c)e^{-K_f t} \quad [7.6]$$

where f = the infiltration capacity at any time t
f_c = the final minimum infiltration rate ≈ saturated hydraulic conductivity (k_s)
f_0 = the initial infiltration rate
K_f = a constant representing the time required for f_0 to reach f_c

This equation is derived from empirical fitting of the infiltration capacity curve. Several approaches can be used to determine K_f. One such approach uses two points on the infiltration curve:

$$K_f = \frac{1}{t_2 - t_1} \ln\left(\frac{f_1 - f_c}{f_2 - f_c}\right) \quad [7.7]$$

where f_1 and f_2 represent the infiltration rates at time t_1 and t_2, respectively. Infiltration measurements are required to determine f_0 and f_c. The Horton equation can be used to fit almost any curve. However, it has no theoretical basis, and infiltration cannot be related to soil characteristics. Also, the curve does not apply when precipitation is less than the infiltration rate.

Green and Ampt Equation. The Green and Ampt infiltration equation is based on Darcy's law.

$$F_s = \frac{-\psi \times IMD}{\dfrac{I}{K_s} - 1} \quad [7.8]$$

where F_s = accumulated infiltration volume at surface saturation
         ψ = capillary potential across the wetting front, and is negative
         I = rainfall intensity
      IMD = initial moisture content deficit, equal to the porosity minus initial moisture content on a volumetric basis
         K_s = saturated conductivity (Skaggs and Khaleel, 1982)

The time to surface saturation (Figure 7.6) can be determined from:

$$t_{sat} = \frac{F_s}{I} \qquad [7.9]$$

and

$$f_p = K_s\left(1 - \frac{\psi \times IMD}{F}\right) \text{ where } F \geq F_s \qquad [7.10]$$

where f_p is the potential infiltration rate.

If $F < F_s$, then $f = I$, and

$$F = F + P\Delta t \qquad [7.11]$$

■ Soil Water

There are two fundamental ways to characterize soil moisture. The first aspect is the amount of water or water content in the soil. The amount of water is important for soil recharge and overland flow. The second aspect is the energy status of soil moisture, which is important for evapotranspiration, tree growth, and water movement in the soil.

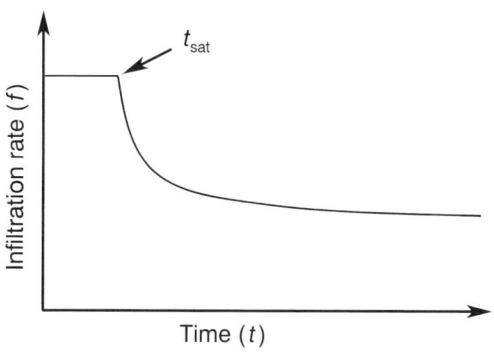

Figure 7.6 Infiltration curve showing time to saturation followed by the decay in infiltration rate.

Amount of Water

The amount of water in soil is expressed in the following common ways (Buckman and Brady, 1960; Gardner, 1965):

Oven-dry water content (θ_{ODW}):

$$\theta_{ODW} = \frac{\text{wet wt} - \text{dry wt}}{\text{dry wt}} \times 100\% \qquad [7.12]$$

where wet wt = the weight of soil and water
dry wt = the weight of soil

Volumetric water content (θ_v)(%):

$$\theta_v = \frac{\theta_{ODW} \times D_b}{\rho = 1} \qquad [7.13]$$

where D_b = the bulk density (g/cm³)
ρ = the density of water (g/cm³)

The depth of water in the soil can be determined from:

$$\theta_{depth} = \frac{\theta_v \times depth}{100} \qquad [7.14]$$

where *depth* is the thickness of soil of interest in the units of depth used.

Soil bulk density (D_b) is the mass of a unit volume of soil (Blake, 1965; Buckman and Brady, 1960) determined from:

$$D_b = \frac{\text{soil dry weight}}{\text{soil volume}} = g/cm^3 \qquad [7.15]$$

Methods of Soil Water Content Measurement. Both direct and indirect methods are used to determine soil water content.

Gravimetric. A soil moisture measurement can be obtained directly by gravimetric (weighing) methods. The soil sample can be collected with a core sampler (Figure 7.7). The sample is placed in a soil tin and weighed in the original wet condition and then again after it is dried 24 hours at 105°C in an oven, using the same soil tin (Gardner, 1965). If the volume of the sample is known, then the bulk density of the soil can also be obtained. This method is simple and has a low initial cost. However, this method is destructive and cannot be repeated over time and depth. Also, this approach is unsuitable for stony soils.

Time Domain Reflectometry. Time domain reflectometry (TDR) was originally used to find faults in coaxial cable (Topp et al., 1980). This approach is based on the dialectric constants for water and soil, the latter of which is a function of the soil water content. A microwave pulse is sent through a steel rod, producing a waveform on an oscilloscope, which also measures the transit time of the pulse.

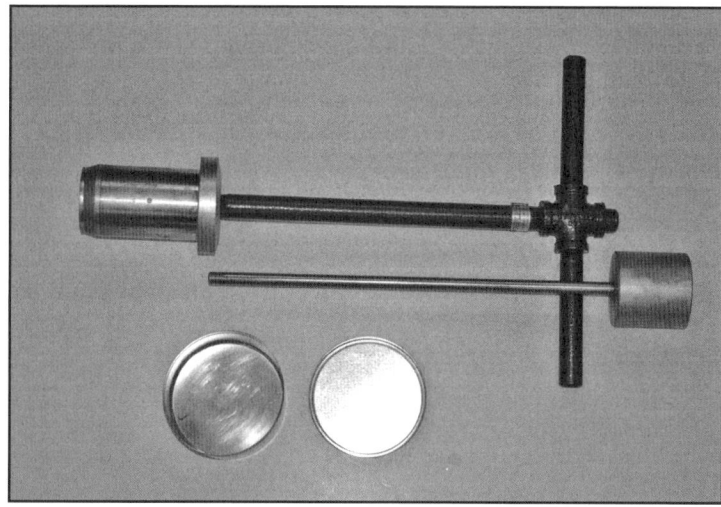

Figure 7.7 Bulk density core sampler and soil tin.

The dielectric constant for water is high ($K' = 81.5$), while that for a vacuum is low ($K' = 1$). Therefore the soil water content can be determined from:

$$\theta_v = f(K'_a) \quad [7.16]$$

where θ_v = the volumetric moisture content
K' = the dialectric constant

subscript a represents apparent permittivity due to potential electrical loss and

$$K_a \approx K' = \left(\frac{ct}{2L}\right)^2 \quad [7.17]$$

where c = a constant and the velocity of an electromagnetic wave in free space
t = the transit time through the rod (times 2 because down and back)
L = the rod length

Then an empirical relationship between the apparent dielectric constant and soil water content is used.

Energy Status of Water

Two forces involved in the energy status of water are (1) cohesion between like particles, such as water molecules, and (2) adhesion, which is the attraction between charged soil particles and the dipolar water molecule (Buckman and Brady, 1960). Energy is needed to move water from layers around soil particles to a root (Figure 7.8).

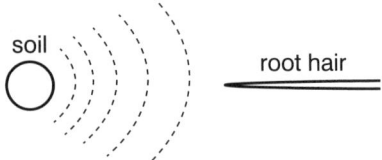

Figure 7.8 Gradient in soil water tension around a soil particle.

Water located in the soil has energy called *specific energy* due to the weight of water and gravity (g). Water moves from regions of high to low energy. The work done is equal to the difference in energy at the two regions. The force acting on water is determined from:

$$F = \frac{w}{s} \qquad [7.18]$$

where F = force (dynes/g)
  w = work
  s = distance

Soil water potential (ψ) is the work required to transfer water from a reference point ($\psi = 0$) to some other ψ. At atmospheric pressure $\psi = 0$. Lower potential exists when $\psi < 0$, which occurs during unsaturated conditions; this potential is also called suction or tension. Higher potential exists when $\psi > 0$, which occurs during saturated conditions.

Factors Determining Soil Water Potential. Several factors influence soil water potential. These factors give rise to different types of potential. **Matric potential** (ψ_m) (capillary potential) is the affinity of soil particles for water. **Osmotic potential** (ψ_o) (solute potential) is due to the affinity of salts for water. Pure water will move toward water containing salts or sugar. Soil evaporation can increase solutes in the soil, resulting in more work needed to remove soil water. Osmotic potential is important for plant roots. **Gravitational potential** (ψ_z) is the work needed to raise water above the earth's surface against gravity, and it increases with height above the earth's surface. **Submergence potential** (ψ_s) occurs under saturated conditions if water is submerged beneath a free water surface or is ponding. Submergence potential cannot exist if there is matric potential because the soil would then be dryer. **Pneumatic potential** (ψ_G) is due to the pressure of the air adjacent to water in the soil. **Pressure potential** (ψ_P) is equal to matric or submergence potential plus pneumatic potential. **Thermal potential** (ψ_T) is due to water moving from low temperature to high temperature, but this is not often encountered. The total potential is shown in Eqn. 7.19.

$$\psi_{H_2O} = \psi_P + \psi_o + \psi_Z + \psi_T \qquad [7.19]$$

Methods of Measurement. There are two common methods to measure soil water potential.

Tensiometer. A tensiometer is used to measure soil water potential (negative potential). An idealized tensiometer is shown in Figure 7.9 in a soil pit. Tensiometers are accurate near saturation, but less so in dry conditions.

For Figure 7.9, head is determined in reference to a datum:

$$H = -h + Z \qquad [7.20]$$

where H = hydraulic head
h = matric potential
Z = gravity

A typical tensiometer resembles Figure 7.10. Tension is determined from:

$$\psi = -\rho g h_m + \rho g h_w \qquad [7.21]$$

where h_m = the height of the mercury
h_w = the height of the water above some datum

Soil Matric Potential Block. Soil water potential can also be determined by measuring the difference in water potential in the soil with a sensor that measures the resistance between two probes. This resistance is a function of water content.

Soil Water Terms

Some additional terms are useful for explaining the different amounts of water in a soil. **Wilting point** (WP) is the moisture content at which plants wilt. **Field capacity** (FC) is the moisture content at which water is held against gravity.

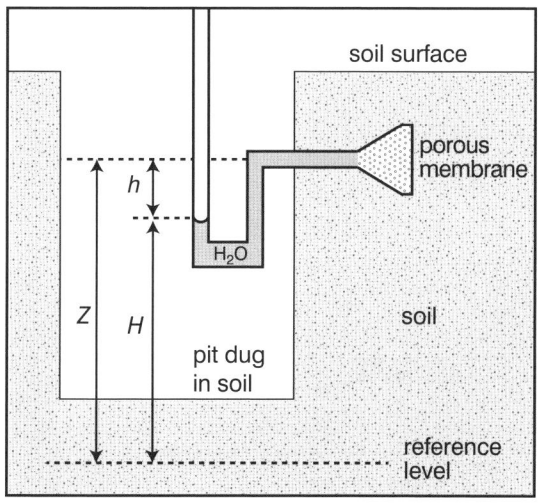

Figure 7.9 Idealized tensiometer in a soil pit.

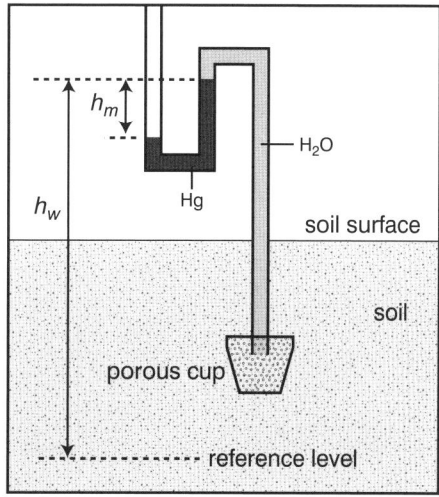

Figure 7.10 Tensiometer without a soil pit.

Gravitational water is the depth or volume of water that is greater than the field capacity. It would drain away over time due to gravity. **Available water** is the depth or volume of water at field capacity minus that at the wilting point. This is the amount of water considered available to the plant. Unavailable water is the moisture content below the wilting point. The amount of available water varies with the soil type (Figure 7.11). Also, soil tension varies with water content (Figure 7.12).

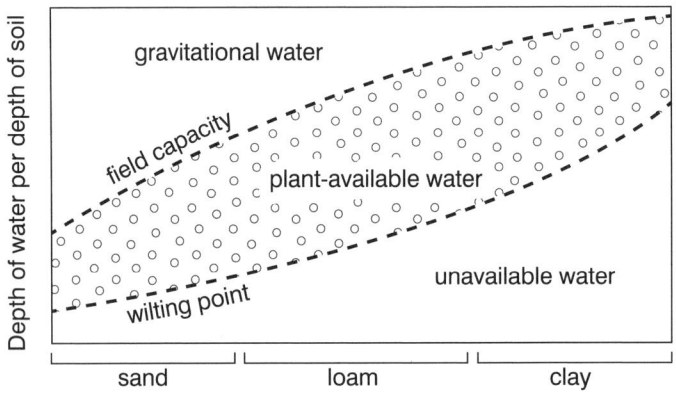

Figure 7.11 Typical water characteristic of soils of various textures.

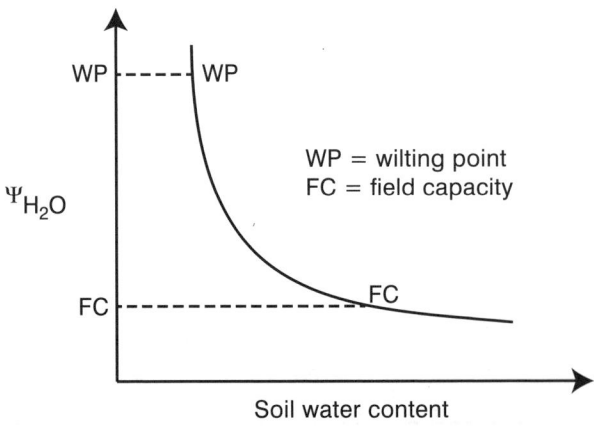

Figure 7.12 Relationship between soil suction (tension) and moisture content.

Problems

7.1 If the wet weight of a soil sample is 80 g and the dry weight is 60 g, what is the percent soil moisture on a dry weight basis?

7.2 If the bulk density of the soil in Problem 7.1 was 1.45 g/cm^3, what would be the volumetric water content of the soil?

7.3 What would be the depth of water in the upper foot of soil in Problem 7.2?

7.4 A bulk density corer (Figure 7.7) was used to collect the soil sample in Problem 7.1. If the diameter of ring used in the corer was 2.25 in OD, and the height of the ring was 3 cm, what was the bulk density of the soil in g/cm^3?

7.5 Fit the Horton equation to the decay portion of the infiltration curve using two points on the curve, using the data in the table below from a double-ring infiltration test in a loam soil. Plot the actual infiltration rate versus time and the calculated rate from the Horton equation on the same graph. The soil has a porosity of 52.3% and a saturated conductivity of 1.27 cm/hr. The field capacity is approximately 38%. The average tension of the wetting front is 31.24 cm.

Time (min)	f (cm/hr)
4.56	10.57
5.34	8.71
6.55	7.47
8.0	6.58
9.9	5.84
12.4	5.23
15.2	4.72
19.3	4.24
24.5	3.84
30.3	3.48
36.9	3.23

7.6 Using the information from Problem 7.5, compute the time to surface saturation, and then starting at this point, use the Green and Ampt equation to calculate accumulated infiltration volume and potential infiltration rates at two-minute intervals for 60 minutes. The initial moisture content is 30% and the rainfall rate is 5.28 cm/hr. Surface saturation occurs at 26.8 minutes.

References

Blake, G. R. 1965. Bulk density. Chapter 30 in *Methods of soil analysis. Part 1. Physical and mineralogical properties, including statistics of measurements and sampling*. Madison, WI: American Society of Agronomy.

Bouwer, H. 1986. Intake rate: Cylinder infiltrometer. Chapter 32 in A. Klute (ed.), *Methods of soil analysis. Part 1. Physical and mineralogical methods*. 2nd ed. Madison, WI: American Society of Agronomy, pp. 825–842.

Brooks, K. N., P. F. Folliott, H. M. Gregersen, and J. L. Thames. 1991. *Hydrology and the management of watersheds*. Ames: Iowa State University Press.

Buckman, H. O., and N. C. Brady. 1960. *The nature and properties of soils*. 6th ed. New York: Macmillan.

Chow, V. T. 1964. *Handbook of applied hydrology*. New York: McGraw-Hill.

Constanz, J., and F. Murphy. 1987. An automated technique for flow measurement from Mariotte reservoirs. *Soil Sci. Soc. Am.* 51(1): 253–254.

Gardner, W. H. 1965. Water content. Chapter 7 in *Methods of soil analysis. Part 1. Physical and mineralogical properties, including statistics of measurements and sampling*. Madison, WI: American Society of Agronomy.

Green, W. H., and G. A. Ampt. 1911. Studies on soil physics: 1. Flow of air and water through soils. *J. Agric. Sci.* 4: 1–24.

Grismer, M. E. 2012. Standards vary in studies using rainfall simulators to evaluate erosion. *California Agriculture* 66(3): 102–107.

Horton, R. E. 1933. The role of infiltration in the hydrologic cycle. *Transactions, American Geophysical Union. Report and Papers, Hydrology*, pp. 446–460.

Horton, R. E. 1940. An approach toward a physical interpretation of infiltration capacity. *Proc. Soil Sci. Soc. Am.* 5: 399–417.

Skaggs, R. W., and R. Khaleel. 1984. Infiltration. Chapter 4 in C. T. Hann, H. P. Johnson, and D. L. Brakensiek (eds.), *Hydrologic modeling of small watersheds*. ASAE Monograph No. 5. St. Joseph, MI: American Society of Agricultural Engineers, pp. 121–166.

Topp, G. C., J. L. Davis, and A. P. Annan. 1980. Electromagnetic determination of soil water content: measurements in coaxial transmission lines. *Water Resources Research* 16(3): 574–582.

Ground Water

Introduction

There are a number of basic terms used in ground water studies that need to be defined. **Ground water** is subsurface water that occupies the saturated zone (Figure 8.1). It is generally regarded as water below the water table. This distinction separates this type of water from soil water, which lies above the saturated zone. Ground water comprises 67% of public water supply withdrawals in the United States and 98% of domestic self-supplied water (Kenny et al., 2009).

An **aquifer** is a body of ground water capable of supplying an appreciable amount of water. There are two main types of aquifers. A **water table aquifer** is unconfined and open vertically to the atmosphere (Figure 8.2). It is made up of permeable material. An **artesian aquifer** (Figure 8.2) is an "aquifer confined between less permeable materials from which water will rise above the bottom of the overlying confining bed if afforded an opportunity to do so" (American Public Health Association et al., 1969).

A **piezometric surface** is "an imaginary surface that everywhere coincides with the static level of the water in an aquifer" (American Public Health Association

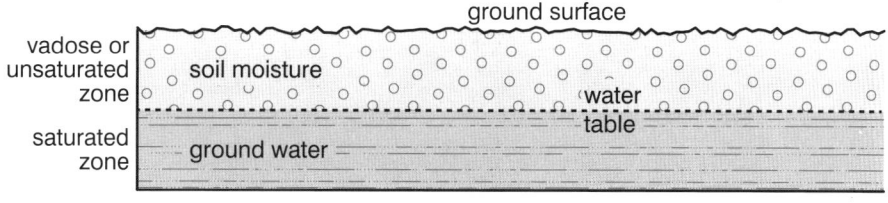

Figure 8.1 Cross-sectional view of the subsurface of the land showing forms of ground water.

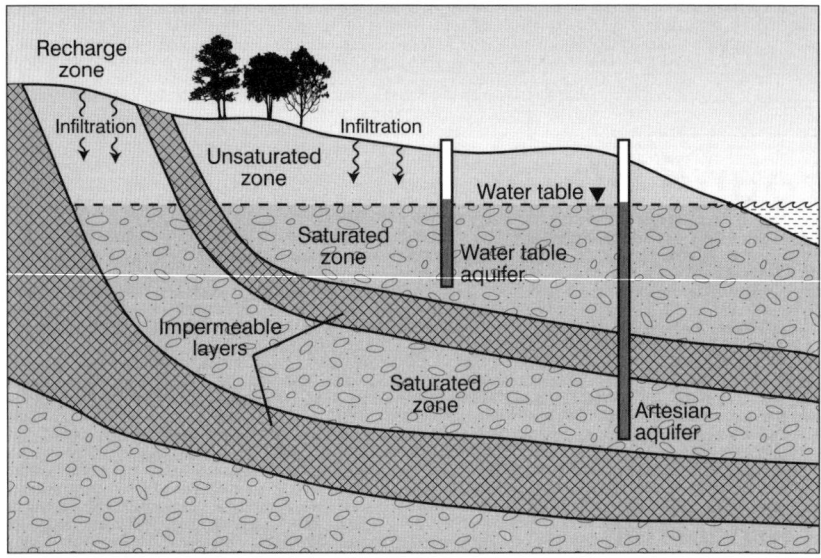

Figure 8.2 Water table aquifer and artesian aquifer.

et al., 1969). A piezometric map shows the shape of the piezometric surface above the aquifer using isopleths or lines of equal head (Figure 8.3).

Head is the energy required to move a unit weight of water from a high point to a lower point. Head is also the height of the free surface of water above any point in a hydraulic system (American Public Health Association et al., 1969). Head is used to determine which directions ground water is flowing. A **discharge zone** is an area where ground water comes to the surface. It may be directly into a water body or on the surface of the land (Figure 8.4). Springs

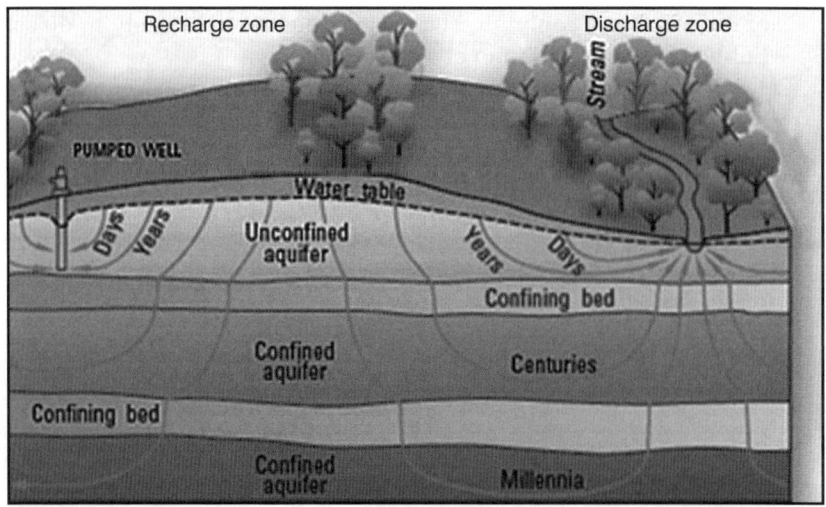

Figure 8.4 Discharge zone (USGS, 2016).

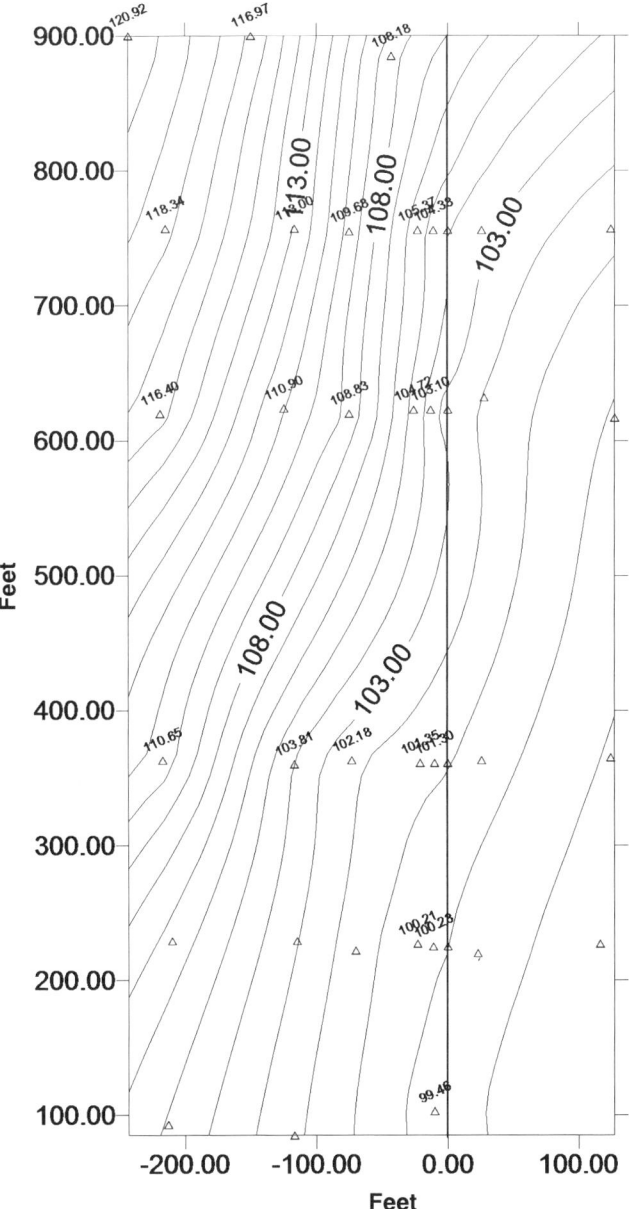

Figure 8.3 Water surface elevation of the ground water in the vicinity of Muddy Brook.

and certain wetlands are examples of ground water discharge areas. A **recharge zone** is an area that contributes to the addition of water to an aquifer, typically from precipitation (Figure 8.2).

Ground Water Flow

Ground water movement is explained by Darcy's law (1856) for saturated flow through porous media (Figure 8.5). The velocity form of the equation is:

$$v = k_s \frac{dh}{dL} \quad [8.1]$$

and the discharge form of the equation from $Q = VA$ (Chapter 9) is:

$$Q = k_s A \frac{dh}{dL} \quad [8.2]$$

where v = Darcy velocity, which ignores porosity
k_s = saturated hydraulic conductivity (cm/s)
dh/dL = hydraulic gradient
h = hydraulic head
L = distance in the direction of flow
Q = discharge
V = velocity
A = the cross section area (L^2) (e.g., Davis and DeWiest, 1966)

The k_s is a function of the porous media through which the water is moving (Table 8.1). Head is gravity (z) plus the pressure potential of water in the medium.

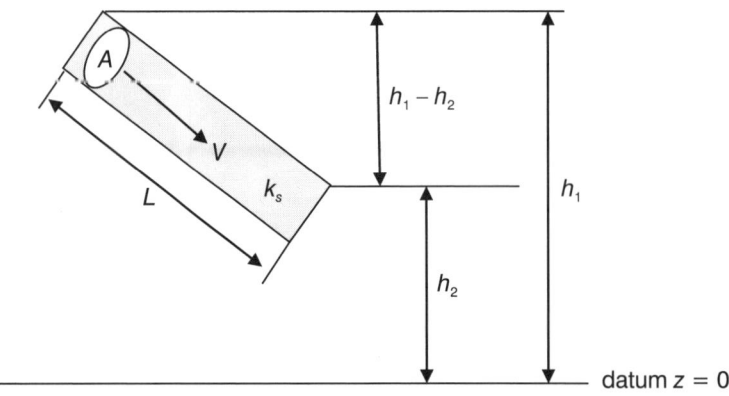

Figure 8.5 Diagram of Darcy's law.

Table 8.1 Porosities and saturated hydraulic conductivities for various materials.

Material	Porosity (%)	Hydraulic Conductivity k_s (cm/s)
Unconsolidated materials		
Soils	50 – 60[c]	$10^{-4} - 10^{-1}$ [c]
Sand	25 – 40[b]	$1 - 10^{-4}$ [a,b]
Silt	35 – 50[b,c]	$10^{-3} - 10^0$ [b]
Clay	45 – 55[b,c]	$10^{-11} - 10^{-1}$ [c]
Gravel	25 – 40[b,c]	$10^6 - 1$ [a,b,c]
Sand and gravel	10 – 35[b,c]	$10^{-3} - 10^{-1}$ [c]
Glacial till	10 – 25[b]	$10^{-6} - 10^2$ [b]
Rocks		
Sandstone	5 – 30[b,c]	$10^{-6} - 10^{-3}$ [c]
Limestone	1 – 10[c]	$10^{-4} - 1$ [b]
Shale	0 – 10[b]	10^{-10} [c]

[a] Davis and DeWiest, 1966.
[b] Driscoll, 1986.
[c] Novotny, 2003.

The following is an example from Brooks et al. (2013) of a typical calculation of ground water flow.

EXAMPLE 8.1   Calculation of Ground Water Flow

For a well-sorted gravel aquifer with a k_s of 0.01 cm/s, a hydraulic gradient of 1 m over 1,000 m, and an aquifer cross section of 500 m², what is the ground water flow?

$$Q = (0.01 \text{ cm/s}) \left(500 \text{ m}^2 \times \frac{10{,}000 \text{ cm}^2}{\text{m}^2}\right) \left(\frac{1 \text{ m}}{1{,}000 \text{ m}}\right) = 50 \text{ cm}^3/\text{s} = 4.32 \text{ m}^3/\text{d}$$

The true velocity, for example for a contaminant, can be estimated by knowledge of the porosity, since:

$$Q = A_p v \qquad [8.3]$$

and

$$A_p = Ap \qquad [8.4]$$

where A_p = the area of the voids
A = the cross-section area
p = the porosity (%)

The velocity of transport is then determined from:

$$v_{\text{pore}} = \frac{v}{p} \quad [8.5]$$

The time of travel for a contaminant can be determined from:

$$t = \frac{L}{v_{\text{pore}}} \quad [8.6]$$

where L = distance.

Ground water flow in a basin is often characterized as being local, intermediate, or regional (Toth, 1963) (Figure 8.6). Local flow systems have adjacent recharge areas and discharge areas that originate from their respective topographic highs and lows. Such systems have the greatest interaction with surface waters (Winter et al., 1998). Intermediate flow systems do not have recharge and discharge areas that occupy the topographic highs and lows and have one or more such highs and lows between the recharge and discharge areas (Figure 8.6). These systems generally lie beneath local flow systems. Regional flow systems lie deeper than local and intermediate systems. The recharge area is located along the watershed divide, and the discharge area is found at the base of the watershed. Flow lines in this system are the longest, and this allows for greater contact time with dissolved constituents (Winter et al., 1998).

■ Effect of a Well

Pumping a well in unconfined conditions induces radial flow to the well that can result in a lowering of the water level in the aquifer, creating a cone of depression (Figure 8.7). Drawdown is the difference between the initial water table level and the level after pumping. Most hydrogeology texts provide equations for relating the well yield to the hydraulic conductivity, drawdown during pumping, the radius of influence, and the well radius (e.g. Driscoll, 1986). These equations are used in pumping tests.

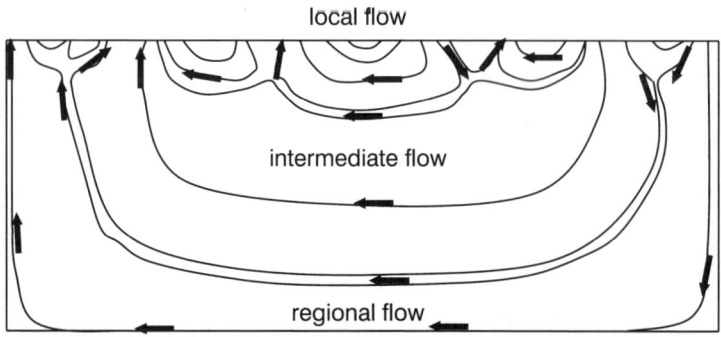

Figure 8.6   Local, intermediate, and regional ground water flow systems (after Toth, 1963).

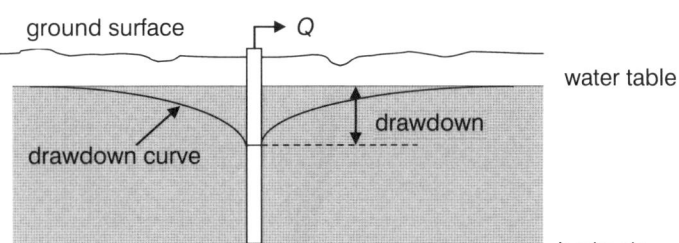

Figure 8.7 Well in a water table aquifer showing drawdown effects (after Davis and DeWiest, 1966).

Flow Nets

A flow net is a two-dimensional diagram that shows how ground water moves (Figure 8.8). It is used to determine the quantity and direction of ground water flow. The flow net is composed of two sets of lines. The first are equipotential lines, which are lines of equal pressure or head. From above, these lines would represent the water table surface (Figure 8.3). The second are flow lines that are perpendicular to the equipotential lines. These represent the lines of water movement. A minimum of three wells is needed to construct the direction of ground water flow (Driscoll, 1986) by triangulation (Figure 8.9).

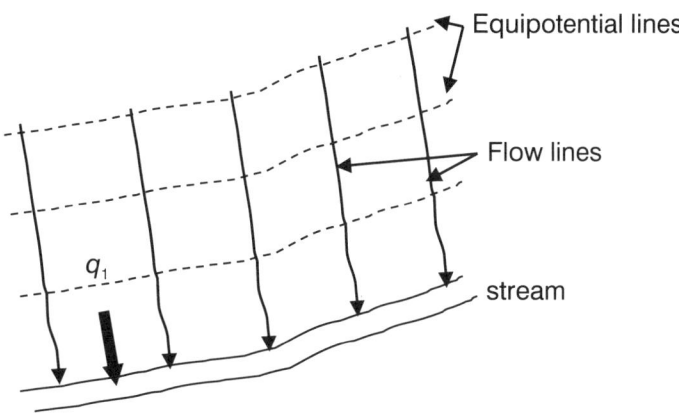

Figure 8.8 Flow net in the vicinity of a stream.

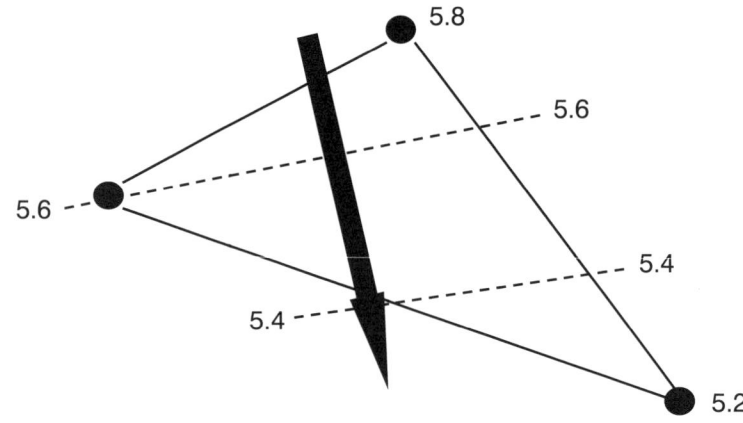

Figure 8.9 Determining direction of ground water flow from water elevations in three wells surrounding a septic drain field.

■ Problem

8.1 A stratified drift aquifer in Connecticut is 1,000 ft wide and is 25 ft thick. Two wells are located 400 ft apart; h_1 = 320 ft, h_2 = 310 ft. Determine the daily ground water flow (ft^3/d), assuming a typical conductivity for stratified drift of 15 ft/day.

■ References

American Public Health Association, American Society of Civil Engineers, American Water Works Association, Water Pollution Control Federation. 1969. *Glossary: Water and wastewater control engineering*. Joint Editorial Board.

Brooks, K. N., P. F. Folliott, H. M. Gregersen, and J. L. Thames. 2013. *Hydrology and the management of watersheds*. 4th ed. Ames: Iowa State University Press.

Darcy, H. 1856. *Les fontaines publiques de la Ville de Dijon*. Paris: Victor Dalmont.

Davis, S. N., and R. J. M. DeWiest. 1966. *Hydrogeology*. New York: John Wiley & Sons.

Driscoll, F. G. 1986. *Groundwater and wells*. St. Paul, MN: Johnson Filtration Systems.

Kenny, J. F., N. L. Barber, S. S. Hutson, K. S. Linsey, J. K. Lovelace, and M. A. Maupin. 2009. *Estimated use of water in the United States in 2005*. U.S. Geological Survey Circular 1344. Denver, CO: USGS. http://pubs.usgs.gov/circ/1344/pdf/c1344.pdf

Novotny, V. 2003. *Water quality: Diffuse pollution and watershed management*. 2nd ed. New York: John Wiley & Sons.

Toth, J. 1963. A theoretical analysis of groundwater flow in small drainage basins. *J. Geophysical Research* 68(16): 4795–4812.

U.S. Geological Survey. 2016. *Groundwater discharge: The water cycle*. Available at http://water.usgs.gov/edu/watercyclegwdischarge.html

Winter, T. C., J. W. Harvey, O. L. Franke, and W. M. Alley. 1998. *Ground water and surface water: A single resource*. U.S. Geological Survey Circular 1139. Denver, CO: USGS. http://pubs.usgs.gov/circ/circ1139/pdf/circ1139.pdf

9

Streamflow

■ Introduction

Flow in streams is an important component of the hydrologic cycle. It is primarily the part of the water balance left over after evapotranspiration. Streamflow is also an important source of water for people. Water reaches rivers through a number of processes (Figure 9.1). The term *runoff* has many meanings. **Runoff** has been defined as **surface runoff** or **overland flow**, which is the part of streamflow that runs over the surface of the land (Hewlett, 1982). **Subsurface runoff**, also sometimes called **subsurface stormflow** or **interflow**, is the part of streamflow that comes from subsurface sources but reaches the stream quickly. **Stormflow**, sometimes called **quickflow**, is the part of streamflow from both surface and subsurface sources that reaches the stream soon enough to produce higher discharge. **Baseflow** or dry-weather flow is that part of streamflow derived from ground water (Dunne and Leopold, 1978). Runoff is often used as a synonym with streamflow for water balances.

Several runoff processes that result in stormflow are recognized. **Hortonian overland flow** is a widely recognized process where rainfall intensity exceeds the infiltration capacity of the soil (Horton 1933, 1940). When surface depressions on the land are filled, rainfall excess will contribute to surface runoff. This

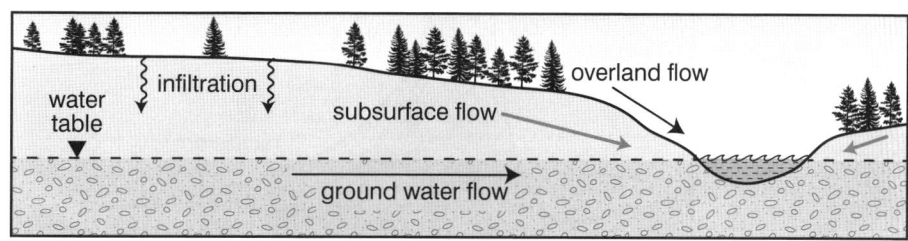

Figure 9.1 Forms of runoff.

phenomenon has been observed to occur in semiarid regions and on compacted and disturbed soils. **Saturated-source area flow** is more commonly observed in humid regions and in forests. These are **partial areas** of watersheds, often close to streams that become saturated during storms. Direct precipitation on these saturated areas produces quick overland flow to the stream (Dunne and Black, 1970). The **variable source area** concept, that streamflow is due to shrinking and expanding source areas adjacent to streams, results in subsurface flow as the main contributor to streamflow in certain parts of the country (Hewlett and Hibbert, 1967). This process occurs in well-drained, permeable deep soils.

■ Components of Streamflow

A **hydrograph** is a plot of discharge over time (Figure 9.2). The rising limb and peak discharge (Q_p) are affected by watershed and weather characteristics. The receding or falling limb is affected by stream characteristics. Watershed characteristics that affect the rising limb are slope, watershed length, antecedent soil moisture, vegetation, soil characteristics, aspect, and elevation. Weather characteristics include the intensity and duration of precipitation, temperature, radiation, area of precipitation, and the type of precipitation, whether snow or rain (Hewlett and Hibbert, 1967; Huggins and Burney, 1982).

■ Time of Concentration

The time of concentration (t_c) is the time required for water to travel from the most remote part of the watershed to the outlet. When the duration of the precipitation event is equal to the time of concentration, all parts of the watershed

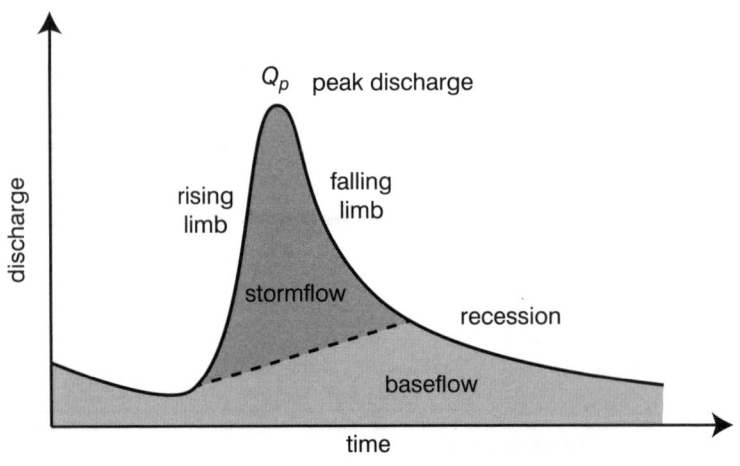

Figure 9.2 Hydrograph and associated terms.

are believed to be contributing to the outlet. The time of concentration can be determined from:

$$t_c = \frac{L^{1.15}}{7700\, H^{0.38}}$$ [9.1]

where t_c = time of concentration (hr)
L = length of catchment (ft)
(along stream from outlet to farthest high point)
H = change in elevation (ft) (Kent, 1972)

■ Basin Lag

Lag time is a theoretically useful value that acts like a fingerprint of a watershed because it incorporates many aspects of runoff generation (Leopold, 1991). The characteristics that affect lag time include watershed size, soils, geology, slope, and land use (Dingman, 2008), precipitation amount and duration (Pawlow, 1977), timing of peak rainfall intensity (Askew, 1968), and antecedent precipitation (Kang et al., 1998).

Four measures of lag time are in common usage: centroid lag-to-peak, centroid lag, lag-to-peak, and peak lag-to-peak (Figure 9.3). The symbols for these terms are shown in Table 9.1. Centroid lag-to-peak is the time from the centroid of precipitation to the peak discharge. The term **centroid** means the center of mass of a figure. Centroid lag is the time from the centroid of precipitation to the centroid of discharge. Lag-to-peak is the time from the beginning of precipitation to the peak discharge. Peak lag-to-peak is the time from the peak rainfall intensity to the peak discharge (Hood et al., 2007).

The centroid of precipitation is determined from:

$$t_{wc} = \frac{\sum_{i=1}^{n} W_i \times t_i}{\sum_{i=1}^{n} W_i}$$ [9.2]

where t_{wc} = centroid of precipitation
W_i = precipitation for period i
t_i = time for period i (Dingman, 2008)

Likewise, the centroid of runoff is determined from:

$$t_{qc} = \frac{\sum_{i=1}^{n} Q_i \times t_i}{\sum_{i=1}^{n} Q_i}$$ [9.3]

where t_{qc} = centroid of runoff
Q_i = runoff for period i
t_i = time for period i

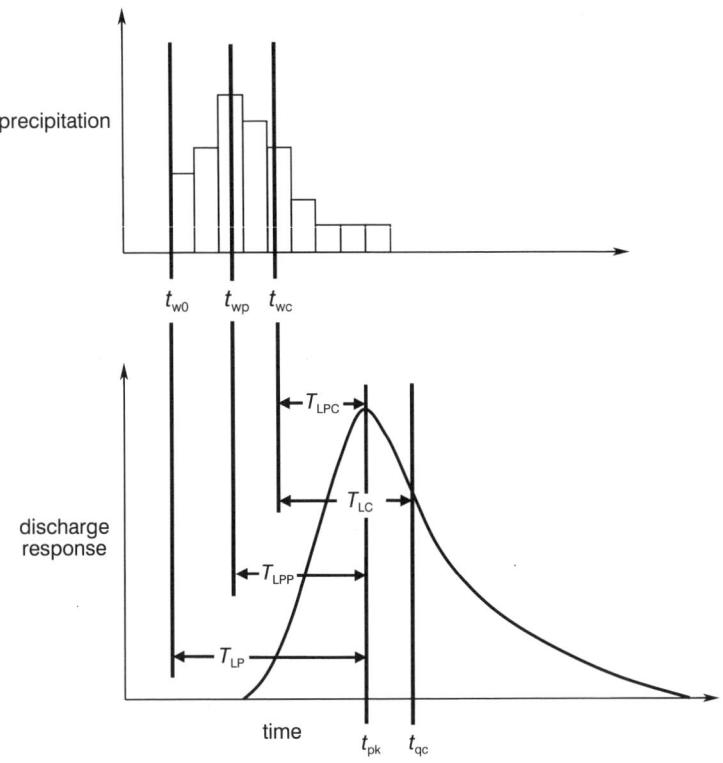

Figure 9.3 Definitions of terms used to describe hyetographs (a graphical representation of the distribution of rainfall over time) and response hydrographs based on Dingman (2008) and Hall (1984).

Table 9.1 Terms used in Figure 9.3

Time Instants		Time Durations	
t_{w0} ≡ beginning of precipitation		T_{LPC} ≡ centroid lag-to-peak	
t_{wp} ≡ peak of precipitation		T_{LC} ≡ centroid lag	
t_{wc} ≡ centroid of precipitation		T_{LP} ≡ lag-to-peak	
t_{pk} ≡ time of peak discharge		T_{LPP} ≡ peak lag-to-peak	
t_{qc} ≡ centroid of runoff			

Hydrograph Separation

Separation of stormflow from baseflow is a common procedure to quantify the amount of stormflow associated with a particular rainfall event. Several methods are used to separate the sources of streamflow displayed in a hydrograph.

The first method (Figure 9.4a) uses a constant slope (0.05 cfs/mi^2/hr) based on watershed area (Hewlett and Hibbert, 1967). Baseflow is termed *delayed flow* and stormflow is termed *quick flow* in their analysis to better portray the sources of water contributing to discharge. This method assumes that baseflow or delayed flow is gradually increasing during the stormflow period as old water is pushed through the soil into the stream by new water from above.

The second approach (Figure 9.4b) uses a projection of baseflow to the time of the peak discharge followed by a rise to the recession limb equal to N days where $N = A^{0.2}$ with A being watershed area in mi^2 (Linsley et al., 1982). This approach assumes that the previous recession rate will continue up to the peak discharge and then baseflow will increase during the latter part of the hydrograph.

The third method (Figure 9.4c) is a projection of the recession curve backward to the time of peak discharge. That point is then joined with a line tangent to the rising limb (Brooks et al., 1991). This method assumes that an increase in baseflow contributes primarily around the time of the peak discharge.

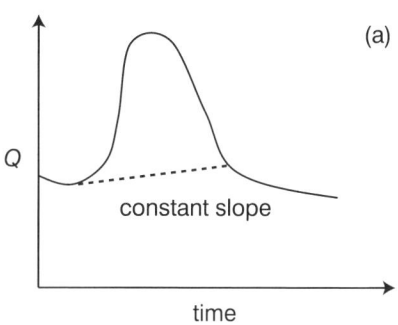

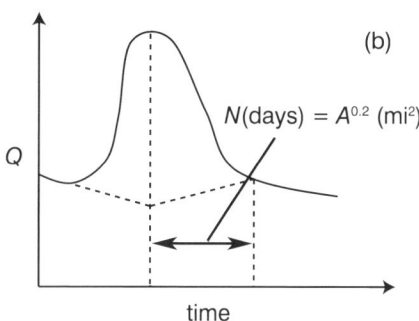

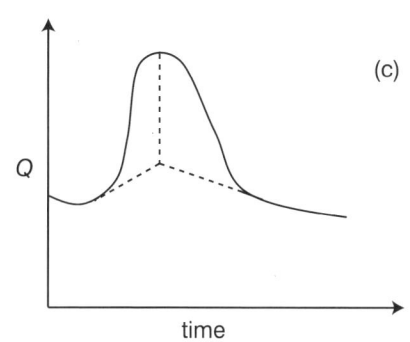

Figure 9.4 Approaches used in hydrograph separation: (a) constant slope method (e.g., 0.05 ft^3/s/mi^2/hr) (Hewlett and Hibbert, 1967); (b) projection of baseflow to peak discharge; and (c) projection of recession back to peak discharge.

Streamflow Measurement

Several methods have been used to measure streamflow. The primary approach for open channels is the velocity-area method, also known as the equation of continuity (Chow, 1964):

$$Q = AV \qquad [9.4]$$

where Q = discharge (m³/s)
 A = area of cross section (m²)
 V = velocity (average) (m/s)

In actual practice, depths are recorded at several distances across the stream (Figure 9.5). A velocity measurement is taken at each distance at the appropriate depth. The area for each width and depth subsection is calculated (Eqn. 9.5). The discharge for each subsection is determined from Eqn. 9.4 and summed across the channel. At each end of the transect, the area is calculated as a triangle and Eqn. 9.6 is used.

$$A = wD \qquad [9.5]$$

where A = cross section area
 w = width
 D = depth

except at the ends of the cross section, where

$$A = \frac{wD}{2} \qquad [9.6]$$

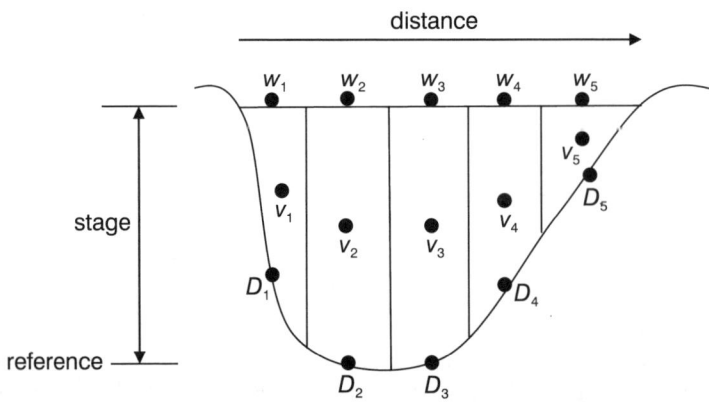

Figure 9.5 Cross section of idealized stream channel showing locations of width, depth, and velocity measurements.

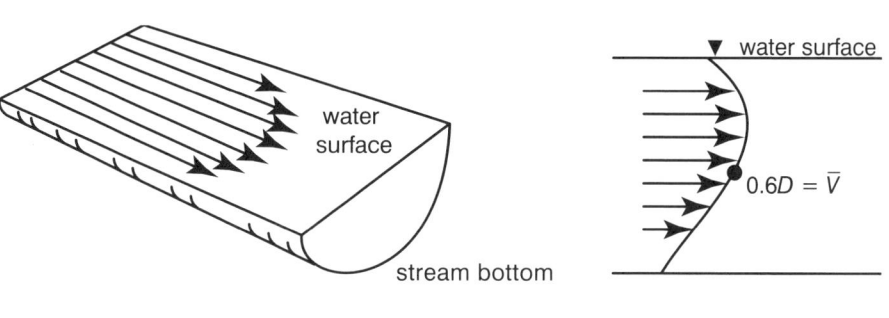

Figure 9.6 Two-dimensional and side (cross-section) views of a stream showing velocity profiles. Arrows indicate vectors of velocity.

Velocity is measured at 0.6D if the depth is 1.5 ft or less. If the depth is greater than 1.5 ft, velocity is measured at 0.2D and 0.8D and averaged (Turnipseed and Sauer, 2010). The depth of the velocity measurement is assumed to be at the average velocity, based on the assumed distributions of velocity in the stream profile (Figure 9.6).

Flumes. Flumes are specially shaped structures that constrict open channel flow in order to determine the relationship between water level and flow rate. Flumes can be used in small streams to measure discharge. They are more accurate than the velocity-area method. One of the most common flumes is the H-flume (Figure 9.7) (Brakensiek et al., 1979). If the dimensions of the H-flume are known, discharge can be calculated by just knowing the stage or height of the water in the device. Some flumes have a stilling well attached to the side for stage measurements. Flumes are useful in channels that have high sediment loads and where the slopes are gentle, because they allow sediment to pass through them and do not pond water behind them. Ponded water would encourage sediment deposition.

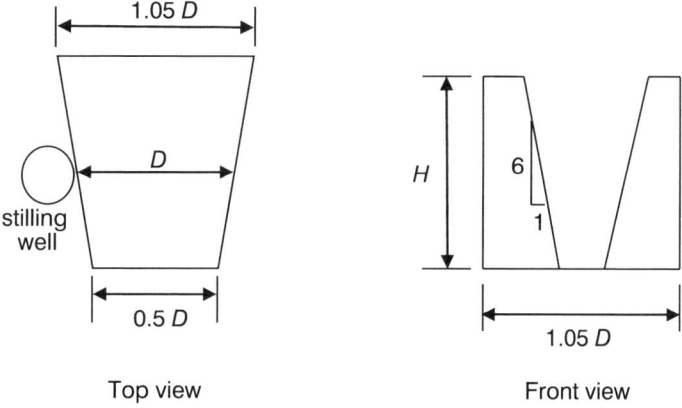

Figure 9.7 Top and front views of an H flume.

Weirs. A weir is a low dam or overflow structure built across an open channel, which causes an increase in water depth as the water flows over the weir. Weirs have specific sizes and shapes with unique head-discharge relationships. The general formula for weir discharge is:

$$Q = CLH^{3/2} \qquad [9.7]$$

where Q = discharge
  C = coefficient for the weir type
  L = weir length
  H = head or height of water flowing over the weir
    (U.S. Department of Interior, Bureau of Reclamation, 2001)

A common weir is the V-notched weir (Figure 9.8a). Other types include the compound, Cipolletti, and rectangular suppressed weirs.

Weirs generally have sharp blades, although broad-crested weirs exist as well. A pond is required behind a weir. The pond length should be $20H$ and the pond width $6H$ (U.S. Department of Interior, Bureau of Reclamation, 1997). The stilling well should be located four to six feet behind the weir blade.

Velocity Measurements

Direct Measurement. Several methods are used to measure velocity in streams. The methods include current meters, such as the Pygmy and Price cup velocity meters, electromagnetic methods, and Doppler methods (Turnipseed and Sauer, 2010). Floats are sometimes used for approximations (Figure 9.9).

For this approach, velocity is obtained from:

$$v = \frac{s}{t} \qquad [9.8]$$

where v = velocity
  s = distance downstream
  t = time of travel

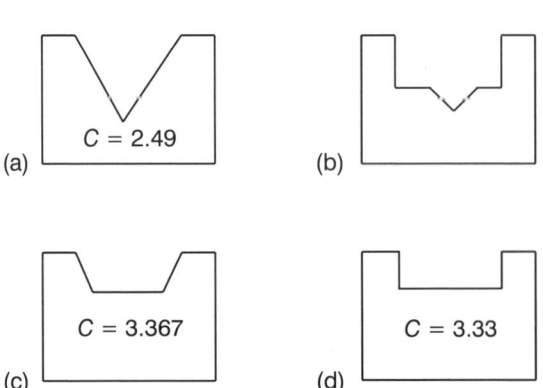

Figure 9.8 Cross-sectional views of (a) V-notched, (b) compound, (c) Cipolletti, and (d) rectangular suppressed weirs.

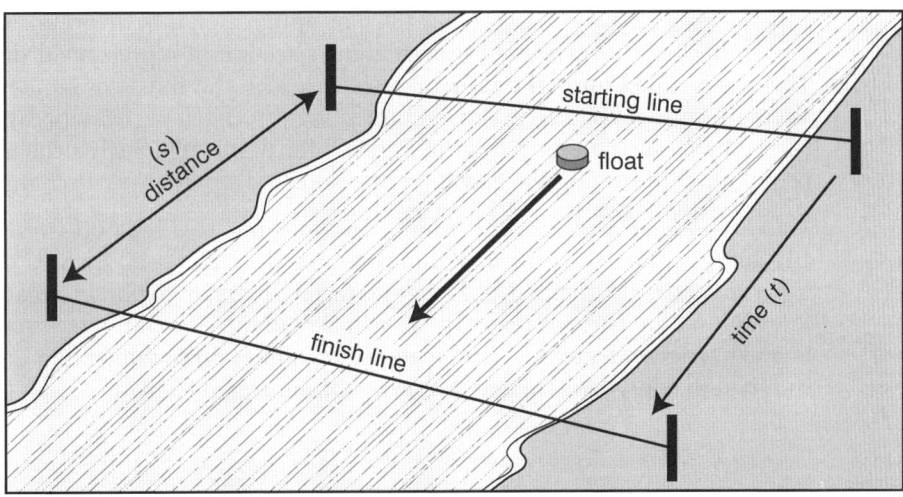

Figure 9.9 View of stream showing measurement of velocity using a float.

Because the surface of the water is faster than the average velocity, the velocity determined from a float is multiplied by a coefficient ranging from 0.66 to 0.80 depending on the channel depth (U.S. Department of Interior, Bureau of Reclamation, 2001).

Formula. Manning's equation can be used to estimate velocity:

$$v = \frac{1.486}{n} R^{2/3} s^{1/2} \qquad [9.9]$$

where v = velocity
$R = A/P$ where A is the cross-sectional area
P = wetted perimeter
s = slope of the streambed
n = Manning's roughness coefficient

The constant 1.486 is for using English units. The roughness coefficient is related to friction and turbulence in the stream. Table 9.2 summarizes the range of Manning's n values for several stream types.

Table 9.2 Manning's *n* for select stream types.

Stream Type	Roughness Coefficient (*n*)
Clean straight	0.025 – 0.033
Clean straight with weeds & stones	0.030 – 0.040
Sluggish with pools and weeds	0.050 – 0.080

Source: Data from Barnes, 1967.

Manning's equation is very useful. One application is to determine the stage or depth of water traveling through a cross section at a prescribed discharge. This use is called **normal depth analysis**. If n, s, v, and the cross section dimensions are known, the height of water traveling through a particular cross section can be back calculated by solving Eqn. 9.9 for depth (D). Such a calculation is useful for determining the elevation of a flood for a particular discharge.

Velocity—Head Rod. Used in mountain streams, this method is only about 10–20% accurate. An edged, stadia rod–type device is used for this measurement of velocity (Figure 9.10). The rod is faced upstream to obtain a reading and then again downstream to obtain a second reading. The difference in readings is due to friction factors forcing water to be higher on the upstream end of the rod than the downstream end. Velocity is determined from:

$$v = \sqrt{2gh} \qquad [9.10]$$

where v = velocity
   g = acceleration due to gravity
   $h = h_1 - h_2$, or the difference between the two height measurements

Salt / Dye Dilution. The salt or dye dilution technique is useful at sites where it is difficult to measure either the cross section of the stream or the velocity. This approach is suitable for relatively small streams, but it might be difficult in a large river. The basis of the method is that there is an identity relationship between the amount of tracer added to a stream and the flow in the stream. Streamflow is determined from (U.S. Department of Interior, Bureau of Reclamation, 2001):

$$Q = q \frac{C_1 - C_2}{C_2 - C_0} \qquad [9.11]$$

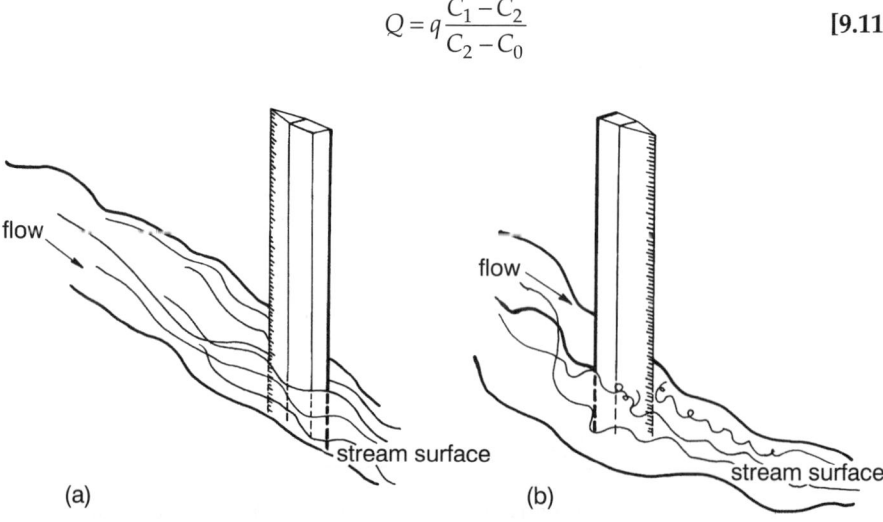

Figure 9.10 Use of the head rod for computing stream velocity. (a) Facing upstream. (b) Facing downstream. (U.S. Department of the Interior, 1980).

where Q = stream discharge
        q = constant inflow rate of the tracer
        C_1 = tracer concentration added to the stream
        C_2 = downstream concentration in the stream
        C_0 = upstream or background concentration of the tracer in the stream

Salt has been a frequently used tracer for this technique, though excess salt can have adverse environmental consequences. A conductivity meter can be used to monitor the rise in salt concentrations. A siphon from a carboy can be used to constantly add the tracer. Sufficient distance downstream is needed to ensure mixing prior to measurement.

Choosing the Stream Gaging Site

The choice of a location to conduct stream gaging is critical to the success of the discharge measurement. The selection is primarily based on the objectives of monitoring as well as the physical features of the site in relation to those objectives. Considerations include whether the monitoring is long- or short-term, for water quantity or quality or both, whether for year-around or just seasonal sampling, and if continuous measurement is needed as compared to just peak flow. Physical features that affect site selection primarily deal with the concept of a **control section** or control of flow at all stages. One consideration is the stability of the bed. It is most desirable to monitor at stable cross sections, such as those found on bedrock or impermeable soils to prevent leaks. A second consideration is the stream gradient. If the stream slope is too steep, turbulent flow is likely and measurement difficult. Also, if the stream gradient is too low, there may be insufficient drop to use certain flow devices, such as weirs. Usually a uniform, straight section is used where discharge is contained within the channel and can be measured at all stages. Other considerations might include ownership, access, and availability of electricity.

■ Flood Frequency Analysis

Similar to precipitation frequency analysis (Chapter 4), there is a probability that a certain peak discharge will occur in a stream. The same equations (Eqns. 4.4 and 4.6) would be appropriate. Often the highest peak discharge for the year is used in the analysis. An alternative approach, termed a partial series, uses all the peak discharges during a year above some cutoff value. In order to attach probability statements to certain peak discharges, the data is assumed to fit a certain type of distribution. Two common distributions used in flood frequency analysis are the Log Pearson Type III and the Gumbel (Brooks et al., 1991), although many different distributions may be used.

Uncertainties in Estimating Discharge

Winter (1981) summarized errors in measuring streamflow for the water balance of lakes. Measurements in weirs and flumes were reported to be within 5%. Stage discharge relationships can have errors of 5–10% if done correctly. Measurements within a channel can also have errors of 5–10%.

Problems

9.1 For the annual peak discharges provided below for the Mt. Hope River in Connecticut, compute the rank, recurrence interval (T), and probability of occurrence for each annual peak discharge. What is the discharge of the mean flood?

Year	Q (cfs)	Year	Q (cfs)	Year	Q (cfs)
1941	1090	1965	415	1989	2320
1942	814	1966	550	1990	1490
1943	814	1967	648	1991	882
1944	950	1968	1410	1992	701
1945	767	1969	1210	1993	1300
1946	469	1970	2250	1994	928
1947	486	1971	610	1995	607
1948	767	1972	1450	1996	3220
1949	444	1973	1340	1997	1280
1950	646	1974	1890	1998	2790
1951	1610	1975	771	1999	1150
1952	1190	1976	1200	2000	1300
1953	990	1977	807	2001	1280
1954	3250	1978	1730	2002	645
1955	5590	1979	3080	2003	813
1956	920	1980	2340	2004	1330
1957	550	1981	819	2005	1040
1958	528	1982	2720	2006	5000
1959	1690	1983	1060	2007	1350
1960	1140	1984	1300	2008	1490
1961	960	1985	491	2009	2480
1962	920	1986	791	2010	1750
1963	565	1987	1350	2011	2450
1964	820	1988	788	2012	979

9.2 Using the following stage and discharge values, determine the stage-discharge rating curve.

Date	Stage (ft)	Discharge (cfs)	Date	Stage (ft)	Discharge (cfs)
4/4	3.69	19.62	5/10	3.19	17.5
4/5	4.60	38.15	5/25	2.13	7.38
4/13	4.42	38.7	6/2	4.40	37.92
4/20	3.69	26.2	6/15	3.47	25.58
4/28	3.28	20.07	8/23	6.65	152.0
5/4	2.81	13.7	9/20	3.60	21.6

9.3 Determine the streamflow (cfs) for the following measurement taken at the Toivola watershed outlet. The cross section was 10 feet wide. A Price current meter was used for the measurement. One ft/s = 60 counts (revolutions) per minute (rpm).

Point	Distance (ft)	Depth (ft)	0.2D Count/min	0.8D Count/min	V_1 (ft/s)	V_2 (ft/s)	$\bar{V}$ (ft/s)	Q_i (cfs)
1	1	3.34	13	32	0.22	0.53		
2	3	3.10	35	37	0.58	0.62		
3	5	3.52	18	48	0.30	0.80		
4	7	2.87	37	62	0.62	1.03		
5	9	2.72	43	61	0.72	1.02		

Total Q =

9.4 Estimate the discharge (cfs) in a stream using Manning's equation. The stream is 52 ft wide, has a mean depth of 5.4 ft, a cross section area of 280 ft², a hydraulic radius of 4.87 ft, a Manning's n of 0.026, and a slope of 0.05 ft per ft.

9.5 The salt dilution technique was used to estimate discharge in a ditch. The following measurements were made:
Background conductivity (C_0) = 50 µ S/cm
Conductivity of addition (C_1) = 18,000 µ S/cm
Downstream conductivity after mixing (C_2) = 210 µ S/cm
Constant rate of addition (q) = 0.008 cfs
Determine the discharge in cfs.

9.6 For the following hydrograph data in 2014, separate the discharge into stormflow and baseflow using the constant slope approach. Determine the discharge at each end of the line of separation in cfs.

Day	Q (cfs)	Day	Q (cfs)
3/21	131	3/31	545
3/22	107	4/1	269
3/23	97	4/2	170
3/24	79	4/3	130
3/25	71	4/4	111
3/26	70	4/5	107
3/27	61	4/6	104
3/28	57	4/7	90
3/29	89	4/8	74
3/30	876	4/9	65

References

Askew, A. J., 1968. *Lag time of natural catchments.* The University of New South Wales, Water Research Laboratory. Report No. 107.

Barnes, H. H., Jr. 1967. *Roughness characteristics of natural channels.* U.S. Geological Survey. Water-Supply Paper 1849.
http://pubs.usgs.gov/wsp/wsp_1849/pdf/backup-2.pdf

Brakensiek, D. L., H. B. Osborn, and W. J. Rawls. 1979. *Field manual for research in agricultural hydrology.* Agricultural Handbook No. 224. U. S. Department of Agriculture, Science and Education Administration.

Brooks, K. N., P. F. Folliott, H. M. Gregersen, and J. L. Thames. 1991. *Hydrology and the management of watersheds.* Ames: Iowa State University Press.

Chow, V. T. 1964. *Handbook of applied hydrology.* New York: McGraw-Hill.

Dingman, S. L., 2008. *Physical hydrology.* 2nd ed. Long Grove, IL: Waveland Press.

Dunne, T., and R. D. Black. 1970. Partial area contributions to storm runoff in a small New England watershed. *Water Resources Research* 6: 1296–1311.

Dunne, T., and L. B. Leopold. 1978. *Water in environmental planning.* San Francisco: W.H. Freeman.

Hall, M. J. 1984. *Urban hydrology.* London, UK: Elsevier Applied Science Publishers.

Hewlett, J. D. 1982. *Principles of forest hydrology.* Athens: The University of Georgia Press.

Hewlett, J. D., and A. R. Hibbert. 1967. Factors affecting the response of small watershed to precipitation in humid areas. In W. E. Sopper and H. W. Lull (eds.), *International symposium on hydrology.* Elmsford, NY: Pergamon Press, pp. 275–290.

Hood, M. J., J. C. Clausen, and G. S. Warner. 2007. Comparison of stormwater lag times for low impact and traditional residential development. *J. American Water Resources Association* 43(4): 1036–1046.

Horton, R. E. 1933. The role of infiltration in the hydrologic cycle. *American Geophysical Union Transactions* 14: 446–460.

Horton, R. E. 1940. An approach toward a physical interpretation of infiltration-capacity. *Proceedings Soil Science Society of America* 4: 399–417.

Huggins, L. F., and J. R. Burney. 1982. Surface runoff, storage and routing. Chapter 5 in C. T. Haan, H. P. Johnson, and D. L. Brakensiek (eds.), *Hydrologic modeling of small watersheds*. ASAE Monograph No. 5. St. Joseph, MI: American Society of Agricultural Engineers.

Kang, S., J. Park, and V. Singh. 1998. Effect of urbanization on runoff characteristics of the On-Cheon stream watershed in Pusan, Korea. *Hydrological Processes* 12: 351–363.

Kent, K. M. 1972. Travel time, time of concentration and lag. Chapter 15 in *National engineering handbook. Section 4. Hydrology*. Washington, DC: USDA-Soil Conservation Service.
http://directives.sc.egov.usda.gov/OpenNonWebContent.aspx?content=27002.wba

Leopold, L., 1991. Lag time for small drainage basins. *Catena* 18(2): 157–171.

Linsley, R. K., Jr., M. A. Kohler, and J. L. H. Paulhus. 1982. *Hydrology for engineers*. 3 Sub Edition. New York: McGraw-Hill.

Pawlow, J. R., 1977. Impact of suburban development on the rainfall-runoff relationship. Paper presented at International Symposium on Urban Hydrology, Hydraulics, and Sediment Control. University of Kentucky, Lexington, July 18–21.

Turnipseed, D. P., and V. B. Sauer. 2010. *Discharge measurements at gaging stations*. U.S. Geological Survey Techniques and Methods Book 3, chapter A8. Reston, VA: U.S. Geological Survey. http://pubs.usgs.gov/tm/tm3-a8/pdf/tm3-a8.pdf

U.S. Department of the Interior, Bureau of Reclamation. 2001. *Water measurement manual*. Washington, DC: U.S. Government Printing Office.
http://www.usbr.gov/tsc/techreferences/mands/wmm/WMM_3rd_2001.pdf

U.S. Department of the Interior, Bureau of Land Management. 1980. *Construction and use of a velocity head rod for measuring stream velocity and flow*. Technical Report 5. https://www.blm.gov/style/medialib/blm/ak/aktest/tr.Par.78682.File.dat/tr5.pdf

Winter, T. C. 1981. Uncertainties in estimating the water balance of lakes. *Water Resources Bulletin* 17(1): 82–115.

10

Watershed Management

■ Introduction

Watershed management is not just the process of managing the biophysical features of watersheds, but it is getting stakeholders together to accomplish stated goals and objectives for watersheds. It typically results in the management of forested or other lands in a drainage basin with objectives to protect, rehabilitate, or enhance its water resources (Black, 1996). Management utilizes the interrelationships among watershed resources, including soil, water, plant, and land use/cover (Brooks et al., 1991). This chapter will focus on water quantity management. The management of water quality within watersheds is covered in later chapters. Tools used in watershed management include soil conservation practices, land use management, vegetation management, and channel or reservoir management. Management can be conducted to either prevent something undesirable from happening or to restore favorable conditions. Effective watershed management relies on knowledge obtained from Chapters 3 through 9 of this book. For example, interception, evapotranspiration, and infiltration in forests can all be manipulated, changing rainfall–runoff relationships. The consequences of watershed management are highly variable and depend on such controlling factors as climate zone, elevation, and topography. The effects of watershed management have been studied in the United States since about 1911 at various experimental watersheds and experimental forests (Table 10.1). These watersheds have generated a wealth of information. For an excellent summary of many of these experimental areas, see Ice and Stednick (2004).

Table 10.1 Experimental watersheds in the United States.

Watershed	Agency	State	Start Date	Reference
Beaver Creek Experimental Watershed	USFS / NAU	Arizona	1955	Ice and Stednick, 2004
Casper Creek Experimental Watershed	USFS	California	1961	Ice and Stednick, 2004
Coshocton (North Appalachian Experimental Watershed)	ARS	Ohio	1935	Harmel et al., 2007
Coweeta Hydrologic Laboratory	ARS / OSU	North Carolina	1934	Ice and Stednick, 2004
Fernow Experimental Forest	USFS	West Virginia	1934	Ice and Stednick, 2004
Fraser Experimental Forest	USFS	Colorado	1937	Alexander et al., 1985
H. J. Andrews Experimental Forest	USFS	Oregon	1948	Ice and Stednick, 2004
Hubbard Brook Experimental Forest	USFS	New Hampshire	1955	Ice and Stednick, 2004
Leading Ridge Experimental Watersheds	PSU / USFS	Pennsylvania	1958	Lynch and Corbett, 1990
Marcell Experimental Forest	USFS	Minnesota	1960	Verry, 1986
Reynolds Creek Experimental Watershed	ARS	Idaho	1960	Slaughter et al., 2000
San Dimas Experimental Forest	USFS	California	1933	Dunn et al., 1988
Sleeper's River Research Watershed	ARS / USGS / CRREL	Vermont	1955	Shanley, 2000
Wagon Wheel Gap Experimental Watershed	USFS	Colorado	1910	Ice and Stednick, 2004
Walnut Gulch Experimental Watershed	ARS	Arizona	1951	Renard et al., 2008

Water Yield

Water yield is defined as the drainage basin's yield of liquid water during some period of time (Hewlett, 1982). Generally, the water yield for a long time period, such as a year, is equivalent to the difference between precipitation and evapotranspiration. As vegetation is modified in a watershed, the amount, timing, and distribution of water yield from that watershed will be changed (Brown et al., 2005). There are several ways that vegetation is altered, such as logging or other forest management techniques, rural development, and land conversions to agriculture. It is generally understood that as forest vegetation is removed, evapotranspiration and interception will decrease, resulting in increases in soil moisture and streamflow (Black, 1996; Brooks et al., 1991; de la Crétaz and Barten, 2007; Hewlett, 1982; Satterlund and Adams, 1992). Such increases occur when forests are thinned, when species are converted from deep-rooted to shallow-rooted, and when high interception species are converted to lower interception species (Brooks et al., 1991). Conversely, when forested areas within watersheds increase, streamflow has decreased (Black, 1996). Several factors have been found to affect water yield changes.

Percent Harvested. Several studies of experimental watersheds have shown that the percentage of forest cut on an area will positively affect the water yield response (Figure 10.1). This finding has also been true for percentage of basal area cut. In addition, the largest increases in water yield have been observed in the first year following harvest (de la Crétaz and Barten, 2007).

In the eastern United States the expected change in yield for hardwoods in the first year following harvest is related to:

$$Y_H = f\left(\frac{BA}{PI}\right) \qquad [10.1]$$

where Y_H = first year increase in yield (in.)
  BA = basal area cut
  PI = potential solar radiation (Douglass, 1983)

The duration of this change in yield follows an exponential decay response (Figure 10.1b) with the change in yield decreasing over time.

Type of Cover. The harvesting of different vegetative cover types will result in varying water yield responses. In general, a greater yield has been observed

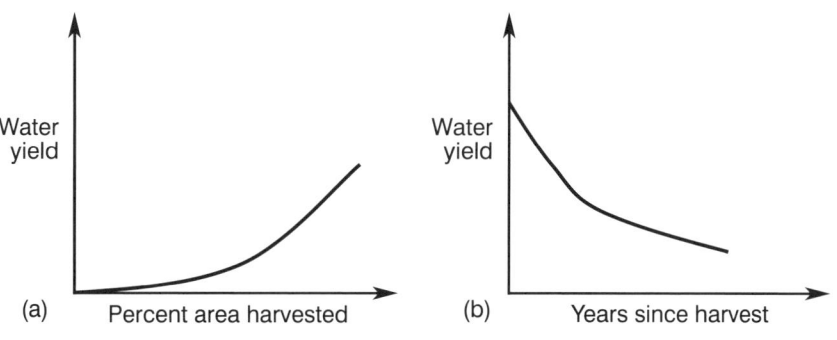

Figure 10.1   Generalized water yield response to varying levels of forest harvest and the years since harvest.

for harvesting conifers than for hardwoods due to greater interception from conifers (de la Crétaz and Barten, 2007). For example, in Minnesota an aspen clearcut resulted in an increase of 3.5 inches in water yield, while a pine clearcut increased water yield by 6 inches (Verry, 1986). Streamflow decreased following conversions from hardwood to pine but increased following conversions of hardwoods to grass (Black, 1996). Conversion of forest to agriculture has produced runoff increases (de la Crétaz and Barten, 2007). Urban development also increases runoff.

Upland vs. Wetland. Timber harvesting on wetlands in Minnesota has resulted in little change in water yield (Verry, 1986) compared to harvesting uplands. However, water table responses have been observed. During wet periods, water tables after harvesting have been higher due to less interception. During dry periods, water tables have been lower due to greater wind and radiation effects at the surface, resulting in higher surface temperatures.

Aspect. The **aspect** is the compass direction that sloping land faces. In the northern hemisphere, water yield responses have been higher on north-facing as compared to south-facing aspects. North-facing slopes have lower evapotranspiration (de la Crétaz and Barten, 2007). They also have higher soil moisture and water tables than south-facing slopes. Wetter soils would have less available storage and would produce higher water yields.

Climate. Climate conditions influence water yield responses. Humid regions have been shown to have greater water yield responses than dryer regions (Brooks et al., 1991). Areas with higher precipitation result in greater water yield increases than dryer areas. And areas with more evapotranspiration result in less increases in water yield. Tree removal in areas with a high amount of fog generally will not increase streamflow, and may decrease it, due to less tree scavenging of the fog (Satterlund and Adams, 1992).

Harvest Methods. Logging that has involved skidding and haul-road building has resulted in higher peak flows than operations with less forest floor disturbance (de la Crétaz and Barten, 2007).

Streamflow Pattern

Peak flow can also change following forest harvesting. Peak discharge increased twofold for five years following an aspen clearcut in Minnesota (Verry, 1986). With increased soil moisture, there was less available storage volume. Snowmelt patterns can also change with forest harvesting. The aspen clearcut in Minnesota increased peak flow by two times, and the peak occurred five days earlier. Less shade on the snowpack allowed greater net radiation.

Forest (Vegetation) Management

There are several alternative forest harvesting techniques that result in differences in water yield responses. A clearcut has been cited as causing the greatest water yield changes, but because of controversies regarding clearcuts in the 1960s, they are now less common in the United States (Bolle, 1989). A patch cut is a small clearcut that can be managed to have potentially beneficial effects on water yield. For example, patches can be configured to desynchronize the timing of peak discharge and actually lower the downstream peak flow (Verry, 1986). Conversion of forests to grasslands has been used to decrease evapotranspiration (Satterlund and Adams, 1992). Strip cuts have been used with the advances in mechanical harvesting equipment. The size of the strip cut, the width of the leave strip, and the orientation of the strip cut can all influence snowmelt. North-south–oriented strips in Minnesota accumulated more snow but melted faster than east-west–oriented strips. The width of the leave strip should be two times the tree heights to allow for shading. Selection cuts, where individual trees are removed, have little effect on water yields. The sizes of openings created by patch cuts influence the amount of snow concentrated in these areas. If openings are too large, wind scour can increase and result in no gain in accumulation. Another consideration is the timing and synchronization of snowmelt runoff. Heterogeneity in watershed cutting is more likely to flatten and broaden snowmelt hydrographs than homogeneous cutting practices (Satterlund and Adams, 1992). The melting of snow is generally accelerated in cut areas when compared to forests. In semiarid areas, the water yield responses to forest and brush harvesting have been found to positively relate to annual precipitation (Satterlund and Adams, 1992), and treatment on moist sites generates more runoff than on dryer sites.

Afforestation of agricultural lands and plantation forests can reduce streamflow (van Dijk and Keenan, 2007). Additional water quality benefits may occur due to this reduction.

Snowpack Management

Snowpacks have been managed to produce water yields in the western United States. Snowpack management involves changing the accumulation or melt patterns of snow. Vegetation management can be used to alter snowpacks. A reduction in tree density with thinning can result in more snow accumulation, but the water yield changes are not great (Brooks et al., 1991). Patch cuts also can result in higher snow accumulation and may increase yield, depending on the type and size of the patch (Black, 1996). Snow fences are used to pile up snow and reduce sublimation. In alpine areas, various techniques are used to retain more snow (Satterlund and Adams, 1992) including snow fences, vegetative shelter belts, and reshaping the terrain. Coloring the snow with carbon black, sawdust, coke, or other chemicals has been used to change the albedo of the snow or reduce sublimation. The general principle is to concentrate the snow, which then delays or extends the melt period. Similarly, snowmelt can be accelerated by cutting large openings. Contour trenches across the landscape in alpine areas have been used to capture surface runoff and encourage infiltration (Satterlund and Adams, 1992) in cases where flood damages are severe.

Urban Watershed Management

Urban watershed management has historically been synonymous with stormwater management for flood protection. However, urban watershed management should consider issues beyond just controlling floods, such as preserving the ecological integrity of water bodies, providing recreation, and supporting other uses such as water supply, navigation, and hydropower (Novotny et al., 2001). As Black (1996) describes, other watershed modifications can occur through a change in watershed slope (flattening, terraces), stream gradient (damming, channeling), and watershed size (diversions, roads). Another component of urban watershed management is stream restoration. Practices used for stormwater management are described in Chapter 18.

Stream restoration has become a common activity in urban watersheds. Four categories of stream restoration projects have been described: riparian restoration, streambank stabilization, water quality management, and in-stream habitat improvements (de la Cretaz and Barten, 2007). Most stream restorations are conducted at a relatively small scale, such as a stream reach. De la Cretaz and Barten (2007) point out that disturbances causing changes in streams are more at a watershed scale. They further suggest that watershed planning should consider the conservation of open space, particularly forests; riparian area conservation and restoration; use of low-impact development principles (Chapter 18), and regulation of stormwater management.

Reservoir Watershed Management

Reservoirs have been constructed primarily for three main purposes: flood control, hydropower, and water supply. However, they also provide many recreational benefits. Reservoir watershed management is often targeted at protecting water quality or managing water yields. Land use management or control is an important tool to protect water quality. The various approaches described previously to increase water yields would be applicable to reservoir watershed management. One example would be forestland conversions to grasslands, which would be expected to increase water yields (Barten et al., 1998). For the Quabbin reservoir in Massachusetts, which supplies water to Boston, uneven-aged, mixed species management is the goal for water quality purposes. Best management practices (Chapter 18) are also advocated to protect water quality. Since many reservoir watersheds are in public ownership, recreation management has also been applied to protect water quality. For example, in the Quabbin reservoir and its watershed, certain recreational activities are restricted (Cohen and Loomis, 2004) to prevent pathogen contamination and other use-related impacts.

■ PROBLEM

10.1 For an in-depth exercise on watershed management, see the "Structured Experiences" section of the online materials at waveland.com/Clausen.

■ REFERENCES

Alexander, R. R., C. A. Troendle, M. R. Kaufmann, W. D. Shepperd, G. L. Couch, R. K. Watkins, and L. D. Love. 1985. *The Fraser Experimental Forest, Colorado: Research program and published research 1937–1985*. General Technical Report RMRS-GTR-118. USDA Forest Service. Rocky Mountain Range and Experiment Station, Fort Collins, CO.

Barten, P. K., T. Kyker-Snowman, P. J. Lyons, T. Mahlstedt, R. O'Connor, and B. A. Spencer. 1998. Managing a watershed protection forest. *J. Forestry* 96(8): 10–15.

Black, P. E. 1996. *Watershed hydrology*. 2nd ed. New York: CRC Press, Taylor & Francis.

Bolle, A. W. 1989. The Bitterroot revisited: A university review of the Forest Service. *Public Land Law Review* 10: 1–18.

Brooks, K. N., P. F. Folliott, H. M. Gregersen, and J. L. Thames. 1991. *Hydrology and the management of watersheds*. Ames: Iowa State University Press.

Brown, A. E., L. Zhang, T. A. McMahon, A. W. Western, and R. A. Vertessy. 2005. A review of paired catchment studies for determining changes in water yield resulting from alterations in vegetation. *J. of Hydrology* 310: 28–61.

Cohen, B. E., and D. K. Loomis. 2004. Outdoor recreation and the Quabbin Reservoir: An exercise in political maneuvering? In J. Murdy (ed.), *Procedures of the 2003 Northeastern Recreation Research Symposium*. Gen. Tech. Rep. NE-317. Newtown Square, PA: U.S. Forest Service Northeast Research Station.

de la Crétaz, A. L., and P. K. Barten. 2007. *Land use effects on streamflow and water quality in the northeastern United States*. New York: CRC Press, Taylor & Francis.

Douglass, J. E. 1983. The potential for water yield augmentation from forest management in the eastern United States. *Water Resources Bulletin* 19(3): 351–358.

Dunn, P. H., S. C. Barro, W. G. Wells II, M. A. Poth, P. M. Wohlgemuth, and C. G. Colver. 1988. *The San Dimas Experimental Forest: 50 years of research*. General Technical Report PSW-104. Berkeley, CA: USDA-Forest Service. Pacific Southwest Forest and Range Experiment Station.

Harmel, R. D., J. V. Bonta, and C. W. Richardson. 2007. The original USDA-ARS experimental watersheds in Texas and Ohio: Contributions from the past and visions for the future. *Transactions of the ASABE* 50(5): 1669–1675.

Hewlett, J. D. 1982. *Principles of forest hydrology*. Athens: University of Georgia Press.

Ice, G. G., and J. D. Stednick. 2004, Fall/Winter. Forest watershed research in the United States. *Forest History Today*, pp. 16–26.

Lynch, J. A., and E. S. Corbett. 1990. Evaluation of best management practices for controlling nonpoint pollution from silvicultural operations. *Water Resources Bulletin* 26(1): 41–52.

Novotny, V., D. Clark, R. Griffin, and D. Booth. 2001. Risk-based urban watershed management under conflicting objectives. *Water Science and Technology* 43(5): 69–78.

Renard, K. G., M. H. Nichols, D. A. Woolhiser, and H. B. Osborn. 2008. A brief background on the U.S. Department of Agriculture Agricultural Research Service Walnut Gulch Experimental Watershed. *Water Resources Research* 44, W05S02. Doi:10.1029/2006WR005691.

Satterlund, D. R., and P. W. Adams. 1992. *Wildland watershed management.* 2nd ed. New York: John Wiley & Sons.

Shanley, J. B. 2000, June. *Sleepers River, Vermont: A water, energy, and biogeochemical budgets program site.* USDI-U.S. Geological Survey Fact Sheet 166-99. Montpelier, VT: U.S. Geological Survey.

Slaughter, C. W., D. Marks, G. N. Flerchinger, S. S. van Vactor, and M. Burgess. 2000. *Research data collection at the Reynolds Creek experimental watershed, Idaho USA.* USDA-Agricultural Research Service. Northwest Watershed Research Center. ARS Technical Bulletin NWRD-2000-2.

van Dijk, A. I. J. M., and R. J. Keenan. 2007. Planted forests and water in perspective. *Forest Ecology and Management* 251: 1–9.

Verry, E. S. 1976. *Estimating water yield differences between hardwood and pine forests: An application of net precipitation data.* North Central Forest Experiment Station. USDA Forest Service Research Paper NC-128. http://www.nrs.fs.fed.us/pubs/rp/rp_nc128.pdf

Verry, E. S. 1986. Forest harvesting and water: The lake states experience. *Water Resources Bulletin* 22(6): 1039–1047.

Part II

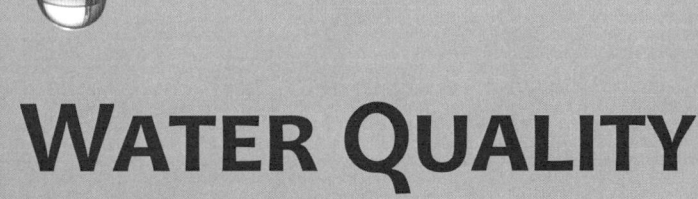

Water Quality

11

Introduction to Water Quality

■ Introduction

Water quality has been a topic of concern for as long as humans have been forming communities. One example dates back to at least the fifth century BC in Greece, where there was a regulation regarding cleanliness in Athens (quoted in Arnaoutoglou, 1998):

> ... it is not permitted to allow hides to rot in the Ilissos above the temple of Herakles; nobody is permitted to tan hides or to throw litter into the river.

In a more recent example, George Perkins Marsh, in his book *Man and Nature; or Physical Geography as Modified by Human Action* (1865), wrote:

> **General Consequences of the Destruction of the Forest**
>
> With the disappearance of the forest, all is changed. ... The soil is bared of its covering of leaves, broken and loosened by the plough, deprived of the fibrous rootlets which held it together. ... [T]he floods which the waters of the sky pour over it hurry swiftly along its slopes, carrying in suspension vast quantities of earthy particles ... fill the beds of the streams ... and thus the earth is rendered no longer fit for the habitation of man.

Two significant events involving water quality led to the creation of the U.S. Environmental Protection Agency (EPA) in 1970. The first was the Santa Barbara oil spill. On January 28, 1969, a blow-out occurred on Platform Alpha, one of Union Oil's offshore drilling rigs located just six miles from the California coast. Over the next ten days, approximately 3 million gallons of crude oil spilled into the Santa Barbara Channel and onto the beaches of Santa Barbara County in southern California before the leak could be successfully sealed (Clarke and Hemphill, 2002). It was the largest oil spill in U.S. waters at the time.

A second event occurred shortly afterward in Ohio. On June 22, 1969, an oil slick on the Cuyahoga River, just southeast of downtown Cleveland, caught fire (Adler, 2003). An article in *Time* magazine (Time, 1969) described the Cuyahoga as the river that "oozes rather than flows" and "anyone who falls into the Cuyahoga does not drown. . . . He decays."

Love Canal in Niagara Falls, New York, became another critical water-quality tragedy in 1976 when corroding chemical waste drums sticking out of the ground, puddles of noxious substances in basements and on lawns, and dying vegetation came to the attention of the general public. This was all due to past storage of industrial chemical wastes in an abandoned canal that was then covered with earth and sold to the city for $1. Later, 98 homes and a school were built on the site. New York offered to purchase the homes and the president and U.S. Congress approved emergency financial aid. Streams and swales also bordered the site (Beck, 1979). In response, in 1980 Congress passed the Comprehensive Environmental Response, Compensation, and Liability Act (CERCLA), the so-called Superfund Act.

This chapter provides important definitions of the common terms used in water quality management. A summary of the status of water quality in the United States is also provided.

Water Quality Definitions

Water quality is defined as a characteristic of water as related to its intended use (Novotny, 2003). Thus water quality can have different meanings for different people. The quality of water desired might also be different for fish and wildlife than for public health. The term **pollution** comes from the Latin *pollutus*, which means to soil or to defile (Krenkel and Novotny, 1980). The term *pollution* has the same general meaning as contamination or degradation. It also means an undesirable change in water quality or an adverse impairment of the beneficial uses of water. Pollution control refers to the regulation of pollutants from various sources.

Water quality management deals with all aspects of water quality problems for all the beneficial uses of water. Pollution and water quality are determined by comparing the chemical, biological, physical, microbiological, and radiological quantities to a set of standards and criteria. A **criterion** is a scientific quantity upon which a judgment can be based. An example of a criterion is an LC_{50} (the lethal concentration at which 50% of the test organisms do not survive). A **standard** is a rule or principle of measure that is established by an authority, such as a state agency. An example of a standard is the drinking water standard of 10 mg/L NO_3–N.

Sources of Pollution

There are two general sources of pollution. **Point pollution** generally refers to pollutants that enter transport routes, such as rivers, at discrete, identifiable locations (Novotny, 2003). The outflow from a pipe is often point pollution. **Nonpoint pollution** enters transport routes at diffuse locations across the landscape. Urban stormwater runoff is regulated separately in the United States. Although stormwater often enters water bodies through a stormwater pipe, it originates from diffuse sources.

Magnitude of the Water Quality Problem

Surface Water

The first compilation of water quality impairments from nonpoint source (NPS) pollution in the United States was reported by the Association of State and Interstate Water Pollution Control Administrators in 1985 (ASIWPCA, 1986) at the request of the EPA. That report summarized information from assessments of about one-fifth of the river miles and one-half of lake and reservoir acres. The results indicated that 31% of assessed river miles were impacted by NPS pollution, and an additional 12% were threatened. Lake acres impacted were 29% of assessed, with an additional 24% threatened by NPS pollution. Overall, about one-half of U.S. estuaries were assessed. Twenty-six percent were impacted by NPS pollution and an additional 16% were threatened.

Sources of Surface Water Pollutants

The Association's report (ASIWPCA, 1986) also included a breakdown of the nonpoint sources of the pollutants causing impairments (Table 11.1) and the types of pollutants causing the impairments (Table 11.2). Agriculture was identified as the major source of pollutants to surface waters resulting in impairments, with sediment being the dominant pollutant causing impairment in rivers (47%) and nutrient runoff being the dominant cause of pollutant impairment to lakes (59%). The results of this report suggested that the 1972 Water Pollution Control Act Amendments (PL 92-500) were insufficient to restore the quality of the waters of the United States. Out of that conversation was born the Water Quality Act of 1987 (PL 100-4), which added statutory provisions for NPS control. These acts, and others, are described in Chapter 19.

Table 11.1 Sources of nonpoint source pollutants causing impairments in rivers and lakes.

Sources	Rivers	Lakes
Agriculture	64%	57%
Hydromodification (drainage, channels)	4%	13%
Resources extraction	9%	1%
Urban runoff	5%	12%
Land disposal (drain fields, landfill)	1%	5%
Construction	2%	1%
Silviculture	6%	1%

Source: Data from ASIWPCA, 1986.

Table 11.2 Types of nonpoint source pollutants in impacted waters.

Pollutant	Rivers	Lakes
Nutrients	13%	59%
Sediment	47%	22%
Pathogens	9%	2%
Habitat alteration (sediment, temperature)	9%	2%
Oxygen demand	4%	3%
Acidity	7%	4%
Salinity (irrigation)	2%	3%
Pesticides	3%	<1%
Toxic substances (Hg)	6%	3%

Source: Data from ASIWPCA, 1986.

Since the ASIWPCA report and subsequent to the Water Quality Act of 1987, the EPA has prepared water quality reports (Section 305[b]) to Congress on the status of impairments in water bodies, generally on a two-year cycle. Although the water bodies assessed and the number of states reporting have varied from year to year, it is interesting to follow the progress in removing water bodies from the impaired lists (Table 11.3). This information suggests that while the major pollutant has changed over time, partly due to additional sampling, the percentage of impaired water bodies has not changed. Although water bodies have been removed from state impaired lists (Section 303[d] of the Clean Water Act, PL 100-4), others have been added due to increased bacterial and mercury sampling.

Table 11.3 Summary of impaired waters in the United States by year.

Year	Threatened or Impacted	Assessed	Major Source	Major Pollutant
Rivers				
1985	43%	20%	Agriculture	(not identified)
1992	44%	18%	Agriculture	Siltation
1996	44%	19%	Agriculture	Siltation
2000	47%	19%	Agriculture	Pathogens
2004	44%	16%	Agriculture	Pathogens
2010	54%	20%	Agriculture	Pathogens
2012	44%	22%	Agriculture	Pathogens
Lakes				
1985	53%	30%	Agriculture	
1992	57%	46%	Agriculture	Metals
1996	49%	40%	Agriculture	Nutrients, metals
2000	47%	43%	Agriculture	Nutrients
2004	64%	39%	Atmosphere	Mercury
2010	67%	37%	Atmosphere	Mercury
2012	75%	54%	Atmosphere	Mercury

Sources: Data from ASIWPCA, 1986; EPA 1994, 1998, 2002, 2009, 2014.

Ground Water

About 53% of the U.S. population relies on ground water as a source. The EPA conducted a five-year study of 1,300 community wells and rural domestic wells for 101 pesticides, 25 degradates, and nitrate (U.S. Environmental Protection Agency, 1990). Nitrate was the most frequently detected pollutant in both community and domestic wells, with nitrate concentrations greater than 10 mg/L (drinking water standard) detected in 1.2% of community wells and 2.4% of rural domestic wells.

For community wells, concentrations of nitrate greater than 0.15 mg/L (analytical minimum reporting limit) were found in 52% of those studied. Ten percent of community wells contained at least one pesticide or degradant, with DCPA (dimethyl tetrachloroterephtalate) being the most common pesticide found (6.4%), followed by Atrazine (1.7%). DCPA has the common name of Dacthal and is used on home lawns, golf courses, and farms for annual grass and broadleaf weed control.

For domestic wells, nitrate concentrations greater than 0.15 mg/L were found in 57% of the wells. DCPA was the second most common pollutant and was found in 2.5% of wells. Atrazine was third most common (0.7%).

Pharmaceuticals, Hormones, Steroids

Recently there have been several studies of organic wastewater contaminants in waters of the United States. The first was a national reconnaissance of 139 streams in 1999–2000 in 30 states (Kolpin et al., 2002). Eighty percent of the streams were contaminated, most frequently by steroids, nonprescription drugs, insect repellant, detergent metabolites, caffeine, plasticizers, antimicrobial disinfectant, fire retardant, and hormones. There was a median of seven and a maximum of 38 contaminants in a given sample.

This study was followed up by two national surveys. The first survey was conducted on ground water, sampling 47 wells in 18 states (Barnes et al., 2008). There were contaminants in 81% of the samples from these sites. The most frequent contaminants were insect repellant, plasticizer, fire retardant, antibiotics, and detergent metabolites; a total of 35 different contaminants were found. No concentration of contaminants occurred above guidelines, but only nine of the 65 substances found have guidelines.

The second survey targeted untreated drinking water sources (Focazio et al., 2008). Investigators sampled 25 ground-water and 49 surface-water sites and found 63 compounds. The most frequently detected were cholesterol, metolachlor, nicotine metabolite, plant sterol, caffeine metabolite, and fire retardant. There was a median of four compounds per site and a maximum of 31.

Soil Quality

Water quality often can also be linked to concentrations of contaminants in soils. Nitrogen mass balances were estimated for each state in the United States for 1987 (National Research Council [NRC], 1993). Inputs were fertilizer, manure, fixation by legumes, and crop residues. Outputs were harvested crops and residues. Nationally, assuming a moderate amount of nitrogen fixation, the nitrogen balance resulted in a residual (inputs – outputs) of +36%. That is, 36% more nitrogen was applied than removed. Individual states varied substantially. Nitrogen mass balances for seslected states are listed in Table 11.4. Similarly, phosphorus mass balances were estimated for each state for 1987. Inputs were fertilizer, manure, and crop inputs. Outputs were harvested crops and crop residues. Nationally, the residual in the mass balance was 63%. Again, balances for individual states varied (Table 11.5). In summary, these balances suggest a buildup of nitrogen and phosphorus in the nation's soils.

Table 11.4 State and national nitrogen mass balance as percent of total mass input.

State	Fertilizer	Harvested	Residual
Hawaii	93	1	99
Florida	90	9	90
Rhode Island	86	19	80
Connecticut	48	28	71
California	63	32	64
Minnesota	36	51	34
Iowa	36	55	27
United States	45	51	36

Source: NRC, 1993.

Table 11.5 State and national phosphorus mass balance as percent of total mass input.

State	Fertilizer	Harvested	Residual
Hawaii	91	<1	99
Florida	94	3	97
Rhode Island	100	6	94
Connecticut	61	7	92
California	76	13	84
Minnesota	80	36	56
Iowa	76	44	45
United States	79	29	63

Source: NRC, 1993.

■ PROBLEMS

11.1 Find a local water quality problem that has been in the news in the past year. Discuss in groups the differing viewpoints on the problem.

11.2 Is the quality of waters in the United States improving, staying about the same, or getting worse? Defend your answer. Why is the trend you identify occurring?

References

Adler, J. H. 2003. Fables of the Cuyahoga: Reconstructing a history of environmental protection. *Fordham Environmental Law Journal* 14: 89–146.

Arnaoutoglou, I. 1998. *Ancient Greek laws: A sourcebook.* New York: Routledge.

Association of State and Interstate Water Pollution Control Administrators (ASIWPCA). 1986. Meeting the challenge of nonpoint source control. *J. WPCF* 58(7): 730–740.

Barnes, K. K., D. W. Kolpin, E. T. Furlong, S. D. Zaugg, M. T. Meyer, and L. B. Barber. 2008. A national reconnaissance of pharmaceuticals and other organic wastewater contaminants in the United States—(I) groundwater. *Science of the Total Environment* 402: 192–200.

Beck, E. C. 1979. The Love Canal tragedy. *EPA Journal* 5(1): 16–19.

Clarke, K. C. and J. J. Hemphill. 2002. The Santa Barbara oil spill: A retrospective. D. Danta [ed.], *Yearbook of the Association of Pacific Coast Geographers*, vol. 64. Honolulu: University of Hawaii Press, pp. 157–162.

Focazio, M. J., D. W. Kolpin, K. K. Barnes, E. T. Furlong, M. T. Meyer, S. D. Zaugg, L. B. Barber, and M. E. Thurman. 2008. A national reconnaissance for pharmaceuticals and other organic wastewater contaminants in the United States—(II) Untreated drinking water sources. *Science of the Total Environment* 402: 201–216.

Kolpin, D. W., E. T. Furlong, M. T. Meyer, E. M. Thurman, S. D. Zaugg, L. B. Barber, and H. T. Buxton. 2002. Pharmaceuticals, hormones, and other organic wastewater contaminants in U.S. streams, 1999–2000: A national reconnaissance. *Environ. Sci. Technol.* 36: 1202–1211.

Krenkel, P. A., and V. Novotny. 1980. *Water quality management.* New York: Academic Press.

Marsh, G. P. 1865. *Man and nature; or physical geography as modified by human action.* New York: Charles Scribner.

National Research Council (NRC). 1993. *Soil and water quality: An agenda for agriculture.* Committee on Long-Range Soil and Water Conservation. Board on Agriculture. Washington, DC: National Academy Press.

Novotny, V. 2003. *Water quality: Diffuse pollution and watershed management.* New York: John Wiley & Sons.

Time, Inc. America's sewage system and the price of optimism. *Time*, Aug. 1, 1969. http://content.time.com/time/magazine/article/0,9171,901182,00.html

U.S. Environmental Protection Agency (EPA). 1990. *National pesticide survey: Summary results of EPA's national survey of pesticides in drinking water wells.* Washington, DC: Office of Water and Office of Pesticides and Toxic Substances.

U.S. Environmental Protection Agency (EPA). 1994. *National water quality inventory. 1992 Report to Congress.* EPA 841-R-94-001. Washington, DC: Office of Water. http://nepis.epa.gov/Exe/ZyPDF.cgi/20004S2F.PDF?Dockey=20004S2F.PDF

U.S. Environmental Protection Agency (EPA). 1998. *National water quality inventory. 1996 Report to Congress.* EPA 841-R-97-008. Washington, DC: Office of Water.

U.S. Environmental Protection Agency (EPA). 2002. *National water quality inventory: 2000 Report to Congress.* EPA 841-R-02-001. Washington, DC: Office of Water.

U.S. Environmental Protection Agency (EPA). 2009. *National water quality inventory: Report to Congress.* EPA 841-R-08-001. Washington, DC: Office of Water.

U.S. Environmental Protection Agency (EPA). 2014. *Water quality assessment and total maximum daily loads information.* Accessed 9/10/2014 from http//www.epa.gov/waters/ir/

12

Physical Characteristics of Water

■ Introduction

The word *physics* comes from the Greek *physika*, which means pertaining to natural things. The physical characteristics of water are those that primarily relate to physical entities in water as distinguished from chemical and biological characteristics. These physical properties are those things that we generally can see or smell. For example, the "muddy Mississippi" conjures an image of a physical characteristic of the river. The physical characteristics of water discussed in this chapter include turbidity, sediment and solids, odor, temperature, color, and conductivity. These follow the normal conventions of physical versus chemical properties as used in common references such as *Standard Methods* (Clesceri et al., 1998). Some of these characteristics are admittedly not just physical and may represent an aggregate of various effects in water.

■ Turbidity

Suspended and colloidal matter in water causes turbidity. Higher turbidity in water results in the reduction of light in water bodies. Turbidity can be created by microorganisms, minerals (e.g. silica), clay and silt, sawdust, and industrial wastes (Figure 12.1). **Turbidity** has been defined as a measure of the extent to which the intensity of light is reduced by suspended matter (McKee and Wolf, 1963). The analytical test for turbidity is based on the comparison of light passing through a sample to that passing through a standard sample. The original units used were Jackson turbidity units (JTUs). The JTU refers to the depth of water at which a candle flame could be clearly distinguished (Figure 12.2a). Because instruments were not able to match the results obtained from the Jackson candle, nephelometric turbidity units (NTUs) are now used. A nephelometer (Figure 12.2c) measures the amount of scattered light at a right angle to the incident light (Figure 12.2b). There is no conversion or relationship between JTUs and NTUs because particle size distributions influence the results obtained.

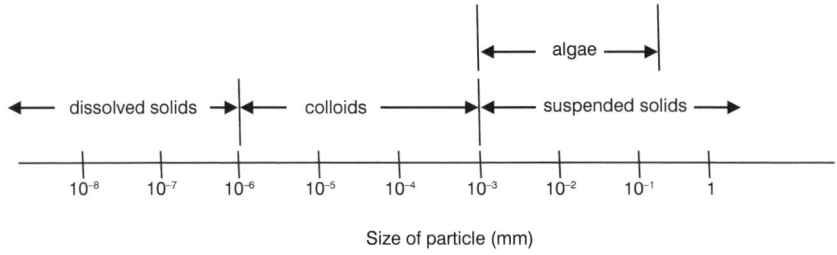

Figure 12.1 Sizes of particles in water (after Tchobanoglous and Schroeder, 1987).

Turbidity can affect several beneficial uses of water, including domestic water supplies, industrial water supplies, and fish and other aquatic life. The U.S. Environmental Protection Agency (EPA, 2003) has adopted the following drinking water regulations for turbidity:

> At no time can turbidity (cloudiness of water) go above 5 nephelolometric turbidity units (NTU); systems that filter must ensure that the turbidity go no higher than 1 NTU (0.5 NTU for conventional or direct filtration) in at least 95% of the daily samples in any month. As of January 1, 2002, turbidity may never exceed 1 NTU, and must not exceed 0.3 NTU in 95% of daily samples in any month.

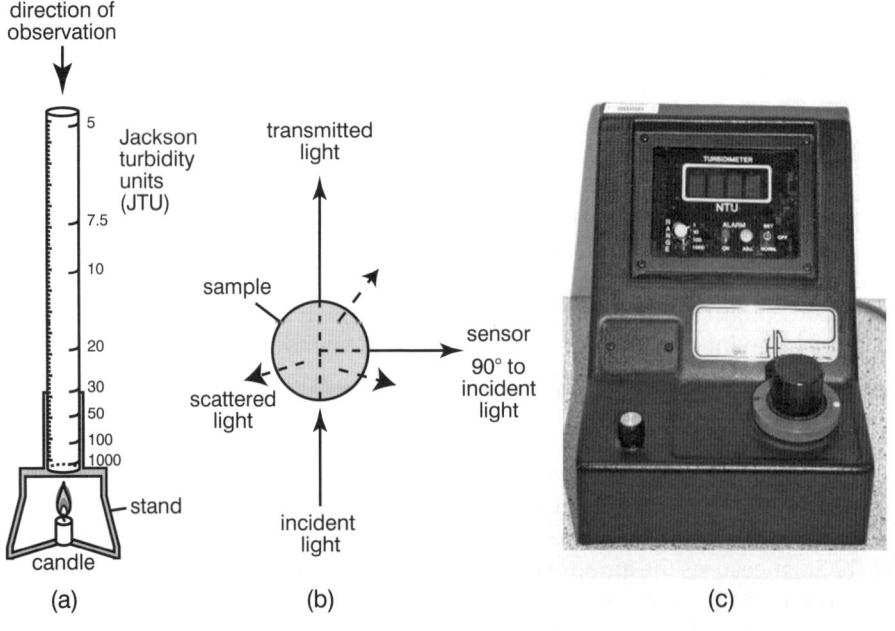

Figure 12.2 Turbidity measurement. (a) Jackson Candle Turbidimeter, (b) principle for measuring scattered light in a nephelometer, and (c) an example of a nephelometer.

CHAPTER 12   Physical Characteristics of Water   119

Industrial water supplies are commonly used for laundry, ice making, bottled beverages, textiles, and pulp and paper. Generally such water needs to be low in turbidity and requires less than 1 to 2 NTU (WHO, 1997).

Turbidity interferes with the penetration of light into water and thus can have several ecological implications. For example, less light could lower the rate of photosynthesis and therefore primary production. Food available for fish could also be lowered. Furthermore, turbid water could make it more difficult for aquatic organisms to find food. Highly turbid water can change the water's albedo and may heat up more easily. High turbidity can be directly lethal to some organisms by clogging gills or covering trout eggs (McKee and Wolf, 1963). Turbidity also inhibits feeding and restricts the growth of some species of oysters and freshwater mussels.

Based on the U.S. Geological Survey's (USGS) National Water-Quality Assessment Program (NAWQA) results, the median turbidity in monitored streams in the United States from 1990 to 2008 was 5 NTU, although values as high as 4,160 NTU have been observed (Table 12.1). The median turbidity of ground water has been reported to be 1.4 NTU with a maximum of 1,339 NTU.

Table 12.1   USGS NAWQA results 1990–2008.

	Ground Water				Surface Water			
	n	Median	Min	Max	n	Median	Min	Max
Turbidity (NTU)	2,225	1.4	0	1,339	536	5.0	0	4,160
Total solids (mg/L)	7,046	294	0	65,000				

■ Solids (Residue)

There are many forms of solids in water. These forms include total solids, dissolved solids, suspended solids, fixed solids, and volatile solids. More recently, the term *suspended solids concentration* has been used. Total solids are based on evaporation from a dish when baked at a predetermined temperature (Figure 12.3). Total solids ("total residue" in EPA [1983] methods) is determined on an unfiltered water sample. Methodologically, total solids equal suspended solids plus dissolved solids (Clesceri et al., 1998). Suspended solids are actually nonfilterable solids. These are solids that would not settle by gravity and are retained on a filter (Figure 12.4). Dissolved solids are those that pass through a filter. Various chemical compounds contribute to dissolved solids, especially carbonate, bicarbonate, chloride, sulfate, calcium, magnesium, sodium, and potassium (McKee and Wolf, 1963). However, in actual field sampling, the method results in the collection of solids that could settle. Fixed solids are the solids remaining after ignition, and volatile solids are those lost during ignition. Volatile solids are generally of organic origin but can also include nonorganic matter. Following is an example of calculations for a total suspended sample analysis.

EXAMPLE 12.1 Total Suspended Sample Analysis

A 365 mL sample of water was filtered using the apparatus in Figure 12.4. The initial weight of the dried filter was 0.1096 g and the final weight of the dried filter and sediment was 0.1182 g. Both filters were dried to a constant weight at 105°C. Determine the total suspended solids (TSS) in mg/L.

$$mg/L = \frac{g \text{ weight (after} - \text{before)} \times 1000 \text{ mg/g}}{\text{volume mL} \times 1 \text{ L}/1000 \text{ mL}} \qquad [12.1]$$

$$TSS = \frac{(0.1182 - 0.1096) \text{ g} \times 1000 \text{ mg/g}}{365 \text{ mL} \times \text{L}/1000 \text{ mL}} = 23.6 \text{ mg/L}$$

To obtain a suspended solids water sample in the field, there are several depth integrating samplers available, such as the DH-81 (Figure 12.5). *D* means depth integrating, *H* means handheld, and the number refers to the year approved. The amount of suspended sediment (settleable solids) in water is a function of the water velocity. In an idealized river system, velocity is stratified from top to bottom and from bank to bank (Figure 12.6, repeated from Chapter 9). The average velocity is said to occur at 0.6 times the depth from the surface. To obtain a representative suspended sediment sample, a compositing or depth-integrated approach is necessary.

Figure 12.3 Evaporation dish.

CHAPTER 12 Physical Characteristics of Water ♦ 121

Figure 12.4 Filtration apparatus.

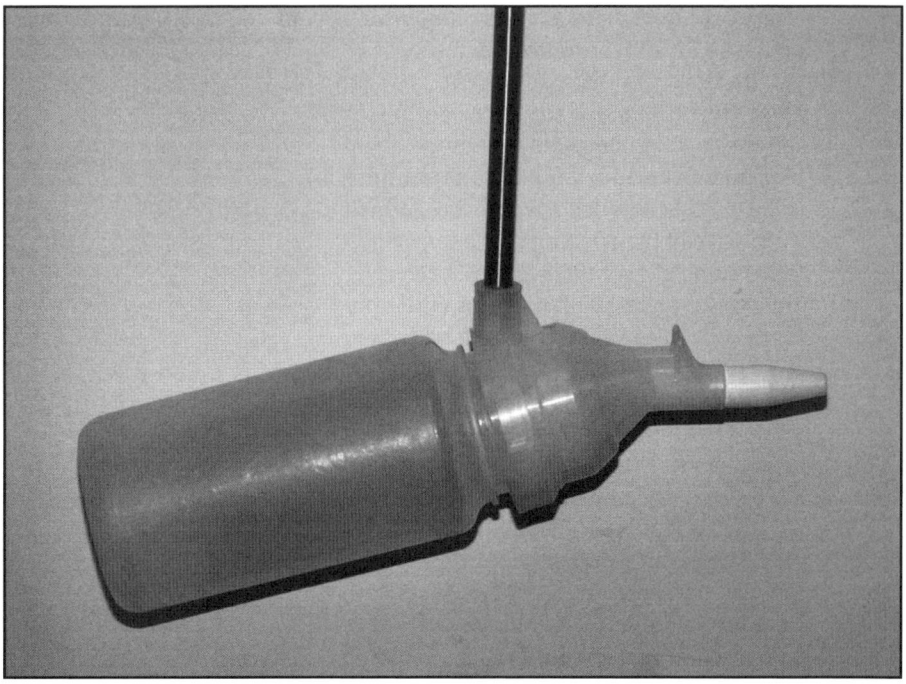

Figure 12.5 DH-81 sampler.

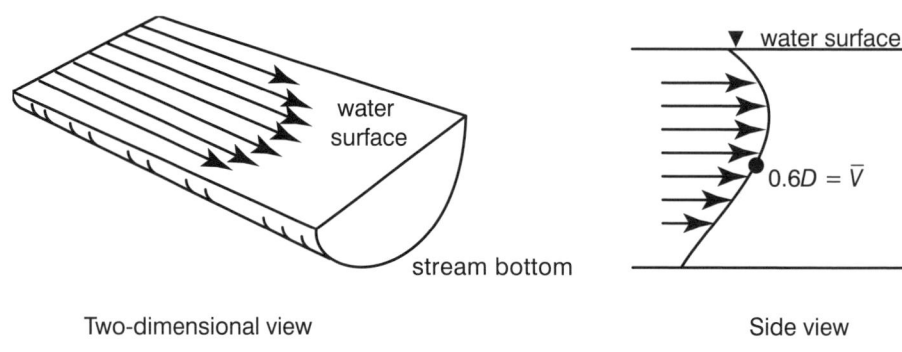

Figure 12.6 Two-dimensional and side views showing stratification of stream velocity.

The USGS utilizes the EWI (equal width increment) or EDI (equal discharge increment) method to measure fluvial sediment (Wilde, 2006). These approaches obtain an integrated sample for the entire cross section of a stream. Automated samplers typically obtain a sample from a discrete point in a stream. Modifications to intakes have been made to obtain a more depth-integrated sample (Eads and Thomas, 1983).

Suspended solids concentration (SSC) has been compared to total suspended solids (TSS) (Gray et al., 2000) and appears to be a more reliable measurement. The major difference in the method is that the total sample, rather than an aliquot, is used to determine SSC. Larger samples are subsampled using a churn splitter (Figure 12.7) or cone splitter, depending on the sediment concentration.

Bedload is the sediment carried along the bottom of a stream by rolling or saltation. A Helley-Smith bedload sampler may be used to collect such samples (Figure 12.8). Bedload would be defined by the size of the opening of the sampler in terms of height off the bottom of the river and size of material allowed into the sampler. Bedload can also be determined using a bedload pan placed in the bottom of the stream, which is removed and weighed at appropriate time intervals. Cross section area changes of stream bottom profiles have also been used to estimate bedload.

Excess solids can have adverse effects on domestic and industrial water supplies and fish and other aquatic life. There is no primary (mandatory) drinking water regulation regarding solids, but the national secondary drinking water regulation (non-mandatory guidelines) for total dissolved

Figure 12.7 Churn splitter.

solids is 500 mg/L (EPA, 2003). Water with higher concentrations may not be palatable. There are no recommended regulations for other forms of solids, such as suspended solids. However, certain crops are injured by high dissolved solids (salt) in irrigation water. Wildlife and livestock have limits in dissolved salts that should occur in their drinking water. Fish and shellfish may be harmed by suspended solids that clog gills and bury eggs and macroinvertebrates on stream bottoms (McKee and Wolf, 1963). Solids also can reduce light penetration into water and affect plant growth.

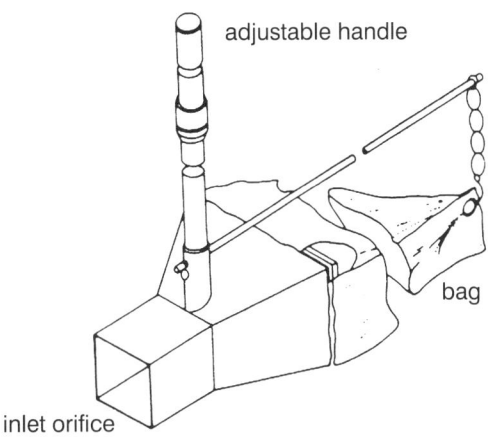

Figure 12.8 Helley-Smith bedload sampler. (USGS, https://water.usgs.gov/admin/memo/SW/sw90.08.att.html)

∎ Odor

Odor is important for drinking water, food preparation, and the aesthetics of water bodies. The sources of odors are primarily from most organic chemicals as well as some inorganic chemicals. These chemicals may come from either natural or municipal/industrial sources. A familiar example of a noticeable odor is that from H_2S, which resembles a rotten egg smell. This odor can also be produced by the decomposition of algae or anoxia in muds and ground water.

The test for odor uses the nose (Clesceri et al., 1998). One test is called the threshold odor test. The principle of this test is to dilute a sample with odor-free water until the least definitely perceptible odor is achieved. The odor test is conducted with a panel of from five to 10 persons. The threshold odor values vary with temperature, and 40°C is the standard test temperature. For hot threshold tests, 60°C is the standard.

The procedure for conducting the test has been standardized (Clesceri et al., 1998). Individuals are selected who have a serious interest in the test. Participants should avoid smoking and eating before the test and should avoid the use of perfumes or shaving lotions. Participants work in an odor-free room. The most dilute sample is presented first. Odor vessels are 500 mL Erlenmeyer flasks, and they should be colored to avoid bias from turbidity or color. Odor-free water is created by passing clean water through activated carbon. Each participant describes the odor. **Threshold odor number (TON)** is defined as the greatest dilution of sample with odor-free water yielding a definitely perceptible odor. The TON is calculated from the ratio of the total volume to the sample volume (Eqn. 12.2). The total volume of sample and odor-free water used is standardized at 200 mL. An example from an odor test is shown in Table 12.2.

$$\text{TON} = \frac{A+B}{A} \quad [12.2]$$

where A = number of mL of sample
B = number of mL odor-free water

Table 12.2 Preparation for a threshold odor test.

Flask	Sample Volume (mL)	TON
A	0	200
B	2.8	70
C	12	17
D	blank	200
E	50	4

The sample volume is added to the 500 mL flask with enough odor-free water to make 200 mL, and the sample is shaken. A retest is done with two blanks of odor-free water inserted randomly.

Temperature

Water temperature can be affected by changes in available sunlight, discharges, overland flow, and ground water inputs. The temperature of water affects the density of water, the solubility of gases, and the rate of reactions. It also affects the organisms living in water. Generally, as the temperature of water increases, the capacity of the water to hold oxygen decreases while the demand for oxygen can increase.

For drinking water purposes, water temperatures should be below 15°C (McKee and Wolf, 1963). Lethal temperatures for fish vary by species and are affected by exposure time. Median tolerance limits generally occur above 25°C to 35°C. Sudden changes in water temperature can be deleterious to some fish. Algal growth is also affected by water temperature.

Brown (1970) developed a simple model to predict the change in stream temperature associated with exposing a stream reach to solar radiation. Exposure might be the result of forest harvesting along the stream. Brown's model is:

$$\Delta T = \frac{AH}{Q} \times 0.000267 \quad [12.3]$$

where ΔT = the temperature increase expected (°F)
A = exposed surface area (ft^2)
H = heat load (solar radiation) received (BTU/ft^2-min)
Q = stream discharge (ft^3/s)

and the constant converts flow from ft^3/s to lb/min. Using this equation, greater temperature increases would occur with greater length exposed, more solar radiation associated with stream orientation, and lower discharge.

Temperature measurements are typically made with a thermometer. Increasingly, recording instruments use thermocouples or thermistors to obtain temperature measurements. A thermocouple is a temperature measuring device based on the voltage difference created by connecting two different metals, such as copper and constantan, a nickel-copper alloy with high resistivity. This voltage difference increases with temperature. Many different metal combinations are used and affect accuracy. A thermistor is a resistor using the principle that resistance changes with temperature. Thermistors are often used in water quality monitoring equipment and are more accurate than thermocouples at temperatures over 0.1°C.

■ Color

Color in water comes from a number of sources, including metallic ions (Fe and Mn), humic materials, plankton, and industrial wastes (Clesceri et al., 1998). Two terms are used when describing color. The term **color** applies when the turbidity of the water has been removed. The term **apparent color** includes suspended matter in the original sample.

The common method of analysis of water for color uses a visual comparison with a known concentration of colored solutions, usually platinum-cobalt standards. A color wheel is one example of a color comparator (Figure 12.9). One color unit is equivalent to 1 mg/L of platinum in water. Fewer than 10 color units are not noticeable to the eye. More than 200 color units characterize swamp water.

Figure 12.9 Color comparator wheel.

The National Secondary Drinking Water Standard for color is 15 color units (EPA, 2003). High color is undesirable for many industrial uses of water. For example, industrial brewing water should be 0 to 10 units (McKee and Wolf, 1963).

■ Conductivity

Conductivity is the ability of water to conduct electricity. Specific conductivity is the conductivity of a cube of water 1 cm on a side. English units for conductivity are μmho/cm. Since the English units for resistance are ohms and conductivity is 1/resistance, the mho is 1/ohm. The S.I. units for conductivity are μSiemens/cm (μS/cm). Conductivity increases with greater dissolved solids in water and at greater temperature. Total dissolved solids has sometimes been related to conductivity through the simple linear regression (Hem, 1985):

$$TDS = A \times \text{conductivity} \quad \quad [12.4]$$

where TDS = total dissolved solids in mg/L
  A = 0.55 to 0.75
and conductivity is in μS/cm.

Conductivity should be reported at 25°C since it varies with temperature. Some instruments measure temperature-compensated conductivity. For cases in which they do not compensate for temperature, conductivity can be adjusted (Clesceri et al., 1998).

Excessive conductivity (greater than 2,000 μS/cm) is not good for fish life (McKee and Wolf, 1963) and greater than 4,000 μS/cm can be toxic. Ground water typically has higher specific conductivity than surface waters. Evaporative waters also show higher conductivity (Clausen et al., 2006). Conductivity has been used to determine the source of water to streams and to classify waters in peatlands (Clausen and Brooks, 1983).

■ Problems

12.1 A 300 mL water sample is filtered on a 0.45 μm glass fiber filter and dried at 105°C for longer than 1 hr. The initial weight of the filter was 0.1034 g and the weight of the dried filter and sediment was 0.1274 g. Determine the total suspended solids in mg/L.

12.2 If the SSC of Long River was found to be 110 mg/L and the average discharge was 7.2 ft³/s, what is the mass export in kg/ha/yr? The watershed is 640 acres in size.

■ REFERENCES

Brown, G. W. 1970. Predicting the effect of clearcutting on stream temperature. *J. Soil and Water Conserv.* 25: 11–13.

Clausen, J. C., and K. N. Brooks. 1983. Quality of runoff from Minnesota peatlands: I. A characterization. *Water Resources Bulletin* 19(5): 763–767.

Clausen, J. C., I. M. Ortega, C. M. Glaude, R. A. Relyea, G. Garay, and O. Guineo. 2006. Classification of wetlands in a Patagonian national park, Chile. *Wetlands* 26(1): 217–229.

Clesceri, L. S., A. E. Greenberg, and A. D. Eaton. 1998. *Standard methods for the examination of water and wastewater*. 20th ed. Washington, DC: American Public Health Association, American Water Works Association, Water Environment Association. http://www.mwa.co.th/download/file_upload/SMWW_1000-3000.pdf

Eads, R. E., and R. B. Thomas. 1983. Evaluation of a depth proportional intake device for automatic pumping samplers. *Water Resources Bulletin* 19(2): 289–292.

Gray J. R., G. D. Glysson, L. M. Turcios, and G. E. Schwarz. 2000. *Comparability of suspended-sediment concentration and total suspended solids data*. USDI, U.S. Geological Survey. Water Resources Investigations Report 00-4191. Reston, VA: U.S. Geological Survey. http://pubs.usgs.gov/wri/wri004191/

Hem, J. D. 1985. *Study and interpretation of the chemical characteristics of natural water*. 3rd ed. Geological Survey Water-Supply Paper 2254. Washington, DC: U.S. Government Printing Office. http://pubs.usgs.gov/wsp/wsp2254/pdf/wsp2254a.pdf

McKee, J. E., and H. W. Wolf. 1963. *Water quality criteria*. 2nd ed. Publ. No. 3-A. Sacramento: California State Water Quality Control Board. http://www.waterboards.ca.gov/publications_forms/publications/general/docs/waterquality_criteria1963.pdf

Tchobanoglous, G., and E. D. Schroeder. 1987. *Water quality characteristics, modeling and modification*. Menlo Park, CA: Addison-Wesley.

U.S. Environmental Protection Agency (EPA). 2003. *National primary drinking water standards*. EPA 816-F-03-016. Washington, DC: Office of Water.

U.S. Geological Survey (USGS). 1990–2008. NAWQA data warehouse. http://cida.usgs.gov/nawqa_www/nawqa_data_redirect.html?p=nawqa:

Wilde, F. D. 2006. Collection of water samples. Chapter A4 in *National field manual for the collection of water-quality data*; Book 9, *Handbooks for water-resources investigations*. U.S. Geological Survey. http://water.usgs.gov/owg/fieldmanual/

World Health Organization (WHO). Guidelines for drinking water quality. 2nd ed., Vol. 3: *Surveillance and control of community supplies*. Geneva, Switzerland.

13

Chemical Characteristics of Water

■ Introduction

Water in its pure state is a chemical compound of hydrogen and oxygen (Hem, 1985). Its dipolar molecule is attracted to many dissolved ions. Dissolved ions in water change the ability of water to conduct electricity, described by a term called *conductivity*. Water is often called the universal solvent because so many substances dissolve in water. Natural water contains numerous chemical substances of both natural and cultural origin. The processes of weathering, soil erosion, and soil and sediment formation influence these chemicals in water (Stumm and Morgan, 1995). Many chemicals affect the uses of water and therefore serve as water quality standards.

This chapter will summarize the common chemical characteristics of water, their classifications, water quality standards, processes controlling chemical composition, and methods of water analysis. Minor mention of water treatment techniques will be made. Certain chemical characteristics will be discussed in greater detail because they are so commonly used in describing water quality. While this chapter is devoted to the chemical characteristics of water, these constituents interact with both physical and biological characteristics and can have both aqueous and gas phases. Thus, these are complex relationships that cannot be considered alone.

Chemicals in water can exist in several states: gaseous, dissolved, and particulate. Particles of very small sizes may exist as colloids, which are almost dissolved because they are so small (5 mμ to 0.2 μm) (Hem, 1985). Waters may also contain suspended particles. Filtering with the common 0.45 μm sized filter will allow particles larger than colloidal material to pass through the filter.

Common Chemical Characteristics of Water

The typical compositions of river water and ground water are summarized in Table 13.1. It is evident that the major constituents in water are the anion bicarbonate, followed perhaps by calcium, sulfate, and sodium in decreasing order of abundance. Ground water is also generally highest in bicarbonate, followed by sulfate, sodium, and calcium. Chloride can be high in certain ground waters. The chemical composition of ground water in particular can vary from place to place due to contact with varying mineral deposits. Residence (or contact) times of ground water also influence its composition. There are several other minor ions found in water (Table 13.2).

Table 13.1 Chemical composition of common waters.

Constituent	River Water[1] (mg/L)	Ground Water[2] (mg/L)
Aluminum (Al^{+3})	0.07	—
Bicarbonate (HCO_3^-)	58	29–302
Calcium (Ca^{+2})	15	1.5–87
Carbonate (CO_3^-)	—	0–8
Chloride (Cl^-)	7.6	4.2–97
Fluoride (F^-)	0.2	0–3.4
Iron (Fe^{+2})	0.67	0.02–0.74
Magnesium (Mg^{+2})	4.1	0.8–34
Manganese (Mn^{+2})	—	0–0.23
Nitrate (NO_3^-)	1	0.7–3.2
Potassium (K^+)	2.3	1.3–6.2
Sodium (Na^+)	6.3	2.4–138
Sulfate (SO_4^{-2})	11	5.8–282

[1] Hem, 1985.
[2] Tchobanoglous and Schroeder, 1987.

Table 13.2 Minor ionic species in water.

Cations	Anions
Aluminum (Al^{+3})	Carbonate (CO_3^{-2})
Ammonia (NH_3)	Fluoride (F^-)
Arsenic (As^+)	Phosphate (PO_4^{-3})
Copper (Cu^{+2})	Sulfide (S^{-2})
Iron, ferrous (Fe^{+2})	Sulfite (SO_3^{-2})
Iron, ferric (Fe^{+3})	
Manganese (Mn^{+2})	

Source: After Tchobanoglous and Schroeder, 1987.

Classification of Chemicals in Water

Standard Methods for the Examination of Water and Wastewaters (Clesceri et al., 1998) classifies the chemical characteristics of water into metals, inorganic nonmetallic, and organic materials (Table 13.3). Inorganic compounds do not contain a carbon atom, whereas carbon is characteristic of organic compounds. The U.S. EPA drinking water standards classify the chemical characteristics of water as inorganic chemicals, organic chemicals, and disinfectants and disinfection by-products (EPA, 2002). A sampling of the National Primary Drinking Water standards is given in Table 13.4. These standards are often presented as the maximum contaminant level (MCL); that is, the highest level of a contaminant allowed in drinking water. There are 16 inorganic chemicals and 54 organic chemicals in the standards.

Table 13.3 Common chemical characteristics of water.

Metals	Inorganic Nonmetallic (no carbon atom)
Aluminum	Boron
Antimony	Bromide
Arsenic	Chloride
Barium	pH
Cadmium	Nitrogen species
Calcium	Dissolved oxygen
Chromium	Sulfate
Copper	Phosphorus
Iron	
Lead	**Organic**
Magnesium	**(contains carbon atom)**
Manganese	BOD_5
Mercury	TOC
Nickel	Oil and grease
Potassium	Phenols
Selenium	Tannin
Sodium	
Zinc	

Table 13.4 EPA selected national primary drinking water standards.

Inorganic Chemicals	MCL (mg/L)	Organic Chemicals	MCL (mg/L)
Arsenic	0.010	Benzene	0.005
Cadmium	0.005	2,4-D	0.07
Mercury	0.002	Dioxin	0.00000003
Nitrate	10	PCBs	0.0005

Source: EPA, 2001, 2002.

Human Influences

Humans and human activities have added chemicals to water typically beyond those introduced by natural processes. For example, urban runoff often contains more Cu, Pb, and Zn than natural waters. Mercury has also appeared in water bodies as a result of combustion processes and releases into the air. Industrial wastewaters can add numerous metals to surface and ground waters, unless treated. Various forms of N and P have appeared in waters in concentrations greater than produced naturally. In addition, a host of organic compounds have been introduced to water from human sources.

Important Chemical Constituents of Water

pH and Carbonates

pH is defined as the negative $\log_{10}$ of the H^+ activity (Eqn. 13.1). The pH scale is generally considered to range from 0 to 14. pH 7 is neutral, less than 7 is acidic (a CO_2 excess), and greater than 7 is alkaline (excess carbonate and bicarbonate). The carbonate system controls the pH in lakes and therefore the composition of certain chemicals found there. pH actually indicates the equilibrium of the carbonate system at any one time. Ground and river water typically have a pH ranging from 6.0 to 8.5 (Hem, 1985). Rivers affected by acidic deposition can have a pH as low as 3.5, at least episodically (Pisanelli, 1985).

$$pH = -\log\left[H^+\right] = \log\frac{1}{\left[H^+\right]} = \frac{1}{2}pK_w \qquad [13.1]$$

where K_w = the dissociation constant of water

Equation 13.2 shows the carbonate system in water. CO_2 is produced in water by plant respiration and also enters water from the atmosphere. Free CO_2 combines with water to form carbonic acid. H_2CO_3 (carbonic acid) dissociates into an H^+ ion and HCO_3^- (bicarbonate). Bicarbonate dissociates into an H^+ ion and carbonate. In the presence of Ca, bicarbonate can precipitate as $Ca(HCO_3)_2$ and carbonate can precipitate in lakes as $CaCO_3$, which is called marl. Bicarbonate is a buffer to pH change. Local soils and bedrock influence the carbonate chemistry of lakes. The proportion of carbonate species present in water is a function of pH (Figure 13.1).

$$
\begin{array}{c}
(CO_2)_g \\
\updownarrow \\
CO_2 + H_2O \leftrightarrow H_2CO_3 \leftrightarrow H^+ + HCO_3^-; \leftrightarrow H^+ + CO_3^{2-} \\
\downarrow \qquad\qquad\qquad\qquad\qquad + Ca \qquad\qquad + Ca \\
\text{Photosynthesis} \qquad\qquad Ca(HCO_3)_2 \qquad CaCO_3 \text{ (marl)}
\end{array}
\qquad 13.2
$$

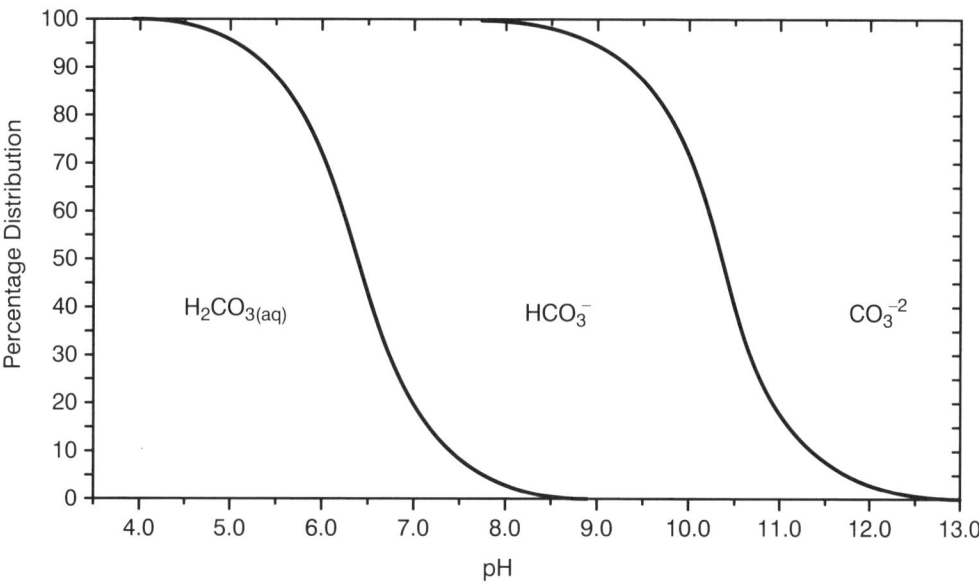

Figure 13.1 Fraction of carbonate species (after Hem, 1985).

The carbonate system thus includes:
  Carbon dioxide $(CO_2)_g$ and $(CO_2)_{aq}$
  Carbonic acid (H_2CO_3)
  Bicarbonate (HCO_3^-)
  Carbonate (CO_3^{2-})
  Carbonate solids (e.g., $CaCO_3$)

Importance of pH. Most fish live within pH limits of 6.5 to 8.4. Toxic limits are less than pH 4.8 or higher than pH 9.2 (McKee and Wolf, 1963). The appropriate pH range in water also depends on the temperature, dissolved oxygen, other ions, and acclimation by the fish. pH has an indirect effect on aquatic life by influencing the dissolution of other compounds, some of which may be harmful.

Acid Precipitation. Rainfall is naturally acidic. Pure rainfall with no pollutants would have a pH of 5.56, which is derived when CO_2 is at equilibrium in water. Following is the calculation of that pH:

Reaction: $CO_{2(aq)} + H_2O_{(l)} \leftrightarrow H_2CO_{3(aq)} \leftrightarrow H^+ + HCO_3^-$

$$\frac{[H^+]^2}{[H_2CO_3]} = K_1 \qquad [13.3]$$

Solving for $[H^+]^2$ gives:

$$[H^+]^2 = (4.47 \times 10^{-7} \text{ mol/L})(1.69 \times 10^{-5} \text{ mol})$$

and
$$[H^+] = 2.7485 \times 10^{-6} \text{ mol/L}$$

therefore
$$pH = \log \frac{1}{[H^+]} = 5.56$$

where K_1 = the equilibrium constant of the ratio of H^+ and H_2CO_3 concentrations

Buffering is the resistance of the change in pH to additions of acids or bases. The presence of bicarbonate in water increases its buffering capacity. pH also influences the availability and therefore the solubility of many other characteristics of water (Figure 13.2). At a low pH most of the substances in Figure 13.2 are less soluble, except Mn and Zn. Remember, acidic precipitation can lower the pH and leach the chemicals that become soluble.

Photosynthesis.   Photosynthesis in lakes or some rivers influences pH by using CO_2 or releasing it during respiration (Eqn. 13.4). During the day, algae use up CO_2 and the pH can increase to greater than 9.0. At night, algae respiration returns the CO_2 to the water and the pH can decrease.

$$6\,H_2O + 6\,CO_2 \leftrightarrow C_6H_{12}O_6 + 6\,O_2 \quad\quad [13.4]$$
$$\text{Respiration} \quad\quad \text{Photosynthesis}$$
$$\leftarrow \quad\quad\quad \rightarrow$$

Determination of pH.   pH is usually determined using an ion electrode, although colorimetric (indicator) methods are sometimes used. pH is an easy measurement to make, but a difficult measurement to make accurately. Appropriate technique is important in pH measurements, including concern about calibration, temperature of the sample, and adequate stirring. pH paper is sometimes used for classroom or laboratory purposes to assess pH. The dissociation constant K_w increases with temperature, and therefore increasing temperature will lower pH (Westcott, 1978). The principle behind electrometric methods is that there is a potential difference between two electrodes in water that can be measured by a galvanometer (pH meter). This potential is proportional to the hydrogen ion activity.

Alkalinity

Alkalinity is the capacity of water to neutralize hydrogen ions (acid). It is often determined by titration with an acid to a fixed end point (e.g., pH 4.6). Titration is the slow addition of a chemical to a water sample until it produces a desired pH or color change. A burette is often used for the titration, although automatic titrators exist. Alkalinity in water is typically caused by the presence of dissolved carbonate and bicarbonate ions (Hem, 1985). Alkalinity is expressed as mg $CaCO_3$/L (Clesceri et al., 1998). The dissolution of limestone is a primary source of alkalinity in many waters (Boyd, 2000). High alkalinity in waters would be from 150 to 300 mg/L, whereas low alkalinity would be 10 to 50 mg/L. Generally, as alkalinity increases, so does pH. Another term applied to alkalinity is acid neutralizing capacity (ANC), which applies to an unfiltered sample.

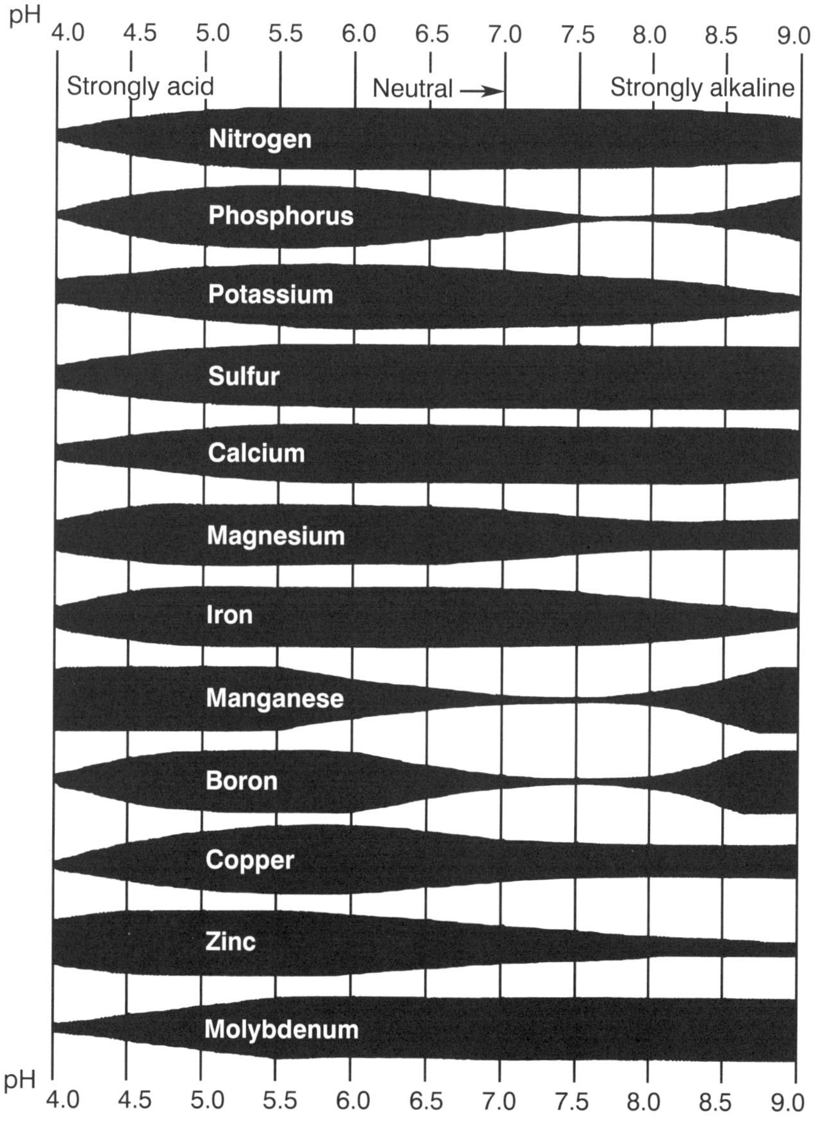

CHAPTER 13 Chemical Characteristics of Water 135

Figure 13.2 Nutrient availability in response to pH (Lucas and Davis, 1961). Used with permission of Wolters Kluwer.

The ANC has been widely used in acid precipitation studies. ANC is determined by preparing a titration curve for pH and determining the equivalence point or by a Gran titration for low-alkalinity waters (USGS, 2006). Inflection points (points of maximum change in pH) determine the equivalence points. An extrapolation of a Gran plot of sample plus titrant volumes times 10^{-pH} versus the titrant volume is used to determine the equivalence point.

Acidity

Acidity is the capacity to neutralize hydroxyl (OH) ions. It is linked to pH and caused by free CO_2, carbonic acid, organic acids, and the oxidation of sulfur (sulfuric acid) in water. Acidity is determined by titration to a fixed end point, often pH 8.3, and is expressed as mg $CaCO_3$/L (Clesceri et al., 1998).

Dissolved Oxygen

The dissolved oxygen content of water is important for aquatic life, including fish. Dissolved oxygen also influences the solubility of a number of chemical characteristics of water. The amount of oxygen dissolved in water is a function of temperature and pressure. Dissolved oxygen is sometimes expressed as percent saturation (Figure 13.3). Saturations greater than 100% are possible due to biological activity in the water.

There is no single threshold of dissolved oxygen suitable for fish life (McKee and Wolf, 1963). Fish consume more oxygen at higher water temperatures. The effect of low dissolved oxygen concentrations are made worse by the presence of toxic substances. Also, different species of fish tolerate different dissolved oxygen thresholds. However, less than 3.0 mg/L is considered harmful, and 5.0 mg/L or higher is considered necessary for a good condition (McKee and Wolf, 1963).

The major processes using oxygen in water are decomposition of biodegradable organics, sediment oxygen demand, nitrification of NH_3 to NO_3, and nighttime respiration by algae and macrophytes. The major source of oxygen in water is the atmosphere through the air–water interface. A second source is through photosynthesis by plants in the water body. A model developed for determining the oxygen balance in streams is presented in Chapter 15 on river water quality.

Dissolved oxygen (DO) is determined by either the Winkler titration or ion electrode method (Clesceri et al., 1998).

Biochemical Oxygen Demand

Biochemical oxygen demand (BOD) is the amount of oxygen used in the metabolism of organic matter (Tchobanoglous and Schroeder, 1987). The method for determining BOD measures the changes in oxygen content of water during a specified incubation period, such as five days (Clesceri et al., 1998). BOD includes both carbonaceous and nitrogenous oxygen demand. Carbonaceous oxidation is due to the decomposition of organic compounds by microorganisms. Nitrification (see below) requires oxygen and thus contributes to BOD. The range of BOD can be from under 5.0 mg/L to over 1,000 mg/L for wastewaters (Boyd, 2000).

Nitrogen

Nitrogen is one of the most important constituents in water. The major sources of nitrogen in water are the weathering of rocks and soils and organic matter, and nitrogen gas in the atmosphere (Hem, 1985). Nitrogen-fixing plants and bacteria can remove atmospheric N and convert it to NO_3–N. Three forms

Chapter 13 Chemical Characteristics of Water

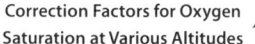

Correction Factors for Oxygen
Saturation at Various Altitudes

Altitude		Pressure	
Feet	Meters	mm.	Factor
0	0	760	1.00
328	100	750	1.01
656	200	741	1.03
984	300	732	1.04
1312	400	723	1.05
1640	500	714	1.06
1970	600	705	1.08
2297	700	696	1.09
2625	800	687	1.11
2953	900	679	1.12
3281	1000	671	1.13
3609	1100	663	1.15
3937	1200	355	1.16
4265	1300	347	1.17
4593	1400	639	1.19
4921	1500	631	1.20
5249	1600	623	1.22
5577	1700	615	1.24
5906	1800	608	1.25
6234	1900	601	1.26
6562	2000	594	1.28
6890	2100	584	1.30
7218	2200	580	1.31
7546	2300	573	1.33
7874	2400	566	1.34
8202	2500	560	1.36

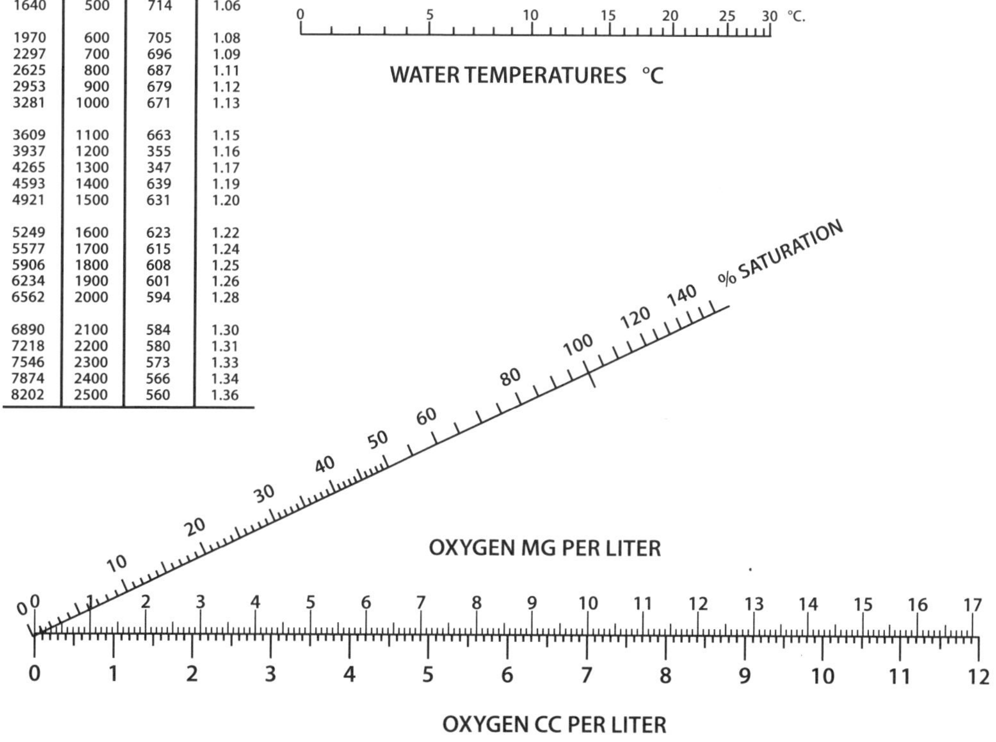

Figure 13.3 Rawson's nomogram (after Welch, 1948).

of nitrogen in water are important for most water quality concerns: nitrate–N (NO_3–N), ammonia–N (NH_3–N), and organic–N.

Nitrite–N (NO_2–N) usually is not a major constituent in water, and nitrogen does not stay in the NO_2–N form for very long. The nitrogen cycle is shown in Figure 13.4. Nitrogen fixation is the process of converting N_2 in the atmosphere to ammonia. Nitrification is the oxidation of ammonia to nitrate, while nitrate reduction is the opposite. Denitrification is the process of reducing NO_3–N to N_2. These processes are dependent on the presence of oxygen and certain bacteria. In low-oxygen waters, more NH_3–N would be observed, while in oxygenated waters, more NO_3–N would be present. Denitrification requires the presence of NO_3–N, carbon, bacteria, and low oxygen levels. It is an important mechanism for removing nitrogen from waters.

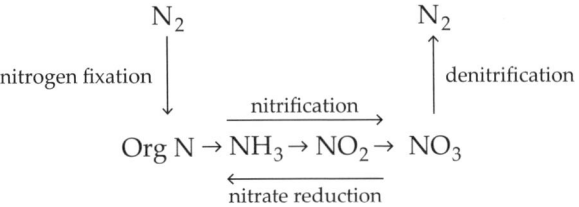

Figure 13.4 Nitrogen cycle.

Some average nitrogen concentration values for streams versus land use in the eastern United States based on the National Eutrophication Survey were reported by Omernik (1976). Streams in agricultural watersheds had the highest total nitrogen and NO_3–N concentrations, while forested watersheds were the lowest (Table 13.5). Wastewaters have even higher nitrogen concentrations. For example, total Kjeldahl nitrogen (TKN) in dairy milkhouse wastewater was reported to range from 48.86 mg/L (Schwer and Clausen, 1989) to 102.64 mg/L (Newman et al., 2000), advanced wastewater was 1 to 3 mg/L, and barnyard runoff was 121.76 mg/L (Schellinger and Clausen, 1992).

The nationwide urban runoff program reported the event median concentration (EMC) of nitrogen at 28 locations (Table 13.6). Differences from storm to storm were generally greater than differences among land-use categories (EPA, 1983).

Table 13.5 Mean nitrogen concentrations and export for land uses in the eastern U.S.

Land Use	Total N (mg/L)	NO_3–N (mg/L)	Percent of total N as NO_3–N	Total N (kg/ha/yr)	NO_3–N (kg/ha/yr)
Forest	0.85	0.23	27	4.40	1.32
Mostly forest	0.88	0.35	39	4.49	1.76
Mixed	1.28	0.68	53	5.52	2.90
Mostly urban	1.29	1.25	98	7.89	5.37
Mostly agriculture	1.81	1.05	57	6.30	3.69
Agriculture	4.17	3.19	76	9.82	7.39

Source: Omernik, 1976.

Table 13.6 Median nitrogen EMCs from the nationwide urban runoff program.

	TKN (mg/L)	$NO_2 + NO_3$–N (mg/L)
Open/nonurban	0.965	0.543
Residential	1.900	0.736
Mixed	1.288	0.558
Commercial	1.179	0.572

Source: EPA, 1983.

Frink (1991) summarized nitrogen export coefficients from numerous studies and reported values for Chesapeake Bay and Long Island Sound (Table 13.7). These values were generally higher than those reported by Omernik (1976).

Table 13.7 Nitrogen export coefficients for Chesapeake Bay and Long Island Sound.

	Chesapeake Bay (kg/ha/yr)	Long Island Sound (kg/ha/yr)
Wooded	0.2 – 5.6	0.1
Urban	5.6 – 28.0	9.6
Agriculture	5.6 – 78.4	20.6

Source: Data from Frink, 1991.

Management of Nitrogen. Knowledge of the nitrogen cycle has allowed the management and reduction of N in wastewaters. For example, nitrogen losses from spray irrigation of wastewater on forested land have been reduced by incorporating a rest-dose management system that encouraged denitrification (Cassell et al., 1979). In wetland treatment systems, nitrogen losses from a wetland were also reduced by introducing alternating saturated and unsaturated conditions, favoring denitrification (Green et al., 1998).

Phosphorus

Phosphorus is an essential nutrient for plants and another important water quality constituent. The sources of phosphorus in water include: (a) apatite in igneous rocks and marine sediments, (b) soil leaching, (c) organic wastes and wastewaters from sewage and animals, (d) the natural decomposition of organic matter, (e) detergents, and (f) phosphate fertilizers (Hem, 1985). The chemical compounds of phosphorus are influenced by pH similar to carbonate species. Orthophosphate (PO_4^{3-}) is the final disassociation product of phosphoric acid (H_3PO_4) that is governed by pH (Eqn. 13.5). The relative proportions of phosphorus species as a function of pH are shown in Figure 13.5.

$$\text{Acid} \qquad\qquad\qquad \text{pH 7} \qquad\qquad\qquad \text{Alkaline}$$
$$H_3PO_4 \leftrightarrow H^+ + H_2PO_4^- \leftrightarrow 2H^+ + HPO_4^{2-} \leftrightarrow 3H^+ + PO_4^{3-} \qquad [13.5]$$

The various forms of phosphorus in water are largely determined by the method of analysis performed (Figure 13.6). Dissolved and particulate forms of phosphorus are determined by filtration. Organic and inorganic fractions are determined by whether the sample is digested or hydrolyzed (Clesceri et al., 1998). Important chemical processes affecting phosphorus concentrations include precipitation reactions. Phosphate can form insoluble salts with several metal ions such as calcium, magnesium, and iron depending on pH (Stumm and Morgan, 1995).

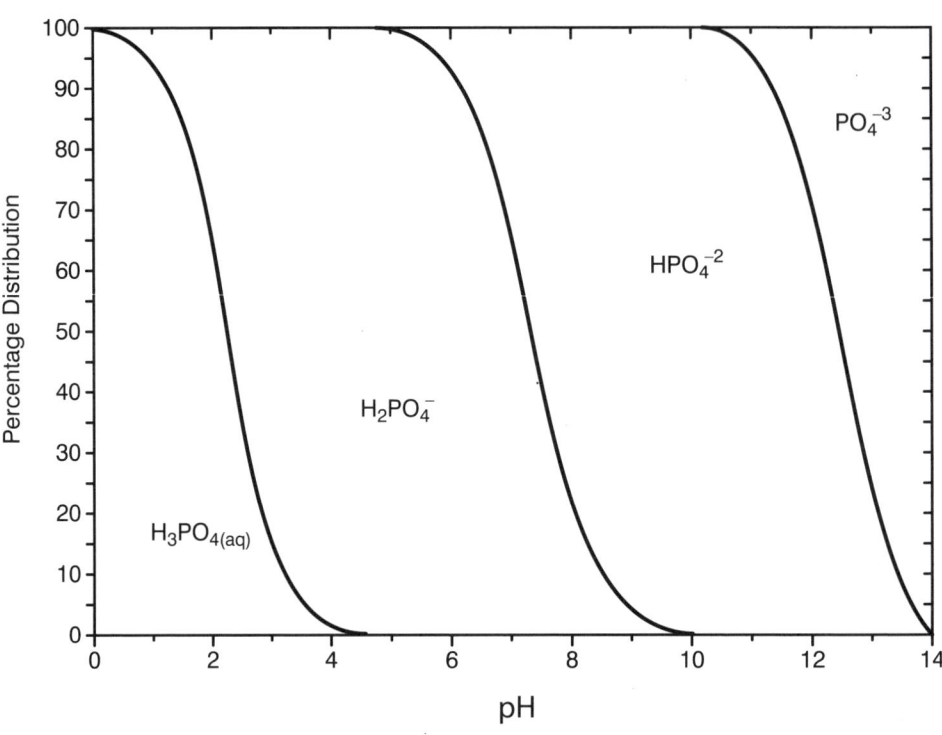

Figure 13.5 Percentages of total dissolved phosphate species in solution as a function of pH (Hem, 1985).

Some average phosphorus values for streams versus land use in the eastern United States were reported by Omernik (1976). These values suggest that ortho–P represents about 40–43% of total phosphorus in these streams (Table 13.8). Both urban and agricultural watersheds were similar in phosphorus export and were the highest of the land-use types. As expected, forested watersheds had the lowest phosphorus export of all land-use types. By comparison, advanced wastewater has about

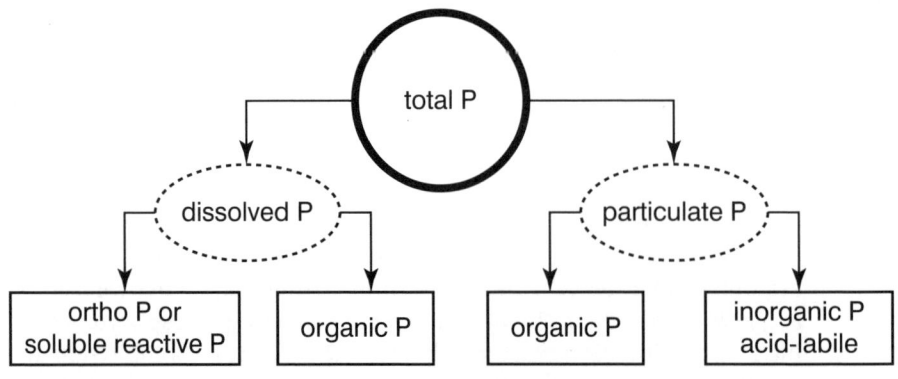

Figure 13.6 The forms of phosphorus in an aquatic environment.

1.0 mg/L, dairy milkhouse waste ranges from 25.7 mg/L (Newman et al., 2000) to 81.8 mg/L (Schwer and Clausen, 1989), and barnyard runoff was 10.0 mg/L (Schellinger and Clausen, 1992). Excess concentrations of phosphorus in water can lead to algal blooms, which is further discussed in Chapter 17. Results from the nationwide urban runoff program (NURP) (EPA, 1983) suggest that residential land use had the highest phosphorus concentrations and open/nonurban the lowest (Table 13.9).

Frink (1991) also summarized phosphorus export coefficients from numerous studies and reported values for Chesapeake Bay and Long Island Sound (Table 13.10). These values generally range higher than reported by Omernik (1976) except for wooded areas.

Table 13.8 Mean phosphorus concentrations and export for land uses in the eastern U.S.

Land Use	Total P (mg/L)	Ortho-P (mg/L)	Total P (kg/ha/yr)	Ortho-P (kg/ha/yr)
Forest	0.014	0.006	0.083	0.041
Mostly forest	0.035	0.014	0.174	0.070
Mixed	0.040	0.017	0.184	0.079
Mostly urban	0.066	0.033	0.301	0.150
Mostly agriculture	0.066	0.027	0.227	0.092
Agriculture	0.135	0.058	0.308	0.133

Source: Omernik, 1976.

Table 13.9 Median phosphorus EMCs from the nationwide urban runoff program.

	Total P (mg/L)	Soluble P (mg/L)
Open/nonurban	0.121	0.026
Residential	0.383	0.143
Mixed	0.263	0.056
Commercial	0.201	0.080

Source: EPA, 1983.

Table 13.10 Phosphorus export coefficients for Chesapeake Bay and Long Island Sound.

	Chesapeake Bay (kg/ha/yr)	Long Island Sound (kg/ha/yr)
Wooded	0.06 – 0.34	0.01
Urban	0.56 – 3.36	1.5
Agriculture	0.28 – 5.60	0.39

Source: Data from Frink, 1991.

Methods of Analysis

There are many ways to measure chemical constituents in water. These methods include:

1. **Stoichiometric.** Titration is a common technique used for acidity and alkalinity determinations. Titration has also been used to measure many other constituents in water, including the Winkler dissolved oxygen test. Titration involves making small additions of either an acid (to determine alkalinity) or a base (to determine acidity) to a point when neutralization of acids or bases present occurs. pH is used to determine these points, although color indicator solutions have also been used. Titration curves can be generated to find the true inflection point in the curve, rather than fixed end-point titration.

2. **Colorimetric.** The colorimetric approach uses a spectrophotometer for a certain wavelength. The wavelength coincides with the point of maximum absorption and the development of a specific color. Visual comparison of a sample with known concentrations of colored solutions is also used, especially for the determination of water color. The apparatus is sometimes called a color wheel.

3. **Atomic absorption.** Atomic absorption (AA) spectrometry is based on a sample being aspirated into a flame and becoming atomized. Light absorbed by the particular element in the flame is detected. AA is used for metals, and each metal has its own absorption wavelength, which is matched to the lamp. The amount of energy absorbed in the flame is proportional to the concentration of the metal at that wavelength. The flame is an air–acetylene mixture.

4. **Flame photometer (emission).** A flame photometer is used in metals analysis. A sample is introduced to a flame and a photometer detects the color of the flame using filters.

5. **Ion-selective electrodes.** Ion-selective electrodes are based on measurement of the potential (mV) between a reference electrode and an electrode designed for the specific ion (e.g., hydrogen electrode for pH). Electrodes are available for several ions, such as chloride.

6. **Plasma emission spectroscopy.** Inductively coupled plasma emission spectroscopy (ICP) is used for metals analysis. This is a form of emission spectroscopy used to excite ions at high temperatures that produce a recognizable electromagnetic spectrum characteristic of a certain element. The intensity of the emission is related to the concentration of the element.

7. **Chromatography.** Chromatography is an analytical chemistry approach that involves the physical separation of water sample components due to absorption and desorption characteristics (Poole and Schuette, 1984). As a sample moves along a stationary phase bed, sorption/desorption will occur at different rates for individual components. There are several types of chromatography.

Gas chromatography uses an inert gas as the mobile phase. Liquid chromatography uses a low viscosity liquid for the mobile phase. Both of these types of chromatography are closed-bed techniques and use pressure through a column to move the gas or liquid. A column is made of glass or metal that includes a sorbent either as granules that fill the column or as a thin film on the column wall. A chromatogram displays the concentrations of sample components over time and shows the number of observed peaks, peak positions, the concentration or amount for each peak, and information about the column performance.

Ion chromatography (IC) is a common approach used to detect anions in water samples (Clesceri et al., 1998). Ion chromatography is used to determine concentrations of Br, Cl, Fl, NO_3, NO_2, PO_4, and SO_4. The advantage of IC is that these anions can be determined rapidly in a single sequential analysis of a single sample. IC is a liquid chromatography technique using a series of ion exchangers to separate the components using a strong acid. A conductivity detector is used to measure the anions, and they are identified based on retention times compared to standards. Peak area or height is used to determine concentrations.

■ PROBLEM

13.1 How would you manage a spray irrigation treatment system of wastewater to remove the maximum nitrogen possible? What if most of the nitrogen is in the form of NH_3–N?

■ REFERENCES

Boyd, C. E. 2000. *Water quality: An introduction*. Boston: Kluwer Academic Publishers.

Cassell, E. A., D. W. Meals, and J. R. Bouzoun. 1979. *Spray application of wastewater effluent in West Dover, Vermont: An initial assessment*. Special Report 79-6. Hanover, NH: U.S. Army Cold Regions Research and Engineering Laboratory.

Clesceri, L. S., A. E. Greenberg, and A. D. Eaton. 1998. *Standard methods for the examination of water and wastewater*. 20th ed. American Public Health Association, American Water Works Association, Water Environment Association.

Frink, C. R. 1991. Estimating nutrient exports to estuaries. *J. Environ. Qual.* 20: 717–724.

Green, M., E. Friedler, and I. Safrai. 1998. Enhancing nitrification in vertical flow constructed wetland utilizing a passive air pump. *Water Research* 32(12): 3513–3520.

Hem, J. D. 1985. *Study and interpretation of the chemical characteristics of natural water*. 3rd ed. Geological Survey Water-Supply Paper 2254. Washington, DC: U.S. Government Printing Office. http://pubs.usgs.gov/wsp/wsp2254/pdf/wsp2254a.pdf

Lucas, R. E., and J. F. Davis. 1961. Relationships between pH values of organic soils and availabilities of 12 plant nutrients. *Soil Science* 92(3): 177–182.

McKee, J. E., and H. W. Wolf. 1963. *Water quality criteria*. 2nd ed. Publication No. 3-A. Sacramento: California State Water Quality Control Board. http://www.waterboards.ca.gov/publications_forms/publications/general/docs/waterquality_criteria1963.pdf

Newman, J. M., J. C. Clausen, and J. A. Neafsey. 2000. Seasonal performance of a wetland constructed to process dairy milkhouse wastewater in Connecticut. *Ecological Engineering* 14: 181–198.

Omernik, J. M. 1976. *The influence of land use on stream nutrient levels.* U.S. Environmental Protection Agency, Office of Research and Development, Corvallis Environmental Research Laboratory, Eutrophication Survey Branch. U.S. EPA-600/3-76-014. http://nepis.epa.gov/Exe/ZyPDF.cgi/9100T18Y.PDF?Dockey=9100T18Y.PDF

Pisanelli, A. J. 1985. Streamflow acidification in Vermont along elevation intervals. Master's thesis, University of Vermont.

Poole, C. F., and S. A. Schuette. 1984. *Contemporary practice of chromatography.* New York: Elsevier.

Schellinger, G. R., and J. C. Clausen. 1992. Vegetative filter treatment of dairy barnyard runoff in cold regions. *J. Environ. Qual.* 21: 40–45.

Schwer, C. B., and J. C. Clausen. 1989. Vegetative filter treatment of dairy milkhouse wastewater. *J. Environ. Qual.* 18: 446–451.

Stumm, W., and J. J. Morgan. 1995. *Aquatic chemistry: Chemical equilibria and rates in natural waters.* 3rd ed. New York: Wiley-Interscience.

Tchobanoglous, G., and E. D. Schroeder. 1987. *Water quality characteristics, modeling and modification.* Menlo Park, CA: Addison-Wesley.

U.S. Environmental Protection Agency (EPA). 1983. *Results of the nationwide urban runoff program.* Water Planning Division. https://www3.epa.gov/npdes/pubs/sw_nurp_vol_1_finalreport.pdf

U.S. Environmental Protection Agency (EPA). 2001. *Arsenic and clarifications to compliance and new source monitoring rule: A quick reference guide.* U.S. EPA 816-F-01-004. Office of Water.

U.S. Environmental Protection Agency (EPA). 2002. *National primary drinking water regulations.* 40 CFR Ch. 1. Section 141. https://www.epa.gov/sites/production/files/2015-11/documents/howepargulates_cfr-2003-title40-vol20-part141_0.pdf

U.S. Geological Survey (USGS). 2006. *Alkalinity and acid neutralizing capacity 6.6.* USGS TWRI Book 9. Chapter A6, Field Measurements. http://water.usgs.gov/owq/FieldManual/Chapter6/Archive/chapter6.6._v3.pdf

Welch, P. S. 1948. *Limnological methods.* Philadelphia: The Blakiston Co.

Westcott, C. C. 1978. *pH measurements.* New York: Academic Press.

14

Biological Characteristics of Water

■ Introduction

Water is a medium for a diverse and rich biological ecosystem with structure and function. This chapter focuses on the identification of the major biological groups in water, some quantitative techniques to measure these groups, and the use of biological indicators of water quality. The groups included in this chapter are the plankton, macroinvertebrates, macrophytes, and pathogens. The use of bioassays is also discussed.

■ Plankton

Plankton are plants and animals suspended in water; they are generally at the mercy of the currents. Two major categories of plankton are the phytoplankton (plants) and zooplankton (animals).

Phytoplankton

The phytoplankton, or algae, are aquatic, photosynthetic, and lack a vascular system (Wehr and Sheath, 2003). They exist in many forms as unicells, some of which are motile; colonies; filaments; and even more complex forms. The algae belong to up to 12 divisions and classes. However, the major groups include:

1. Chlorophyta – green algae
2. Cyanobacteria – blue-green algae
3. Bacillariophyceae – diatoms
4. Pyrrhophyta – dinoflagellates

Chlorophyta

The Chlorophyta, or green algae, are unicellular plants that are colonial or filamentous. They can be floating, swimming, or attached. These algae contain chloroplasts with chlorophyll. Examples of Chlorophyta include *Desmodesmus*, *Pediastrum*, *Spirogyra*, *Staurastrum*, *Ulothrix*, *Volvox*, and *Hydrodictyon* (Figures 14.1 and 14.2).

Desmodesmus has oval cells that are adjoined to form colonies of two to 16 cells. On some species, there are also one or two spines. *Spirogyra* has spiraled chloroplasts like ribbons. This genus forms green clouds of filaments below the water or as a floating mat. *Staurastrum* has arms extending out from each semicell, with a deep median constriction between the two semicells. *Pediastrum* has a plate-like arrangement of cells, some with holes (Prescott, 1978). Cells on the outer edge often have two lobes (Wehr and Sheath, 2003). *Ulothrix* has cells that are cylindrical and longer than they are wide. The chloroplast is a broad band covering most of the cell wall. *Ulothrix* can be found in flowing streams or wave-washed shores as clumps. *Volvox* can form colonies up to 1 mm in diameter that are visible with the unaided eye. They can contain as many as 50,000 cells

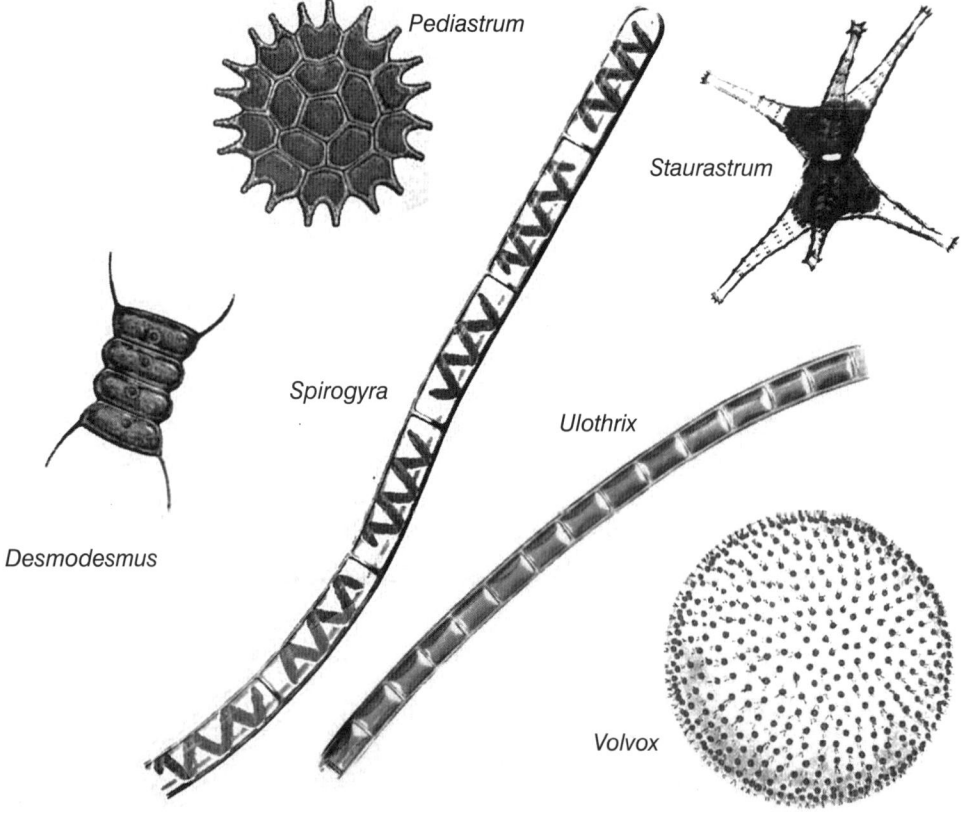

Figure 14.1 Chlorophyta (Palmer, 1962).

in a globular colony. *Hydrodictyon* (Figure 14.2) is composed of connected cylindrical cells that form macroscopic floating clumps of "water net" (Prescott, 1978) that almost resemble hairnets.

Cyanobacteria

The Cyanobacteria, or blue-green algae, have a bacteria-like cell structure and are unicellular and colonial and have simple or branched filaments. Chloroplasts are lacking, and the pigment is distributed throughout the cell rather than in a membrane. This characteristic is the primary way to separate them from the Chlorophyta.

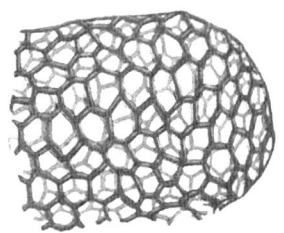

Figure 14.2 *Hydrodictyon reticulantum* (water net) showing hexagonal arranged cells (Palmer, 1962).

Some species fix atmospheric nitrogen, can form stromatolites, and can produce toxins. They can occur in several **lentic** (still water) and **lotic** (flowing) aquatic environments, including planktonic, benthic, and periphytic habitats (Wehr and Sheath, 2003). Examples of the Cyanophyta are *Anabaena, Microcystis, Oscillatoria,* and *Aphanizomenon* (Figure 14.3).

Anabaena is a filamentous alga that has multicellular trichomes (filament without sheath) of beadlike or barrel-shaped cells, with a larger heterocyst that is present. *Anabaena* forms blooms in lakes, but they are suspended throughout the water column, rather than at the surfaces of lakes and ponds. They can liberate a toxin that is fatal to cattle. *Microcystis* has numerous cells that are crowded

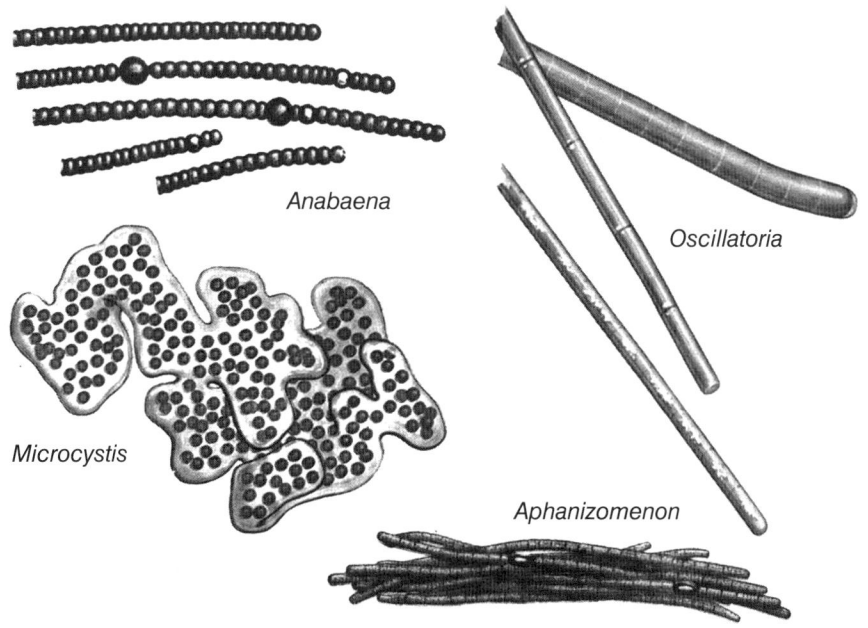

Figure 14.3 Cyanobacteria (Palmer, 1962).

within a colonial mucilage that itself may not be visible. They form irregularly shaped colonies, and some are almost globular. Their blooms result in surface scums due to pseudovacuoles (gas pockets). They also can produce toxins. *Oscillatoria* has solitary trichomes without sheaths that sometimes can move in an oscillating fashion. These trichomes can be found singly or in great masses of interwoven filaments. *Oscillatoria rubescens* causes water to become blood red. *Aphanizomenon* is filamentous and sometimes resembles grass clippings at the surface of a lake. Some species exhibit a conspicuous larger heterocyst.

Bacillariophyceae

The Bacillariophyceae, or diatoms, are unicellular or colonial plants that are yellow-brown to golden brown and have frustules (shells) composed of silicon dioxide (SiO_2) that form two valves. Motile cells have flagella. Diatoms are specific to certain habitat conditions and therefore serve as habitat indicators. Their silica shells also are well preserved in sediments, making them excellent indicators of past conditions. Examples of diatoms are *Fragilaria, Navicula, Tabellaria,* and *Synedra* (Figure 14.4).

Fragilaria has rectangular frustules that are attached side by side to form ribbons or bands. *Navicula* is cigar-shaped and symmetrical as are many other genera. The striae converge somewhat toward a clear center. *Tabellaria* has rectangular frustules (the shell, cell wall of a diatom) that form zig-zag chains or radiating colonies. These can break apart and be confused with other genera. *Synedra* are solitary or clustered cells that are needle-like.

Pyrrhophyta

Dinoflagellates. This group of organisms contains flagella and swims in a whirling fashion. These are the source of the red tide in marine environments. *Ceratium* is a distinctive example (Figure 14.5). It has horns and a flagellum in a transverse groove.

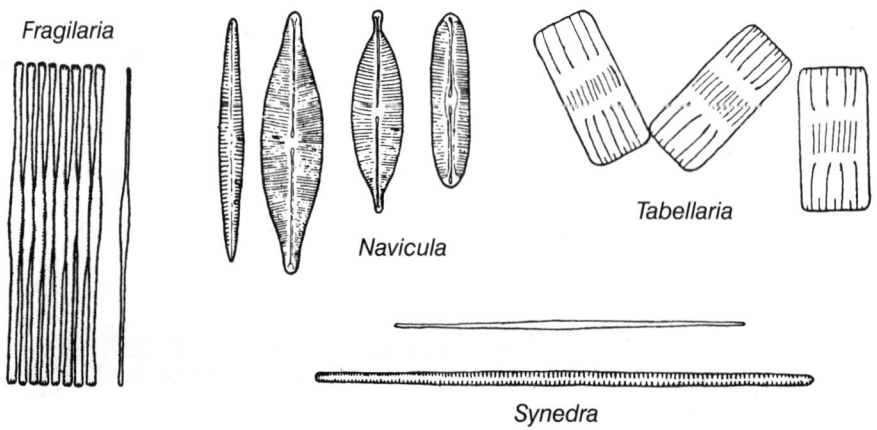

Figure 14.4 Bacillariophyceae (after Needham and Needham, 1962).

Box 14.1 contains a dichotomous key to the major algal groups.

Ecological Habitats

Algae occupy several different niches in water bodies. The **neuston** are the organisms, including algae, that occupy the surface film on lakes and other water bodies (Cole and Weihe, 2016). The assemblage of neuston resembles a city skyscape with filaments resembling skyscrapers. The community extends both upward into the air and downward in the water and includes many invertebrates as well as algae. The **periphyton (Aufwuchs)** are the organisms attached to the substrate (Cole and Weihe, 2016). The types of substrates can include rocks and plants. The periphyton are sometimes visible along the shores of streams and lakes.

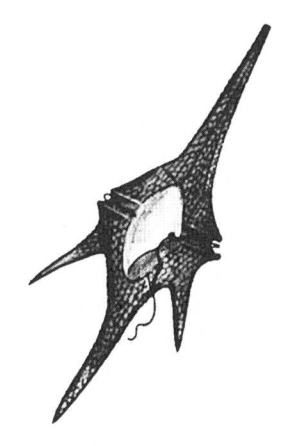

Figure 14.5 The dinoflagellate *Ceratium* (Palmer, 1962).

BOX 14.1

Dichotomous Key to the Major Algal Groups

1. Cells without chloroplasts, bluish green pigment throughout cell . . . . Cyanobacteria
1. Cells with chloroplasts, green, brown, or red 2
   2. Plant grass green . . . . Chlorophyta
   2. Plant yellow or brown 3
      3. Cell wall siliceous, wall in two sections . . . . Bacillariophyceae
      3. With flagella . . . . Dinoflagellates

Phytoplankton Sampling

Phytoplankton can be collected using a number of methods. One of the most common techniques is to use a plankton net, such as the Wisconsin plankton net (Figure 14.6). Plankton nets can be deployed by towing horizontally behind a boat or by a vertical tow. If the tow height is known, the volume of water passing through the net can be calculated. Tow height is sometimes set to be at the compensation point in lakes, which is assumed to be 2.2 to 2.7 times Secchi disk transparency (Figure 14.7) (O'Sullivan and Reynolds, 2004). Plankton collected with a net are termed net plankton, and their size will depend on mesh sizes for either the net or collection bucket.

A second common way to collect a plankton sample is to collect a water sample. Several devices have been used to collect water samples from lakes, including the Van Doran and Kemmerer bottles (Figure 14.8). These samplers can

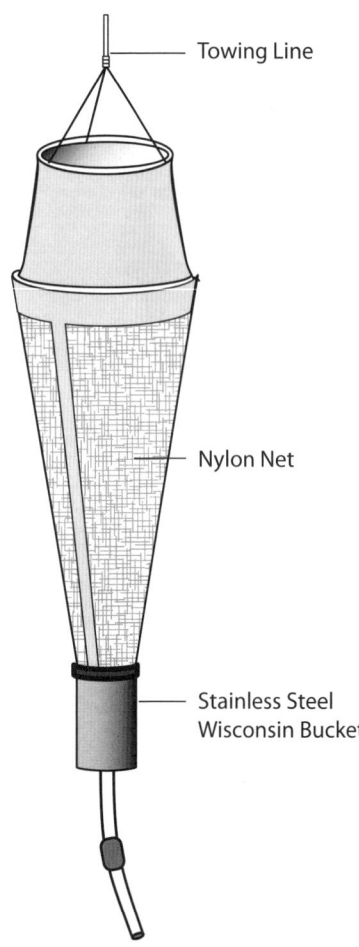

Figure 14.6 Wisconsin plankton net.

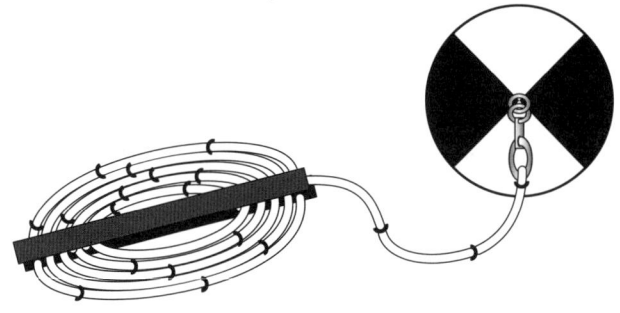

Figure 14.7 Secchi disk.

be used to collect a sample at a certain water depth. These are made of a variety of materials and are triggered with a messenger sent down on the tether rope or chain. These samplers have the advantage of collecting small plankton that might pass through a net.

Another alternative is to collect a large sample with the use of a pump. Once a water sample has been collected, plankton can be concentrated by sedimentation, filtration, or centrifugation.

Phytoplankton can be enumerated (counted) using counting cells such as the Sedgewick-Rafter cell (Figure 14.9) and a microscope with eyepiece grid. This cell holds 1 mL of water. The procedure involves counting all the algae within many fields (e.g., 10) across the cell. Then the number of organisms per liter can be determined from knowing the size of the eyepiece grid and the size of the counting cell (Clesceri et al., 1998). Other counting techniques include using a membrane filter or an inverted microscope.

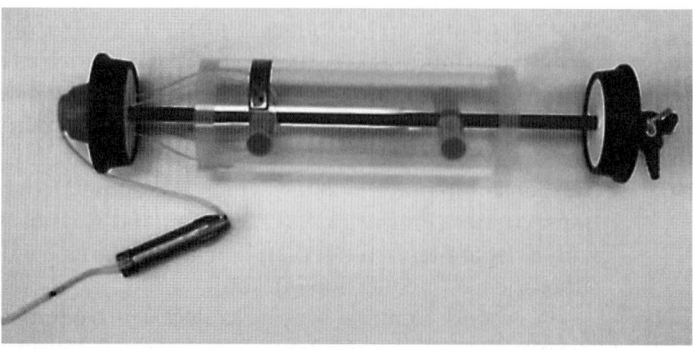

Figure 14.8 Kemmerer sampler.

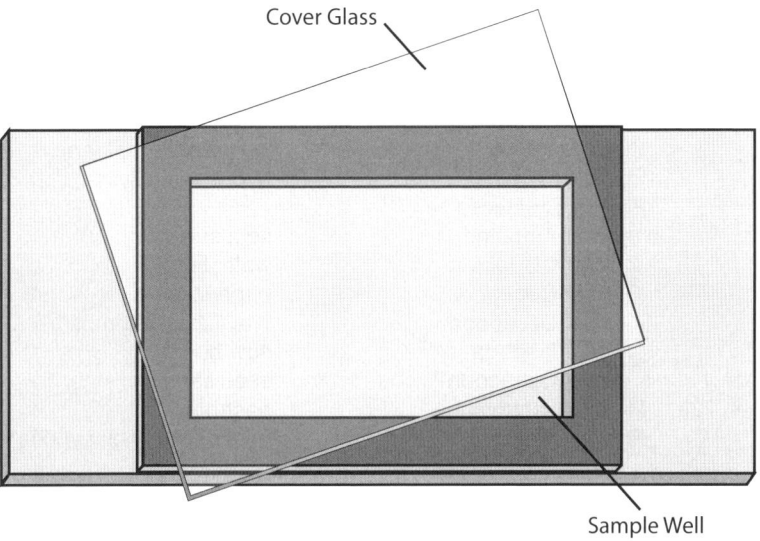

Figure 14.9 Sedgewick-Rafter counting cell.

Zooplankton

A wide variety of aquatic invertebrates exist in aquatic habitats (Table 14.1). Of these, this chapter will include those commonly encountered in plankton communities, such as rotifers, crustaceans, Cladocera, copepods, and ostracods.

Rotifers

Rotifers are minute aquatic animals with one or two rings of cilia at the anterior end of the body (Figure 14.10). These cilia resemble a pair of revolving wheels because the beating of the cilia is synchronized (Smith, 2001). The body is usually cylindrical and somewhat elongated and generally contains regions resembling a head, trunk, and foot. The cilia assist in both feeding and locomotion. Most rotifers observed are females, as the males are small and short lived. The major parts of a rotifer are the antennae, corona (cilia rings), mastax (unique internal grinding jaws), toes terminating the foot, and the lorica (hardened shell-like covering).

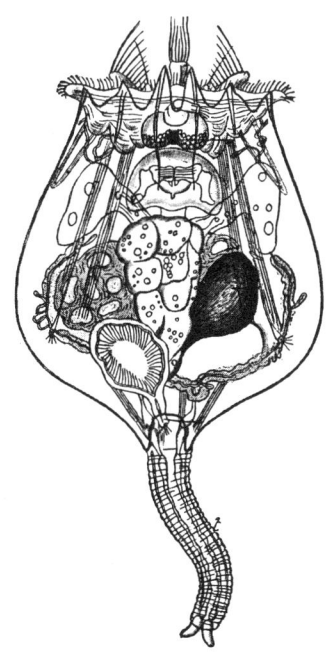

Figure 14.10 Rotifer *Brachionus* (after Hudson and Gosse, 1886; Parker, 1900).

Table 14.1 Freshwater invertebrates.

Phylum, Class, or Order	Common Name
Phylum Annelida	oligochaetes, leeches
Class Arachnida	water mites, spiders
Phylum Cnidaria	hydra and jellyfish
Phylum Crustacea	
Order Amphipoda	scuds
Order Cladocera	water fleas
Order Copepoda	copepods
Order Decapoda	crayfishes, shrimps*
Order Isopoda	sow bugs
Order Ostracoda	seed shrimp
Phylum Gastrotricha	gastrotrichs
Phylum Mollusca*	gastropods, pelecypods*
Order Gastropoda	snails
Order Pelecypoda	clams, mussels
Phylum Nematoda	roundworms
Phylum Nematomorpha	horsehair worms, gordian worms
Phylum Nemertea	proboscis worms
Phylum Platyhelminthes	flatworms
Phylum Porifera	freshwater sponges
Phylum Rotifera	rotifers
Phylum Tardigrada	water bears

* macroscopic

Crustacea

Members of the phylum Crustacea are arthropods, have a head with antennae, and have paired jointed appendages. Common crustaceans include Cladocera, Copepoda, Ostracoda, and Amphipoda (scuds, sideswimmers) (Smith, 2001).

Cladocerans, or water fleas, are minute crustaceans with large antennae and a post-abdominal claw, and a conspicuous large compound eye (Figure 14.11). Examples include *Daphnia*, *Bosmina*, and *Leptodora*. *Daphnia* exhibits changing variations in head forms during the year. It generally starts with a rounded head in the spring and then becomes elongated, and then hooded (helmet) as the water warms (Smith, 2001). Cladocerans generally migrate upward during darkness and downward during light, although there are exceptions. *Bosmina* is similar in appearance to *Daphnia* except it has a trunk. *Leptodora* resembles a flying dragon (Figure 14.11).

The class Copepoda includes a segmented body that is elongated and cylindrical. The body is divided into a head, thorax, and abdomen, which has three to five segments (Smith, 2001). Copepoda have jointed trunk (body) appendages and are distinguished by the number of segments and length of their antennae. Common copepods include *Cyclops* and *Diaptomas* (Figure 14.12). *Cyclops* has a prominent eye spot and the antennae are shorter than the main body. *Diaptomas* has antennae about as long as the body.

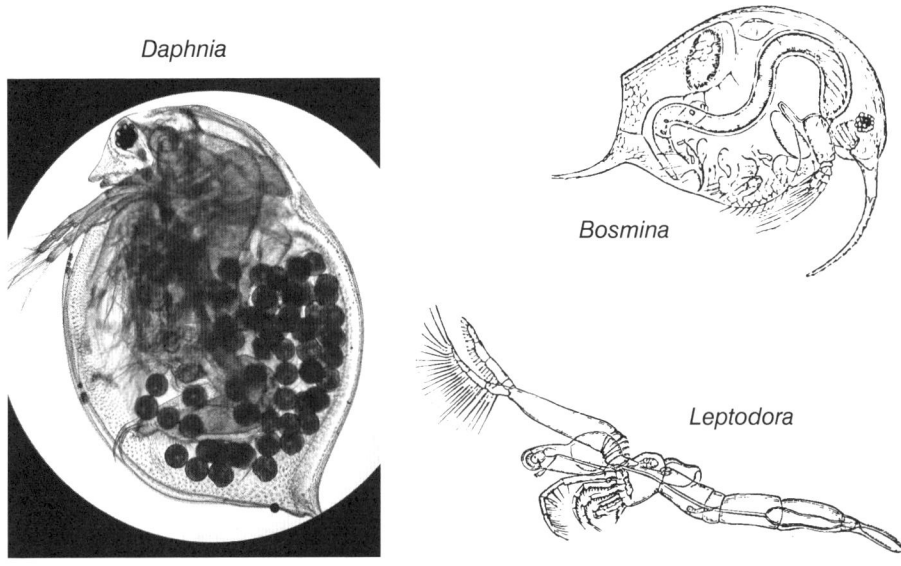

Figure 14.11 Cladocerans (*Daphnia*: USGS photo by Shari Greseth; *Bosmina* and *Leptodora*: after Smith and Weldon, 1909).

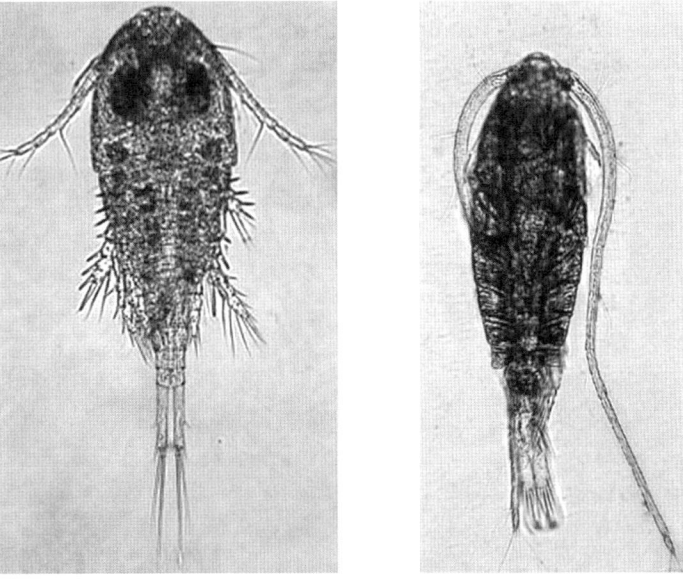

Figure 14.12 Copepoda examples: Cyclops (*Diacyclops thomasi*, left) and Diaptomas (*Leptodiaptomus minutus*, right) (USGS, Great Lakes Science Center).

The Ostracod is a crustacean that has opaque bivalve shells (Figure 14.13) and is often found in small temporary pools of water.

The Amphipoda include scuds and sideswimmers (Figure 14.14); they have a six-segmented abdomen and thoracic legs. They often swim on their sides, especially *Gammarus*.

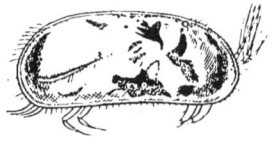

Figure 14.13 Ostracod (after Smith and Weldon, 1909).

Macroinvertebrates

Common aquatic insects include the dragonfly, caddisfly, mayfly, stonefly, and various other insects (Figure 14.15). The macroinvertebrates are large enough to be seen by the unaided eye. There are several that are sensitive to pollution and are thus used as indicators of water conditions. These include caddisflies, mayflies, stoneflies, Hellgrammites, and clams. Macroinvertebrates tolerant to pollution include the midges, leeches, cranefly and horsefly larvae, aquatic worms, and the rat-tailed maggot.

Beck's Biotic Index (Box 14.2) is one tool to assess the water quality or habitat condition of a water body (Beck, 1954; Terrell and Perfetti, 1996). This approach was initially developed for use in Florida. The index is calculated from:

$$BI = 2n_I + n_{II} \qquad [14.1]$$

where BI = Beck's Biotic Index
n_I = the number of species in Class I
n_{II} = the number of species in Class II

To use this index, a sample of the macroinvertebrates would be obtained with a kick net (aquatic net). Collected organisms would be identified to genera,

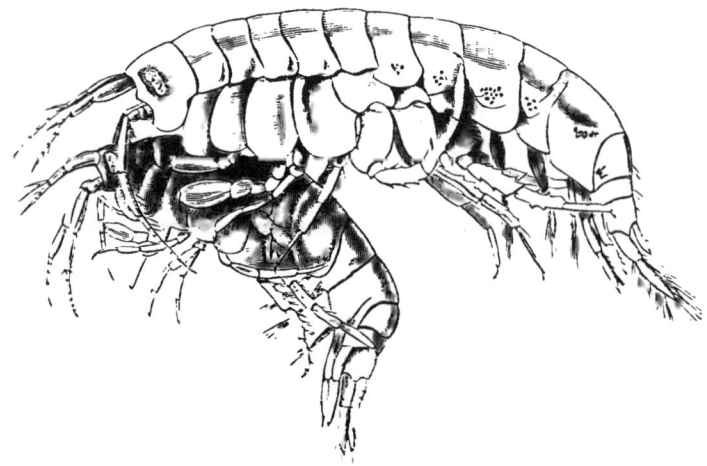

Figure 14.14 *Gammarus* (scud or sideswimmer) (after Smith and Weldon, 1909).

CHAPTER 14   Biological Characteristics of Water   155

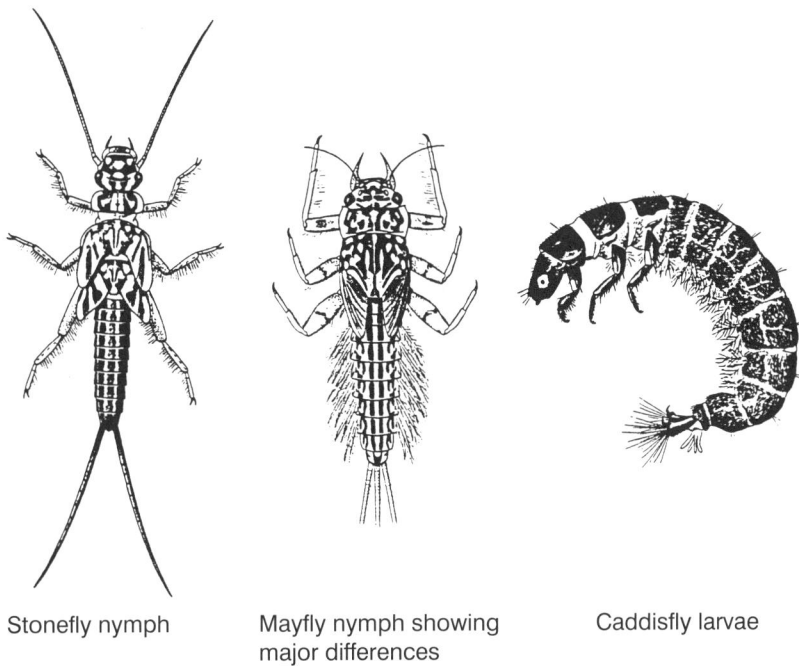

Stonefly nymph   Mayfly nymph showing   Caddisfly larvae
                   major differences

Figure 14.15   Macroinvertebrates (Courtesy of S. Jensen, Missouri State University).

Class I, II, or III determined using Table 14.2, and the number of species in each Class counted. Following the calculation of the BI, Table 14.3 would be used to determine the condition of the stream based on the index.

BOX 14.2

Beck's Biotic Index

- **Class I Organisms** (Sensitive or Intolerant)
   These are organisms that tolerate no appreciable organic pollution and are the more sensitive forms. Their presence indicates the water is clean.

- **Class II Organisms** (Facultative)
   Organisms that tolerate a moderate amount of pollution, but not anaerobic conditions.

- **Class III Organisms** (Tolerant)
   Organisms are those that can be found in heavily polluted areas, as well as clean waters, moderately polluted waters, or grossly polluted waters.

- **Class IV Organisms**
   These are air-breathing forms.

- **Class V Organisms**
   Organisms in the class are uncertain, perhaps due to insufficient numbers or knowledge about their habitat needs.

Table 14.2 Beck's Biotic Index of benthic macroinvertebrates.

Class I–Sensitive	Class II–Facultative	Class III–Tolerant
Ephemeroptera (Mayflies)	Aselidae (Isopods, sowbugs)	Chironomidae (Midges)
Plecoptera (Stoneflies)	Odonata (Damselflies, dragonflies)	Hirundinea (Leeches)
Tricoptera (Caddisflies)	Planariidae (Flatworms)	Oligochaeta (Worms)
Helligrammites	Simulidae (Blackflies)	Psychodidae (Moth flies)
Coleoptera (Beetles)	Tabanidae (Horseflies)	
	Tipulidae (Crane flies)	

Table 14.3 Beck's Biotic Index and stream condition.

Index	Condition
0	Stream grossly polluted
1–5	Stream moderately polluted
6–9	Stream clean, but with a monotonous habitat
10+	Stream clean

■ Macrophytes

Macrophytes are herbaceous aquatic plants that are large enough to be visible to the eye. The major growth forms are floating, submerged, and emergent. Floating plants may be free-floating or rooted. Common free-floating plants include duckweed (*Lemna spp.*) and water-meal (*Wolffia*) (Figure 14.16). Duckweed is a small floating plant that can completely cover some ponds. It is identified by the fronds (modified stem) being veined and having one root per frond (Crow and Hellquist, 2000). Water-meal has no roots and is small and globular.

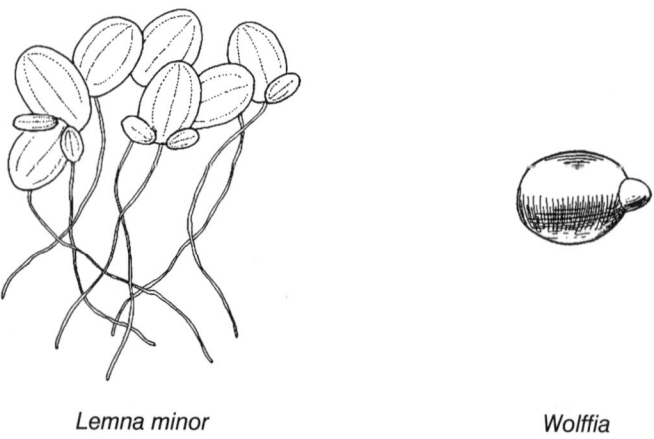

Lemna minor   *Wolffia*

Figure 14.16 Free-floating plants: *Lemna minor* (duckweed) with one root per frond, and *Wolffia* (watermeal) with no roots (USDA/NRCS Plants Database, 2016).

CHAPTER 14   Biological Characteristics of Water   157

Floating-leaved plants that are rooted in the substrate include the waterlilies (*Nymphaea* and *Nuphar*), water-shield (*Brasenia*), and some of the pondweeds (*Potamogeton spp.*) (Figure 14.17). White waterlily (*Nymphaea*) has flowers that range in color from white to pink. The leaves have a deep cleft, often with pointed tips, with veins that radiate from the center. The petiole is located somewhat in the center of the leaf. Yellow waterlily, or spatterdock (*Nuphar*), has yellow flowers. The leaves are kidney shaped, deeply lobed with rounded lobes. Veins radiate from a central midrib. The petiole is located at the end of the

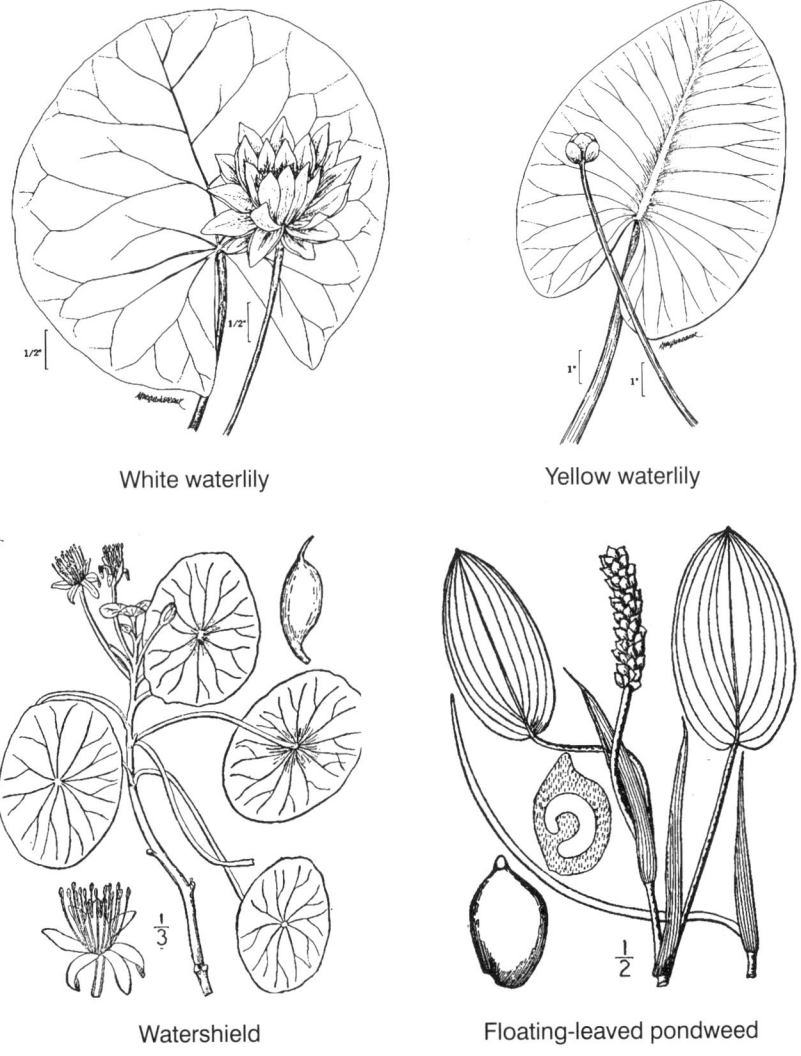

Figure 14.17 Floating-leaved plants (USDA/NRCS Plants Database, 2016).

leaf notch, generally not in the center of the oblong leaf. Water-shield (*Brasenia*) is alternate leafed with several floating leaves for the same plant. The leaves are not lobed, and the petiole is centered on the leaf.

The pondweeds are a large group of aquatic plants with many different forms, although all are alternate leaved and have a distinctive midvein (Crow and Hellquist, 2000). Floating-leaved pondweed (*P. natans* L.) has oblong floating leaves with many veins, with the petiole located at the end of the leaf (USDA/NRCS, 2016). Often the pondweeds have two kinds of leaves, with submerged leaves being thin. The floating leaf for *P. natans* is often heart-shaped at the base.

The submerged plants include waterweeds (*Elodea*), pondweeds, milfoil, and coontail (Figure 14.18). Waterweed is a submerged, free-floating aquatic plant that has the appearance of entire (smooth margin) leaves in whorls of three (Fassett, 1975). Coontail (*Ceratophyllum*) is a submerged aquatic plant but is free floating with no roots. It gets its name from its resemblance to a raccoon's

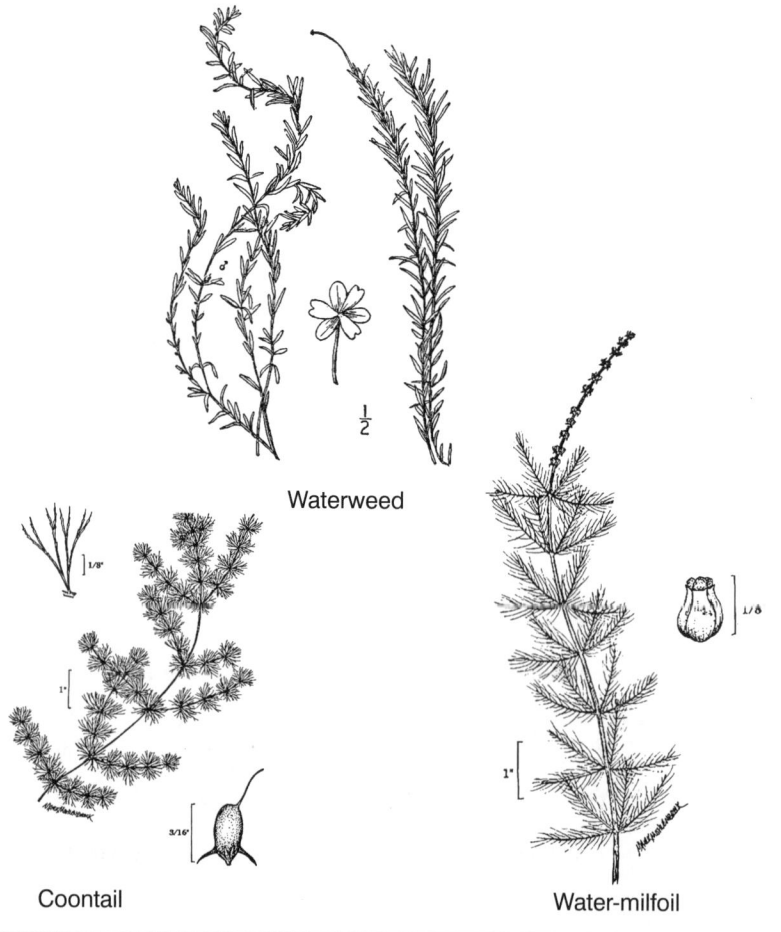

Figure 14.18 Submerged plants (USDA/NRCS Plants Database, 2016).

tail when under water. The leaves are also whorled along the forked stem. The leaf blades have noticeable teeth along one margin. Water-milfoil (*Myriophyllum*) is largely a submerged aquatic plant with usually whorled leaves (can be alternate) that are finely divided into leaflets on opposite sides of the leaf. For some species, the leaflet resembles a parrot's feather (Figure 14.18).

Emergent macrophytes include arrowhead, cattail, phragmites, and wild rice (Figure 14.19). Arrowhead, or duck-potato (*Sagittaria*), can have several different types of leaves depending on the species, but an arrow-shaped leaf is commonly associated with this plant. Cattail (*Typha*) has the characteristic cylindrical spike containing the flowers, with the male portion above and the female portion below, and long, narrow leaves that are twisted (Fassett, 1975). Phragmites is a grass and therefore hollow with nodes, and the leaves are two-ranked. Wild rice is a grass that grows along the margins of lakes and is harvested commercially.

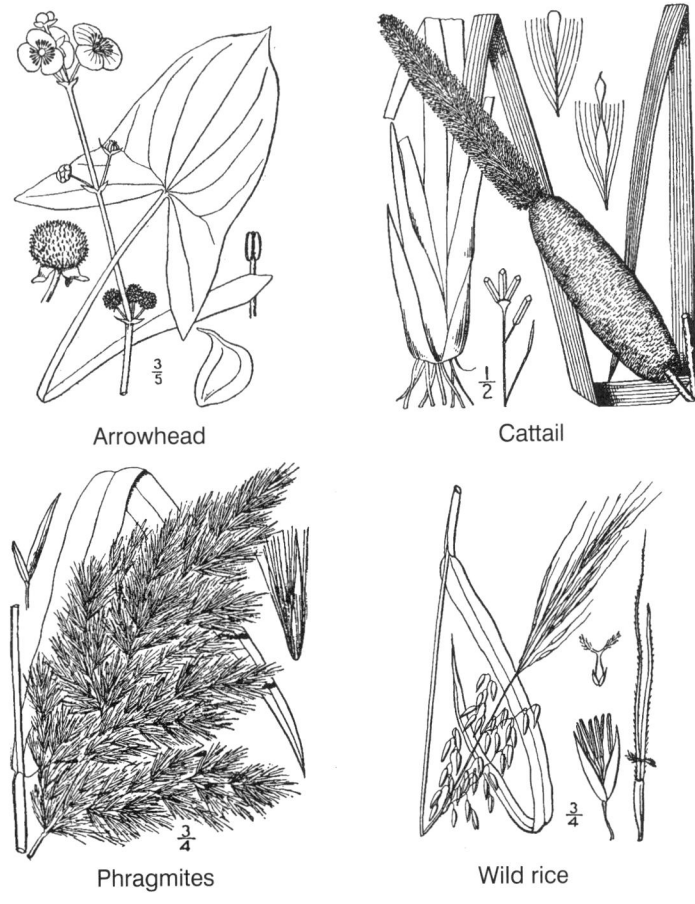

Figure 14.19 Emergent macrophytes (USDA/NRCS Plants Database, 2016).

Pathogens in Water

Waterborne diseases are estimated to cause 842,000 diarrheal deaths per year (WHO, 2016). In the United States, there are an estimated 4 to 32 million cases of acute gastrointestinal illness each year associated with public drinking water systems (Colford et al., 2006). Several disease- and infection-causing pathogens may be found in water. These may be grouped as bacteria, protozoa, and viruses. The bacteria include Acinetobacter, Campylobacter, Escherichia coli, Salmonella, and Shigella. Additionally, Cyanobacteria (blue-green algae) may produce toxins that are harmful to animals. Some of the protozoans include Cryptosporidium, Giardia, and several amoeba. Viruses include Hepatitis A, Norovirus, and Rotavirus. Many of these pathogens affect children and the elderly more severely than they do the rest of the population. Most are more prevalent in developing countries than developed countries. Detection methods vary and many pathogens are found in water in low concentrations. Therefore, some means of concentrating the water is used, such as filtration or centrifugation. Most pathogens are not routinely sampled in either drinking or recreational waters, except for E. coli. Table 14.4 summarizes the more common waterborne bacteria, protozoans, and viruses that affect humans. This table was constructed from information found in Percival et al. (2014). Most pathogens are found in contaminated water and are transmitted by drinking, although some are acquired by contact in recreational waters. Many can be further spread by person-to-person contact. Many of the pathogens become apparent by causing an outbreak within a certain area. All but E. coli are not routinely sampled, and detection requires labs that can perform culturing and microscopy. Some can only be truly identified by microbiological DNA techniques, which are not generally available, especially in developing countries. Escherichia coli is used as the indicator of contamination for most of these pathogens, even though most strains of E. coli are not pathogenic. The current procedure is that if E. coli is present, then fecal contamination is assumed.

Bacteria

Bacteria in water are used as an indicator of contamination with human or animal excreta. Normally the test is for an indicator organism rather than the actual pathogen that may be harmful to humans. Examples of indicators include the coliform group and Escherichia coli. There are several methods for enumerating (counting) bacteria. One method uses membrane filtration. The basics of this test is to filter a sample of water, place the filter on an agar, incubate for 24 hr at 44.5°C, and count the red or magenta colonies on the filter (U.S. EPA, 2002). Dilution of the sample may be required if the number of colonies are too many for an adequate count. Another common method is the multiple tube fermentation test. Results from this test are expressed as most probable number (MPN), which is an estimate of bacterial density. Using five or ten tubes for each dilution in a test, the tubes with sample and broth are incubated for 24 hr at 35°C (Clesceri et al., 1998). Each tube contains an inverted smaller tube. The presence of a bubble in the inverted tube at the end of the test indicates a positive presumptive test. MPN/100 mL is calculated from the number of tubes showing a positive reaction at the highest dilution. Additional techniques are through the use of enzyme substrates, bioluminescence, radiometric detection, and PCR (polymerase chain reaction) (U.S. EPA, 2012b). Bacteria are commonly tested for the presence of fecal streptococcus, fecal coliform, heterotrophic plate count (total number of viable bacteria), Staphylococcus, Pseudomonas, and Escherichia coli (E. coli). The coliform group are organisms that are capable of producing gas from lactose in a culture medium at 44.5°C.

There are several water quality standards for bacteria depending on the use and type of water. The criterion for bathing in fresh, recreational waters is 126 colony-forming units (CFU) per 100 mL for E. coli or 33 CFU per 100 mL for Enterococci (U.S. EPA, 2012a). For marine waters, the criteria is a mean of 35 CFU per 100 mL Enterococci for five samples in 30 days.

Protozoans

Protozoans are not routinely sampled in waters but the EPA regulates surface water supply systems to remove and treat for Cryptosporidium and Giardia.

Viruses

Viruses are dilute in most water samples, and the sample must be concentrated in order to detect them. Primary methods of concentration include filtration/adsorption and centrifugation. Detection is accomplished by infection of a cell culture or PCR techniques. To identify the type of virus, isolation is required. The EPA requires treatment of public drinking waters to reduce viruses.

■ Bioassay

Bioassays are commonly used in toxicological studies. A **bioassay** is a test using organisms to detect the presence or effect of substances or conditions (Weber et al., 1973). These tests are conducted either in the laboratory or *in situ* using containers. The goal of the test is often to determine the concentration of a substance lethal to 50 percent of the organisms during a short period of time. Two commonly used bioassays use *Daphnia* or the fathead minnow (*Pimephales promelas*), although a wide variety of test organisms have been used. Acute tests are short-term and are conducted over two to four days. Chronic tests are long term and are conducted for at least one-tenth of the life span of the test organism (Clesceri et al., 1998).

■ Problem

14.1 Develop a dichotomous key for the following floating-leaved plants: white waterlily, yellow waterlily, watershield, and floating-leaved pondweed.

Table 14.4 Summary of waterborne pathogens.

Bacteria	Source	Transmission	Infections/diseases	Detection Method	Risk
Acinetobacter	Ubiquitous: soils, water, animal hosts, hospitals	Person-to-person	Urinary tract, eye, skin, wounds, meningitis, brain & lung abscess	Culture media	50–100/100,000 capita/yr
Campylobacter	Contaminated drinking water and sewage, animals	Fecal-oral	Acute diarrhea	Filter & culture media	50–100/100,000 capita/yr
Escherichia coli*†	Contaminated drinking water and recreational waters	Fecal-oral & contact in recreational water	None to diarrhea or bloody diarrhea to meningitis to death	Many methods: filtration, multiple tube, culturing, PCR	
Salmonella*	Contaminated drinking water, more commonly food	Fecal-oral	Typhoid-like, diarrhea, fever, abdominal pain to organ failure and death	Concentration and culture media or PCR	1.4 M cases/yr in U.S.
Shigella	Contaminated drinking water and contact recreational water	Fecal-oral	Dysentery – watery or bloody diarrhea	Culture media or PCR	

Table 14.4 Summary of waterborne pathogens. (cont.)

Protozoa	Source	Transmission	Infections/diseases	Detection Method	Risk
Cryptosporidium	Farmland manure, drinking & recreational waters	Fecal-oral	Watery diarrhea, nausea, vomiting	Concentration and microscopy	185 outbreaks since 1985
Entamoeba*	Contaminated drinking water, especially untreated	Oral and person-to-person	Dysentery and diarrhea	Microscopy + cultivation, PCR	100,000 deaths/yr
Giardia*†	Contaminated drinking water	Fecal-oral cyst ingestion	Diarrhea, nausea, vomiting, weight loss	Demonstrate cysts in stool samples, PCR, water concentration then stain & fluorescence microscopy	280 M/yr

Virus	Source	Transmission	Infections/diseases	Detection Method	Risk
Hepatitis A*	Water contaminated from sewage	Fecal-oral	Malaise, fever, nausea, vomiting, diarrhea, jaundice	PCR	
Norovirus	Contaminated water & food	Fecal-oral	Nausea, vomiting, diarrhea	PCR	20 M/yr in U.S.
Rotavirus	Contaminated water and wastewater		Diarrhea, can be fatal in children	PCR	110 M/yr

Source: Derived from data in Percival et al., 2014.
PCR = polymerase chain reaction; DNA molecular amplifying process
* higher in developing countries
† higher in children

References

Beck, W. M., Jr. 1954. Studies in stream pollution biology I: A simplified ecological classification of organisms. *Quart. J. of the Florida Academy of Sci.* 17(4): 211–227.

Clesceri, L. S., A. E. Greenberg, and A. D. Eaton. 1998. *Standard methods for the examination of water and wastewater.* 20th ed. American Public Health Association, American Water Works Association, Water Environment Association. http://www.mwa.co.th/download/file_upload/SMWW_1000-3000.pdf

Cole, G. A., and P. E. Weihe. 2016. *Textbook of limnology.* 5th ed. Long Grove: Waveland Press.

Colford, J. M., S. Roy, M. J. Beach, A. Hightower, S. E. Shaw, and T. J. Wade. 2006. A review of household drinking water intervention trials and an approach to the estimation of endemic waterborne gastroenteritis in the United States. *Jour. of Water and Health* 4, Suppl. 2: 71–88.

Crow, G. E., and C. B. Hellquist. 2000. *Aquatic and wetland plants of northeastern North America. Vol. 2. Angiosperms: Monocotyledons.* Madison: University of Wisconsin Press.

Fassett, N. C. 1975. *A manual of aquatic plants.* Madison: University of Wisconsin Press.

Hudson, C. T., and P. H. Gosse. 1886. *The rotifera.* London: Longmans.

Jensen, S. L. Introduction to aquatic insects. Lab 15 in J. E. Havel, *Laboratory exercises for freshwater ecology*, pp. 103–117. Long Grove, IL: Waveland Press.

Needham, J. G., and P. R. Needham. 1962. *A guide to the study of freshwater biology.* Oakland, CA: Holden-Day.

O'Sullivan, P. E., and C. S. Reynolds (eds). 2004. *The lakes handbook: Limnology and limnetic ecology.* Vol 1. Oxford, UK: Blackwell Science.

Palmer, C. M. 1962. *Algae in water supplies. An illustrated manual on the identification, significance, and control of algae in water supplies.* Public Health Service Publication No. 657. Washington, DC: U.S. Department of Health, Education, and Welfare, Public Health Service, Division of Water Supply and Pollution Control.

Parker, T. J. 1900. *A manual of zoology.* New York: Macmillan.

Percival, S. L., M. V. Yates, D. W. Williams, R. M. Chalmers, and N. F. Gray. 2014. *Microbiology of waterborne diseases.* 2nd ed. London: Elsevier.

Prescott, G. W. 1978. *How to know the freshwater algae.* 3rd ed. Dubuque, IA: Wm. C. Brown.

Smith, D. G. 2001. *Pennak's freshwater invertebrates of the United States.* 4th ed. New York: John Wiley and Sons.

Smith, G., and W. J. F. Weldon. 1909. Crustacea. *The Cambridge natural history*, vol. 4: 1–217. London: Macmillan.

Terrell, C. R., and P. B. Perfetti. 1996. *Water quality indicators guide: Surface waters.* 2nd ed. Washington, DC: Terrene Institute.

USDA/NRCS. 2016. *The PLANTS Database.* National Plant Data Team, Greensboro, NC 27401-4901 USA. http://plants.usda.gov

U.S. Environmental Protection Agency (EPA). 2002. *Method 1603: Escherichia coli (E. coli) in water by membrane filtration using modified membrane-thermotolerant Escherichia coli Agar (modified mTEC).* U.S. EPA 821-R-02-023. Washington, DC: Office of Water. http://nepis.epa.gov/Exe/ZyPDF.cgi/P1008MZV.PDF?Dockey=P1008MZV.PDF

U.S. Environmental Protection Agency (EPA). 2012a. *2012 recreational water quality criteria.* EPA-820-F-12-061. Washington, DC: Office of Water.

U.S. Environmental Protection Agency (EPA). 2012b. *Method 1611:* Enterococci *in water by TaqMan® quantitative polymerase chain reaction (qPCR) assay*. U.S. EPA-821-R-12-008. Washington, DC: Office of Water.
https://www.epa.gov/sites/production/files/2015-08/documents/method_1611_2012.pdf

Weber, C. I. (ed.). 1973. *Biological field and laboratory methods for measuring the quality of surface waters and effluents*. U.S. EPA-670/4-73-001. Cincinnati, OH: Office of Research and Development.
http://nepis.epa.gov/Exe/ZyPDF.cgi/2000JIC8.PDF?Dockey=2000JIC8.PDF

Wehr, J. D., and R. G. Sheath (eds.). 2003. *Freshwater algae of North America*. San Diego, CA: Academic Press.

World Health Organization (WHO). 2016. *Quantitative microbial risk assessment: Application for water safety management*. Geneva, Switzerland.

15
River Water Quality

■ Introduction

Rivers have long been an important resource to human culture. Their use in transportation, food supply, irrigation, and readily available drinking water has shaped the patterns of human cultures from their beginnings. Thus, even now, much development is focused along rivers. Rivers have been the focus of water quality studies because they also typically have been used to dispose of wastewaters from a wide variety of sources. Excess disposal of wastewaters have led to undesirable effects in river ecosystems. Rivers are also used for water supply for municipalities, industry, and agriculture, as well as recreation, fishing, and hydropower production. Thus there are many conflicting uses of rivers. This chapter summarizes the water quality aspects of rivers. The important physical, chemical, and biological characteristics and concepts specific to rivers will be included.

■ Physical Processes in Rivers

The physical characteristics of streams influence river water quality (Kittrell, 1969). Important physical characteristics include the depth and velocity of flow; streambed types; slope and roughness; turbulence; and the physical aspects of the water itself, such as temperature and turbidity (see Chapter 12). These characteristics are highly interrelated; for example, slope influences velocity. Together such physical aspects govern important water quality functions, such as mixing, reaeration, and sedimentation. It is also important to understand that watershed and climate processes (Chapter 10) have profound influences on each of these characteristics. Geology, topography, soils, and vegetative cover all influence streamflow as land processes. Climate patterns, such as precipitation seasonality and snowmelt, equally influence the flow regime in rivers (Poff et al., 1997). Flooding and drought have great consequences on water quality.

Mixing

The mixing that occurs when a substance is added to a stream is largely a physical process (Figure 15.1). To determine the concentration that results from the addition of an inflow to a stream, Eqn. 15.1 may be used. This equation assumes that instantaneous mixing occurs at the point of discharge.

$$C_0 = \frac{Q_r C_r + q_w C_w}{Q_r + q_w} \qquad [15.1]$$

where C_0 = initial concentration at point of discharge, g/m³
Q_r = river discharge, m³/s
C_r = river concentration before mixing, g/m³
q_w = wastewater discharge, m³/s
C_w = concentration in wastewater, g/m³

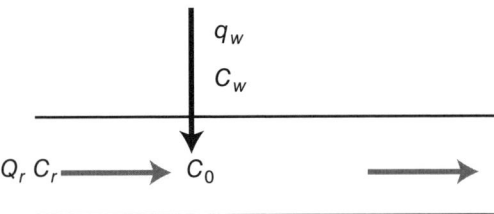

Figure 15.1 Stream mixing diagram.

Longitudinal Dispersion Coefficient

Another physical process that operates in a stream is related to dispersion (spreading out) as material flows downstream. The longitudinal dispersion coefficient may be determined from the information derived from a dye test. To conduct the test, a dye such as Rhodamine WT is injected into the stream. This dye is fluorescent at low concentrations (10 µg/L), and therefore a flourometer (field version) can be used (Thomann and Mueller, 1987).

Kilpatrick and Wilson (1989) describe planning a dye study:

A. The volume of dye needed can be determined from:

$$V = 3.4 \times 10^{-4} \left(\frac{Q_m x}{U}\right)^{0.93} [C_p] \qquad [15.2]$$

where V = volume of Rhodamine WT (20%) (liters) needed to produce a peak concentration (C_p) in µg/L at distance downstream (x) in miles from injection point
Q_m = maximum discharge in cfs
U = average velocity (fps)

B. The time to peak is determined from:

$$t_p = 1.47 \frac{x}{U} \quad [15.3]$$

where t_p is time to peak (hr).

Assumptions used for a field dye study include:

1. The reaction coefficients $K_1 = K_2 = 0$ since the dye is a conservative substance.
2. Loading $W = 0$ because there is only the dye and no other loading.
3. The volume (V) is constant.
4. The discharge (Q) is constant.
5. The cross-sectional area (A) is constant.
6. There is only one longitudinal dispersion coefficient (D_L) and it is constant.

A simplified mass balance equation is applicable for this calculation (Thomann and Mueller, 1987):

$$C = \frac{M}{A(4\pi D_L t)^{1/2}} \exp\left[-\frac{(S-Ut)^2}{4 D_L t}\right] \quad [15.4]$$

where M = mass of dye added
 S = downstream distance
 D_L = longitudinal dispersion coefficient
 t = time

There are several approaches to determine the D_L:

1. A single monitoring point downstream of the input can be used.
2. The single point downstream can be repeated and the average determined.
3. Using the two-point method, two distributions of the dye can be examined at two locations downstream.
4. The peak concentration at three or more points can be used.

For the two-distributions method, D_L is determined from:

$$D_L = \frac{U^2(\sigma_2^2 - \sigma_1^2)}{2(\bar{t}_2 - \bar{t}_1)} \quad [15.5]$$

where U = average velocity between stations (mi/hr), and

$$\sigma_t^2 = \frac{\Sigma(t - \bar{t}_i)C_i}{\Sigma C_i} \quad [15.6]$$

where σ = variance in the concentration at station i
 $\bar{t}$ = centroid of the distribution determined for each station from:

$$\bar{t}_i = \frac{\Sigma tC}{\Sigma C} \quad [15.7]$$

To calculate the dispersion coefficient from three sites, Eqn. 15.4 becomes:

$$C_p = \frac{M}{2A\sqrt{\pi D_L t_p}} = \text{slope} \times \frac{1}{\sqrt{t_p}} \qquad [15.8]$$

and

$$\text{Slope} = \frac{M}{2A\sqrt{\pi D_L}} \qquad [15.9]$$

where C_p = the peak concentration
 M = mass of dye added
 t_p = time to peak
 $A = Q/U$

The slope can be determined from a graph of peak dye concentration and the time to peak (Figure 15.2).

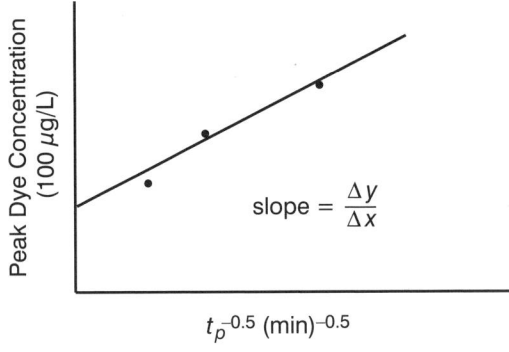

Figure 15.2 Graph to determine the slope term for calculating the longitudinal dispersion coefficient in a stream.

Other River Processes

Several processes are unique to rivers and are combinations of physical, chemical, and biological actions. Rivers and streams constantly move particles and chemicals downstream. Nutrient cycling occurs within and along streams. For example, **nutrient spiraling** is a term used to describe the cycling of nutrients from the water into the benthic environment, where it is temporarily retained, and then mineralized back into the water column (Ensign and Doyle, 2006). Both biochemical reactions and stream velocity/residence time influence nutrient uptake. Headwater streams have been found to be greater in nutrient retention than larger rivers because a greater proportion of water interacts with benthic substrates (Alexander et al., 2000). Transient storage can occur as hyporheic flow, in macrophytes, and in side pools. However, the rate of spiraling along a stream appears to vary with the constituent and form of the nutrient involved (Ensign and Doyle, 2006).

The **river continuum concept** is the idea that rivers display biological community changes along a longitudinal continuum downstream in the form of a gradient (Vannote et al., 1980). These changes are regulated largely by geomorphic processes. The concept is that biological communities become established in concert with the dynamic physical conditions of the river. These physical characteristics include changing width, depth, velocity, and shading as well as temperature differences. For example, headwater streams are often influenced mostly by riparian vegetation that provides allochthonous (external) inputs. Downstream, the riparian vegetation has much less influence, and autochthonous (internal) processes of primary production occur. Associated with this gradient is the type of macroinvertebrates found. Upstream, shredders would be dominant, whereas downstream there would be more collectors.

Another major concept is that of a graded stream. A **graded stream** means that its slope is adjusted to provide the velocity needed to transport the sediment load input (Mackin, 1948). Thus changes to the slope of a stream will result in reactions that migrate both upstream and downstream. This is a process that occurs over a period of years. It also is a function of available discharge and the dominant channel characteristics. Some examples of changes include an increase in load, which results in an increase in slope below an influx. A decrease in load can result in downcutting and a lowering of slope downstream. A decrease in discharge should increase slope, whereas the opposite occurs with an increase in discharge. A barrier in the stream, such as that caused by a dam or sometimes a culvert, decreases the slope upstream and results in deposition.

Biological Characteristics of Rivers

Water Quality Zones

When wastewater with a high BOD is discharged into a river, several zones of self-purification can be identified (Figure 15.3) (Bartsch, 1948):

1. Zone of cleaner water

2. Zone of degradation (below input)

3. Zone of active decomposition

4. Zone of recovery

5. Zone of cleaner water

A zone of cleaner water would exist upstream of the discharge point. The zone of degradation is typically short, has high turbidity, and a gray color. Sunlight can be shut out. Oxygen is reduced to 40% saturation at the lower end, or about 3.5 mg/L during summer. CO_2 increases as does chloride. Most N is present as organic N. Green and blue-green algae occur, and ciliate protozoa abound.

172 ◆ PART II Water Quality

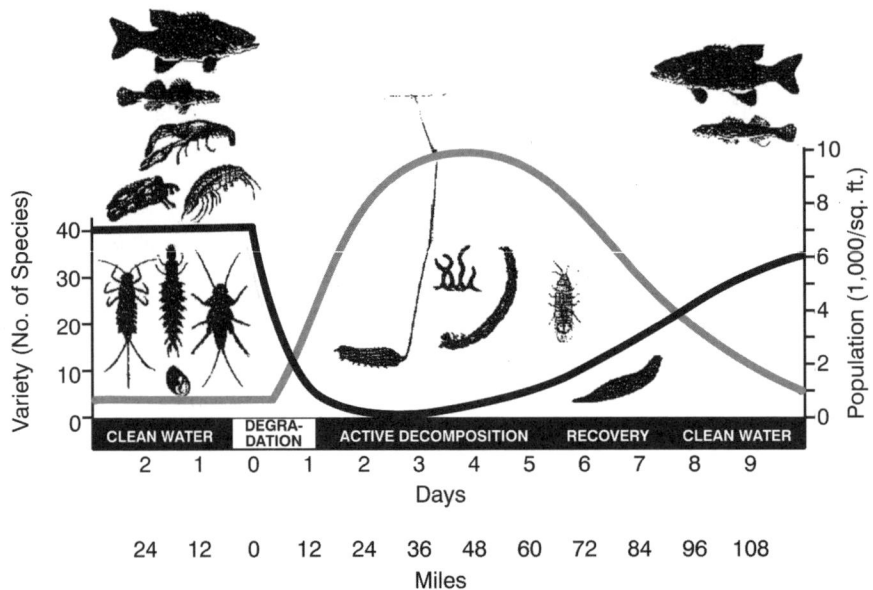

Figure 15.3 Biota representative of the water quality zones in a river receiving wastewater with a high BOD (Bartsch, 1948).

The zone of active decomposition is present when pollution is severe but absent when pollution is light. The water is gray to black, odors are offensive, and gas bubbles appear. The sediment is sticky and offensive. The upper and lower ends of this zone have about 40% oxygen saturation; saturation is lower in between. H_2S, CO_2, CH_4, and NH_3 evolve. Bacteria flourish and green plants are absent. Rat-tail maggots thrive and fish are absent.

The zone of recovery is the opposite of the zone of degradation. This zone is relatively long with gradually clearing water. Oxygen is greater than 40% saturation and may extend to 100% saturated. Bacteria decrease in numbers and rotifers and crustaceans are present. Blue-green and green algae appear. Diatoms are numerous at the lower end and larger aquatic plants appear. Mussels, snails, and a few fish appear.

The zone of cleaner water is characterized by the presence of large and small green plants, microscopic animals, insect larvae, mussels, crayfish, and game fish. Macroinvertebrates and algae have long been used as indicators of the water quality of rivers (Chapter 14).

■ Chemical Characteristics of Rivers

Reaction Kinetics

Various chemicals in rivers (also lakes and ground water) undergo reactions and form new products. An example of such a reaction would be a compound disassociating into two products. Another example would be the nitrogen cycle (Chapter 13). Understanding the rates of these reactions is important to understanding the mechanisms that control the fate of pollutants in rivers. The rate of product formation is dependent on the number of substances involved in the reaction. These reactions are termed zero-order, first-order, second-order, and higher-order or complex reactions (James, 1993; Tchobanoglous and Schroeder, 1987). Collectively these reactions are termed *kinetics*, which is derived from the Greek *kenetikos*, meaning to move. Only zero- and first-order reactions are discussed here because they are the most commonly applied. This discussion also assumes that the river system or segment is well-mixed, a concept discussed later in this chapter.

Zero-Order Reactions

For zero-order reactions, the rate of the reaction of C_i is a constant and is independent of the concentration following the equation:

$$\frac{-d[C]}{dt} = k_0 \qquad [15.10]$$

where k_0 = a constant (1/time) and is obtained as the slope of C versus t
C_0 = the initial concentration (C) (Figure 15.4).

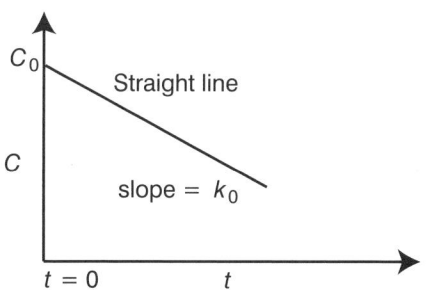

Figure 15.4 Zero-order reaction rate.

The first-order differential equation is solved by integration:

$$C = k_0 t + \text{constant} \qquad [15.11]$$

This equation resembles the equation of a straight line:

$$y = mx + b \qquad [15.12]$$

A decrease in concentration is indicated by a minus sign. A positive sign would indicate an increase in concentration.

First-Order Reactions

For a first-order reaction, the rate of the reaction of C_i is proportional to C_i (Figure 15.5) following the equation:

$$\frac{-d[C]}{dt} = k_1[C] \qquad [15.13]$$

where k_1 = a new constant and is obtained from the plot of log $[C] / [C_0]$ as a function of time

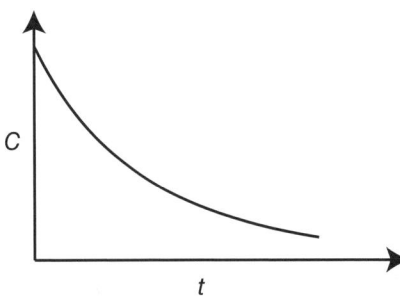

Figure 15.5 First-order reaction rate.

Equation 15.13 is solved by integration, as shown here in several steps:

$$\ln [C] = -k_1 t + \text{constant} \qquad [15.14]$$

and

$$\log [C] = 0.434\, k_1 + \text{constant} \,(= \log [C_0]) \qquad [15.15]$$

The constant is the y-intercept or $\log[C_0]$ as shown in Figure 15.6, so that:

$$\log \frac{[C]}{[C_0]} = -k_1 t \qquad [15.16]$$

$$[C] = [C_0] 10^{-k_1 t} \qquad [15.17]$$

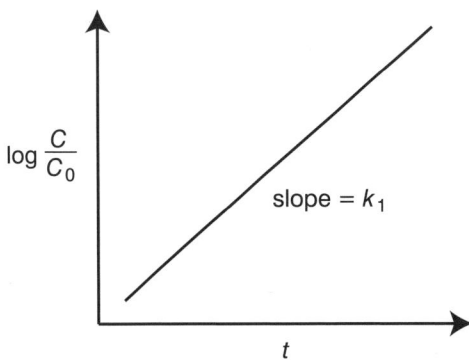

Figure 15.6 First-order reaction semi-log of the ratio of concentration to initial concentration as a function of time.

CHAPTER 15   River Water Quality   175

The following example will illustrate the use of logs for first-order reaction constant calculations:

EXAMPLE 15.1   Determining k and Reaction Order

Given the following data, determine the reaction rate constant.

Time (s)	Concentration (mmol/L)	$Log_{10}(C_i / C_0)$
0	2.35 (C_0)	0
5	1.75	−0.128
10	1.20	−0.292
15	0.90	−0.417
20	0.70	−0.526

The log_{10} of the ratio (C_i / C_0) is plotted against time in the figure below. The slope of the linear regression is the reaction rate constant k_1, in this case -0.027 s^{-1}.

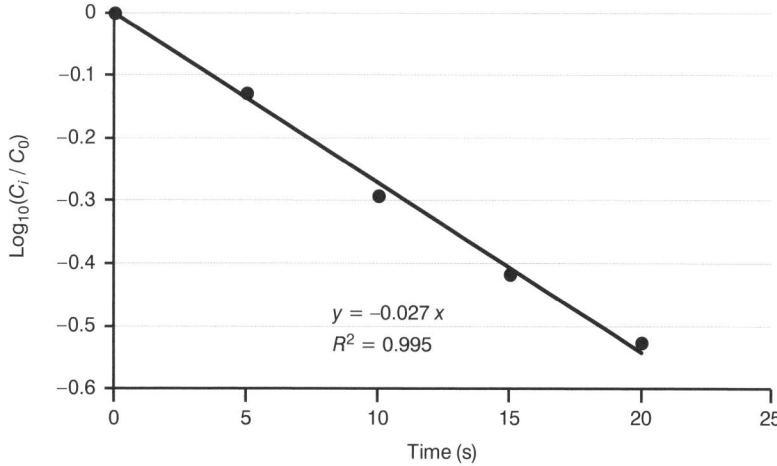

Reactors

Another important concept in river systems is the assumption of the type of mixing in a river segment and its consequences in terms of pollutant transport. The relationship between influent to and effluent from a river segment is a function of the reactor type and the kinetics as described previously. The term *reactor* is used to describe the river segment. There are three reactor types (James, 1993; Tchobanoglous and Schroeder, 1987):

1. Plug flow
2. Well or completely mixed
3. Intermediate mixed flow

Plug Flow Reactor. A plug flow reactor assumes that the influent flows through the segment without any mixing (Figure 15.7). This reactor type is appropriate for rivers or pipes when they are long and have a small cross-section in relation to their length. Plug flow assumes pure **advection**, which is transport due to the flow of water (James, 1993). The concentration of a substance will be transported downstream as a material front. If a dye were being used, the color of the river would change as the dye passed by.

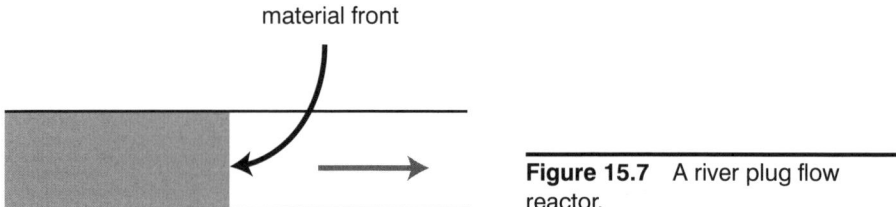

Figure 15.7 A river plug flow reactor.

Completely Mixed Reactor. In a completely mixed reactor, also termed *well-mixed reactor*, increments of influent are instantaneously dispersed throughout the system when the influent enters (Figure 15.8). The effluent properties are identical to the contents of the system. This reactor type is appropriate for river run lakes that are not stratified.

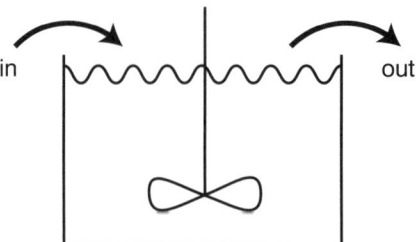

Figure 15.8 A completely mixed reactor.

Intermediate Mixed Flow. Intermediate mixed flow assumes that there are both advection and some mixing occurring in the system. This reactor represents a combination of the previous two types and is more representative of most natural systems.

Reactor Response to Different Inputs

Each reactor type will respond differently to different types of inputs. The change in the concentration of a substance entering a reactor might occur in two different ways:

1. Impulse input
2. Step input

An impulse input might be represented by a spill of a pollutant, such as that generated by a wastewater treatment plant release, or an accidental spill next to a river. The impulse will begin and then end.

A step input might be generated by a constant change in the concentration of a substance, such as that generated by allowing a new wastewater treatment plant to be added in a watershed. The effluent from each reactor type will vary depending on the type of input.

Impulse Input. Assuming an impulse input, the effluent from a plug flow reactor would be identical to the influent (Figure 15.9a). The residence time in the reactor would be the reactor volume (V) divided by the flow rate (Q). The effluent from a well-mixed reactor would initially be the input concentration, but it would decline exponentially over time (Figure 15.9b). The intermediate mixed flow reactor would show properties of both reactors, resulting in a normal distribution of the concentration in the effluent (Figure 15.9c).

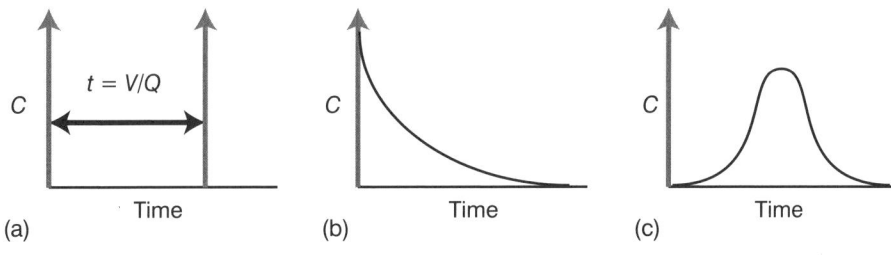

Figure 15.9 Responses of reactors to an impulse input. (a) Plug flow, (b) Well mixed, and (c) Intermediate mixed flow.

Step Input. Assuming a step input, the effluent from a plug flow reactor would be at the same concentration as the input after the plug traveled through the reactor, which would be governed by the residence time (Figure 15.10a). Effluent from a completely mixed reactor would begin with the background concentration and then the concentration would increase exponentially, eventually becoming asymptotic to the step input concentration (Figure 15.10b). Effluent from the intermediate mixed reactor would follow a sigmoid curve (Figure 15.10c).

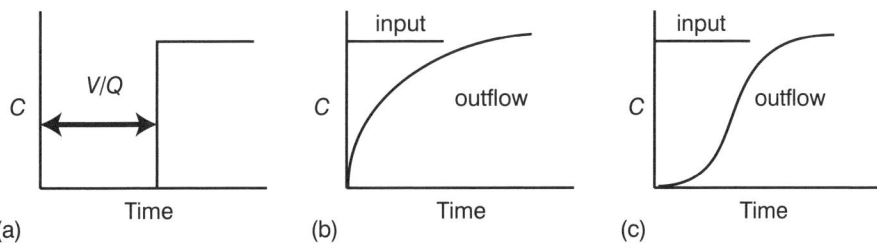

Figure 15.10 Responses of reactors to a step input. (a) Plug flow, (b) Well mixed, and (c) Intermediate mixed flow.

Dissolved Oxygen

One of the most important river water quality variables that has been impacted by wastewater discharges is dissolved oxygen. The biochemical oxygen demand (BOD) of the wastewater causes an "oxygen sag" curve to develop downstream from the discharge (Figure 15.11). Initially, there is a deficit (D_0) of oxygen from what the water could hold at saturation (C_s) right below the input of the wastewater. The biological decomposition that occurs uses oxygen at a greater rate than reaeration, which results in a lowering or sag in the oxygen concentration in the river to a critical minimum (D_c) at a downstream distance (X_c). Reaeration of the water at a greater rate than decomposition results in an increase in dissolved oxygen downstream of this location. Meanwhile, the BOD declines downstream from the wastewater input. The Streeter-Phelps model predicts the oxygen deficit in rivers caused by the discharge of wastewater (James, 1993; Tchobanoglous and Schroeder, 1987), and it will be explained later in this section.

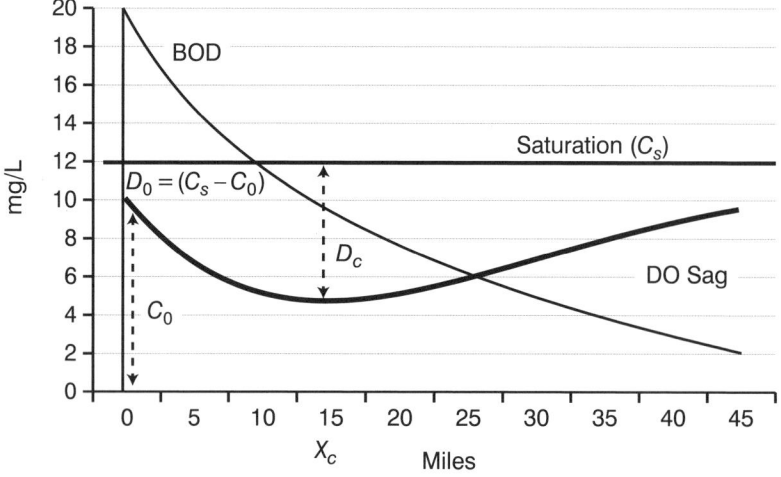

Figure 15.11 Dissolved oxygen and BOD concentrations representative of the water quality zones in a river receiving wastewater with a high BOD.

The mass balance of oxygen in a stream, assuming plug flow, is (Tchobanoglous and Schroeder, 1987):

$$\frac{\partial C_{O_2}}{\partial t} \Delta V = QC_{O_2 \text{ in}} - QC_{O_2 \text{ out}} + r_{O_2} \Delta V + r_k \Delta V \qquad [15.18]$$

This partial differential equation may be read as:

Accumulation = inflow − outflow + deoxygenation + reoxygenation

The discharge of wastewater is assumed to be well mixed at the point of discharge. The initial concentration in the stream at the point of discharge of the wastewater can be calculated from Eqn. 15.1. See Figure 15.12 below, which repeats the stream-mixing diagram of 15.1.

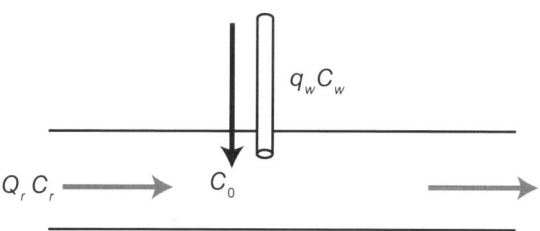

Figure 15.12 Initial mixing of dissolved oxygen at the point of a wastewater discharge.

The concentration of oxygen in a river is a function of deoxygenation and reoxygenation processes, as described in the following sections.

Deoxygenation

Deoxygenation is the depletion of oxygen by:

1. Bacterial decomposition

2. Sediment oxygen demand

The rate of deoxygenation is a function of the velocity of flow, turbulence, and the amount of BOD remaining. The BOD is the primary source of depletion. The rate of deoxygenation can be determined from (Tchobanoglous and Schroeder, 1987):

$$r_{O_2} = -kL_i e^{-k\theta_H} \qquad [15.19]$$

where r_{O_2} = rate of deoxygenation (g/m³/d)
k = first-order reaction rate constant (d⁻¹)
L_i = BOD at point of input (g/m³)
θ_H = time (d)

The constant k is determined in the laboratory, and 20°C is the standard base temperature. To adjust k to the ambient temperature, use:

$$k_{T_1} = k_{T_2} \theta^{(T_1 - T_2)} \qquad [15.20]$$

where T_2 = 20°C
T_1 = any other temperature
θ = a temperature coefficient (1.025) for $T > 20°C$ (Novotny, 2003)

Reoxygenation

Reoxygenation is the addition of oxygen by:

1. tributaries, surface runoff, and ground water inflow
2. atmosphere absorption (also termed reaeration)
3. photosynthesis

Reaeration is a function of stream characteristics such as velocity, depth, diffusion, and temperature. Reaeration (r_k) can be determined from:

$$r_k = k_2 \left(C_s - C_{O_2}\right) \quad [15.21]$$

where r_k = the rate of reaeration (g/m³/d)
k_2 = a reaeration constant (d⁻¹)
C_s = the dissolved oxygen (DO) concentration at saturation (g/m³)
C_{O_2} = the DO concentration (g/m³) (Tchobanoglous and Schroeder, 1987)

The reaeration constant k_2 is determined from:

$$k_2 = \frac{294(D_L u)^{1/2}}{\bar{H}^{3/2}} \quad [15.22]$$

where D_L = molecular diffusion for oxygen (m²/d)
u = stream velocity (m/s)
$\bar{H}$ = average flow depth (m) (Tchobanoglous and Schroeder, 1987)

Since D_L is a function of temperature, it can be adjusted for any temperature from:

$$D_{LT} = D_{L20} \times 1.037^{(T-20)} \quad [15.23]$$

where D_{LT} = molecular diffusion at temperature T (°C) (m²/d)
D_{L20} = molecular diffusion at 20°C
= 1.760 × 10⁻⁴ m²/d (Tchobanoglous and Schroeder, 1987)

Streeter-Phelps Oxygen Sag Equation

The oxygen deficit in the stream is determined from:

$$D_{O_2} = \left(C_s - C_{O_2}\right) \quad [15.24]$$

where C_s = saturated concentration of DO in the river (g/m³)
C_{O_2} = actual concentration of DO in the river (g/m³) (Tchobanoglous and Schroeder, 1987)

Then the dissolved oxygen can be calculated from:

$$D_{O_2} = \frac{kL_i}{k_2 - k}\left(e^{-k\theta_H} - e^{-k_2\theta_H}\right) + D_i e^{-k_2\theta_H} \quad [15.25]$$

where D_i = initial oxygen deficit at the point of discharge (g/m³),
and all other terms have been previously described

The critical (maximum) dissolved oxygen deficit can be determined from:

$$D_c = \frac{k}{k_2} L_i e^{-k\theta_H^*} \quad [15.26]$$

where θ_H^* is the flow time required to reach the critical point and is determined from (Tchobanoglous and Schroeder, 1987):

$$\theta_H^* = \frac{1}{k_2 - k}\ln\left[\frac{k_2}{k}\left(1 - D_i \frac{k_2 - k}{kL_i}\right)\right] \quad [15.27]$$

The distance (X_c) to the critical dissolved oxygen deficit can be determined from:

$$X_c = \theta_H^* u \quad [15.28]$$

where u = velocity (Tchobanoglous and Schroeder, 1987)

Alternatively, the dissolved oxygen in the stream can be determined from:

$$D = D_o e^{-k_a(x/u)} + \frac{k_r}{k_a - k_r}\left(e^{-k_d(x/u)} - e^{-k_a(x/u)}\right)L_o$$

$$+ \left[\frac{k_d}{k_a k_r}\left(1 - e^{-k_a(x/u)}\right) - \frac{k_d}{(k_a - k_r)}\left(e^{-k_r(x/u)} - e^{-k_a(x/u)}\right)\right]L_r \quad [15.29]$$

$$+ \left(1 - e^{-k_a(x/u)}\right)\frac{S_B}{k_a H}$$

where $D = C_s - C$ deficit at end of reach (mg/L)
D_o = initial oxygen deficit (mg/L)
L_o = initial ultimate BOD concentration (mg/L)
L_r = ultimate BOD concentration lateral input (mg/L/d)
k_r = overall BOD removal coefficient (d⁻¹)
k_a = reaeration coefficient (d⁻¹)
k_d = BOD deoxygenation coefficient (d⁻¹)
X = length of reach (m)
u = average stream velocity (m/d)
S_B = sediment oxygen demand (g/m²/d)
H = average depth of flow (m) (Novotny, 2003)

An example will be used to illustrate the calculations.

Example 15.2 Streeter-Phelps Oxygen Sag Equation

Determine the dissolved oxygen concentration for Fenger Brook as it flows into Alewife Cove after passing through an urban community. We will use the two-year storm of 5 cm in 6 hours and assume a runoff coefficient of 50% that follows a period of the 7Q10. The 7Q10 is the average low discharge that is expected to occur once every 10 years for seven consecutive days. The BOD concentration in urban stormwater is 30 mg/L. The length of the brook passing through the town is 4 km, and the area contributing to the brook is 4 km². The stream has an average width of 2 m and is 0.5 m deep. During August, the water temperature is 25°C. Assume that the lateral flow input is 0.09 m³/s-km with a BOD of 2.5 mg/L. The 7Q10 at the upstream end of the town (Q_o) is 0.3 m³/s. At the time of the 7Q10, the brook has a BOD of 1.2 mg/L and a DO concentration of 7.6 mg/L. Assume that $k_r = k_d = 0.30$ d⁻¹ and $k_a = 18.6$ d⁻¹. The sediment oxygen demand is 1.8 g/m²/d.

Step 1: Flow calculations

$$\text{Stormflow} = 0.5 \times \frac{5 \text{ cm}}{6 \text{ hr}} \times \frac{0.01 \text{ m}}{\text{cm}} \times 4 \text{ km}^2 \times \frac{10^6 \text{ m}^2}{\text{km}^2} \times \frac{1 \text{ hr}}{3600 \text{ s}} = 4.63 \text{ m}^3/\text{s}$$

$$Q_o = \text{river} = 0.3 \text{ m}^3/\text{s}$$

$$Q_e = Q_o + \text{stormflow} + (\text{dist.} \times \text{lateral flow})$$

$$= 0.3 \text{ m}^3/\text{s} + 4.63 \text{ m}^3/\text{s} + \left(4 \text{ km} \times 0.09 \text{ m}^3/\text{s/km}\right)$$

$$= 5.29 \text{ m}^3/\text{s}$$

$$Q_{ave} = \frac{Q_o + Q_e}{2}$$

$$= \frac{0.3 \text{ m}^3/\text{s} + 5.29 \text{ m}^3/\text{s}}{2}$$

$$= 2.80 \text{ m}^3/\text{s}$$

Step 2: Velocity

$$u_{ave} = \frac{Q_{ave}}{B \times H} = \frac{2.80 \text{ m}^3/\text{s}}{2 \text{ m} \times 0.5 \text{ m}} = 2.8 \text{ m/s} \times \frac{1 \text{ km}}{1000 \text{ m}} \times \frac{86,400 \text{ s}}{\text{d}} = 241.9 \text{ km/d}$$

Step 3: C_s at 25°C (Novotny, 2003)

$$C_s = 14.652 - 0.41022\,(25) + 0.007991\,(25)^2 - 0.0000777747\,(25)^3$$
$$= 8.18 \text{ mg/L}$$

Step 4: Lateral BOD load

$$L_r = \frac{1.4\left(\text{lateral flow} \times \text{BOD}_{\text{conc}}\right)}{x - \sec \text{ area}}$$

$$= \frac{1.4\left(\dfrac{0.09 \text{ m}^3}{\text{s} \times \text{km}} \times \dfrac{3 \text{ g}}{\text{m}^3} \times \dfrac{0.001 \text{ km}}{\text{m}} \times \dfrac{86,400 \text{ s}}{\text{d}}\right)}{(2 \text{ m})(0.5 \text{ m})}$$

$$= 32.7 \text{ g/m}^3/\text{d}$$

Step 5: Initial downstream BOD

$$L_o = 1.4\left(\frac{\text{stormwater BOD load}}{Q_0} + \text{upstream BOD}\right)$$

$$= 1.4\left[\left(\frac{\dfrac{30 \text{ g}}{\text{m}^3} \times 4.63 \text{ m}^3/\text{s}}{0.3 \text{ m}^3/\text{s}}\right) + 1.2 \text{ g/m}^3\right]$$

$$= 649.9 \text{ mg/L}$$

Step 6: Initial DO deficit

$$D_0 = C_s - C_0$$

$$= 8.2 \text{ g/m}^3 - 7.6 \text{ g/m}^3$$

$$= 0.6 \text{ g/m}^3$$

Step 7: Deficit at critical point:

$$D_c = C_s - C_c$$

$$= 8.2 \text{ g/m}^3 - 5 \text{ g/m}^3$$

$$= 3.2 \text{ g/m}^3$$

Step 8: Coefficients

$$k_{a25} = k_a \theta^{(T-20)} = 18.6 \text{ d}^{-1} \times 1.025^{(25-20)} = 21 \text{ d}^{-1}$$

$$k_{r25} = k_r \theta^{(T-20)} = 0.3 \times 1.047^{(25-20)} = 0.377 \text{ d}^{-1}$$

Step 9: Travel time

$$t = \frac{x}{u} = \frac{4 \text{ km}}{241.9 \text{ km/d}} = 0.0165 \text{ d}$$

Step 10: DO deficit

$$D = 0.6e^{-21(0.0165)} + \frac{0.377}{21-0.377}\left(e^{-0.377(0.0165)} - e^{-21(0.0165)}\right)(649.9)$$

$$+ \left[\frac{0.377}{21(0.377)}\left(1-e^{-21(0.0165)}\right) - \frac{0.377}{(21-0.377)}\left(e^{-0.377(0.0165)} - e^{-21(0.0165)}\right)\right](32.6)$$

$$+ \left(1 - e^{-21(0.0165)}\right)\frac{1.8}{21(0.5)}$$

$$= 0.425 + 3.410 + 0.283 + 0.050 = 4.17 \text{ mg/L}$$

Step 11:

$$C = C_s - D = 8.18 - 4.17 = 4.01 \text{ mg/L}$$

This value is below the 5.0 mg/L desired.

■ PROBLEMS

15.1 Determine the first-order reaction constant for the following data:

Time (min)	Concentration (mmol/L)	Log10(C_i / C_0)
0	20 (Co)	
5	15	
10	11	
15	9	
20	7	

15.2 For Example 15.2, what reduction in stormwater runoff would be needed to prevent the DO concentration from decreasing below 5 mg/L?

15.3 For Example 15.2, what would be the effect of adding a municipal discharge of 1.75 m³/s with a BOD of 30 mg/L?

15.4 Determine the volume of Rhodamine WT (20%) (liters) needed to produce a peak concentration (C_p) of 50 μg/L downstream 2 miles from the injection point. The maximum discharge is 50 cfs, and the average velocity is 2 ft/s.

15.5 Determine the longitudinal dispersion coefficient for a large river. You perform a dye test by adding 550 lbs of Rhodamine WT 20%. You monitor at two locations: Station A at 30.3 miles downstream and Station B at 36.3 miles downstream with 6 miles between stations. The following information was determined:

Time (hr)	Station A Concentration (μg/L)	Station B Concentration (μg/L)	Time (hr)	Station A Concentration (μg/L)	Station B Concentration (μg/L)
0	0.00		32	0.14	7.50
2	0.00		34	0.10	6.80
4	0.10		36		5.10
6	0.30		38		3.70
8	5.40		40		2.40
10	22.00		42		1.68
12	13.00		44		1.21
14	4.25		46		0.88
16	1.83		48		0.65
18	1.16		50		0.50
20	0.83		52		0.37
22	0.63	0.00	54		0.29
24	0.45	0.14	56		0.24
26	0.34	1.30	58		0.17
28	0.25	5.00	60		0.13
30	0.18	9.00	62		0.10

References

Alexander, R. B., R. A. Smith, and G. E. Schwarz. 2000. Effect of stream channel size on the delivery of nitrogen to the Gulf of Mexico. *Nature* 403(17): 758–761.

Bartsch, A. F. 1948. Biological aspects of stream pollution. *Sewage Works Journal* 20(2): 292–302.

Ensign, S. H., and M. W. Doyle. 2006. Nutrient spiraling in streams and river networks. *J. Geophysical Research* 11. Go4009, doi:10.1029/2005JG000114.

James, A. 1993. *An introduction to water quality modelling*. 2nd ed. Chichester, England: John Wiley & Sons.

Kilpatrick, F. A., and J. F. Wilson, Jr. 1989. *Measurement of time of travel in streams by dye tracing. Techniques of water-resources investigations of the United States Geological Survey*. TWI 3-A9. Denver, CO: U.S. Geological Survey. https://pubs.usgs.gov/twri/twri3-a9/pdf/twri_3-A9.pdf

Kittrell, F. W. 1969. *A practical guide to water quality studies of streams*. U.S. Dept. of the Interior. Federal Water Pollution Control Administration. CWR-5. Washington, DC: U.S. Government Printing Office. http://files.eric.ed.gov/fulltext/ED044302.pdf

Mackin, J. H. 1948. Concept of the graded river. *Bulletin of the Geological Society of America* 59: 463–512.

Novotny, V. 2003. *Water quality: Diffuse pollution and watershed management*. 2nd ed. New York: John Wiley & Sons.

Poff, N. L., J. D. Allan, M. B. Bain, J. R. Karr, K. L. Prestegaard, B. D. Richter, R. E. Sparks, and J. C. Stromberg. 1997. The natural flow regime: A paradigm for river conservation and restoration. *BioScience* 47: 769–784.

Tchobanoglous, G., and E. D. Schroeder. 1987. *Water quality characteristics, modeling and modification*. Menlo Park, CA: Addison-Wesley.

Thomann, R. V., and J. A. Mueller. 1987. *Principles of surface water quality modeling and control*. New York: Harper & Row.

Vannote, R. R, G. W. Minshall, K. W. Cummins, J. R. Sedell, and C. E. Cushing. 1980. The river continuum concept. *Canadian Journal of Fisheries and Aquatic Sciences* 37: 130–137.

16

Lakes and Reservoir Water Quality

■ Introduction

Limnology is the study of inland waters (Ruttner, 1971), and it is often limited to the study of inland lakes. This chapter will focus on inland lakes, ponds, and reservoirs. It will include a review of the physical, biological, and chemical aspects of limnology. Methods for predicting lake trophic status will be reviewed. Lake restoration techniques also will be discussed.

■ Physical Limnology

Physical Origin of Lakes

Lakes have originated from several different causes. Following are 11 possibilities.

1. **Tectonic.** Tectonic lakes are formed by the movement of the earth's crust (Hutchinson, 1957). Such movement can cause uplift, tilting or folding, and subsidence, and it can leave a depression that can become a lake. Lake Victoria in Africa, Lake Baikal in Russia, and Lake Champlain and Lake Tahoe in the United States are examples of tectonic lakes. These lakes may also form along faults.

2. **Volcanic.** Volcanic lakes form in the old craters of volcanoes and by collapse of a crater (Hutchinson, 1957). Crater Lake in Oregon is an example of a volcanic lake, which occurred by collapse.

3. **Landslides.** Landslides may create dams in valleys, which subsequently fill with water and form lakes (Hutchinson, 1957).

4. **Glaciers.** Glaciers have formed lakes in several ways (Hutchinson, 1957; Zumberge, 1952).

   a. Lakes may form directly on a glacier.

   b. A glacier in a valley downstream may block streamflow and create a lake upstream.

   c. Glaciers may scour rock basins and preglacial valleys. For example, many lakes in the Boundary Waters Canoe Area of Minnesota were created by glacial scour forming parallel long lakes along tilted bedrock layers.

   d. Cirques and fjords are created by glaciers.

   e. Moraine outwash may create a dam with a lake behind it.

   f. Kettle lakes are formed by melted ice blocks in outwash.

   g. The irregular deposition of till can create shallow lakes.

5. **Solution.** Solution lakes, such as those found in Florida, can form in karst topography where soluble limestone may dissolve (Hutchinson, 1957).

6. **Fluviatile.** River processes may result in oxbow lakes or the damming of lakes when tributary actions create an alluvial fan (Zumberge, 1952). Lakes have formed behind natural levees in floodplains and in deltas (Lake Pontchartrain in Louisiana). A meander scroll is another example of a lake formed by erosion and deposition in a floodplain.

7. **Wind action.** Winds may create lakes such as pans, playas, or blowouts (Hutchinson, 1957), typically in dry or historically dry areas.

8. **Shoreline lakes.** Littoral drift along shorelines can isolate a bay and develop a separate lake. It can also cause the growth of a point and cut off a bay (Zumberge, 1952).

9. **Organic accumulation.** The growth of vegetation, for example peat or other vegetation, can dam an area (Hutchinson, 1957).

10. **Higher organisms.** Beaver dams may in some cases create lakes (Hutchinson, 1957; Zumberge, 1952). Lakes have also been formed or enlarged by artificial dams. Though not originally intended, in some cases lakes have formed in abandoned mining and quarrying operations.

11. **Meteorites.** Meteorite impacts create very round lakes (Hutchinson, 1957).

Physical Characteristics of Lakes

Lakes are described by several characteristics or measurements of their size. **Lake depth** is shown on bathymetric maps. **Lake length** is the shortest water distance along the most distant points on its shore (Hutchinson, 1957). **Lake breadth** is the width perpendicular to the line describing the length. **Mean lake depth** is the lake volume divided by lake surface area. **Lake area** is the surface area as determined from maps and photos. **Lake volume** is determined from a plot of depth versus area of each depth contour, and from the area under the curve that is equal to the volume. **Shore length** is the total length along the shoreline of a lake and is determined using digitizers or map wheels. **Shore development** is a measure that relates shoreline length to the circumference of a circle and is determined using the following equation (Hutchinson, 1957):

$$D_L = \frac{L}{2(\pi A)^{0.5}} \qquad [16.1]$$

where D_L = shore development index, a value >1
L = lake length
A = lake surface area

Insulosity is the percentage of the surface area occupied by islands (Hutchinson, 1957). **Volume development** is the lake volume divided by the volume of a cone and is a value greater than 1. **Shape** is a description that, when applied to a lake, may include such terms as circular, elliptical, or dendritic. **Open lakes** have an inlet and an outlet, whereas **closed lakes** have no outlet.

Light

Sunlight is an important source of energy, photosynthesis, organism movement, and heating. Light on a lake can be reflected, or it can penetrate the water and then become absorbed or transmitted. The reflected light is similar to sunlight in its spectral composition, and therefore a lake can act as a mirror in true color. Light decreases exponentially with depth in lakes (Figure 16.1) following the expression:

$$I = I_0 e^{-\varepsilon h} \qquad [16.2]$$

where I_0 = light intensity at the surface
ε = an extinction coefficient
h = depth or length of the light path in the water column
(Ruttner, 1971)

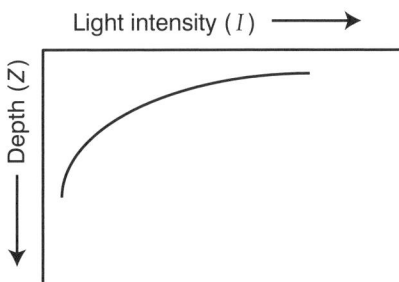

Figure 16.1 Exponential light penetration.

The percentage of components of the visible light spectrum that are transmitted through the water varies (Ruttner, 1971). The transmission is highest for the shortest wavelengths in the visible spectrum (blue) and decreases greatly for the longer wavelengths (yellow, orange, red). This property explains the color of lakes. The visible color spectrum can be remembered using the acronym ROY G BIV for red, orange, yellow, green, blue, indigo, violet. The color blue is least absorbed by water, and thus penetrates deeper (Figure 16.2). Light that is scattered back by particles in the water has relatively more blue than sunlight. Particles suspended in the water and dissolved materials can also affect the transmission of light, and thus not all lakes are blue, but some are greenish or aqua.

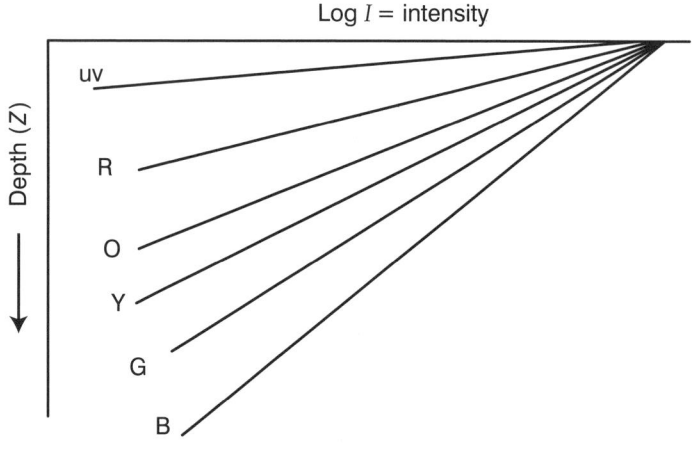

Figure 16.2 The intensity of light at different depths in a lake.

Thermal Stratification

One of the physical properties of water is that it has different densities at different temperatures (Ruttner, 1971). Water is most dense at 4°C (3.98°C) as shown in Figure 16.3. Like most substances, its density increases with decreasing temperature, but only to the maximum of 4°C. At lower temperatures, its density decreases until it freezes. This property explains why ice floats.

Lakes may thermally stratify in layers due to this property (Figure 16.4). In northern climates, lakes become isothermal in the winter and have the same density throughout. In spring, winds can move the entire lake and mix it, a term called the **spring turnover** (Ruttner, 1971). As lakes warm in spring and summer they begin to stratify, with lower-density warm water overlying denser colder waters. Such stratification has water quality implications. Once stratified into layers, the waters in each layer do not mix. The upper layer is termed the **epilimnion** (Figure 16.5). The middle layer is termed the **metalimnion** and the lower layer is termed the **hypolimnion**. Because these layers have different densities, they do not mix well depending on the differences in density and the

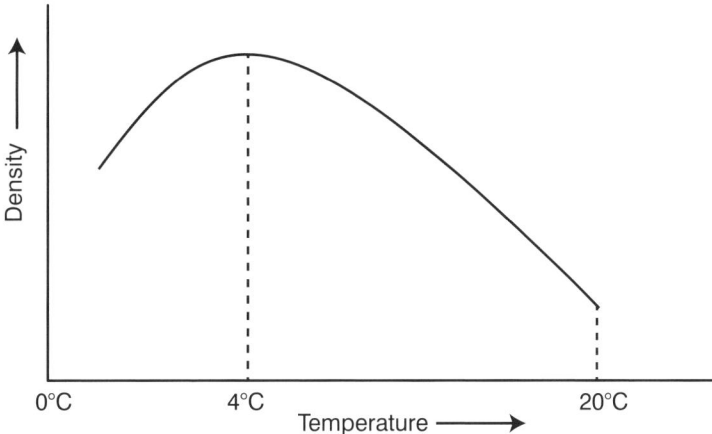

Figure 16.3 The density of water as a function of water temperature.

thickness of the layers. The term **thermocline** refers to the plane through the lake of the maximum change in temperature with depth (Hutchinson, 1957). There are physical and chemical implications of the waters in these layers not mixing that are discussed later.

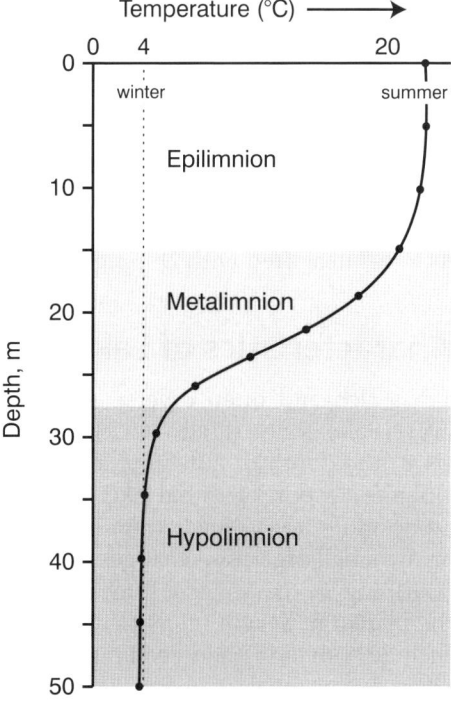

Figure 16.4 Temperature as a function of depth in a thermally stratified lake.

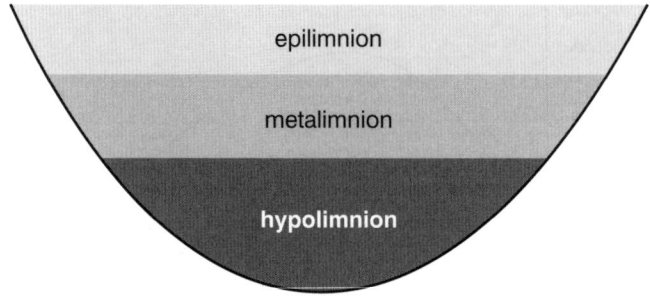

Figure 16.5 Layers of a lake during thermal stratification.

Seiche

A **seiche** is an oscillation of a lake caused by a buildup of water at one end of a lake due to wind or air pressure differences (Hutchinson, 1957). This imbalance in water level results in a movement of waters to seek equilibrium. There are two types of seiches: surface and internal. A surface seiche is the movement of surface water, flowing from the higher lake elevation to the lower elevation (Figure 16.6a). The period of such seiches is characteristic of an individual lake and sometimes a bay. Examples of seiche periods include 112 minutes for Lake Michigan, 289 minutes for Lake Huron, and 786 minutes for Lake Erie (Hutchinson, 1957). In lakes with bays, the seiche in the bay is often different from that of the main part of the lake. Internal seiches occur between the epilimnion and the hypolimnion along the thermocline, and may continue to occur after the surface seiche has ceased (Figure 16.6b). Such oscillations also result in the transport of plankton and chemical constituents in the water.

Lake currents can be measured using poles of different lengths and vanes. They are typically released at a point and tracked over time. A distribution of currents at different depths can thereby be obtained. Present technology allows lake currents to be measured with Doppler velocity meters.

■ Biological Characteristics of Lakes

Lakes contain a rich and often diverse assemblage of biota. Organisms are found in several lake zones (Figure 16.7) that have been named. The **littoral** zone extends to the depth of autotrophic plants (Ruttner, 1971). The **pelagic** zone is the open water portion of the lake. The **profundal** zone is located below the pelagic zone and refers to the bottom in the deep part of the lake.

Plankton are small organisms that generally are at the mercy of the currents or passively drifting in the water (Hutchinson, 1957). There are several terms applied to the plankton. **Seston** refers to all particulate matter present in water. The seston include both living and dead material. The **nekton** are organisms that can travel where they want, such as fish. The **neuston** are organisms found in the surface film of lakes (Ruttner, 1971). There are two general types of plankton: **phytoplankton** (plants) and **zooplankton** (animals). Plankton often exhibit a seasonal

Chapter 16 Lakes and Reservoir Water Quality 193

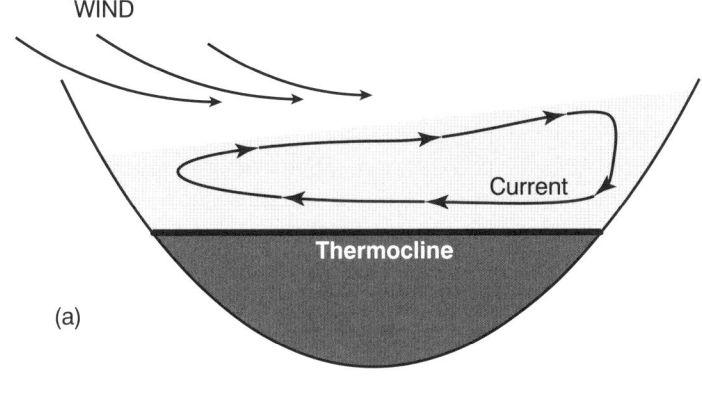

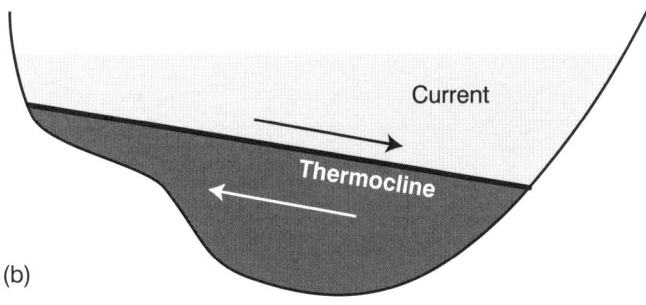

Figure 16.6 Seiches in lakes and bays. (a) Surface, (b) Internal (not to scale).

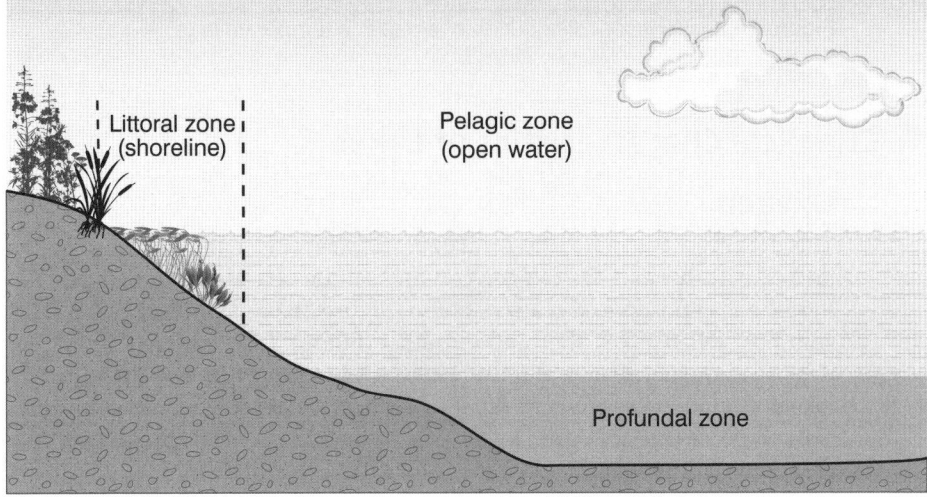

Figure 16.7 Lake zones.

distribution in lakes (Figure 16.8). In unproductive lakes, the pattern is typically an increase in abundance in the spring, increasing to a maximum in midsummer and then decreasing through the fall. This difference in quantity and type of phytoplankton is influenced by temperature and the concentration of substances in water (Hutchinson, 1967). Many lakes exhibit a spring and fall peak in the diatoms. Grazing by zooplankton, the availability of silica and nutrients, and the timing of rainfall events also influence the abundance and type of plankton present.

Paleolimnology is the study of the sediment stratigraphy (Ruttner, 1971). Commonly used methods include pollen and diatom identification as well as some chemical characteristics for undisturbed sediments. *Ambrosia* (ragweed) pollen has been considered an indicator of European colonization and has been used in lake sediments to estimate sediment loading to the lake.

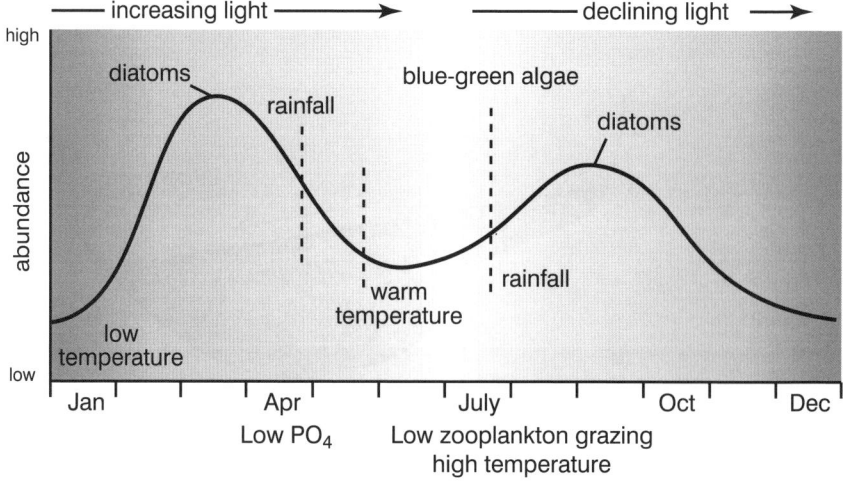

Figure 16.8 Seasonal distribution of algae in a temperate lake.

Chemical Characteristics of Lakes

Oxygen

The dissolved oxygen content of lakes varies seasonally and diurnally. When lakes are isothermal, the oxygen content is often near saturation, especially when the lake is exposed to the atmosphere (Figure 16.9a) (Ruttner, 1971). During the summer, when lakes thermally stratify (Figure 16.4), oxygen levels generally decline in deeper waters (Figure 16.9b). Oxidation processes operating near the lake bottom decrease oxygen levels. During the day, oxygen concentrations typically increase due to higher levels of photosynthesis. At night, the concentration of oxygen in the water can be lowered during respiration. In highly productive lakes, this diurnal lowering of oxygen can be catastrophic, resulting in fish kills (Hutchinson, 1957).

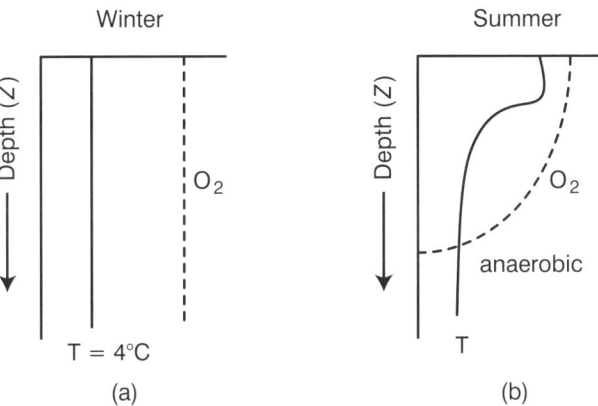

Figure 16.9 Temperature and oxygen profiles in lakes in winter and summer (T - temperature).

Productivity

The productivity of a lake is a measure of the rate of organic matter production (Ruttner, 1971). There are several methods for determining productivity.

1. Light and dark bottle—measure of O_2 production (Figure 16.10). For this method, two bottles are used, one is clear (light) and the other is darkened (dark) such as with aluminum foil (Clesceri et al., 1998). Both bottles are filled with a water sample and incubated in situ or in the laboratory. The dissolved oxygen (DO) concentration is measured at the beginning and end of the incubation period. Net photosynthesis or net production is the difference between the DO concentrations obtained in the original sample and in the light bottle. Respiration is the difference between the DO concentrations obtained in the original sample and in the dark bottle. Gross photosynthesis is the difference between the DO concentrations found in the light and dark bottles.

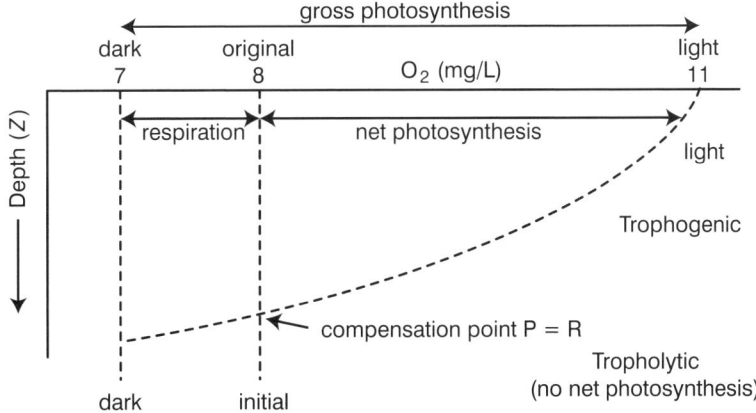

Figure 16.10 Oxygen profile in a lake showing oxygen zones.

2. Carbon-14—the amount of C-14 assimilated by plankton in a sample of water. For this method, radioactive carbonate ($^{14}CO_3^{2-}$) is added to both the light and dark bottles and incubated as in method 1 above (Clesceri et al., 1998). The samples are then filtered and the C-14 is extracted and tested for radioactivity. This method measures net photosynthesis.

3. Standing crop—measurement of biomasses in a lake by weighing the dried organic matter. This method is not considered reliable due to detritus and silt (Ruttner, 1971).

4. Chlorophyll *a*—measure of a photosynthetic pigment as a measure of productivity. Phytoplankton and all green plants contain chlorophyll *a* and it is a measure of the biomass present. Chlorophyll *a* is determined using a fluorometer (Clesceri et al., 1998). This method is not considered reliable for productivity due to differences in chlorophyll among species and at very high concentrations.

Eutrophication

The term **eutrophication** means well-nourished and has been defined as the addition of nutrients to bodies of water (National Academy of Sciences, 1969). Natural eutrophication occurs when a lake goes from low to high productivity with a decrease in size and depth. Cultural eutrophication occurs when there is no change in size or depth but the lake becomes more productive. The primary causes of eutrophication are nutrients such as nitrogen and phosphorus, with phosphorus being most important. Lakes are commonly classified by trophic status as **eutrophic** (rich in nutrients) and **oligotrophic** (poor in nutrients) (Ruttner, 1971). The term **mesotrophic** has been applied to lakes that have characteristics that are between oligotrophic and eutrophic. **Dystrophic** lakes, which means out of phase, refers to a lake that does not fit this classification, perhaps due to a dark color (Hutchinson, 1967). The differences between the characteristics of oligotrophic and eutrophic lakes are summarized in Table 16.1.

Table 16.1 Characteristics of the trophic status of lakes.

Characteristic	Oligotrophic	Eutrophic
Depth	Deep, >20 m	Shallow, <20 m
Secchi disk transparency	>6 m	<4 m
Nutrients (N, P)	Low	High
Sediments	Inorganic	Organic
Blooms	None	May have blue-green
Plankton	Many spp., few in number	Few spp., abundant numbers
Benthos	Rich	Qualitatively low, quantitatively rich
Dissolved oxygen	High all depths	Depleted in hypolimnion
Color	Blue to green	Green to yellow
Conductivity	<200 µS/cm	>200 µS/cm

Carlson Trophic State Index (TSI)

Several indices have been developed to describe the water quality of lakes. One of these, the Carlson Trophic State Index (TSI), is a numerical index for lakes (Carlson, 1977). This index can range from 0 to 100, with 100 representing poor water quality. The index can be computed from Secchi disk transparency (SD), chlorophyll *a* (Chl), or total phosphorus (TP) (see Table 16.2).

Table 16.2 Carlson's Trophic State Index (TSI) with values for Secchi disk transparency, total phosphorus, and chlorophyll *a*.

TSI	Secchi Disk (m)	Total Phosphorus (mg/m³)	Chlorophyll a (mg/m³)
0	64	0.75	0.04
20	16	3	0.34
40	4	12	2.6
60	1	48	20
80	0.25	192	154
100	0.062	768	1183

The index for each can be computed from:

$$\text{TSI (SD)} = 10\left(6 - \frac{\ln \text{SD}}{\ln 2}\right) \qquad [16.3]$$

$$\text{TSI (Chl)} = 10\left(6 - \frac{2.04 - 0.68 \ln \text{Chl}}{\ln 2}\right) \qquad [16.4]$$

$$\text{TSI (TP)} = 10\left(6 - \frac{\ln \frac{48}{\text{TP}}}{\ln 2}\right) \qquad [16.5]$$

where SD = Secchi disk transparency (m)
  Chl = chlorophyll *a* concentration (mg/m³)
  TP = total phosphorus concentration (mg/m³)

Prediction Model

The relationship between total phosphorus loading and mean lake depth has been used to predict lake trophic status (Figure 16.11) (Vollenweider and Dillon, 1974). Data from several lakes throughout the world were used to develop the relationship. In a later model Vollenweider added flushing rate to the relationship and plotted load versus the depth divided by the residence time (Figure 16.12).

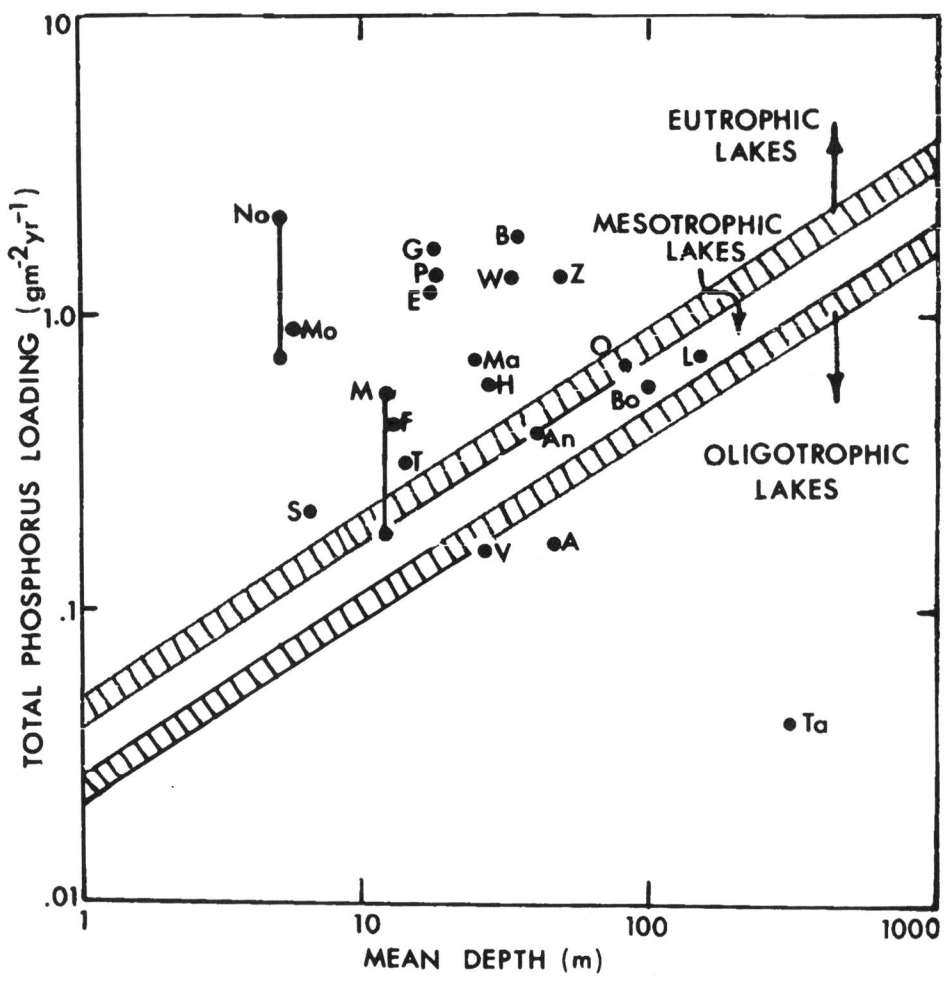

Figure 16.11 Vollenweider's total phosphorus loading as a function of mean depth (Vollenweider and Dillon, 1974; based on Vollenweider, 1968). Used with permission of the Organization for Economic Cooperation and Development.
U.S. lakes: Ta–Tahoe O–Ontario M–Mendota E–Erie W–Washington.

The actual model is:

$$[P] = \frac{L(1-R)}{\bar{Z}\rho}$$ [16.6]

where $[P]$ = spring phosphorus concentration of a lake (mg/m^3)
  L = total lake loading on an areal basis (g/m^2/yr)
  R = retention
  $\bar{Z}$ = mean lake depth
  ρ = flushing rate (yr^{-1})

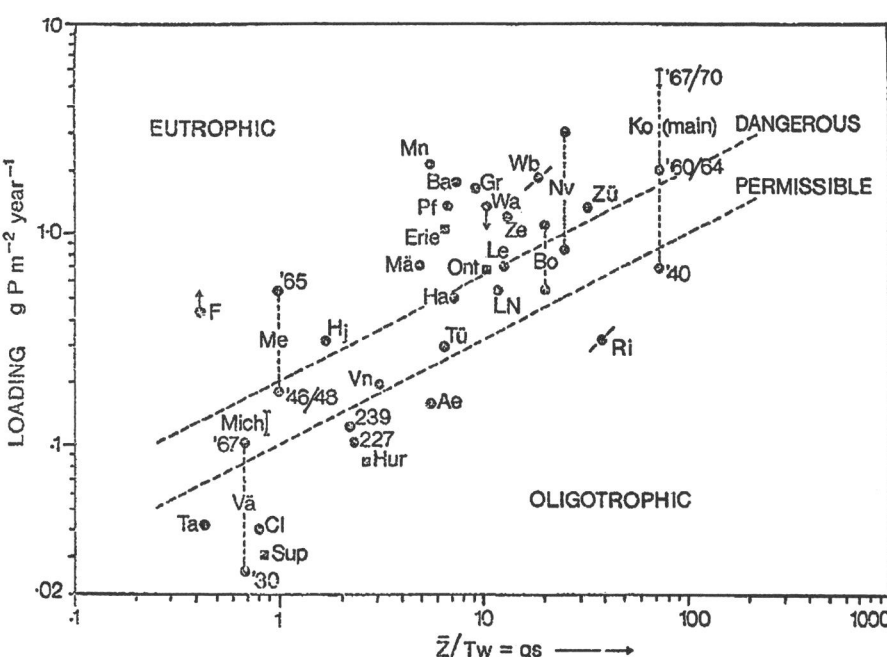

Figure 16.12 Phosphorus loading versus depth/retention time (Vollenweider, 1975). Used with permission of Birkhauser Verlag.

North America lakes:

Me–Lake Mendota, WI	Mn–Lake Monona, WI
Wa–Lake Washington, WA	Sup–Lake Superior, MN
Mich–Lake Michigan, MI	Hur–Lake Huron, MI
Erie–Lake Erie, OH	Ont–Lake Ontario, NY
Ta–Lake Tahoe, CA	Cl–Clear Lake, ONT

Retention (R) is the amount of phosphorus retained by the lake and is calculated as:

$$R = \frac{P_{in} - P_{out}}{P_{in}} \quad [16.7]$$

where P_{in} = phosphorus loading to the lake
 P_{out} = phosphorus mass leaving the lake; or

$$R = 0.46e^{(-0.271q_s)} + 0.574e^{(-0.00949q_s)} \quad [16.8]$$

where q_s = areal water loading (m); or

$$R = \frac{13}{13 + q_s} \quad [16.9]$$

Areal water loading (q_s) is determined as:

$$q_s = \frac{\bar{Z}}{T_w} = \frac{Q}{A_L} \qquad [16.10]$$

where $\bar{Z}$ = mean lake depth
Q = outflow volume
T_w = phosphorus residence time
A_L = lake area (m²)

The outflow volume is assumed to equal inflow volume and is determined as:

$$Q = A_d \times RO \qquad [16.11]$$

where A_d = drainage area (m²)
RO = watershed runoff (m/yr)

If the lake area is greater than 10% of the drainage area, then Q is adjusted for the difference between precipitation and lake evaporation as:

$$Q = A_d \cdot RO + A_L (Pr - Ev) \qquad [16.12]$$

where Pr = lake precipitation
Ev = lake evaporation

The flush rate is determined as:

$$\rho = \frac{Q}{V} = \frac{1}{T_w} \qquad [16.13]$$

where Q = outflow (m³/yr)
V = lake volume (m³), which can be determined as:

$$V = A_L \bar{Z} \qquad [16.14]$$

Equation 16.6 can be solved for L to determine the maximum permissible loading given a phosphorus concentration, such as a eutrophication criterion that is part of a water quality standard. Critical phosphorus concentrations are shown in Table 16.3.

Figure 16.12 is useful for illustrating the potential effects of lake restoration approaches. For example, lake trophic status can be improved by reducing loading, increasing lake depth, or increasing the flushing rate.

Table 16.3 Example of eutrophication water quality criteria for lakes.

Concentration (mg/L)	Trophic Status
> 0.030	Eutrophic
0.010 – 0.030	Mesotrophic
0 – 0.010	Oligotrophic

Source: CT DEEP, 2013.

■ Lake Restoration

There are a number of lake restoration and management techniques that have been used to deal with eutrophication and other nuisance issues (Cooke et al., 2005; Holdren et al., 2001; Moore and Thornton, 1988). These approaches can be grouped as those that treat algal problems or those that deal with excessive or undesirable macrophytes.

Algae Techniques

Phosphorus Precipitation and Inactivation. If the major source of phosphorus into a lake is from the sediments, then the addition of alum (aluminum sulfate) can strip the phosphorus from the water column as well as control phosphorus release from sediments (Moore and Thornton, 1988). This practice will only work in the long term if external loading of phosphorus has been reduced or is not important.

Sediment Removal. In-lake sources of phosphorus can also be reduced by removing nutrient-rich sediments. Hydraulic dredging is the most common method of removal, although draglines and clamshells are also used. Other benefits may occur with sediment removal, including macrophyte control and lake deepening.

Dilution and Flushing. Water low in nutrient concentrations can be added to a lake to reduce the lake concentration and turn over the lake volume more quickly.

Artificial Circulation. The addition of air at the bottom of the lake can be used to upset stratification and oxygenate sediments, possibly preventing phosphorus release.

Hypolimnetic Circulation. By adding air near the lake bottom, colder hypolimnetic water can be brought to the surface through piping and then returned to the bottom with a higher oxygen content.

Hypolimnetic Withdrawal. A deep outlet behind a dam can be used to remove nutrient-rich and low-oxygen hypolimnetic waters. This would lower the phosphorus concentration in the lake at turnover.

Sediment Oxidation. This approach uses the addition of chemicals directly to the sediments to cause the oxidation and decomposition of organic matter in the sediments.

Food Chain Manipulation. Zooplankton communities can be promoted by the management of fish populations. Certain fish species are more likely to feed on zooplankton, which graze on algae.

Algicides. Copper sulfate is a common algicide. This practice does not solve the cause of algal problems and therefore it is usually short lived. Nontarget fish and zooplankton can also be adversely affected by algicides.

Macrophyte Techniques

Sediment Removal and Sediment Tilling. Deepening a lake will reduce light penetration to the bottom and remove organic sediments suitable for macrophytes. The sources of sedimentation should also be controlled.

Water Level Drawdown. Exposing the sediments to drying and freezing conditions can damage certain aquatic plants. However, some plants are not affected, and some can be invigorated.

Shading and Sediment Covers. Placing covers on the bottoms of lakes can reduce rooted macrophytes. Often these are some type of plastic, although sands and gravels have been used. Such treatments are usually only applied in small areas because of cost.

Biological Controls. Herbaceous fish, such as the grass carp, have been used in several states but are banned in others (Moore and Thornton, 1988). Not all plants are preferred by these fish, and some undesirable plants may be avoided. There are several negative impacts resulting from the use of these fish. Insects have also been used for some plant control, particularly in southern states.

Harvesting. Harvesting of plants has been shown to be successful. However, if just the top of the plant is cut and removed, regrowth can occur rapidly. There are also cases in which harvesting spread fragments of plants and increased infestation.

Herbicides. Pesticide use in lakes to control aquatic plants has been common. However, such use is typically short term and does not address the cause of the excessive weed problem. The plant material is left to decompose in the lake, which can consume oxygen and release nutrients. The use of pesticides in lakes is regulated by the U.S. EPA and the states. Some pesticides are specific to certain species. Effects on nontarget aquatic organisms have been reported.

■ Problems

16.1 Phosphorus balance of Unlucky Lake.

Unlucky Lake has been characterized as showing signs of accelerated eutrophication. Very high phosphorus concentrations have been observed in the lake.

Chapter 16 Lakes and Reservoir Water Quality

Phosphorus has been determined to be the chief limiting factor to algal growth in the lake. The high phosphorus concentrations are believed to be the result of nutrient loading from the City of Responsibility sewage treatment facility.

Currently there are two efforts underway to reduce phosphorus loading to the lake. One proposal is to upgrade the sewage treatment plant. Another is to reduce agricultural nonpoint sources of phosphorus by the implementation of best management practices.

Your goal is to evaluate the effect of these actions on the quality of Unlucky Lake given the following characteristics of Unlucky Lake:

Physical	
Surface area	7.0×10^6 m^2
Volume	2.3×10^7 m^3
Mean depth	3.3 m

Annual Water Input	
Sewage effluent	5.53×10^6 m^3/yr
Runoff	52.80×10^6 m^3/yr
Precipitation	6.40×10^6 m^3/yr
Total	64.73×10^6 m^3/yr

Annual Water Output	
Outflow = Inflow − Evaporation	
Evaporation = 3.6×10^6 m^3/yr	

Annual Phosphorus Input	
Wastewater treatment plant	$25{,}013 \times 10^6$ mg/yr
Precipitation	65×10^6 mg/yr
Septic tanks	16×10^6 mg/yr
Major brooks	$5{,}804 \times 10^6$ mg/yr
Minor tributaries	$1{,}849 \times 10^6$ mg/yr
Total	$32{,}747 \times 10^6$ mg/yr

Year	Mean Phosphorus Concentration (mg/m^3)
2005–2006	23
2009	29
2010	37

a. What was the average annual rate of increase in phosphorus concentration from 2005 to 2010?

b. Using Vollenweider's model, what reduction in loading would be needed to achieve a spring [P] concentration of 20 mg/m^3 (mesotrophic)?

c. Using Vollenweider's model, what is the resulting spring [P] concentration if the NPS loading is cut in half?

d. Using Vollenweider's model, what is the resulting spring [P] concentration if the point source loading is cut in half? What if the wastewater treatment plant (WWTP) is upgraded to tertiary treatment with a [P] effluent concentration of 1 mg/L?

References

Carlson, R. E. 1977. A trophic state index for lakes. *Limnology and Oceanography* 22(2): 361–369.

Clesceri, L. S., A. E. Greenberg, and A. D. Eaton. 1998. *Standard methods for the examination of water and wastewater.* 20th ed. American Public Health Association, American Water Works Association, Water Environment Association.

Connecticut Department of Energy and Environmental Protection (CT DEEP). 2013. *Connecticut water quality standards.* Regulations of Connecticut State agencies. Sec. 22a-426-6. Lake tropic categories. https://eregulations.ct.gov/eRegsPortal/Browse/RCSA/%7B2328E62B-7982-48A7-AF52-F3F382A821FA%7D

Cooke, G. D., E. B. Welch, S. A. Peterson, and S. A. Nichols. 2005. *Restoration and Management of Lakes and Reservoirs.* 3rd ed. Boca Raton, FL: CRC Press.

Holdren, C., W. Jones, and J. Taggart. 2001. *Managing lakes and reservoirs.* 3rd ed. U.S. Environmental Protection Agency EPA 841-B-01-006. Madison, WI/Alexandria, VA: North American Lake Management Society/Terrene Institute.

Hutchinson, G. E. 1957. *A treatise on limnology. Vol. I. Geography, physics, and chemistry.* New York: John Wiley & Sons.

Hutchinson, G. E. 1967. *A treatise on limnology. Vol. II. Introduction to lake biology and the limnoplankton.* New York: John Wiley & Sons.

Moore, L., and K. Thornton (eds.). 1988. *Lake and reservoir restoration guidance manual.* U.S. Environmental Protection Agency EPA 440/5-88-002. Madison, WI: North American Lake Management Society.

National Academy of Sciences. 1969. Introduction, summary, and recommendations, in *Eutrophication—Causes, consequences, correctives.* Washington, DC: National Academy of Sciences, pp. 3–4.

Ruttner, F. 1971. *Fundamentals of limnology.* Toronto: University of Toronto Press.

Vollenweider, R. A. 1968. The scientific basis of lake and stream eutrophication, with particular reference to phosphorus and nitrogen as eutrophication factors. Tech. Rep. OECD. Paris. DAS/CSI/68, 27: 1–182.

Vollenweider, R. A. 1975. Input-output models. *Schweizerische Zeitschrift für Hydrologie* 37(1): 53–84.

Vollenweider, R. A., and P. J. Dillon. 1974. *The application of the phosphorus loading concept to eutrophication research.* National Research Council of Canada, Associate Committee on Scientific Criteria for Environmental Quality. Canada Centre for Inland Waters. Burlington, Ontario: Environment Canada.

Zumberge, J. H. 1952. *The lakes of Minnesota: Their origin and classification.* Minnesota Geological Society Bulletin 35. Minneapolis: The University of Minnesota Press.

17

Soil and Ground Water Quality

■ Introduction

Both soil and ground water quality are important for water supply and transport of waters to streams. Soils are often a storage reservoir for pollutants that can remain long after surface treatments are applied. This chapter summarizes the basic principles associated with contamination of soils, soil water, and ground water quality.

■ Soil Water

The role of soils in water quality is to retain, modify, decompose, or adsorb pollutants (Novotny, 2003). Transport from soils occurs in two forms: (1) particulate—where pollutants that are absorbed by soil particles are transported with the soil particles through erosion, and (2) soluble—where pollutants in solution are transported with water movement. A sorption equilibrium can be established between these adsorbed and soluble forms.

There are two groups of pollutants based on their reactability: (1) **Conservative**—these substances persist over time and are not subject to bacterial degradation, volatilization, or chemical breakdown (Novotny, 2003). These substances can be used as tracers. Some examples of conservative substances include chloride and bromide. (2) **Nonconservative**—these substances change their mass with time. An example includes nitrate (NO_3-N).

Particulate Pollutant Transport

Since a pollutant is often a part of soils and sediments, many studies use a proportionality factor to describe particulate pollutant transport (Novotny, 2003). This relationship has been called the potency factor (p_i), which is included in:

$$Y_i = p_i \times Y_s \qquad [17.1]$$

where Y_i = loading or concentration of pollutant i
  Y_s = load or concentration of sediment

To determine p_i, the following is used:

$$p_i = S_{is} \times ER_i \qquad [17.2]$$

where S_{is} = soil concentration of pollutant i (µg/g of soil)
  ER_i = enrichment ratio, the ratio of the concentration in the stream to the concentration in soil

There are several disadvantages to the use of enrichment ratios. These ratios are not readily available for common pollutants. They also assume steady-state conditions, whereas future conditions cannot be predicted. Also, the potency factor is hard to obtain, and pollutants are more commonly associated with fine materials than with coarse materials.

Adsorption of Pollutants on Soil Particles

Many pollutants are immobilized by soils by (1) sorption onto soil particles, (2) precipitation reactions, and (3) transformation by bacteria. Adsorption is a function of the concentration of the pollutant in solution. Two approaches are used commonly to express the proportion adsorbed by soils:

1. Langmuir

$$S_e = \frac{Q^o \times b \times C_e}{1 + b \times C_e} \qquad [17.3]$$

where S_e = concentration in solid phase (µg/g)
  C_e = equilibrium solution concentration (mg/L)
  Q^o = adsorption maximum at temperature t (µg/g)
  b = a constant related to the energy of adsorption (L/mg)
  (Novotny, 2003)

The time to saturation can be determined by dividing the maximum saturation by the rate of application.

2. Freundlich

$$S_e = k \times C_e^{1/n} \qquad [17.4]$$

where k and n are fitted constants.

The test is conducted by preparing a series of beakers with soil and water with a range of concentrations of the pollutant of interest and shaking them until equilibrium occurs in the fraction of dissolved and particulate forms. The relationship between the concentrations is shown in Figure 17.1. The inverse of S_e and C_e would become a straight line, whereby the intercept would be the inverse of Q^o and the slope would be the inverse of $Q^o b$ (Novotny, 2003).

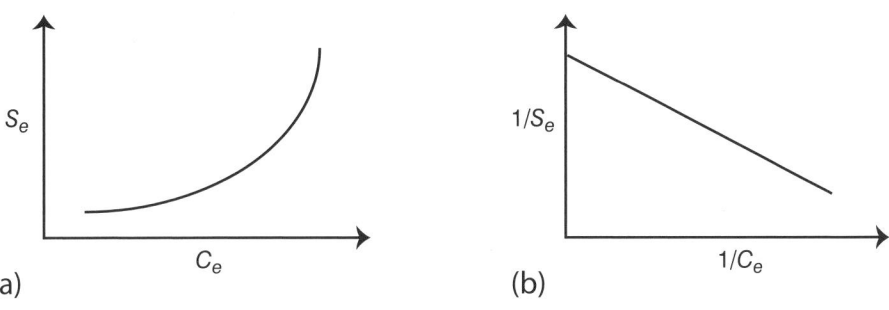

Figure 17.1 Relationship between sorbed (S_e) concentration and dissolved (C_e) concentration of a pollutant. (a) Plotted as concentrations and (b) plotted as the inverse of the concentrations.

As an example, the Langmuir isotherm was determined for phosphorus in milkhouse wastewater being applied to a filter strip in Vermont (Schwer and Clausen, 1989). The filter strip received 2.9 cm/wk of wastewater with a concentration of 55 mg/L PO_4. Using the Langmuir relationship, the sorption ability of the soil was determined to be 250 µg/g soil. Based on this ability it should have taken 0.7 year to fill up all of the sorption sites, but the filter strip continued to remove phosphorus from the wastewater. The reason that treatment continued was due to precipitation reactions also occurring in the soil. Phosphorus solubility in a soil is a function of pH, the concentration of P, and the presence of Ca and other ions, such as Al and Fe (Stumm and Morgan, 1970). The solubility diagram in Figure 17.2 indicates at pH > 7, phosphorus precipitates with Ca and Mg. At a pH < 5, P adsorption occurs with Al and Fe oxides. The maximum dissolved P occurs at a concentration of 10^{-5} mol/L, which is equivalent to 0.3 mg/L.

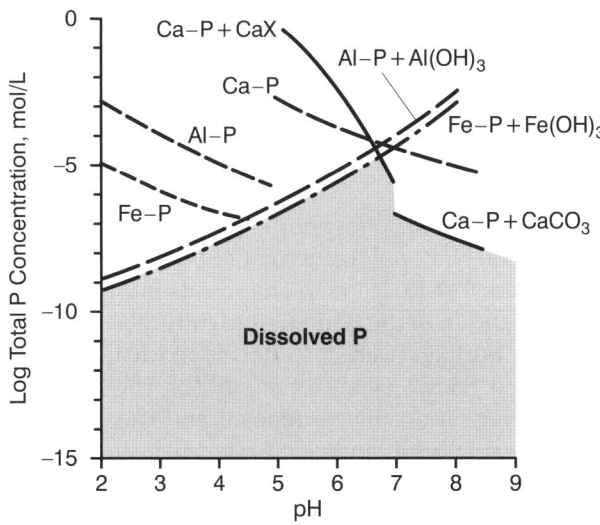

Figure 17.2 Solubility diagram for phosphorus (Hsu and Jackson, 1960. Used with permission of Wolters Kluwer).

The partitioning of P between dissolved and adsorbed phases can be described by:

$$[P_{total}] = S\rho + C\theta \qquad [17.5]$$

where P_{total} = concentration of total phosphorus
S = adsorbed concentration (μg/g soil)
C = dissolved concentration (mg/L)
ρ = density (g/cm^3)
θ = moisture content, which equals the porosity at saturation (Novotny, 2003)

Phosphorus Soil Index

USDA-NRCS developed an index to assess the potential risk of phosphorus movement to water bodies from agricultural fields (Lemunyon and Gilbert, 1993). The index is presented in an eight-by-five matrix. There are eight factors considered, some with different multiplier weights (times X). These are:

1. Soil erosion (1.5 X)

2. Irrigation erosion (1.5 X)

3. Runoff class (0.5 X)

4. Soil phosphorus test (1.0 X)

5. Phosphorus fertilizer application rate (0.75 X)

6. Phosphorus fertilizer application method (0.5 X)

7. Organic phosphorus application rate (1.0 X)

8. Organic phosphorus application method (1.0 X)

Each factor can receive one of five ratings: none, low, medium, high, and very high. The phosphorus index has been widely adopted in several states and modified in some. A nitrogen index has also been developed (Delgado et al., 2008).

Soil Mass Balance

State mass balances for phosphorus (Table 17.1) and nitrogen (Table 17.2) were presented in the National Academy Report on Soil and Water Quality (National Research Council [NRC], 1993). The results indicated that, in general, there is a buildup of P and N in the nation's agricultural soils (Chapter 11).

Nitrogen budgets were also developed for 16 large watersheds in northeastern United States (Boyer et al., 2002). The estimated inputs, in order of magnitude, were atmospheric deposition (31%), food and feed (25%), nitrogen fixation on agricultural lands (24%), fertilizer inputs (15%), and nitrogen fixation in forests (5%). Riverine export only accounted for 25% of the total inputs, indicating high amounts of either storage in the watersheds or losses through denitrification. Inputs varied significantly in different portions of the region, and forested watersheds had different inputs than agricultural watersheds.

Table 17.1 Phosphorus in soils as percentage of total mass input, selected states.

	Inputs			Outputs		Net Balance
	Fertilizer	Manure	Residual	Crop	Residue	
CT	61	39	<1	7	<1	92
MN	80	12	8	36	8	56
FL	94	6	<1	3	<1	97
WI	66	30	5	27	5	68

Source: Data extracted from NRC, 1993.

Table 17.2 Nitrogen in soil as percentage of total mass input (medium scenario), selected states.

	Inputs				Outputs		Net Balance
	Fertilizer	Manure	Legumes	Residual	Crop	Residue	
CT	48	36	16	1	29	1	71
MN	39	6	38	17	58	17	28
WI	31	21	38	11	56	11	33
U.S.	45	8	33	14	51	14	36

Source: Data extracted from NRC, 1993.

Toxic Metals in Soils

Toxic metals can enter soil from atmospheric deposition and road runoff; smelters, ore deposits, and mines; and sewage sludge on agricultural lands (Novotny, 2003). There are two types of metals based on their use by organisms. These include:

1. Biogenic metals—essential metals for living organisms (Fe, Cu, Mg, Cl)

2. Nonbiogenic metals—can accumulate in tissue and are toxic (Hg, Pb, Cd, Cr)

Metal Processes. Many metals precipitate or are adsorbed by soil. These include: Mn, Fe, Al, Cr, As, Pb, and Hg. Some metals, such as Cd, Cu, Mo, Ni, and Zn, are taken up by plants easily, depending on the pH. At a higher pH there is lower metal mobility.

Processes Operating in Soils. There are several processes operating in soils that modify and remove pollutant concentrations. **Adsorption** occurs when ions on the surface of soil particles attract the charges on ions or molecules of chemicals in solution. **Chemical precipitation** is a reaction that results in the formation of insoluble products. **Hydrolysis** is the reaction between a pollutant and water. **Volatilization** is the transfer of a chemical from soil to air. **Biological degradation** is the decomposition of organic compounds by microorganisms. **Plant uptake** of dissolved chemicals in soils occurs as part of the transpiration process.

Ground Water

Ground water is the source of about 23% of fresh water withdrawals in the United States, most (68%) of which is used for irrigation (Kenny et al., 2009). Ground water is the source of 19% of the U.S. public water supply. The quality of ground water at various locations throughout the United States has been affected by various contaminants. A U.S. EPA (1990) study found that concentrations of nitrate greater than 0.15 mg/L were found in 52% of community wells. Ten percent of community wells contained at least one pesticide or degradant. For domestic wells, nitrate concentrations greater than 0.15 mg/L were found in 57% of the wells. Dimethyl tetrachloroterephthalate (DCPA), also called Dacthal, was the second most common pollutant and was found in 2.5% of wells. It is a preemergent herbicide used to kill crabgrass and broadleaved weeds in many applications. Atrazine was the third most common pollutant (0.7%). It is widely used in agriculture for pre- and postemergent weeds. Nitrate concentrations greater than 10 mg/L were detected in 1.2% of community wells and 2.4% of rural domestic wells. The major sources of contaminants in ground water are spills, agrochemicals, road salt, landfills, and leaky underground storage tanks (Table 17.3).

Table 17.3 Sources of ground water contaminants.

Sources	Contaminants
Atmosphere	Hg, Cd, NO_x, SO_x
Agriculture	NO_3, pesticides, P, pharmaceuticals
Hazardous waste sites	Metals, VOCs
Landfills	VOCs, metals
Mining	Metals, acid mine drainage
Road salt	Na, Cl
Septic tanks	N, P, bacteria, pharmaceuticals
Spills	Organic and inorganic chemicals
Underground storage tanks	VOCs, petroleum

Sources: Tchobanoglous and Schroeder, 1987; Novotny, 2003.

Contaminant Transport

Three main processes governing contaminant transport are advection, diffusion, and reactions.

1. **Advection** is transport caused by the flow of water. The rate of contaminant spread is governed by the velocity of ground water flow. Because the velocity of flow is not uniform due to heterogeneity in the aquifer, the contaminant spreads out (Figure 17.3). This process is called **dispersion**.

2. **Diffusion** is the rate of contaminant spread governed by the concentration gradient. In ground water flow terminology, diffusion is usually not separated from dispersion.

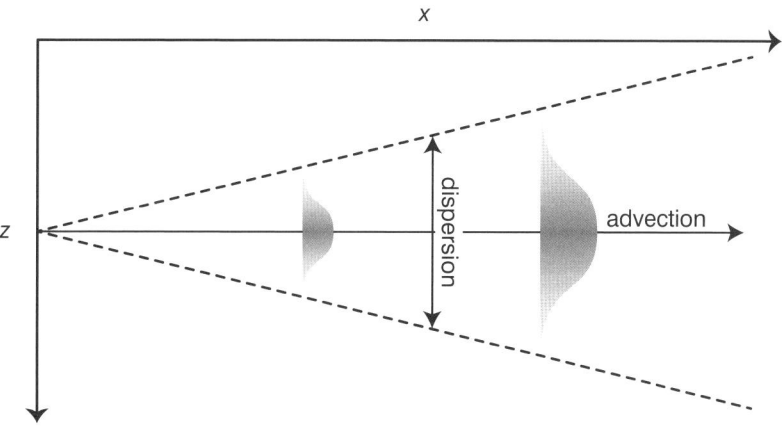

Figure 17.3 Effect of advection and dispersion on contaminant spread (after Novotny, 2003).

3. **Reactions.** Various reactions can occur in ground water systems that will reduce the concentration of the pollutant. These reactions are similar to those operating in soils and include adsorption, precipitation, and hydrolysis.

With regard to time, contamination sources are usually classified as continuous (released over a long period of time) or instantaneous (a one-time release such as that which occurs with a spill).

Continuous Sources. An example of a continuous source is a landfill. This type of source produces a plume downstream because the contaminant follows the flow of water (advection), while spreading out (dispersion) as a result of the heterogeneity of pore spaces in the subsurface zone (Figure 17.4).

The concentration at any point downstream from a continuous source assuming one-dimensional flow can be predicted from:

$$C = \frac{C_0}{2}\left[erfc\left(\frac{L-V_x t}{2\sqrt{D_t t}}\right) + \exp\left(\frac{V_x L}{D_L}\right) erfc\left(\frac{L+V_x t}{2\sqrt{D_t t}}\right)\right] \qquad [17.6]$$

where C = pollutant concentration
  L = distance
  t = time
  C_0 = source concentration
  D_L = longitudinal dispersion coefficient
  V_x = velocity in the x direction
  D_t = transverse dispersion coefficient
  erfc = error function complementary, which is $1 - erf(x)$, which is the error function (Novotny, 2003)

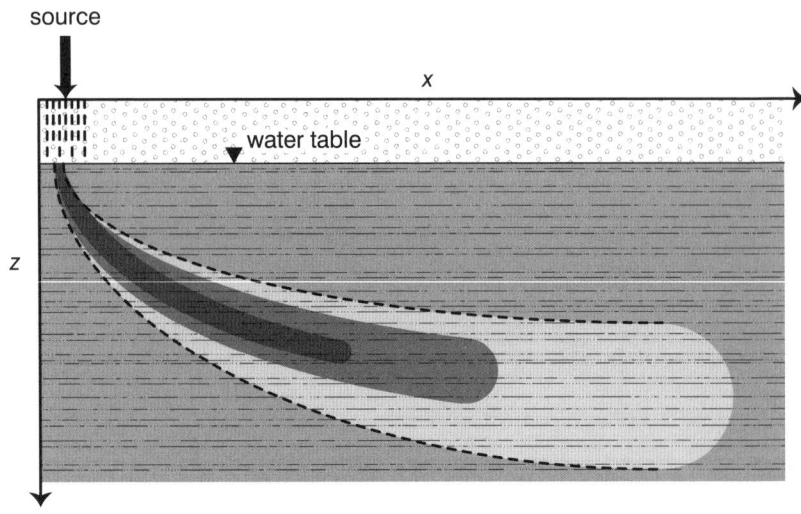

Figure 17.4 Plume of contaminant downstream of continuous source (after Novotny, 2003).

Contaminant velocities can be determined from:

$$v = \frac{k(h_1 - h_2)}{p}$$ [17.7]

where p = porosity (%)

Typical porosities and hydraulic conductivities (k) are summarized in Table 17.4.

EXAMPLE 17.1 Contaminant Velocity

For a sandstone aquifer with ground water slope(s) of 1%, how fast would the contaminant velocity be?

$$v = \frac{ks}{p} = \frac{10^{-4} \times 0.01}{0.15} = 6.67 \times 10^{-6} \text{ cm/s} = 210 \text{ cm/yr}$$ [17.8]

Instantaneous Sources. A spill can produce instantaneous sources. The spill moves as a plug downstream while it spreads out (Figure 17.5). The concentration downstream from the point of discharge assuming two-dimensional flow can be estimated from:

$$C(x,y,t) = \frac{m}{4\pi p (D_L D_t)^{0.5} t} \exp\left(-\frac{(x-Vt)^2}{4D_L t} - \frac{y^2}{4D_t t}\right)$$ [17.9]

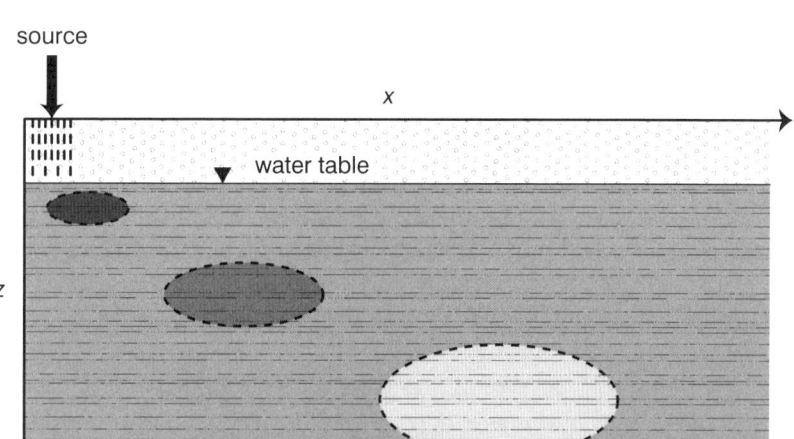

Figure 17.5 Contaminant spread downstream from a spill (after Novotny, 2003).

where m = mass of released contaminant/unit thickness of aquifer
x = distance in the x direction
y = distance in the y direction
p = porosity (Novotny, 2003)

At the point of the center of the plume, the concentration would be:

$$C(x,y,z,t) = \frac{M}{8(\pi t)^{0.5} p\sqrt{D_x D_y D_z}} \exp\left(-\frac{x^2}{4D_x t} - \frac{y^2}{4D_y t} - \frac{z^2}{4D_z t}\right) \quad [17.10]$$

where M = total mass of the contaminant (Novotny, 2003).

Table 17.4 Typical porosities and hydraulic conductivities for various aquifer materials.

Material	Porosity (%)	Hydraulic Conductivity (cm/s)
Sandstone	10–20	10^{-6}–10^{-3}
Sand & gravel	20–35	10^{-3}–10^{-1}
Gravel	30–40	1–100
Sand	30–45	10^{-4}–10^{-1}
Silt	40–50	10^{-6}–10^{-4}
Clay	45–55	10^{-9}–10^{-6}

Source: Data extracted from Novotny, 2003.

Contaminant Remediation

Three main approaches are used to remediate contaminated ground water (Novotny, 2003; Tchobanoglous and Schroeder, 1987).

1. **Containment.** Containment is used to control the spread of the contaminant. This can be achieved by surface sealing, such as a clay cap used for landfills. The cap prevents infiltration of precipitation, which could move contaminants downward. A physical barrier can be added to contain ground water, for example, a plastic liner placed in a trench. Or a hydraulic barrier can be created by using pumping and injection wells (Figure 17.6).

2. **Removal.** Removal of the contaminant can be achieved by pumping ground water, dredging sediment, or excavating soils. Sometimes the treated water can be reinjected. The removed water and soil can then be treated by a variety of means.

3. **Treatment.** Treatment of contaminated ground water can occur in place. Various chemicals have been added to ground water to change the chemical structure of the contaminant. Other additions assist microorganisms in breakdown of the pollutant.

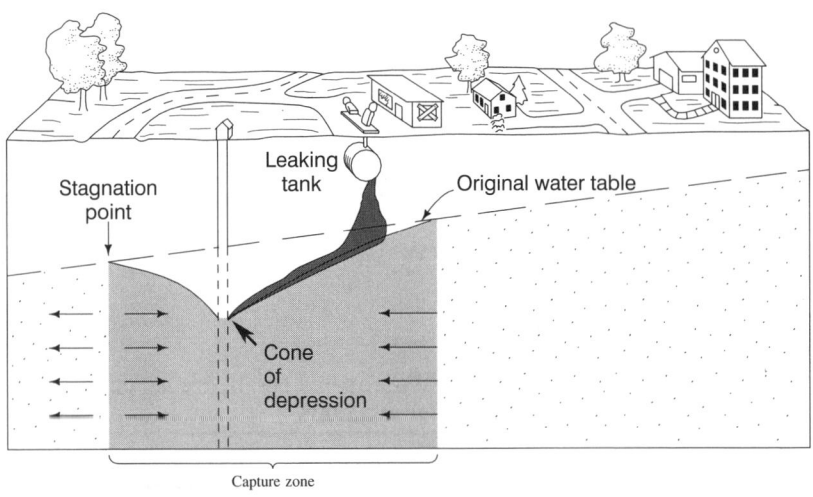

Figure 17.6 Barrier well downstream from a leaking underground tank (Fetter, 1999).

■ Problems

17.1 Determine the time of travel for a contaminant to reach a river from surface-applied wastewater using Darcy's law. Assume no reactions along the way. The head is 10 m and the length of flow is 500 m. The contaminant is traveling through sand alluvium with a hydraulic conductivity of 10^{-3} cm/s and a porosity of 0.4.

CHAPTER 17 Soil and Ground Water Quality   215

17.2 Determine the contaminant velocity in a sand and gravel aquifer near a stream. The slope of the ground water table surface is 0.5%. Assume there are no reactions with the contaminant.

17.3 Determine the phosphorus retention capacity (g P) in a filter strip assuming that its reaction follows a Langmuir isotherm. The dimensions of the filter strip are 10.6 m wide, 26 m long, and 1 m deep. The bulk density of the soil is 1.32 g/cm^3. The sorption capacity was determined to be 250 µg/g.

17.4 If the rate of application of phosphorus in Problem 17.3 is 3.15 cm/wk at a concentration of 55 mg/L, how long would it take to saturate the soil with phosphorus?

17.5 For Problem 17.1, if the initial concentration of the contaminant at the source was 50 mg/L, what would be the concentration discharged to the river assuming a first-order reaction coefficient k of 0.008/d? See Eqn. 15.14.

REFERENCES

Boyer, E. W., C. L. Goodale, N. A. Jaworski, and R. W. Howarth. 2002. Anthropogenic nitrogen sources and relationships to riverine nitrogen export in the northeastern U.S.A. *Biogeochemistry* 57/58: 137–169.

Delgado, J. A., M. Shaffer, C. Hu, R. Lavado, J. Cueto-Wong, and P. Joosse, et al. 2008. An index approach to assess nitrogen losses to the environment. *Ecological Engineering* 32: 108–120.

Fetter, C. W. 1999. *Contaminant Hydrogeology*. 2nd ed. Reissued 2008. Long Grove, IL: Waveland Press.

Hsu, P. H., and Jackson, M. L. 1960. Inorganic phosphate transformations by chemical weathering in soils as influenced by pH. *Soil Science* 90(1): 16–24.

Kenny, J. F., N. L. Barber, S. S. Hutson, K. S. Linsey, J. K. Lovelace, and M. A. Maupin. 2009. *Estimated use of water in the United States in 2005*. U.S. Geological Survey Circular 1344. Reston, VA: U.S. Geological Survey.

Lemunyon, J. L., and R. G. Gilbert. 1993. The concept and need for a phosphorus assessment tool. *J. Product. Agric.* 6: 483–496.

National Research Council (NRC). 1993. *Soil and water quality: An agenda for agriculture*. Committee on Long-Range Soil and Water Conservation. Board on Agriculture. Washington, DC: National Academy Press.

Novotny, V. 2003. *Water quality: Diffuse pollution and watershed management*. 2nd ed. New York: John Wiley & Sons.

Novotny, V., and G. Chesters. 1981. *Handbook of nonpoint pollution: Sources and management*. New York: Van Nostrand Reinhold.

Schwer, C. B., and J. C. Clausen. 1989. Vegetative filter treatment of dairy milkhouse wastewater. *J. Environ. Qual.* 18: 446–451.

Stumm, W., and J. J. Morgan. 1970. *Aquatic chemistry: An introduction emphasizing chemical equilibria in natural waters*. New York: Wiley-Interscience.

Tchobanoglous, G., and E. D. Schroeder. 1987. *Water quality characteristics, modeling and modification*. Menlo Park, CA: Addison-Wesley.

U.S. Environmental Protection Agency. 1990. *National pesticide survey: Summary results of EPA's national survey of pesticides in drinking water wells*. Office of Water and Office of Pesticides and Toxic Substances. Cincinnati, OH: U.S. EPA National Service Center for Environmental Publications.

18

Best Management Practices

■ Introduction

A **best management practice (BMP)** is defined as a method for preventing or reducing nonpoint source pollution to a level compatible with water quality goals (Novotny and Olem, 1994). These practices have also been called acceptable management practices as part of a regulatory program in Vermont (10 V.S.A. 1259, 1986). The term **management measure** was used in Section 6217 of the Coastal Zone Reauthorization Act (U.S. EPA, 1993). Management measures were defined in this act as:

> economically achievable measures for the control of the addition of pollutants from existing and new categories and classes of nonpoint sources of pollution, which reflect the greatest degree of pollutant reduction achievable through the application of the best available nonpoint pollution control practices, technologies, processes, siting, criteria, operating methods, or other alternatives.

In this chapter, the various BMPs used are described as well as their effectiveness, if known. The chapter is organized by major land use category where the BMP might be applied and includes urban, agricultural, and silvicultural BMPs.

■ Urban Stormwater BMPs

The quantity and quality of stormwater runoff from impervious areas have resulted in significant environmental degradation (Chapter 12). A large array of BMPs have been developed to deal with stormwater runoff and its subsequent effects. Practices used for stormwater control are also called stormwater management practices (SWM) (National Research Council, 2009), and green infrastructure (GI). The U.S. EPA (2014) states that "green infrastructure uses natural hydrologic features to manage water and provide environmental and community benefits." However, prior definitions of this term usually refer to an interconnected network of green space that conserves natural ecosystem function and value (Benedict and McMahon, 2002).

There are two general approaches to manage stormwater nonpoint source pollution. One is to control the sources, the other is to control delivery. The control of sources involves onsite prevention. General methods to control sources are to increase infiltration, retain runoff (rather than detain), reduce erosion, and reduce atmospheric deposition. General methods to control delivery include changing the storm drainage system, adding infiltration and sedimentation basins, adding storage basins (detention), and treating the physical, chemical, and biological characteristics of runoff. Ferguson (1998) describes five management alternatives for stormwater control: conveyance, detention, extended detention, infiltration, and water harvesting onsite. There are four general goals or principles in stormwater management:

1. **Reduce runoff.** Runoff prevention or reduction is the foremost tool in stormwater management. If runoff can be reduced, then nonpoint source pollution is also reduced from a downstream loading perspective. Methods to reduce runoff are aimed at increasing infiltration, and sometimes evapotranspiration, and include grid pavers, porous pavement, rain gardens/bioretention, dry wells, infiltration trenches, infiltration basins, and off-line trenches (Schueler, 1987).

2. **Trap oil and sediment.** Oil-grit separators of various designs are used to capture larger particles and floatable materials, including oils and grease. Collected materials may be viewed as hazardous materials, and disposal can be a problem.

3. **Pollution prevention.** The first consideration in the management of stormwater quality is to prevent pollutants from entering the stormwater system in the first place. Some of these approaches are general good housekeeping practices, such as preventing fertilizers from being applied to impervious areas (e.g., sidewalks). Other examples include vegetating exposed soils, preventing erosion, and managing lawns with reduced fertilizers and pesticides. Washing vehicles on impervious areas can be another source of pollutants. The National Research Council (2009) report on stormwater also describes product substitutions, such as phosphorus-free fertilizers, to reduce inputs to stormwater runoff.

4. **Pollution treatment.** Once other methods have been applied and pollutants enter the stormwater system, additional treatment approaches are needed to mitigate pollution. Common approaches include extended detention ponds, wet ponds (Figure 18.1), stormwater wetlands, multiple ponds, dry in-filter systems, sand filters, grassed swales (Figure 18.2), filter strips, and to a certain extent, rain gardens.

CHAPTER 18 Best Management Practices   219

Figure 18.1 Wet pond in Maryland (author photo).

Figure 18.2 Grassed swale in a residential neighborhood (author photo).

Given these four principles, urban stormwater BMPs are described for the planning or pre-construction period, the construction period, and the post-construction or operation period.

Planning and Construction Period

Watershed planning theoretically should be able to manage the amount of stormwater runoff, but few examples of this approach exist (National Research Council, 2009). BMPs have been developed for urban areas for use before and during construction. Practices should start with planning the project to minimize stormwater potential and may include zoning approaches. Cluster designs, the use of open space, reserves, narrow roads, and reduced setbacks from roads can all help reduce imperviousness. Stormwater utilities or districts are increasingly being used as a mechanism to control stormwater while providing a legal and funding mechanism through user fees (National Research Council, 2009). In some cases, reduced user fees can be used as an incentive for developers to implement BMPs and thereby reduce their stormwater runoff. Various types of reserves and conservation areas can be another mechanism to preserve open space and reduce stormwater runoff. These can include stream, wetland, and coastal buffers. During the construction of new developments, the BMPs are mostly erosion and sediment control practices. These BMPs are organized by general practices, vegetation stabilization, perimeter controls, traps and basins, extraordinary control, and erosion and sediment control.

General Practices. Planning of new construction is perhaps the most important step in preventing runoff and nonpoint source pollution. The design of the project should fit the site, rather than remake the site to fit the project. Examples of important planning considerations include the size of the development, alterations to topography, and the connectedness of impervious areas. It is desirable to minimize the area disturbed to maintain existing soil structure for infiltration. Keeping as much intact forest and soil as possible will allow infiltration and prevent excess runoff. Consideration of offsite runoff onto the site should be incorporated into the development plan to minimize runoff problems. Such clean runoff should be diverted around the construction site. Final slopes on a development can accelerate erosion, funnel water to impervious areas, and make installation of bioretention difficult.

Vegetation Stabilization. Several approaches are available for establishing vegetation on disturbed areas. These include: temporary seeding, mulching, using vegetative buffer strips, and protecting trees and shrubs with fencing.

Perimeter Controls. A perimeter control can be used to surround the disturbed area either to contain it or to prevent runoff from entering it. A diversion of clean runoff around an area will reduce erosion of disturbed areas. An earthen berm with grass can be used to contain runoff on the site, allowing ponding behind the berm (Bedan and Clausen, 2009). Silt fences, sometimes with straw bales, are a common perimeter device. They partly contain the disturbed area and also provide some level of treatment.

Traps and Basins. When erosion and sedimentation are inevitable, it may be necessary to collect and trap the sediment onsite. Criteria for sizing a sediment trap can be based on the volume of 3,600 ft^3/acre (Maryland Department of the Environment, 2011) for drainage areas up to 10 acres. Sediment basins are designed based on the expected erosion rate (50 tons/ac/yr for construction sites), the delivery ratio, drainage area, sediment density, and trap efficiency (80%) (Connecticut Council on Soil and Water Conservation and Connecticut Department of Environmental Protection, 2002). Often, a sediment basin is used following construction as a detention basin after it is cleaned out. Sediment bags (silt bags, dewatering bags) can also be used. These filter out the sediment in a removable bag and allow water to pass through.

Extraordinary Controls. Sensitive watersheds may need even more controls to protect downstream areas. Examples of such practices include oversized basins, immediate stabilization of exposed soils, and onsite inspections and cleanup after each storm.

Erosion and Sediment Control. Urban construction projects routinely use sediment and erosion control practices. Some of these practices entail little or no cost, such as storing excavated soils away from watercourses or using only one route to a building site. Soil grading practices are important. The concept of phased grading means that only the area that needs to be exposed for the day is opened up (e.g., stripped of vegetation or leveled). At the end of that work day, the exposed area is protected with erosion control. Phased grading is suggested in contrast to the common practice of stripping the entire site at once. Generally, rough grading of the site is preferred to smoothing because it encourages surface storage and infiltration. Stockpiles of earthen materials should be protected with temporary vegetation and sometimes perimeter controls. Other common practices include temporary revegetation of exposed sites, protection of stormwater catch basins with filter fabric and hay bales (Figure 18.3), silt fence, erosion control fabric, mulch, and sediment traps. Roof downspout extenders may be used across exposed soils to prevent erosion. Post-storm maintenance and frequent street cleaning are good housekeeping practices.

The effectiveness of various erosion and sediment control practices are summarized in Table 18.1.

Post-Construction Period

A wide variety of practices can be employed to treat or prevent stormwater runoff as part of urban development or as a retrofit. Schueler (1987) presents excellent summaries of many of these practices. A discussion of several practices follows, given in order of stormwater origin in a treatment train approach.

First, to prevent stormwater runoff from impervious areas, various kinds of grid pavers (Figure 18.4) and porous pavements (Figure 18.5) can be used. Roof runoff can be directed into a dry well for infiltration. Rain barrels/cisterns (Figure 18.6) are also used for rainwater harvesting (National Research Council, 2009). Adding green roofs can reduce roof runoff (Gregoire and Clausen, 2011).

Table 18.1 Effectiveness of erosion and sediment control practices in removal of total suspended solids (TSS).

Practice	% Removal	
	Average	Range
Sod	99	98–99
Seed	90	50–100
Seed & mulch	90	50–100
Mulch		0–100[1]
Terraces	—	55–70
All erosion and sediment control (E&SC)	85	—
Sediment basin	70	55–100
Sediment trap	60	–7–100
Silt fence	70	0–100[2]
Straw bale	70	—
Filter strip	70	20–80

[1] Function of soil, slope, and mulch material
[2] Function of soil type

Sources: Clausen and Dietz, 2014; U.S. Environmental Protection Agency, 1993.

Figure 18.3 Catch basin sediment protection (author photo).

CHAPTER 18 Best Management Practices   223

Figure 18.4 Grid pavers allow infiltration (author photo).

Figure 18.5 Porous asphalt in a parking lot (photo by Michael Dietz, UConn Center for Land Use Education and Research).

Figure 18.6 Rain barrel on residential property (author photo).

Runoff from paved areas can be treated with a perimeter (infiltration) trench or swale, a bioretention (rain garden) area (Figure 18.7), or filter strips if near a body of water. Based on several studies, bioretention has been shown to decrease runoff volume by a median of 75% (National Research Council, 2009). Second, once water enters the stormwater drainage system, it can be treated with a perforated stormwater pipe, an oil-grit separator, or an off-line trench. Subsurface infiltration systems can also be used, and sometimes are installed underneath impervious parking lots. An alternative stormwater conveyance system to traditional curb-and-gutter systems is to use swales with check dams, which allow infiltration. Third, at the end of the stormwater pipe, various types of wet ponds, extended detention basins, and wetlands can be used for treatment.

The effectiveness of these various stormwater management practices in reducing pollutants in stormwater runoff is presented in Table 18.2.

Road and Highway BMPs

Roads and highways require unique stormwater management practices because of their long, linear features. These practices are organized into planning, construction, and operation and maintenance sections.

Planning. Like many urban projects, the appropriate planning, siting, and design of road and highway projects can prevent excess runoff and nonpoint source pollution. New and widened roads should be located away from sensitive water bodies, should limit the disturbance to natural drainage patterns, and should limit clearing, grading, and cut-and-fill areas (U.S. EPA, 1993). Adequate buffers should be used to separate roads from water bodies. The susceptibility of soils to erosion should also be considered in site design. Structural controls most likely will have to be located within the highway corridor, and adequate space is needed in the layout design for such practices.

Figure 18.7 Bioretention rain garden in a residential lawn to collect roof and driveway runoff (author photo).

Table 18.2 Average effectiveness of stormwater management practices on pollutant removal.

Practice	% Removal			
	TSS[1]	TP[2]	TN[3]	Zn[4]
Infiltration basin	75	65	60	65
Infiltration trench	75	60	55	65
Vegetated filter strip	65	40	40	60
Grass swale	60	20	10	60
Porous pavement	90	65	85	100
Concrete grid pavers	90	90	90	90
Sand filter	80	50	35	65
Water quality inlet	35	5	20	5
Water quality inlet & sand filter	80	—	35	65
Oil/grit separator	15	5	5	5
Extended detention dry pond	45	25	30	20
Wet pond	60	45	35	60
Extended detention wet pond	80	65	55	20
Constructed wetland	65	25	20	35

[1] TSS Total suspended solids
[2] TP Total phosphorus
[3] TN Total nitrogen
[4] Zn Zinc

Sources: Clausen and Dietz, 2014; U.S. Environmental Protection Agency, 1993.

Construction. Many of the erosion and sediment controls used in other urban developments are appropriate for road and highway projects. Construction of bridges can be particularly important because they often occur at a water body crossing and therefore have the potential for nonpoint source impacts. In addition to the actual roadway area, road construction often utilizes "borrow areas" for a source of fill material, and disposal areas to get rid of cut materials and rock, which can also have nonpoint source impacts. It is particularly important to stabilize cut-and-fill areas.

Operation and Maintenance. Most erosion and sediment control practices require periodic inspection and maintenance. Roads and highways also require maintenance of slopes, periodic cleaning of road surfaces, deicing salt management, and snow-disposal management. Pesticide and fertilizer management in roadway corridors is also appropriate. Frequent sweeping of streets (≥1 pass/week) has been reported to remove 20% of the total suspended solids (U.S. EPA, 1993).

Stormwater management practices are also appropriate for road and highway operation. Common practices include filter strips, grassed swales, check dams, detention basins, constructed wetlands, and infiltration trenches (U.S. EPA, 1993).

Agricultural Practices

The Natural Resources Conservation Service (NRCS) uses the term "conservation practices" rather than "BMPs" for methods to control nonpoint source pollution (U.S. Department of Agriculture, Natural Resources Conservation Service, 2014). There are six main categories of agricultural conservation practices that pertain to nonpoint source pollution, and each of these categories will be discussed:

1. Erosion and sediment control
2. Confined animal facility management
3. Nutrient management
4. Pesticide management
5. Grazing management
6. Irrigation water management

Erosion and Sediment Control

This category includes a variety of practices aimed at reducing field erosion. Within fields they include conservation cropping, crop residues, delayed planting, terraces, grassed waterways, strip cropping, cover crops, and conservation tillage. At the edges of fields are diversions, field borders, filter strips, wetlands, and riparian zones. The practices are listed below with a brief description of each; numbers in parentheses are practice code numbers. Detailed technical guides for the NRCS conservation practices can be found at http://www.nrcs.usda.gov/wps/portal/nrcs/detailfull/null/?cid=nrcs143_026849

Practice	Code	Description
• Conservation cover	(327)	establishing and maintaining permanent vegetation on lands retired from agriculture
• Conservation cropping	(328)	planned sequence of crop rotations for organic maintenance of soil
• Conservation tillage	(329)	30% residue after planting
• Constructed wetland	(656)	constructing an artificial wetland ecosystem to treat wastewater and contaminated runoff or improve the quality of stormwater runoff
• Contour systems	(330)	use of ridges, furrows, etc. on sloped land to control direction and velocity of water flow
• Cover & green manure crop	(340)	e.g., winter rye for seasonal vegetative cover

Chapter 18 Best Management Practices

Practice	Code	Description
• Critical area planting	(342)	plant trees, shrubs, or other vegetation on highly erodible soil
• Crop residue use	(344)	retain plant residues to protect cultivated fields during critical erosion periods
• Delayed seed bed preparation	(354)	leave residue until three weeks before planting
• Diversion	(362)	channel across the slope with a supporting ridge on the lower side
• Field border	(386)	plant perennial vegetation at edge of or around perimeter of a field
• Filter strip	(393)	strip of vegetation for removing sediment, organic matter, and pollutants from runoff and wastewater
• Grade stabilization structure	(410)	in channels, control grade or head cutting, prevent advance of gullies
• Grassed waterway	(412)	vegetated channels to convey runoff at non-erosive velocities
• Grasses and legumes in rotation	(411)	produce organic matter
• Riparian forest buffer	(391)	trees and shrubs adjacent to watercourses or water bodies
• Sediment basins	(350)	built to collect and store sediment, preserve capacity of ditches, etc. (mostly on construction sites)
• Strip cropping systems:		
◊ Contour strip cropping	(585)	bands of grass on the contour alternating with a tilled crop
◊ Field strip cropping	(586)	bands of grass across the general slope (not on contour) alternating with a tilled crop
• Terraces	(600)	earthen embankment, channel, and ridge-channel combination, located across the slope, which reduces the slope length
• Water and sediment control basin	(638)	earthen embankment across the slope to trap sediment and detain water (across minor watercourses)

Confined Animal Facility Management

Confined animal facility operations (CAFOs) occur where a large number of animals are confined to buildings or feedlots. Conservation practices are aimed at treating runoff from the site and properly storing animal wastes. Waste utilization is included with nutrient management. Practices at the site include:

Practice	Code	Description
• Dike	(356)	an earthen or constructed barrier to contain runoff
• Diversion	(362)	channel constructed across the slope with a supporting ridge on the lower side
• Grassed waterway	(412)	vegetated channel to carry water at non-erosive velocity
• Heavy use area protection	(561)	vegetation or other materials provide a stable surface for areas frequented by animals, people, or vehicles
• Lined waterway or outlet	(468)	erosion-resistant lining of concrete or rock
• Roof runoff management	(558)	gutters that collect, control, and convey precipitation runoff
• Terrace	(600)	earthen embankment, channel, and ridge-channel combination, located across the slope, which reduces the slope length

Practices to store wastewaters require an engineering design:

Practice	Code	Description
• Waste storage facility	(313)	impoundment or structure to temporarily store wastes
• Waste treatment lagoon	(359)	impoundment by excavation or embankment to treat wastes

Nutrient Management

Nutrient management (590) involves soil testing and determining the timing, amount, and method of application (e.g., split, banding) as well as the incorporation methods for nutrients and manure. It may also include the use of cover crops to scavenge nutrients, and the form and amount of nutrients applied. An underlying principle is pollution prevention; that is, to use only what is needed by the crop.

The effectiveness of nutrient management practices varies greatly by the type of practice used (Table 18.3). The most effective practices for phosphorus control relate to the method of fertilization, manure incorporation, and the use of conservation tillage. Implementation of a wide range of practices across a watershed has shown a reduction of 43% of dissolved phosphorus event loading (Bishop et al., 2005).

Table 18.3 Effectiveness of agricultural nutrient management practices.

Management Practice	Total Phosphorus Load Reduction (%)
Proper rate of fertilizer application	3
Optimum timing of fertilization	20
Optimum method of fertilization	Up to 90
Timing of manure applications	11–30
Incorporation of manure	80
Conservation tillage	80–90
Edge-of-field buffers	24–72
Riparian restoration / fencing	30–50

Sources: Jokela et al., 2004; Nonpoint Source Control Task Force, 1983.

Pesticide Management

Pesticide management practices can include integrated pest management (IPM) (595) as well as field management. IPM is a site-specific strategy that combines pest prevention, pest avoidance, pest monitoring, and pest suppression (NRCS, 2010). Reducing pesticide losses is another goal through efficient application and timing methods and the use of nonpersistent or low-mobility pesticides. Crop management includes resistant strains, crop rotations, cover crops, trap crops, and diversified habitat. Following are a number of practices for pesticide management.

- Efficient application methods — spot spray
- Resistant crop systems
- Nonpersistent pesticides
- Low-mobility pesticides
- Time field operation
- Scouting (looking for damage)
- Biological control:
  ◊ Natural enemies
  ◊ Preserve predator habitat
  ◊ Release sterile male insects
- Use pheromones

- Crop rotations
- Cover crops to prevent leaching
- Destroy pest overwintering sites
- Use trap crops
- Diversify habitat

The effectiveness of various pesticide management practices is summarized in Table 18.4. For most of the practices listed there is a wide range in the pesticide-loss reduction. This wide range is because the summary includes results from many studies, on different soil types, receiving water inputs in different ways; and includes many different pesticides, which by themselves react differently in the environment. Some loss reductions are a single number because they represent a single study. The most studied practice in use seems to be the edge-of-field vegetated buffer strip (Reichenberger et al., 2007).

Table 18.4 Effectiveness of agricultural pesticide management practices.

Management Practice	Pesticide Loss Reduction (%)
Proper rate of pesticide application	50–75
Minimum persistence & volatility types	100
Optimum method of application	50–75
Optimum timing of application	50
Integrated pest management	Up to 100
Safe handling, storage, disposal	Up to 50
Conservation tillage	42–70
Vegetated filter strips	18–100
Constructed wetlands	20–99

Sources: Nonpoint Source Control Task Force, 1983; Reichenberger et al., 2007; Sabbagh et al., 2009.

Grazing Management

Most grazing management practices can be classified as either animal management or crop management. Animal management practices include deferred grazing, calculated grazing use, planned water locations, and exclusion. Crop management includes improved vegetation cover. Conservation practices include:

- Prescribed grazing (528) – managing the harvest of vegetation with grazing (no. of animals/time/area)
- Watering facility (614) – provide water away from streams
- Fencing (382) – exclude livestock from streambanks and riparian areas
- Improve vegetation cover:
  ◊ Pasture and hayland planting
  ◊ Range seeding

The water quality effectiveness of various grazing management conservation practices is summarized in Table 18.5. Both exclusion fencing and providing an alternative source of water for livestock have been shown to have several water quality benefits. Livestock exclusion from streams generally has a quick response effect on stream phosphorus, with changes occurring within one year (Meals et al., 2010).

Table 18.5 Effectiveness of grazing management conservation practices.

Management Practice	Sediment Load Reduction	Total P Load Reduction
Permanent vegetative cover	<1 T/ac/yr	Very high
Reforestation of erodible crop / pastureland	<1 T/ac/yr	Very high
Offstream water source	90%	81%
Exclusion fencing	82%	42–78%

Sources: Agouridis et al., 2005; Meals, 2001; US EPA, 1993.

Irrigation Water Management

Conservation practices for irrigation water management include scheduling the rate, amount, and timing of irrigation; the method of irrigation (drip, trickle, sprinkler, surface, subsurface, field ditch, flooding); irrigation water transport systems (ditch, pipeline); and tailwater recovery. Irrigation practices include:

- Irrigation water management (449) – planning the volume, frequency, and application rate of irrigation water:
  ◊ Rate, amount, and timing of irrigation water
  ◊ Water measuring
  ◊ Soil and crop water-use data

- Transportation systems:
  ◊ Ditch/canal lining (428)
  ◊ Pipeline (430)
  ◊ Water-control structures

- Proper application is a function of crop, topography, and soil. Methods include:
  ◊ Drip or trickle
  ◊ Sprinkler
  ◊ Surface and subsurface
  ◊ Field ditch
  ◊ Land leveling

- Tailwater recovery (447) – use of runoff waters

- Management of drainage waters:
  - ◊ Filter strip – tailwater
  - ◊ Field ditch (388)

The effectiveness of these practices is summarized in Tables 18.6 and 18.7.

Table 18.6 Average effectiveness of irrigation BMPs on sediment removal.

Management Practice	Sediment Removal Efficiency (%)
Sediment basin	87
Buried pipe w/ mini-basins	83
Vegetative filters	50
Straw in furrows	50

Source: U.S. Environmental Protection Agency, 1993.

Table 18.7 Efficiencies of irrigation systems.

System	Efficiency (%)	Runoff Fraction (%)
Conventional furrow	60	22
Gated pipe	68	18
Shorter run	70	17
Tailwater recovery	73	6
Hand move sprinkler	80	11
Lateral move sprinkler	88	7
Drip	95	1

Source: U.S. Environmental Protection Agency, 1993.

■ Silvicultural Practices

Best management practices for silvicultural activities are usually designed for different parts of the operation, including: truck roads, skid trails, log landings, and stream crossings. Many states provide guidance or requirements to use best management practices or acceptable management practices.

Truck Roads. Truck roads are used to move logs from landings to a public road. Road design should minimize cut and fill. Truck roads should be constructed so that they are not too steep (less than 10% for 300 ft). They should include broad-based dips and culverts. They may also require temporary water bars. Broad-based dips should be at least 120 feet long and outsloped (Figure 18.8). Water bars should be constructed from 6 to 12 inches deep, 6 to 12 feet in length with a downslope berm (Figure 18.9). Spacing depends on the slope (Table 18.8). Turn-ups are outsloped turns across the slope that prevent water from running down the road (Figure 18.10).

CHAPTER 18　Best Management Practices　233

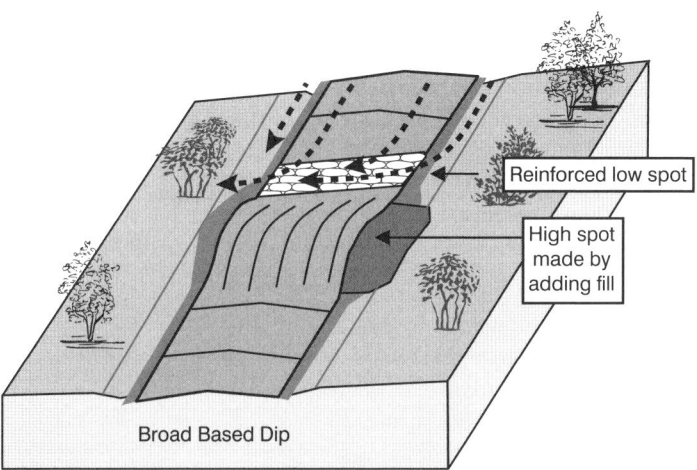

Figure 18.8 Broad-based dip on truck road. (Based on graphic by Steve Bloser, Sept. 2008 Technical Bulletin, Center for Dirt & Gravel Road Studies, Penn State University. Used with permission.)

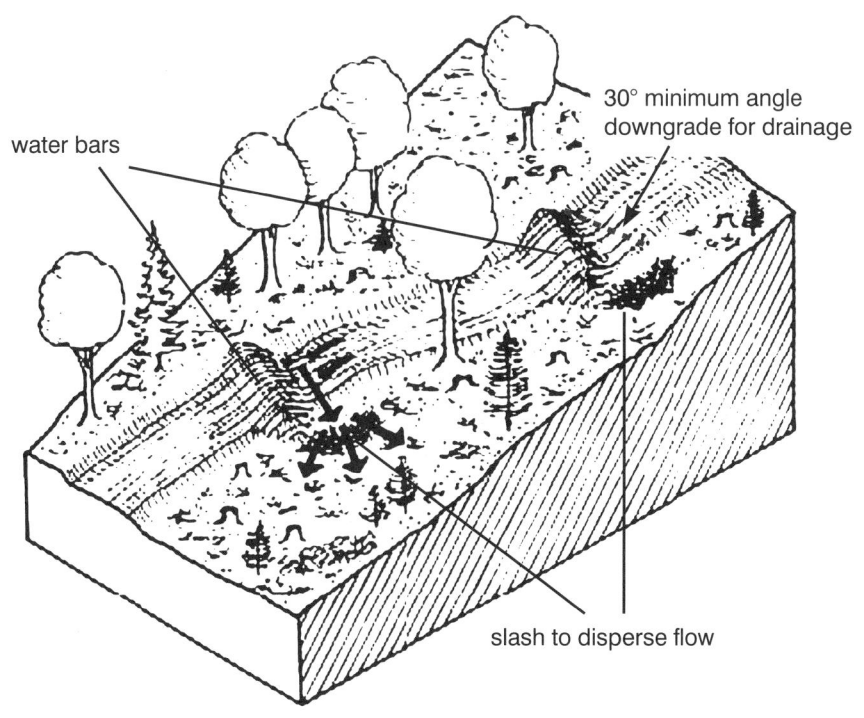

Figure 18.9 Water bar on skid trail. (New York State *BMP Field Guide*, 2011.)

Skid Trails. Skid trails should not have a slope greater than 20% for more than 300 feet. Ruts should be filled in to prevent gullying. Water bars should be installed at prescribed intervals, depending on the slope.

Log Landings. Landings are areas where forest products are brought for processing, sorting, and loading onto trucks (Connecticut Resource Conservation & Development Areas Forestry Committee, 1990). Log landings should be located on fairly level or slightly crowned, stable, and well-drained areas away from water bodies and outside protective strips. Tracking pads should be used where log trucks enter public roads.

Table 18.8 Water bar spacing on a skid trail.

Road Grade (%)	Water bar Spacing (ft)	Culvert Spacing (ft)	Dip, Turn-up Spacing (ft)
1	400	450	450–500
2	250	300	300
5	135	200	160–200
10	80	140	140
15	60	130	130
20	45	120	120
25	40	65	—
30	35	60	—

Sources: Connecticut Resource Conservation & Development Areas Forestry Committee, 1990; Vermont Department of Forests, Parks, and Recreation, 1987.

Stream Crossings. Stream crossings should be conducted only when necessary since they are the major source of sediment to streams (Brynn and Clausen, 1991). Crossings should be bridges on permanent streams. Skid trail fords should occur only in stable locations; however, this practice is easy to abuse and should be used with caution. Turn-ups in the approach roads should be used

Figure 18.10 Turn-up sloping out on truck road. (Connecticut *BMP Field Guide*, 2007.)

before stream crossings. Streams should be crossed at right angles. At harvesting closeout, nonpermanent structures should be removed and the banks and approach roads stabilized. Culverts may have to be designed by a hydrologist.

Stream Corridors. Streams should be kept free of all slash, and there should be no logging in the stream. A protective strip or buffer should be maintained along the stream in which either no machinery is allowed or selective cutting is permitted (Table 18.9).

Filter Strips. A protective strip is often used to keep machinery out of the stream as well as to prevent sedimentation. A strip also provides shade and coarse woody debris to the water body (Figure 18.11).

Table 18.9 Recommended width for buffer strip between truck roads and streams.

Land Slope (%)	Buffer Width (ft)
0	25
10	45
20	65
30	85
40	105
50	125
60	145
70	165

Source: Connecticut Resource Conservation & Development Areas Forestry Committee, 1990.

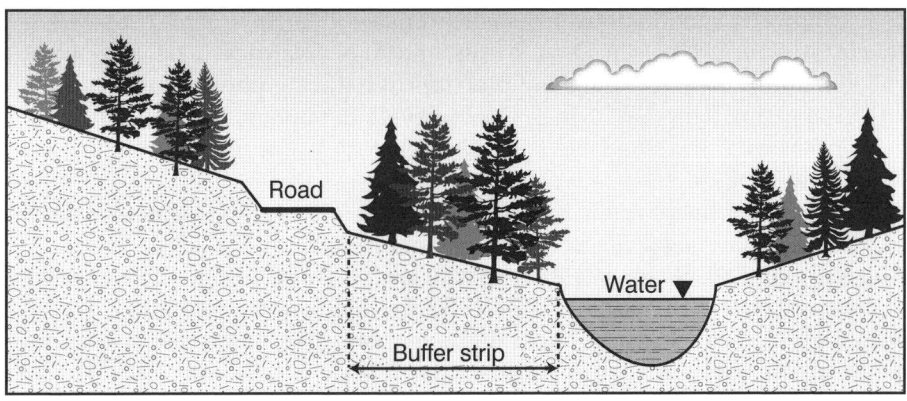

Figure 18.11 Diagram of a protective buffer strip.

Problem

18.7 For an in-depth exercise utilizing urban BMPs, see the "Structured Experiences" section of the online materials at waveland.com/Clausen.

References

Agouridis, C. T., S. R. Workman, R .C. Warner, and G. D. Jennings. 2005. Livestock grazing management impacts on stream water quality: A review. *JAWRA* 41(3):591–606.

Bedan, E. S., and J. C. Clausen. 2009. Stormwater runoff quality and quantity from traditional and low impact development watersheds. *J. Amer. Water Res. Assoc.* 45: 998–1008.

Benedict, M. A., and E. T. McMahon. 2002. Green infrastructure: Smart conservation for the 21st century. *Renewable Resources J.* 20(3): 12–17.

Bishop, P. L., W. D. Hively, J. R. Stedinger, M. R. Rafferty, J. L. Lojpersberger, and J. A. Bloomfield. 2005. Multivariate analysis of paired watershed data to evaluate agricultural best management practice effects on stream water phosphorus. *J. Environ. Qual.* 34:1087–1101.

Brynn, D. J., and J. C. Clausen. 1991. Postharvest assessment of Vermont's acceptable silvicultural management practices and water quality impacts. *Northern J. of Applied Forestry* 8(4): 140–144.

Clausen, J. C., and M. E. Dietz. 2014. Stormwater management. *Encyclopedia of Natural Resources* DOI: 10.1091/E-ENRW-120047552. Pages 436–442. Taylor & Francis.

Connecticut Council on Soil and Water Conservation and Connecticut Department of Environmental Protection. 2002. *Connecticut guidelines for soil erosion and sediment control.* DEP Bulletin 34. Hartford, CT.

Connecticut Resource Conservation & Development Areas Forestry Committee. 1990. *Timber harvesting and water quality in Connecticut.* King's Mark and Eastern Connecticut RC&D Areas.

Ferguson, B. K. 1998. *Introduction to stormwater: Concept, purpose, design.* New York: John Wiley & Sons.

Gregoire, B. G., and J. C. Clausen. 2011. Effects of a modular extensive green roof on stormwater runoff and water quality. *Ecological Engineering* 37: 963–969.

Jokela, W. E., J. C. Clausen, D. W. Meals, and A. N. Sharpley. 2004. Effectiveness of agricultural best management practices in reducing phosphorus loading to Lake Champlain. Pages 39–53 in T. O. Manley, P. L. Manley, and T. B. Mihuc (eds.), *Lake Champlain: Partnerships and Research in the New Millennium.* Boston: Kluwer Academic Publishers.

Maryland Department of the Environment. 2011. *Maryland standards and specifications for soil erosion and sediment control.* Baltimore, MD.

Meals, D. W. 2001. Water quality response to riparian restoration in an agricultural watershed in Vermont, USA. *Water Science and Tech.* 43(5):175–182.

Meals, D. W., S. A. Dressing, and T. E. Davenport. 2010. Lag time in water quality response to best management practices: A review. *J. Environ. Qual.* 39:85–96.

National Research Council. 2009. *Urban stormwater management in the United States.* Washington, DC: National Academies Press.

National Resources Conservation Service (NRCS). 2010. *National Conservation Practice Standards*. Accessed 01/15/2017 at http://www.nrcs.usda.gov/wps/portal/nrcs/main/national/technical/cp/ncps/

Nonpoint Source Control Task Force. 1983. *Nonpoint source pollution abatement in the Great Lakes Basin. An overview of post-PLUARG developments*. Report to the Great Lakes Water Quality Board. Windsor, ON: International Joint Commission.

Novotny, V., and H. Olem. 1994. *Water quality: Prevention, identification, and management of diffuse pollution*. New York: Van Nostrand Reinhold.

Reichenberger, S., M. Bach, A. Sktschak, and H.-G. Frede. 2007. Mitigation strategies to reduce pesticide inputs into ground and surface water and their effectiveness: A review. *Science of the Total Environment* 384:1–35.

Sabbagh, G. J., G. A. Fox, A. Kamanzi, B. Roepke, and J.-Z. Tang. 2009. Effectiveness of vegetative filter strips in reducing pesticide loading: Quantifying pesticide trapping efficiency. *J. Environ. Qual.* 38:762–771.

Schueler, T. R. 1987. *Controlling urban runoff: A practical manual for planning and designing urban BMPs*. Washington, DC: Department of Environmental Programs, Metropolitan Washington Council of Governments.

10 V.S.A 1259. 1986. Vermont Statutes. Title 10: Conservation and Development. Chapter 47: Water Pollution Control. §1259. Prohibitions.

U.S. Department of Agriculture, Natural Resources Conservation Service. 2014. Conservation practices. Accessed 10/23/2014 from http://www.nrcs.usda.gov/wps/portal/nrcs/detailfull/null/?cid=nrcs143_026849

U.S. Environmental Protection Agency. 1993. *Guidance specifying management measures for sources of nonpoint pollution in coastal waters*. USEPA 840-B-92-002. Washington, DC: Office of Water.

U.S. Environmental Protection Agency. 2014. *Green infrastructure basics*. Accessed 11/10/2014 from http://water.epa.gov/infrastructure/greeninfrastructure/index.cfm

Vermont Department of Forests, Parks, and Recreation. 1987. *Acceptable management practices for maintaining water quality on logging jobs in Vermont*. Waterbury, VT.

Part III

Water and Society

19

Water Laws, Regulations, and Standards

■ **Introduction**

Water quantity and quality is largely managed and protected through laws, regulations, and standards. A **law** is a body of rules of conduct of binding legal force and effect enforced by an authority (Baldwin, 1940). Laws in the United States are promulgated by federal, state, and local legislatures. Written laws are also termed **statutes**. Decisions by judges also have the force and effect of law, and are called **case** or **common law**. Various administrative agencies have been given the authority to create law through regulations, a process called promulgation. Usually such authority is granted by a statute. A **regulation** is a rule of order having the force and effect of law (Baldwin, 1940). The terms *rules* and *regulations* are synonyms. A **standard** is a rule, principle, or measure established by an authority (Novotny, 2003). A **criterion** is a scientific quantity upon which a judgment is based (Novotny, 2003). An example of a criterion would be the drinking water concentration of 10 mg/L nitrate-N. The president of the United States also can create laws through **executive orders**. Federal and state agencies have the power to issue orders requiring actions by groups or individuals to comply with specific laws and regulations. Such orders have penalties if not followed. Various federal acts are codified in the United States Code (U.S.C.). The acts of Congress are published as session laws in the statutes at large (**Stat**). Each Congress has two to four sessions. Acts in each session were numbered consecutively as chapters until 1957. A statute at large citation, for example, would be 86 Stat. 816, which means: volume 86, page number 816. Since 1957, acts of Congress have also been termed Public Laws (PL) X-Y, where X is the number of the Congress, and Y is the chronological number of the act

---

Note that the full text of the original acts mentioned in this chapter are available online at waveland.com/Clausen.

within that Congress. The Code of Federal Regulations (CFR) contains regulations including those pertinent to water quality and quantity. Citations to the code are read as "Title No., CFR, Part No." For example, the federal water quality standards regulations are found in 40 CFR 131, or Title 40, Part 131.

For convenience, water laws can be classified as either water quality laws or water quantity laws. This chapter therefore is divided into these two areas and summarizes the important federal legislation in the United States on water quality and quantity. This chapter also includes a summary of their contents. The language in original acts reflects the mood of the Congress, and often the country, at the time. The signing of acts is usually a public event. The statements made by presidents at the signing ceremonies provide additional information about the importance of the water issues of the time and are interesting reading.

Water Quality

Water quality laws in the United States have their foundation in the various Clean Water Acts and the total maximum daily load (TMDL) process. Table 19.1 provides a chronological list of important water quality legislation. The water quality act is codified in 33 U.S.C. §1251-1387. There are several other laws related to the water quality acts. These acts include the National Environmental

Table 19.1 Summary of federal water quality legislation.

Year	Act	Act Name
1899	30 Stat. 1121	Rivers and Harbors Appropriations Act
1944	PL 78-410	Public Health Service Act
1948	PL 80-845	Water Pollution Control Act of 1948
1956	PL 84-660	Water Pollution Control Act Amendments of 1956
1961	PL 87-88	Water Pollution Control Act Amendments of 1961
1965	PL 89-234	Water Quality Act of 1965
1966	80 Stat. 1608	Reorganization Plan No. 2
1966	PL 89-753	Clean Water Restoration Act of 1966
1970	PL 91-224	Water Quality Improvement Act of 1970
1970	84 Stat. 2086	Reorganization Plan No. 3 of 1970
1972	PL 92-500	Water Pollution Control Act Amendments of 1972
1977	PL 95-217	Clean Water Act Amendments of 1977
1981	PL 97-117	Municipal Wastewater Treatment Construction Grant Amendments of 1981
1987	PL 100-4	Water Quality Act of 1987
1990	PL 101-508	Coastal Zone Act Reauthorization Amendments of 1990

CHAPTER 19 Water Law   243

Protection Act of 1969 (NEPA), the Safe Drinking Water Act of 1974, and sometimes the Endangered Species Act.

The following paragraphs summarize the history of federal water quality legislation.

1. **Rivers and Harbors Appropriations Act (1899) 30 Stat. 1121** This act, which originally was the River and Harbor Act (1882) (22 Stat. 191), is considered the first piece of federal legislation addressing water quality. The original act, signed by President McKinley on March 3, 1899, mostly provided for the funding of improvements to specific rivers and harbors. It was also called the Refuse Act and controlled refuse disposal in rivers and harbors.

2. **Public Health Service Act (1944) (PL 78-410) 58 Stat. 682** The Public Health Service Act (42 U.S.C. 301) enacted July 1, 1944, enabled studies of pollution in lakes and streams by the Surgeon General (Krenkel and Novotny, 1980). This addition was a small paragraph in the 39-page bill.

3. **Water Pollution Control Act of 1948 (PL 80-845) 62 Stat. 1155** This act, dated June 30, 1948, is considered the first water pollution control legislation (Krenkel and Novotny, 1980). All future water pollution acts amended this one, although the Rivers and Harbors Act of 1899 is also commonly referenced. The major provisions of the act were to give a role to the federal government for interstate water pollution. Appropriations were to be $22.5 million annually for five years for a treatment works construction loan program that was never funded. Studies by states were funded at $1 million annually. The act recognized the rights of states in controlling water pollution.

4. **Water Pollution Control Act Amendments of 1956 (PL 84-660) 70 Stat. 518** The amendments of July 9, 1956, promoted water pollution jurisdiction by the states and limited the federal role to interstate waters. In Section 4, additional direction was given regarding studies, including disseminating information on chemical, physical, and biological water quality. Appropriations were authorized for planning grants and construction grants for treatment works. This law was administered by the Surgeon General of the Public Health Service. The act could be cited as the "Federal Water Pollution Control Act."

5. **Water Pollution Control Act Amendments of 1961 (PL 87-88) 75 Stat. 204** These amendments were signed July 20, 1961, by President Kennedy. The amendments transferred the program from the Surgeon General to the secretary of HEW (Health, Education and Welfare). Agencies were instructed to consider water quality in reservoir planning. HEW was instructed to study wastewater treatment to restore water quality. The act increased construction grants. The definition of interstate waters was expanded beyond just state boundaries to all waters (Sec. 9. [e]). The act established regional research labs and studies of the Great Lakes and waste treatment.

6. **Water Quality Act of 1965 (PL 89-234) 79 Stat. 903** This act, signed October 2, 1965, by President Johnson, restated the national policy for water pollution. It increased construction grants, included combined sewer systems, and provided additional monies for research and development. The program was administered by a newly created assistant secretary of HEW and named the Federal Water Pollution Control Administration (FWPCA). Under this act, each state was required to submit water quality standards for interstate waters for approval.

7. **Reorganization Plan No. 2 of 1966. 80 Stat. 1608** The FWPCA was moved into the Department of Interior through Reorganization Plan No. 2 by President Johnson on May 10, 1966, who stated, "One agency should assume leadership in our clean water effort. That agency should be the Department of the Interior."

8. **Clean Water Restoration Act of 1966 (PL 89-753) 80 Stat. 1246** This act provided grants to the states for comprehensive water quality planning on a basin basis and research and development grants (Krenkel and Novotny, 1980). The act called for a comprehensive estuary study and a study of pollution from watercraft. The term *basin* was defined. The Oil Pollution Act of 1924 was also amended.

9. **Water Quality Improvement Act of 1970 (PL 91-224) 84 Stat. 91** This act, signed April 3, 1970, added the control of pollution by oil and other hazardous substances, and simultaneously repealed the Oil Pollution Act of 1924. It added the control of sewage from vessels. Demonstrations of new methods to develop plans for the control of pollution in the watersheds of the Great Lakes were included. The demonstration of methods to control acid or other mine water pollution was also added. Training grants for treatment works operators were made available. The FWPCA was changed to the FWQA (Federal Water Quality Administration). A study of methods to control the release of pesticides into the water environment was included.

10. **Reorganization Plan No. 3 of 1970. 84 Stat. 2086** President Richard M. Nixon transmitted Reorganization Plan No. 3 on July 9, 1970, to Congress. The plan created the Environmental Protection Agency and transferred the Federal Water Quality Administration from the Department of the Interior to the EPA.

11. **Water Pollution Control Act Amendments of 1972 (PL 92-500) 86 Stat. 816** This important 89-page act was a major overhaul of the Water Pollution Control Act. It declared national goals to eliminate discharges of pollutants by 1985 (Sec. 101). Sec. 208 required state- and area-wide water treatment management programs, especially in areas with substantial water quality problems for both point and nonpoint sources. Plans were required to be completed before EPA would provide funds for construction grants. Plans must ensure that discharges were not in

excess of the natural waste assimilation capacity of the receiving waters. Point source discharges were declared unlawful (Sec. 301), and effluent limitations were established. Water quality standards were required (Sec. 303). The states were required to identify waters for which effluent limitations were not stringent enough to implement water quality standards (Sec. 303 [d][1]). The states also were required to establish, using priorities, the **total maximum daily load** for certain pollutants (Sec. 303 [d][1][C]). Sec. 305 required a water quality inventory of all point sources of discharge of pollutants and identification of the quality of waters meeting and not meeting uses, and the nature and extent of nonpoint sources of pollutants. Sec. 311 included the provisions regarding oil pollution. The clean lakes program was added in Sec. 314. The National Pollution Discharge Elimination System (NPDES) was created (Sec. 402). Point source dischargers were required to obtain a NPDES permit. The permit set effluent limitations, a compliance schedule, and required monitoring. Permits were initially issued by EPA but were then taken over by the states. EPA retained the power to veto a permit. Permits for disposal of dredged or fill materials into navigable waters were created (Sec. 404). The terms "pollutant," "navigable waters," "point source," and "pollution" were defined (Sec. 502).

The act was returned to the Senate with President Nixon's objections, but they were overridden by the Senate and the House with two-thirds majorities on October 18, 1972.

12. **Clean Water Act Amendments of 1977 (PL 95-217) 91 Stat. 1566** This 47-page act extended the appropriations beyond 1975. Grants for privately owned treatment works serving one or more residences were allowed. The ability to collect service charges was added and included industrial users. Construction grants were extended. The National Wetlands Inventory was funded. Contracts between operators and SCS (Soil Conservation Service) were allowed to promote best management practices to control nonpoint source pollution from agricultural operations with a 50% cost share. State 305(b) reports were changed from annually to biennially. The act identified a list of toxic pollutants and required effluent limitations using best available technology that was economically achievable for each pollutant listed. The act gave authority to states for permits issued under Section 404.

13. **Municipal Wastewater Treatment Construction Grant Amendments of 1981 (PL 97-117) 95 Stat. 1623** This amendment of the Federal Water Pollution Control Act limited grants to secondary or more stringent treatment and directed funds to address water quality problems in estuaries due to combined sewer overflows. Water quality management planning was extended. Secondary treatment was defined. Grants were not allowed unless water quality standards were submitted by the states.

14. **Water Quality Act of 1987 (PL 100-4) 101 Stat. 7** The biggest change provided in the Water Quality Act of 1987 was the addition of Section 319 covering nonpoint source pollution. In summary, that section required: state assessment reports that included information on (1) threatened navigable waters, (2) categories of nonpoint sources, (3) a process to identify BMPs to control nonpoint sources, and (4) state and local programs to control nonpoint source (NPS) pollution. It also required state management programs that (1) identified BMPs to reduce NPS pollution, (2) identified programs (e.g., regulatory, education, financial) to achieve implementation of BMPs by category, and (3) a schedule of milestones for implementation. The act provided a grant program for states to implement the management program; the federal share was 60%. Annual reports by the states were required on their progress in reducing NPS pollution, and by EPA to Congress on the progress being made. These reports are now biennial and are called 305(b) reports, or water quality reports, rather than reports to Congress. This act also created the national estuary program (Secs. 317 and 320). Municipal and industrial stormwater discharge permits were required.

15. **Coastal Zone Act Reauthorization Amendments of 1990 (PL 101-508) 104 Stat. 1388** The original Coastal Zone Management Act (CZMA) was passed in 1972. Section 6217 of the 1990 amendments required states with coastal zone management programs approved under CZMA to implement a coastal NPS control program. States were required to submit a program to NOAA/EPA for approval or lose funding. They were also required to adopt management measures, declare the coastal zone boundary, and develop enforceable policies to implement management measures. A guidance document was required by the act.

16. **Since 1990** There have been no major changes to the Water Pollution Control Act (Water Quality Act) since 1987, although changes have been proposed. Approved legislative changes have largely been for reauthorizing certain components of the act, such as the National Estuary Program (PL 106-457 and PL 108-399). Coastal water quality standards and monitoring were approved through PL 106-284, and the Great Lakes Legacy Act (PL 107-333) provided for contaminated sediment remediation in the Great Lakes.

■ Federal Regulations and Rules

There are a number of important rules and regulations that affect water quality management. Major rules are the water quality standards, stormwater regulations, and guidance on total maximum daily loads (TMDLs).

Water Quality Standards

Regulations for water quality standards are found in 40 CFR 131. These regulations define **criteria** as "elements of state water quality standards, expressed as constituent concentrations, level, or narrative statements, representing a quality of water that supports a particular use." **Standards** are defined as "provisions of state or federal law which consist of a designated use or uses for the water of the United States and water quality criteria for such water based upon such uses." State water quality standards must include as a minimum: (a) use designations, (b) methods used and analyses conducted to support water quality standards revisions, (c) water quality criteria sufficient to protect the designated uses, (d) an antidegradation policy, (e) certification by the state attorney general that the standards were properly adopted, and (f) general policies and information. The states can adopt narrative criteria based on biomonitoring where numerical criteria cannot be established. The antidegradation policy is to protect the level of water quality necessary to maintain existing uses. High-quality waters must also be maintained and protected.

Stormwater Regulations

Stormwater became regulated as a point source following the Clean Water Act Amendments of 1987. These regulations are found in 40 CFR 122.26. Phase I of the stormwater regulations was promulgated in 1990. Phase I used the National Pollution Discharge Elimination System (NPDES) and covered the following categories: medium and large municipal separate storm sewer systems (MS4s) serving populations of 100,000 or more, construction sites disturbing five acres or more of land, and various categories of industrial dischargers. Phase II of the stormwater regulations, published in 1999, expanded the program to small MS4s in urbanized areas, as defined by the Bureau of the Census, not already covered by Phase I, and small construction sites from one to less than five acres. The small MS4s were required to obtain permits and implement a stormwater management program. The overall purpose of the program is to reduce the discharge of pollutants to the maximum extent practicable, protect water quality, and comply with the Clean Water Act.

Total Maximum Daily Loads (TMDL)

A TMDL is a quantitative assessment of a water quality problem in an impaired water body to ensure that water quality standards are attained. It is the amount of a pollutant allowable in a water body and includes the allocation of allowable pollutant loads among sources. TMDLs are required by Sec. 303(d) of the Clean Water Act. There are 10 required elements of a TMDL (U.S. Environmental Protection Agency, 1999):

- water body identification
- pollutant identification and the maximum loading capacity of the water body
- present status of pollutant loading

- source identification
- wasteload allocation to point sources
- load allocation to nonpoint sources and background sources
- margin of safety
- seasonal variations
- future growth
- implementation plan

TMDLs include load allocations (LAs) and wasteload allocations (WLAs). An LA identifies the portion of the loading capacity attributed to existing and future nonpoint sources and the natural background. WLAs identify the portion of the loading capacity allocated to individual existing and future point sources. TMDLs generally do not apply to loss of aquatic habitat or flow regulation (e.g., dams). In Example 19.1, a TMDL for Long Island Sound between New York and Connecticut is presented.

Water Quantity

Laws discussed in this chapter related to water quantity include those surrounding basic water rights, floodplain management, and instream flows (see Table 19.2).

Water Rights (Law)

The term **water right** refers to the legal powers or privileges existing under the appropriate law to use water (Ingram et al., 1969), even though the actual water is owned by the state (Goldfarb, 1984). Water rights are considered "property" and therefore are protected by the Constitution from a "taking" without "just compensation." In some cases, water rights may be exchanged or traded. There are two main approaches to the right to use water in the United States: riparian and prior appropriation, although some states apply elements of both. The **riparian** (Latin, meaning "bank") doctrine applies to owners of land adjacent to water and means that they have a right to use the water (Cech, 2010; Goldfarb, 1984). This is also termed the common law approach to water appropriation. This type of water law is common in the eastern United States. Generally, the riparian right follows ownership and can be passed on to subsequent landowners. These landowners are even called "riparians" in some cases (Griffin, 2006). Two principles have been applied to the riparian doctrine. The first is the concept of **reasonable use**. A riparian landowner has the right to a reasonable amount of allocation or diversion with respect to other users of the water. During drought, the concept of what is a reasonable use may change. Permits are often used to determine what is a reasonable amount and timing of the appropriation. The second principle is that of **correlative rights**. A riparian landowner has the right to share the total amount of water available based on length of shoreline or sometimes proportion of watershed area. Private water companies can with-

EXAMPLE 19.1   Long Island Sound TMDL

Long Island Sound is impaired because of low oxygen levels caused by excess nitrogen loading. The goal of this TMDL is to reduce nitrogen loading by 58.5% from in-basin sources. The percentage is based partly on cost and reducing the unhealthy hypoxic area by 76% and the duration of hypoxia by 85%. The TMDL calls for a 10% reduction in nonpoint source loading. The base load was 47,788 tons/year in 1990. The goals were a reduction of 43.9% by August 2009 and 58.5% by August 2014.

TMDL for Long Island Sound, NY and CT

In-Basin Loads:

	N Load (tons/yr)	Percent of Total
WWTP	38,006	71
CSO	893	
Total point sources	38,899	73
Pre-colonial nonpoint	5,765	
Terrestrial nonpoint	1,843	3.5
Atmospheric nonpoint	6,764	13
Total nonpoint	14,372	27
Total	53,271	

Including boundary in and out of basin:

	N Load (tons/yr)	Percent of Total
Boundary fluxes	33,600	33.5
Pre-colonial	22,900	
Human activities	10,700	
Point Sources		41.7
Nonpoint sources		12.9
Atmospheric direct		5.5
Atmospheric indirect		6.4

draw water away from riparian land when they have been given "prescriptive rights" by the states (Goldfarb, 1984). The water rights are considered common property; that is, held among the other riparians in common (Griffin, 2006).

The **prior appropriation** doctrine allows water to be diverted for use on nonriparian lands, and the right is given by priority date of usage. This doctrine has been called "first in time, first in right" (Goldfarb, 1984). These rights are considered private property and can be sold or leased to others independent of the land on which the water is used. This prior use doctrine is common in the western United States. In addition to these basic principles, states may require

Table 19.2 Summary of federal water quantity legislation.

Year	Act	Importance
1920	41 Stat. 1063	Federal Power Act provided for licenses for dams and other related facilities.
1968	PL 90-448	National Flood Insurance Act authorized flood insurance program. (82 Stat. 572)
1972	PL 92-500	Sec. 401 required state certification of compliance with the Clean Water Act. (86 Stat. 816)
1973	PL 93-234	Flood Disaster Protection Act required flood-prone communities to participate, adopt an ordinance, and mandate flood insurance for property owners receiving loans. (87 Stat. 975)
1986	PL 99-495	Electric Consumers Protection Act amended the Federal Power Act to allow protection of, mitigation of damage to, and enhancement of fish and wildlife (including related spawning grounds and habitat), the protection of recreational opportunities, and the preservation of other aspects of environmental quality. Review by the U.S. Fish and Wildlife Service and state agencies was required. (100 Stat. 1243)

permits to withdraw water and may set limits on the allocation. Also, during emergency conditions, such as those experienced during a drought, states may have established priority allocations that supersede some of these rights. For example, human use may have priority over agricultural use. Minimum flow restrictions may also apply to some of these water rights. Water governed under prior appropriation can be lost by nonuse.

For ground water, land ownership is commonly used to determine water rights (Cech, 2010). A landowner has the right to install a well to withdraw that water, sometimes with no regard to neighboring users (Goldfarb, 1984). This principle is similar to the riparian doctrine. Both the reasonable use and correlative-rights principles, as described above, are also applied to ground water in some areas. However, reasonable use for ground water means that there can be no waste (Goldfarb, 1984). For ground water correlative rights, water is prorated among overlying landowners. Some states apply the prior appropriation doctrine using appropriation permits. The authority for ground water rights lies with the individual states. There are often limits on the minimum distance between wells.

The federal government has the right to reserve water for the federal lands that have been set aside for various purposes, such as parks. These so-called **reserved rights** are generally exempt from withdrawals (Goldfarb, 1984), but the amount set aside is limited to the purpose of use on the federal lands (Griffin, 2006). Instream flow rights are increasingly becoming common uses of water, and some government agencies are acquiring these rights by declaration or through water markets.

Basin Transfers

Large interbasin transfers take place in the United States, and most of these occur within a state. Many states prohibit the export of state water or highly regulate it. There have been many proposals to transport waters from one state to another, but most of these have not occurred (Goldfarb, 1984).

One of the largest and most famous interbasin transfer projects is the Colorado River Compact of 1922. The compact was enabled by federal legislation called "An Act to permit a compact or agreement between the States of Arizona, California, Colorado, Nevada, New Mexico, Utah, and Wyoming, respecting the disposition and apportionment of the waters of the Colorado River, and for other purposes" (42 Stat. 171). This Act gave the consent of Congress to the states to negotiate and enter into a compact to divide and apportion the water supply of the Colorado River and its tributaries among the seven states. Each state appointed a commissioner to negotiate on its behalf, while then-Secretary of Commerce Herbert Hoover served as the representative of the U.S. government.

The Compact divided the Colorado River watershed into the Upper Basin and Lower Basin, each receiving an equal allocation of 7.5 million acre-feet of water per year. The Upper Basin states are Colorado, New Mexico, Utah, and Wyoming; the Lower Basin states are Nevada, Arizona, and California. A long-running dispute between Arizona and California resulted in the U.S. Supreme Court apportioning 4.4 million acre-feet to California, 2.8 million acre-feet to Arizona, and 300,000 acre-feet to Nevada, plus all the water each state had in its tributaries (Gelt, 1997). The states in the Upper Basin agreed to assign their apportionment by percentage.

The Colorado River Compact provided a major allocation out of the basin to southern California through the Colorado River Aqueduct and the All American Canal. In Colorado, portions of the Colorado River are diverted across the continental divide, through the Rocky Mountains via a series of tunnels to the eastern slope (Warnick, 1969). This diversion feeds Denver, Ft. Collins, and Colorado Springs and neighboring communities.

Drainage Law

Drainage is a common practice in several states, particularly in the Midwest. In such states there exist statutory draining organizations, such as drainage districts. These laws govern the maintenance of ditches and drains and may tax district members. There is no federal drainage law, although section 404 of the Clean Water Act provides for regulation of dredging and filling in wetlands.

Floodplain Management

Floodplain management has largely arisen out of the destruction to life and property that has occurred throughout the United States as the result of flooding. The congressional response has been for the federal government to partner with private insurance companies and share the costs of flood insurance. The following acts and executive order have also required the purchase of flood insurance and the adoption of ordinances in floodplains to control development.

1. **National Flood Insurance Act of 1968 (PL 90-448) 82 Stat. 572**
   This act authorized a flood insurance program and required states and local governments to restrict development in flood-prone areas. It also

required identification of flood-risk zones and criteria to guide land development in floodplains.

2. **Flood Disaster Protection Act of 1973 (PL 93-234) 87 Stat. 975**
   This act expanded the National Flood Insurance program by increasing the coverage but also by requiring known flood-prone communities to participate in the program and adopt floodplain ordinances, and it required the purchase of flood insurance by property owners assisted by federally supervised institutions (including banks).
3. **Executive Order 11988 – Floodplain Management**
   In 1977 President Carter required federal agencies to restrict proposed actions in floodplains and to require the construction of federal structures and facilities to be consistent with floodproofing and other flood protection measures. The order also defined the base flood as having a probability of occurrence of 1% in a year, and the floodplain was the area inundated by that flood.

Instream Flows

Instream flows are regulated under a number of federal and state laws (Zellmer, 2008). The Federal Power Act of 1920 for hydropower resources as amended (now 16 U.S.C. Chap. 12, Subchapter I regulation of the development of water power and resources) originally did not provide for setting minimum flows. However, license renewals have allowed for setting of minimum flows for various beneficial public uses of water. A later amendment, the Electric Consumers Protection Act of 1986, required the Federal Energy Regulatory Commission to include license conditions that provide for the equal consideration to the enhancement of fish and wildlife, protection of recreation opportunities, and the preservation of other aspects of environmental quality. The Endangered Species Act provides protection to "listed" endangered species from harm or jeopardy, including providing for adequate water quantity. The Wild and Scenic Rivers Act of 1968 also provides flow protection to "designated" rivers. The Clean Water Act (originally PL 92-500) in Sec. 401 requires that "any facility which may result in any discharge of pollutants to navigable waters shall obtain a certification from the state" that the discharge will comply with the Clean Water Act. This provision has also allowed the inclusion of minimum instream flow stipulations by the states (Zellmer, 2008). Several states also regulate instream flows in some way for certain purposes.

■ **REFERENCES**

Baldwin, W. E. 1940. *Bouvier's law dictionary*. Cleveland, OH: Banks-Baldwin Publishing Company.

Cech, T. V. 2010. *Principles of water resources: History, development, management and policy*. 3rd ed. New York: John Wiley & Sons.

Gelt, J. 1997. *Sharing Colorado River water: History, public policy and the Colorado River Compact*. Arizona Water Resources Research Center. Tucson: University of Arizona.

Goldfarb, W. 1984. *Water law*. Boston: Butterworth Publishers.
Griffin, R. C. 2006. *Water resource economics: The analysis of scarcity, policies, and projects.* Cambridge, MA: MIT Press.
Ingram, W. T., R. A. Gerber, W. Martin, and M. A. Shapiro. 1969. *Glossary: Water and wastewater control engineering.* APHA, ASCE, AWWA, WPCF. Washington, DC: Joint Editorial Board.
Krenkel, P. A., and V. Novotny. 1980. *Water quality management.* New York: Academic Press.
Novotny, V. 2003. *Water quality: Diffuse pollution and watershed management.* 2nd ed. New York: John Wiley & Sons.
U.S. Environmental Protection Agency. 1999. *Draft guidance for water quality-based decisions: The TMDL process.* 2nd ed. EPA 841-D-99-001. Washington, DC: Office of Water.
Warnick, C. C. 1969. Historical background and philosophical basis of regional water transfer. In W. McGinnies and B. Goldman (eds.), *Arid Lands in Perspective.* Tucson: University of Arizona Press and American Association for the Advancement of Science.
Zellmer, S. 2008. Legal tools for instream flow protection. Chapter 12 in A. Locke, C. Stalnaker, S. Zellmer, K. Williams, H. Beecher, T. Richards, C. Robertson, A. Wald, A. Paul, T. Annear, and Instream Flow Council, *Integrated approaches to riverine resource stewardship: Case studies, science, law, people, and policy.* Instream Flow Council.

Water Laws, Regulations, and Standards (for the complete text, see the online materials at waveland.com/Clausen):

30 Stat. 1121. 1899. Rivers and Harbors Appropriations Act.
41 Stat. 1063. 1920. Federal Water Power Act.
58 Stat. 682. 1944. Public Health Service Act. PL 78-410.
62 Stat. 1155. 1948. Water Pollution Control Act of 1948. PL 80-845.
70 Stat. 518. 1956. Water Pollution Control Act Amendments of PL 84-660.
75 Stat. 204. 1961. Water Pollution Control Act Amendments of 1961. PL 87-88.
79 Stat. 903. Water Quality Act of 1965. PL 89-234.
80 Stat. 1608. 1966. Reorganization Plan No. 2 of 1966.
80 Stat. 1246. 1966. Clean Water Restoration Act of 1966. PL 89-753.
82 Stat. 572. 1968. National Flood Insurance Act of 1968. PL 90-448.
84 Stat. 91. 1970. Water Quality Improvement Act of 1970. PL 91-224.
84 Stat. 2086. 1970. Reorganization Plan No. 3 of 1970.
86 Stat. 816. 1972. Water Pollution Control Act Amendments of 1972. PL 92-500.
87 Stat. 975. 1973. Flood Disaster Protection Act of 1973. PL 93-234.
91 Stat. 1566. 1977. Clean Water Act Amendments of 1977. PL 95-217.
42 FR 26951, 3 CFR (44 CFR 9). 1977. Executive Order 11988: Floodplain Management.
95 Stat. 1623. 1981. Municipal Wastewater Treatment Construction Grant Amendments of 1981. PL 97-117.
100 Stat. 1243. 1986. Electric Consumers Protection Act of 1986. PL 99-495.
101 Stat. 7. 1987. Water Quality Act of 1987. PL 100-4.
104 Stat. 1388. 1990. Coastal Zone Act Reauthorization Amendments of 1990. PL 101-508.
33 U.S.C. §1251-1387. 2011. Navigation and navigable waters.

20

Water Policy

■ Introduction

A **policy** is a statement intended to guide actions to a desirable outcome. **Water policy** encompasses a range of approaches that can be applied to water management. Water policy mostly involves governance and the public sector, although private policies also exist. Common policy instruments include legislation, regulations, legal agreements, and criteria (Lawford et al., 2003). Water policies often originate from prominent water issues or problems, such as inadequate water supply, flooding, or poor water quality. As Figure 20.1 illustrates, policy is influenced by many elements in a complicated web of competing interests that includes politics, budget availability, public opinion and values, fragmentation of policy communities, personal interests, bargaining, the available policy window, and system capacity (Kingdon, 2003).

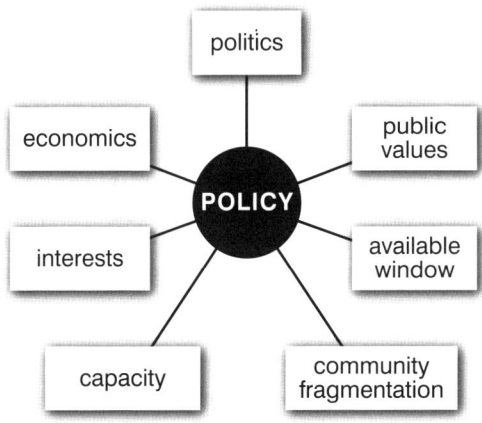

Figure 20.1 Factors influencing policy.

Different governmental jurisdictions in the world have unique concerns for water resources. Some examples of these are shown in Table 20.1. There are some basic characteristics of government in the United States that influence all environmental policy, including water policy. States maintain several roles pertinent to water policy. First, as compared to the federal government, they regulate private land, sometimes sharing this role with local governments (Klyza and Sousa, 2008). States also implement national water pollution control laws in concert with the federal government. States can be characterized as being policy innovators, finding new and unique ways to manage water problems. Increasingly, state ballot measures are being used to create policy. The effect of some of these characteristics is that management, policy, and enforcement vary greatly from state to state. However, states are not very effective in solving issues that cross state borders.

This chapter focuses on how water policy is formulated. Water availability and use are also included because use is strongly associated with water rights. A section is provided on international water policy, and the topic of water and environmental justice is also included.

Table 20.1 Examples of governmental jurisdiction's focus on water resources.

Jurisdiction	Focus	Example
Global—United Nations	World	Intergovernmental Panel on Climate Change
Trans-boundary multination	Boundary waters	International Joint Commission (U.S. and Canada)
Federal government	National	Clean Water Act
U.S. states	State waters	Water allocation
U.S. states	Basins	Sec. 208 program

Policy Formulation

There are many approaches to formulating policy. Often there is an absence of a formal approach to policy formulation, or an ad hoc process. However, a more directed approach is more useful for formulating a policy that meets the needs of a particular problem. The process of creating policy usually begins with an understanding of the **present system**. In some cases the present system is undirected, and a more managed approach is needed (Figure 20.2). There may be conflicting uses and needs for the water resources. This conflict leads to a **problem definition**, asked in the form of a question. For example, "What is the prudent use of the water resource?" The problem would generate the **identification of key issues**. For example, an inventory of the available water resources would be appropriate, as would the demands for water. Analyzing institutional problems and the environmental, social, and economic impacts

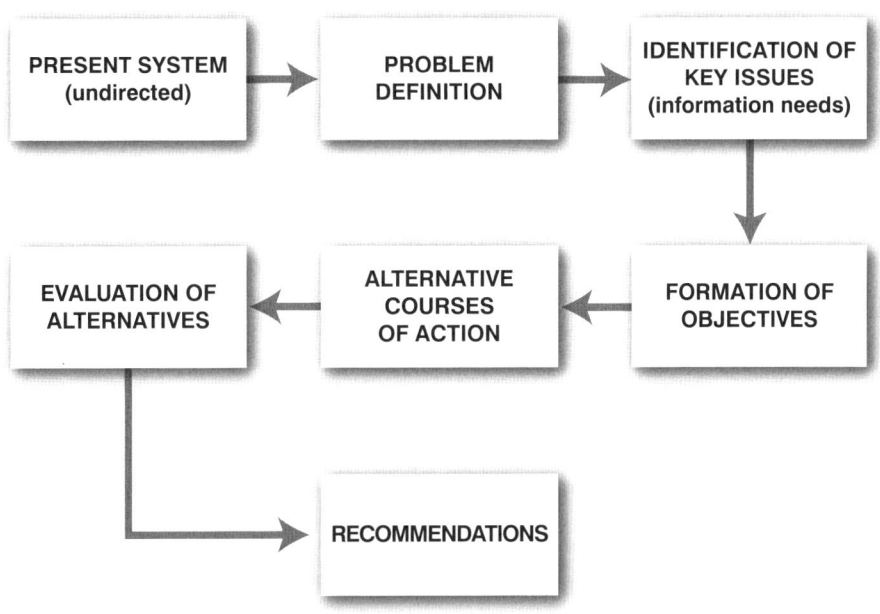

Figure 20.2 Program-planning steps for policy formulation.

could also be key issues. Examples of institutional problems could be the lack of regulatory powers, or powers divided among many agencies. Different stakeholders (someone with a stake in the decision being made) may have differing needs to be addressed. Examples of stakeholders could be urban interests and agricultural producers. Several **management objectives** could be formed based on the information obtained. Example objectives might be: "To ensure the proper utilization of water" or "To ensure future water-use capabilities." Such objectives would serve as a basis for determining **alternative courses of action**. Such alternatives might include proposing legislation, doing nothing, or proposing mitigated actions. Finally, **recommendations** are made after the analysis of alternatives. For example, "Meeting water-use needs will be prioritized based on a hierarchy established by law." Or, "Proposals to increase water withdrawals will be subject to existing permit statutes." Additional steps could be added to Figure 20.2, including implementation, monitoring the results, and modifying the policy as needed.

■ Water Availability and Use

The water-use industry has a number of specialized terms. Water **withdrawal** refers to ground water and surface water taken from local sources or water transported by large infrastructure projects (Christian-Smith, 2012). This term is sometimes called water use. **Consumptive use** is water that is unavailable for reuse because it has evaporated or transpired, has become part of plant material, or is contaminated. **Nonconsumptive use** is water that is available for reuse, for example as irrigation return flows. **Conjunctive use** is the combination of surface and groundwater resources (National Research Council, 1997).

Trends in water withdrawals indicate a rise in total withdrawals up to the 1980s, followed by a leveling in withdrawals thereafter, even though population has continued to increase (Figure 20.3). Withdrawals for thermoelectric power generation are the largest single use, but this use is nonconsumptive and can be further used downstream. Irrigation use is considered largely consumptive. Over three-quarters of water withdrawals in the United States are from surface water sources (Figure 20.4).

The trend in the amount of land irrigated shows a general increase over the years, based on the USDA Census of Agriculture (Figure 20.5). However, the amount of water withdrawn for irrigation has remained relatively steady since 1956 due to irrigation efficiencies (Figure 20.6).

The concept of water availability is complex. To be "available" water must be of sufficient quantity and quality while being legally, socially, and technologically accessible. In general, the amount of water that might be available would be determined by precipitation minus evapotranspiration. Water availability compared to water use in the United States is mostly a local/regional issue. There are water surplus and water deficit areas (Reilly et al., 2008).

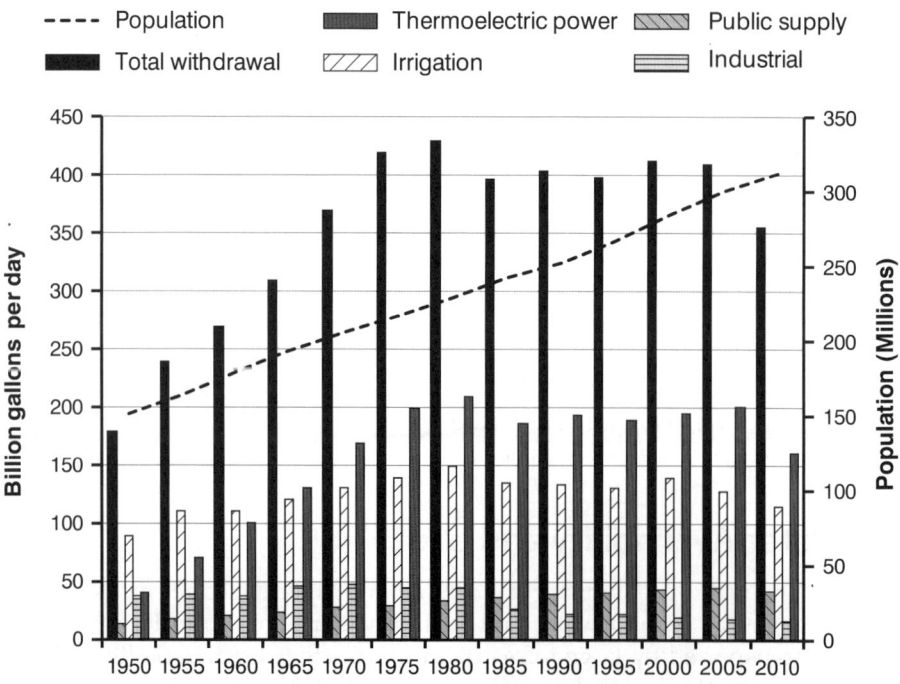

Figure 20.3 U.S. water withdrawals and population (data from Maupin et al., 2014).

CHAPTER 20 Water Policy   259

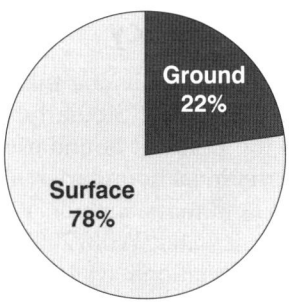

Figure 20.4 Proportion of water withdrawals by source (from Maupin et al., 2014).

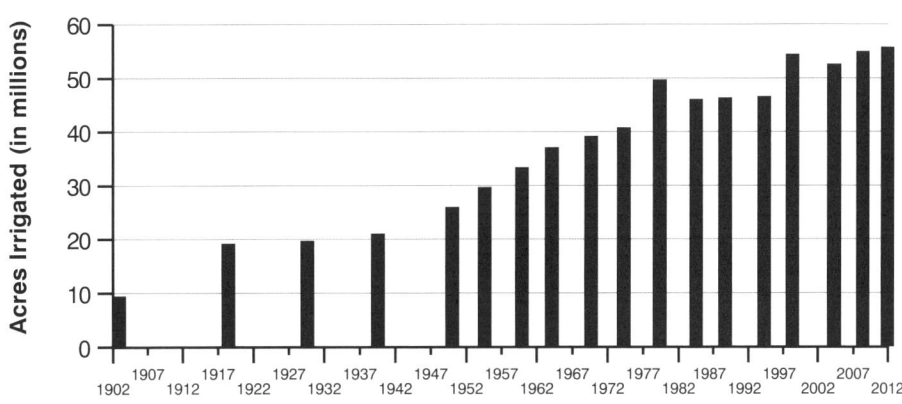

Figure 20.5 Acres irrigated (U.S. Department of Commerce/U.S. Department of Agriculture, *Census of Agriculture*, multiple years).

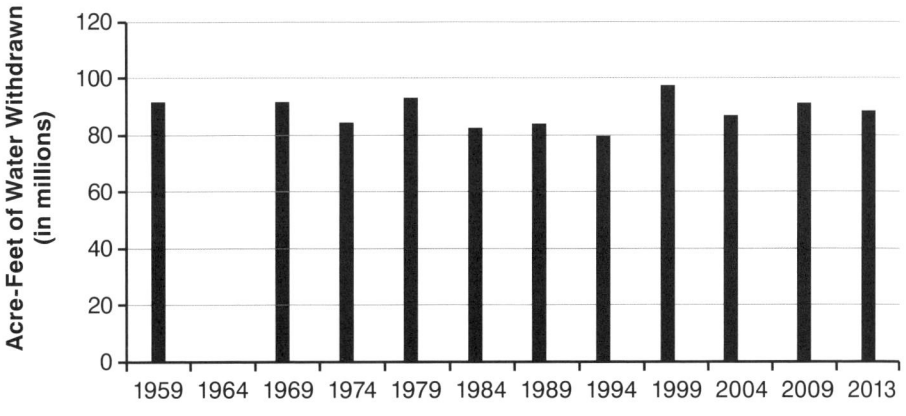

Figure 20.6 Acre-feet of water withdrawn (U.S. Department of Commerce/U.S. Department of Agriculture, *Census of Agriculture*, multiple years).

International Water Policy

An **international watercourse** is one that has parts in different nations, such as a river or lake (Wolf, 2007). Similarly, an **international watershed** (basin, catchment) crosses the political boundaries of at least two nations. Globally, 263 rivers cross international boundaries. The watersheds that feed these rivers cover 47% of earth's land mass, include 40% of earth's population, and supply 60% of the world's fresh water (Wolf, 2007). There are currently 145 nations that have land within an international watershed. Many of these watersheds include multiple nations. For example, the Danube watershed includes 17 nations (Wolf, 2007). Several problems have occurred with international watercourses. Generally, these are upstream versus downstream issues and include:

- Dam construction
- Diversions
- Irrigation withdrawals
- Water quality (salt, nutrients, sediment)
- Wastewater inputs

About 60% of the U.S. land area is part of an international watershed (Gleick, 2012). The shared river basins include the Mississippi, Columbia, Rio Grande, and Colorado. There are two notable treaties covering most of the U.S. international watersheds: (1) the U.S.–Mexico 1944 treaty on the Colorado, Tijuana, and Rio Grande rivers (U.S. and Mexico, 1946), and (2) the 2005 Great Lakes–St. Lawrence River Basin Sustainable Water Resources Agreement (Great Lakes Compact Council, 2005). The U.S.–Mexico treaty created the International Boundary and Water Commission (IBWC). The treaty governs allocations of river waters to each nation, management of water quality, flood control, and reservoir storage. The Canada–U.S. agreement has evolved over the years and is now legally binding. It facilitates planning, water management, and the exchange of data, and prevents large withdrawals.

On a global basis, the United Nations adopted the Millennium Declaration in 2000 that called for reducing the proportion of people unable to reach or afford safe drinking water, stopping unsustainable exploitation of water resources, and promoting equitable access and supplies of water (United Nations, 2000). The U.S. Agency for International Development (USAID) provides funding for water and sanitation-related projects in a variety of countries throughout the globe.

Water and Environmental Justice

Environmental justice studies indicate that low-income communities and certain economically disadvantaged rural areas have a disproportionate number of environmental problems, including contaminated ground water (Vanderwarker, 2012). These problems affect human health and the value of these communities. The concept of environmental justice means that public policy should be based on respect and justice for all people, with no discrimination or bias. Water justice responds to the need for access to an adequate amount and quality of water for various intended uses, including drinking, aquatic life support, and recreation. Water supplies for migrant workers in a North Carolina study showed higher levels of coliform bacteria than those for other farm workers (Evans and Kantrowitz, 2002). Low-income nonwhite farm workers also exhibit greater body burden of chlorinated hydrocarbons and pesticides. Higher levels of coliform have also been observed in rural drinking water supplies to low-income households when compared to others. Socioeconomic status also has been associated with the consumption of contaminated fish or swimming at polluted beaches. Other examples of water-related environmental justice issues are listed below (Vanderwarker, 2012).

- The siting of major water-related structures like dams
- The siting of toxic facilities (e.g., hazardous waste storage, refineries)
- Higher exposure to contaminated fish and higher fish consumption
- Lead contamination in drinking water
- Lower enforcement of water regulations
- Contaminated (nitrate) ground water in rural poor agricultural communities
- Violations of drinking-water standards on Native American reservations
- Affordability of water service
- Delegation of the poor to flood-prone lands
- Less access to healthy waters and water-based recreation sites

Sustainable Water Management

Water management refers to decisions about the use, storage, allocation, delivery, or treatment of water (Jacobs and Pulwarty, 2003). **Sustainable water resources systems** are those that are managed to contribute to the objectives of society now and in the future, while maintaining their integrity (Loucks, 2000). Water needs to be available and of sufficient quality to be sustainable. Much of water resources sustainability involves land management, often termed watershed management (Chapter 10). Adaptive management is believed to be a key in sustainable water resources management because it is so difficult to predict future technology and water needs. The success of sustainability can be measured in terms of increased reliability and resilience and reduced vulnerability. Many efforts for sustainable water management are aimed at these three measures. Supply and demand management are equally important considerations in sustainability (Chapter 21).

Water resources sustainability is also applied to green buildings (EPRI, 2010). The Leadership in Energy and Environmental Design (LEED) rating system considers low-water-use landscaping, efficient plumbing fixtures, stormwater generation, water reuse, irrigation, and indoor water use. Other approaches include rainfall collection, wastewater reclamation, and stormwater collection.

Problems

20.1 Research a local water quality problem that has been in the news in the past year. Discuss in groups the different perspectives on the problem.

20.2 Determine water availability for your state. Compare the availability to the water use.

References

Christian-Smith, J. 2012. Water and agriculture. Chapter 8 in J. Christian-Smith and P. H. Gleick (eds.), *A twenty-first century U.S. water policy*. New York: Oxford University Press.

Electric Power Research Institute. 2010. *Sustainable water resources management*. Vol. 1: Executive summary. Palo Alto, CA: EPRI.

Evans, G. W., and E. Kantrowitz. 2002. Socioeconomic status and health: The potential role of environmental risk exposure. *Ann. Rev. Public Health* 23: 303–331.

Gleick, P. H. 2012. United States international water policy. Chapter 11 in J. Christian-Smith and P. H. Gleick (eds.), *A twenty-first century U.S. water policy*. New York: Oxford University Press.

Great Lakes–St. Lawrence River Basin Compact Council. 2005. Great Lakes–St. Lawrence River Basin Water Resources Compact. Accessed 11/6/2014 from www.glslcompactcouncil.org.

Jacobs, K., and R. Pulwarty. 2003. Water resources management: Science, planning and decision-making. Chapter 9 in R. Lawford, D. Fort, H. Hartmann, and S. Eden (eds.),*Water: Science, policy and management*. Water Resources Monograph 16. Washington, DC: American Geophysical Union.

Kingdon, J. W. 2003. *Agendas, alternatives, and public policies*. 2nd ed. Boston: Addison-Wesley.

Klyza, C. M., and D. J. Sousa. 2008. *American environmental policy: Beyond gridlock*. Cambridge, MA: The MIT Press.

Lawford, R., D. Fort, H. Hartmann, and S. Eden (eds.). 2003. *Water: Science, policy and management*. Water Resources Monograph 16. Washington, DC: American Geophysical Union.

Loucks, D. P. 2000. Sustainable water resources management. *Intern. Water Res. Assoc.* 25(1): 3–10.

Maupin, M. A., J. F. Kenny, S. S. Hutson, J. K. Lovelace, N. L. Barber, and K. S. Linsey. 2014. *Estimated use of water in the United States in 2010*. U.S. Geological Survey Circular 1405. Reston, VA: USGS.

National Research Council. 1997. *Valuing ground water: Economic concepts and approaches*. National Academy Press. Washington, DC.

Reilly, T. E., K. F. Dennehy, W. M. Alley, and W. L. Cunningham. 2008. *Groundwater availability in the United States.* U.S. Geological Survey Circular 1323. Reston, VA: USGS.

United Nations General Assembly. 2000. 55/2. United Nations Millennium Declaration.

United States of America and Mexico. 1946. *Utilization of waters of the Colorado and Tijuana Rivers and of the Rio Grande: Treaty between the United States of America and Mexico.* Treaty Series 994. Washington, DC: U.S. Government Printing Office.

U.S. Department of Agriculture, National Agricultural Statistics Service. Multiple years. *Census of agriculture: Farm and ranch irrigation survey.* (1978, 1984, 1987, 1992, 1997, 2004, 2010, 2014). Washington, DC: U.S. GPO.

U.S. Department of Commerce, Bureau of the Census. Multiple years. *Census of Agriculture: Irrigation of agricultural lands.* (1943, 1952, 1961). Washington, DC: U.S. GPO.

U.S. Department of Commerce, Bureau of the Census. 1955. *Census of agriculture: Irrigation in humid areas.* Washington, DC: U.S. GPO.

U.S. Department of Commerce, Bureau of the Census. 1965. *1964 Census of agriculture: Irrigation, land improvement practices, and use of agricultural chemicals.* Washington, DC: U.S. GPO.

U.S. Department of Commerce, Bureau of the Census. Multiple years. *Census of agriculture: Irrigation and drainage on farms.* (1973, 1978). Washington, DC: U.S. GPO.

Vanderwarker, A. 2012. Water and environmental justice. Chapter 3 in J. Christian-Smith and P. H. Gleick (eds.), *A twenty-first century U.S. water policy.* New York: Oxford University Press.

Wolf, A. T. 2007. Shared waters: Conflict and cooperation. *Ann. Rev. Environ. Resour.* 32: 3.2–3.29.

21

Water Economics

■ Introduction

Economics is "the study of how society manages its scarce resources" (Mankiw, 2009). Therefore, **water economics** is the study of how society manages water. The value of water is a consequence of water scarcity (Griffin, 2006). Water scarcity is a comparison of water demand and water availability. This chapter is mostly about the economics associated with supplying water for various uses, primarily agriculture and municipal. It will review the key concepts in microeconomics as applied to water resources issues. Although many students have taken economics courses, this chapter does not make that assumption, and basic economic principles are introduced. Water is generally viewed as a commodity; that is, it can be marketed as a good to satisfy wants and needs, although the flow of water from place to place complicates its value in the marketplace. The reuse of water, such as return flows in a river, also introduces unique considerations in water economics, not typical for most goods. Water also is considered both a private good and a common resource. That is, owning water rights makes the water a private good, and there are **rival** users to this good. Also, users can be prevented from using this water, a term called **excludability**. However, some uses of water are **nonrival**, such as the aesthetic beauty of a water body, recreation, or maintaining biodiversity in the water. Nonrival users are not in competition for water with each other (Griffin, 2006). Thus water can switch from a private good to a common resource, depending on the circumstances.

This chapter provides a summary of the foundations of water economics, including an introduction to the market, the supply and demand of water, elasticity, water externalities, the costs of production, economic policy analysis, water pricing, cost-benefit analysis, water marketing, and consideration of both direct and indirect economic effects. In addition, examples are provided on pollution trading and the effect of installing water conservation devices. Throughout this chapter the terminology commonly used in economics is explained.

The Water Market

A market is formed from a collection of buyers and sellers of a good or service (Mankiw, 2009). Likewise, water or water rights can be bought and sold. The buyers create the demand for water, and the sellers determine the supply of water. Water marketing is the lease or sale of water rights (Brown, 2006; Cech, 2010). It is called a market because it allocates resources through the decisions of many users, called agents by economists (Mankiw, 2009). However, it would be difficult to assume that these markets are competitive because often there are not a lot of buyers and sellers, especially in a local region. In some cases the water supplier is a **monopoly**. That is, the supplier is the sole seller of a product, and the product does not have close substitutes (Mankiw, 2009). Water transfers most often occur between irrigators and municipalities, between individual irrigators, and between irrigators and industry. Increasingly, government agencies are entering water markets for environmental reasons, such as supporting low flows, aesthetics, and recreation. Water marketing applies mostly to surface water, but there are examples of ground water markets. **Water banking** also occurs when a public institution (e.g., a water district) leases water from owners and then re-leases it to other water users (Griffin, 2006). Auctioning is then sometimes used to set the water prices.

Economists use the term *efficiency* to describe how well a market is working. **Efficiency** means that maximum benefits are being obtained from the scarce resources (Mankiw, 2009). Efficiency is desirable in an economic sense. **Market failure** is a situation when resources are not allocated efficiently (Mankiw, 2009). The primary example of market failure in the water industry is that water allocations are not controlled by market forces.

Within watersheds, market transfers can sometimes be either upstream or downstream. Transferring a withdrawal upstream has the potential to injure third-party downstream users (externalities—explained later). It allows more withdrawal upstream. Some users may be related to nonrival instream flow values (externalities), and be harmed by such a transfer. In the western United States there are state agencies that oversee such transfers and must approve them before they can go forward (Griffin, 2006). Third-party agents may be notified and a hearing conducted as part of the process. Transfers resulting in an increase in consumptive use are often denied. Transfers between watersheds have the potential to cause greater problems. Table 21.1 summarizes the purchases of water for 12 western states from 1990 to 2003. Municipal purchases are the greatest in number and value.

Demand for Water

The quantity of water demanded is the amount that buyers are willing and able to purchase (Mankiw, 2009). A fundamental principle is that the demand for water is largely a function of price, although other factors may also influence demand, such as the water use sector involved, climate effects, and government regulations. If the price of water goes up, agents buy less water, and

Table 21.1 Western (12 states) water market purchases and median prices, 1990–2003.

Purpose	Leases (number)	Sales (number)	Leases (median $/ML/yr)	Sales (median $/ML)[1]
Municipal	286	453	56	2,120
Irrigation	199	123	12	1,917
Environmental	113	37	38	706
All			38	1,955

[1] 1 ML = 1 million liters = 1,000 m^3 = 0.81074 acre-feet.

Source: Data from Brown, 2006.

when prices fall they buy more. Water demand is actually different from water "requirements," which are calculated from water accounting numbers. And requirements may not actually be requirements at all. The economist's view of demand also adds the scarcity effects to the demand function. Because the relationship between price and quantity demanded is so universal, economists call this the **law of demand** (Mankiw, 2009), and the relationship between price and quantity demanded is called the **demand curve**. The demand curve is also called the **marginal benefit** curve or the willingness to pay curve (Griffin, 2006). An example of a demand curve is shown in Figure 21.1a for single-family home water use.

Shifts in the Demand Curve

Shifts in demand can occur due to changes in technology that foster water conservation, such as improved irrigation techniques or water conservation devices in urban areas. Or new research could suggest greater water consumption is associated with longer longevity. Figure 21.1b shows a downward shift in demand for water at all prices. An increase in the cost of water would result in movement upward and along the demand curve in Figure 21.1a, also resulting in less demand.

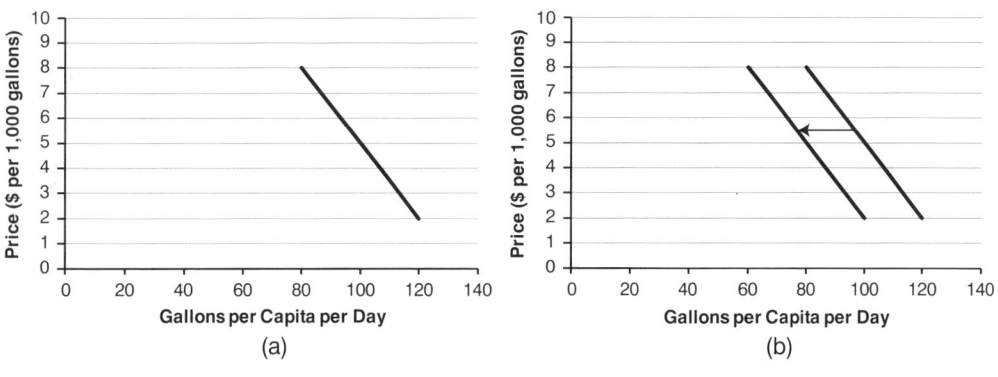

Figure 21.1 Example demand curve for water (a), and a shift in demand curve (b).

> **Water Economics Units**
>
> **BOX 21.1**
>
> This is a reminder of the units used for the quantity of water. Because such large volumes of water are involved in water use, unusual units are used. Common units include acre-feet, liters, gallons, cubic feet, and cubic meters.
>
> An acre-foot is one foot of water over an acre of land.
>
> $$1AF = 3.26 \times 10^5 \text{ US gal} = 1.223 \times 10^6 \text{ L}$$
>
> There are 7.481 US gal per ft^3

Supply of Water

The quantity of water supplied is the amount that sellers are willing and able to sell (Mankiw, 2009). The supply of water is somewhat affected by price but only to a certain extent, unlike many other goods. Theoretically, when the price of water is high, it becomes more profitable, and the quantity of water supplied is greater. When the price of water is low, the quantity supplied should be low because sellers may not be able to meet their costs. This association between price and the quantity supplied is called the **law of supply**, and the relationship between price and the quantity of water supplied is called the **supply curve** (Figure 21.2). Often the price of water is set by the government and not necessarily by the market. Therefore, in certain cases price changes little with the quantity supplied, except perhaps at very high prices. Also, the quantity supplied is sometimes limited, such as during a drought, or even sometimes not supplied at all. An exception to these constraints is bottled water, which acts like all other goods and services in the market.

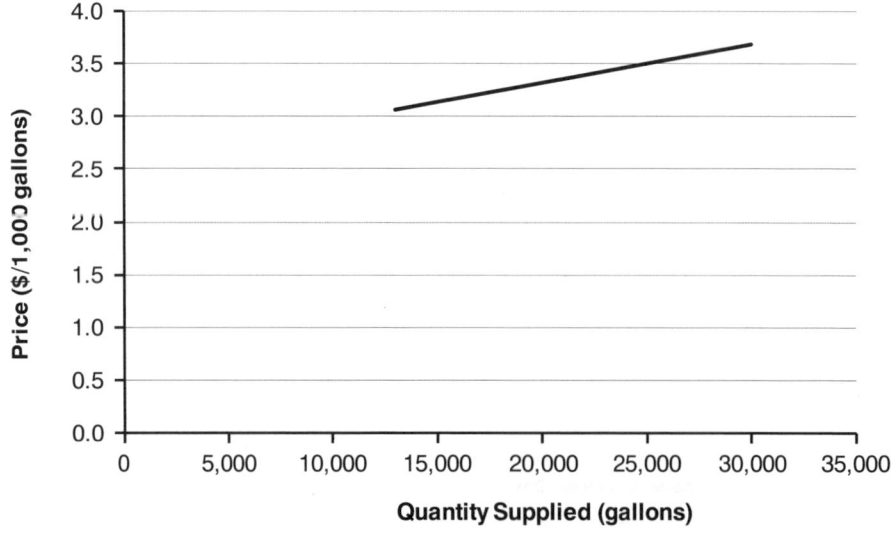

Figure 21.2 Example of a water supply curve for single-family residential use.

Shifts in the Supply Curve

A shift in the supply curve can occur when one of the factors controlling the price of water changes. An example would be the cost of electricity used to pump water. If, for example, the cost of electricity fell, selling water should be more profitable, and sellers would be willing to supply more water. More efficient technologies in obtaining or distributing water could also reduce costs.

Supply and Demand

We will now consider both demand and supply together. If the demand curve and supply curve are combined, the point where the two curves intersect is termed market **equilibrium** (Mankiw, 2009). In other words, the price is such that the quantity demanded equals the quantity supplied. The price at this point is termed the equilibrium price, and the quantity supplied at this point is termed the equilibrium quantity. If the market price is greater than the equilibrium price, the quantity supplied exceeds the quantity demanded, and a **surplus** exists. Similarly, if the market price is below the equilibrium price, the quantity supplied is less than the quantity demanded, and a **shortage** exists. Generally, prices gravitate toward their equilibrium value as the quantity supplied is adjusted. This is called the **law of supply and demand**—that the price will adjust to bring the quantity supplied equal to the quantity demanded (Mankiw, 2009).

Shifts in Supply and Demand

Both shifts in demand and shifts in supply will influence the market equilibrium. Water scarcity can be addressed by either supply enhancement or demand management (Griffin, 2006). Water conservation can reduce demand, and it illustrates economic efficiency in water use.

Elasticity

Elasticity describes how much buyers and sellers respond to changes in the market (Mankiw, 2009). The **price elasticity of demand** is the percent change in quantity demanded for a percent change in price (Griffin, 2006). This concept is similar to the slope of a function, except it is the ratio of the percentage changes of two variables rather than the ratio of the changes in two variables. Elasticity of demand is negative because demand falls as prices rise (Figure 21.1a). Demand is said to be **elastic** when the amount demanded changes greatly in response to a change in price. For example, elasticity is less than −1 (e.g., −1.8). This also means that the quantity demanded changes more than the change in price. Similarly, demand is **inelastic** if the amount demanded changes only slightly (between 0 and −1) in response to a change in price. Elasticity also changes with price, becoming more elastic at higher prices. Some economics texts adopt the convention of dropping the negative sign when describing elasticity. Use of the negative sign will be retained in this chapter.

The price elasticity of demand (ε) is computed from:

$$\varepsilon = \frac{\%\ \Delta D}{\%\ \Delta P} \qquad [21.1]$$

where % ΔD = percentage change in quantity demanded
% ΔP = percentage change in price (Griffin, 2006)

For example, if the price of water were to increase by 5% and the demand were to decrease by 10%, the elasticity of demand would be:

$$\varepsilon = \frac{-10\%}{5\%} = -2$$

Estimating Demand

Several approaches are used to estimate the demand for water, many of which are only appropriate for economic experts. One such approach is called the point expansion method. To use this method, a point on the price versus water demand function is needed. The slope (price elasticity of demand) of the function is then obtained from prior studies. The demand function is given by the following forms of equations:

$$w = mp + b \qquad [21.2]$$

$$w = kp^\varepsilon \qquad [21.3]$$

where p = price per unit quantity of water
w = units of water
ε = elasticity
m, b = constants for the slope and intercept of a linear regression, respectively
k = constant for the exponential relationship between price and quantity

Both of these equations can be solved for p, which is the marginal benefit. See Example 21.1.

The **price elasticity of supply** is the percent change in the quantity supplied for a percent change in price (Mankiw, 2009). Similar to demand, supply is elastic when the quantity supplied changes greatly in response to a change in price. Supply is inelastic when the quantity supplied changes only slightly in response to a change in price. The supply of water is generally inelastic because the amount available is somewhat limited, and it is difficult to produce more water.

EXAMPLE 21.1 Irrigated Corn Demand

The marginal cost for irrigated corn at this location is $2.50/ac-in. If the price were to increase to $3.50/ac-in, what would be the effect on demand using the point expansion method? The quantity of water is 160 MG. Assume the elasticity equals −0.4.

Using Eqn. 21.2:

$$160 = -0.4\,(2.5) + b$$

Solving for $b = 161$ MG

If the price rises to $3.50/ac-in,

$$w = -0.4(3.5) + 161$$

$$w = 159.6 \text{ MG}$$

Therefore the demand would fall by 400,000 gallons.

Water Externalities

Sometimes there are consequences of market decisions that are beyond the laws of supply and demand. An **externality** is a consequence (cost or benefit) of an activity that affects a party (agent) without regard to the agent's welfare. An **agent** can be a consumer, producer, government, or water authority. An externality is the uncompensated impact of an action on the well-being of a bystander (Mankiw, 2009). These impacts can be either positive or negative. An example of a negative externality is the lowering of the ground water table in an area by the actions of one well, thus increasing pumping costs or drying up wells for other users of the same aquifer or even causing land subsidence (Griffin, 2006). Another example of a negative externality is the pollution of water used by many users as the result of some other user or even a nonuser. An example of a positive externality is the recreation provided on a water-supply or flood-control reservoir.

For a negative externality, there is a social cost that includes the cost to the producer and the cost to the bystander(s) who are affected (Mankiw, 2009). To mitigate externalities, a corrective tax is sometimes used to shift the supply curve upward and to serve as an incentive to producers to minimize their impact. A government can also regulate a negative externality, making it illegal or setting limits. Economists generally prefer a corrective tax over regulation because it is more efficient from a market perspective. For a positive externality, a social value is added. A subsidy also can be used to shift the demand curve upward. Subsidies are commonly used in the water industry.

Water Pollution Trading

Another mechanism for responding to externalities that involve the market is through pollution trading. Sulfur dioxide (SO_2) emissions in air are often cited as a success story for pollution trading. For water quality externalities, the total maximum daily load (TMDL) process (Chapter 19) has led to a system of pollution trading. The TMDL analysis establishes a load allocation (LA) and a wasteload allocation (WLA) to achieve a water quality standard for a given water body. In Chapter 19, I used the example of nitrogen in Long Island Sound, located between New York and Connecticut. A system of trading of pollution permits can lead to economic efficiency and thus encourage pollution reductions. A new market for a scarce resource—that is, pollution permits—has been created. These allocations are initially credited to each polluter without regard to economics. For the wasteload allocations, some treatment plants may be able to reduce their nitrogen discharges at a low cost and will sell their permits, while others can reduce nitrogen only at a high cost and will buy those permits. Pollution permits can also be auctioned off in the market to allow a certain level of pollution by the highest bidder.

Trading between point sources (WLA) and nonpoint sources (LA) is also suggested (Ribaudo et al., 2014; U.S. Environmental Protection Agency, 2004). However, this trading between point and nonpoint sources assumes that nonpoint sources from a known source can be reduced at a known cost. Often it is difficult to identify the true source of a nonpoint pollutant. Also, the economics and science of nonpoint source pollution reduction are inexact, and there exists a substantial and unknown lag time between treatment application and effect on nonpoint pollutant exports, unlike those for point sources.

Costs of Production

The cost to supply water includes all the opportunity costs for a supplier to make its output of water. An **opportunity cost** is the value of the next best selection that could have been made (Griffin, 2006), or in other words, what you give up to obtain the item (Mankiw, 2009). An example is whether a given amount of water could be applied to a more valuable crop. Efficient water use is about water's opportunity cost.

Production Function

Productivity is the amount of goods and services produced from a unit of labor (Mankiw, 2009). Units of water are an example of goods produced. A **production function** shows the relationship between the quantity of inputs to make a good and the quantity of outputs of that good (Mankiw, 2009).

Measures of Cost

The costs to supply water depend in part on the various transformations that occur along the way. These might include impounding the water, pumping and piping the water, treating the water, and administrative costs such as planning and accounting. Costs might be associated with new production activities, such as building impoundments or drilling wells, storage facilities, and treatment facilities. These costs can be a function of the amount of water supplied and are termed **total costs** (Figure 21.3). Some of these costs are termed **fixed costs**. These are the costs that occur whether water is supplied or not and include machinery and rent; they do not vary with the quantity of water supplied (Griffin, 2006). **Variable costs** increase with the quantity of water supplied and might include wages, utilities, and transportation. Thus, fixed costs plus variable costs equal total costs.

The cost of a unit quantity of water is called the **average total cost** and is total cost divided by the quantity of water. Similarly, **average fixed cost** is the fixed cost divided by quantity of water produced, and **average variable cost** is the variable cost divided by the quantity of water produced. Because the total cost varies with the quantity produced, the **marginal cost** is the change in total cost divided by the change in quantity produced, or the slope of the total cost function (Figure 21.3). Marginal costs often increase with greater quantity produced. It is the cost to produce an additional unit of water. The supply that minimizes average total cost is termed the *efficient scale*, and the marginal cost curve crosses the average total cost curve at its minimum.

Supply Analysis

Supply analysis of water involves determining the marginal costs (MC) of converting natural water into retail water (Griffin, 2006). The marginal, or average costs, can be estimated simply by using the rate that is charged for a unit of water. For municipal applications, the water supply cost function can be determined by adding the individual costs associated with (1) the number of new connections, (2) the volume of water delivered, and (3) the number of active connections.

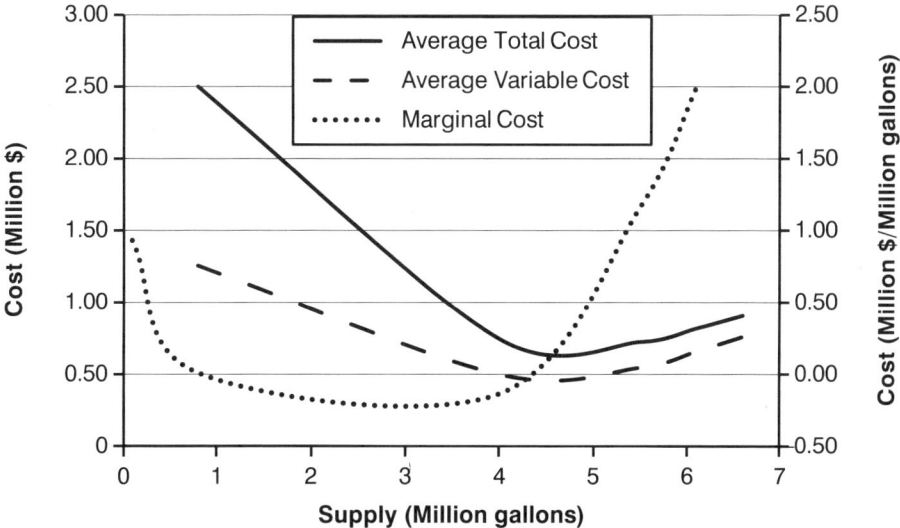

Figure 21.3 Costs of water supply per unit quantity of water.

More on Efficiency

We have discussed market efficiency from a number of perspectives, and we know that efficiency means maximum benefits are being obtained from scarce resources, such as water (Mankiw, 2009). For any given amount of supplied water, the cost function is the lowest total costs of supplying that water. Efficiency exists when suppliers operate on a total cost function and not above it. Efficiency requires cost-effectiveness, and all levels of water supply must be provided at minimum cost (Griffin, 2006). Economic efficiency also occurs when water is apportioned among users so that net benefits are maximized. There are two additional measures that are used to evaluate efficiency and guide whether a certain decision is appropriate. These are the net present value and the benefit–cost ratio.

The **net present value** (NPV) is the sum of all net benefits occurring as the result of an activity discounted to a current value (Griffin, 2006). It is considered over an appropriate time period. The NPV is determined from:

$$\text{NPV} = \sum_{t=0}^{T} \frac{\text{NB}_t}{(1+d)^t} \qquad [21.4]$$

where t = time period (usually year)
T = total time periods
NB_t = net benefits (or net cash flow) in period t
d = discount rate

If NPV is positive, the investment adds value; if negative it loses value, and if equal to zero, then the project adds no value. Example 21.2 illustrates the usefulness of the NPV by determining the effects of converting to a low-flow toilet.

Benefit–cost ratio (BCR) is the present value of benefits (B_t) divided by the present value of costs (C_t). The BCR is determined from:

$$BCR = \frac{\sum_{t=0}^{T} \frac{B_t}{(1+d)^t}}{\sum_{t=0}^{T} \frac{C_t}{(1+d)^t}} \qquad [21.5]$$

Economic Policy Analysis

Water resources problems, such as shortages, often prompt the analysis of policies used to manage water. Some of these policies involve water rate structures and water use restrictions. Economists believe that rule changes must provide positive net benefits to improve economic efficiency. Thus social benefits need to exceed social costs, or the change in net benefits (NB) must be positive. There are four mechanisms for affecting net benefits associated with water use management: price rationing, quantity rationing, demand shifting, and supply shifting (Griffin, 2006). Each of these approaches will be explained, and they are summarized in Table 21.2. An increase in the water rate might be desired by a utility because current marginal costs are too high, there is a water supply

EXAMPLE 21.2 Buying a Low-Flow Toilet

A low-flow toilet costs about $200. The estimated cost of the water saved is about $90 per year if you buy the water from a municipality. Assume the discount rate is 15% and the toilet is warranted for three years. Should you buy the toilet? Assume that the cost of installation is zero because you will install it yourself. See the table below.

Year (T)	Net Benefit ($)	Net Present Value (NPV) ($)	Accumulated NPV ($)
0	−200	−200	−200
1	+90	+78.26	−121.74
2	+90	+68.05	−53.69
3	+90	+59.18	+5.49

Since the sum of NPV is greater than zero by year 3, it would be better to purchase the toilet than to do nothing at all. Since toilets typically last beyond three years, the NPV should continue to increase.

For our example using a water-saving toilet, the sum of benefits would be 78.26 + 68.05 + 59.18 = $205.49, and the cost is $200. Therefore the BCR = 205.49/200 = 1.03, which is acceptable because it is greater than 1.

---

shortfall, or the utility wants to increase revenue. The users' net benefits would decrease, and they would probably use less water (law of demand). The utility would sell less water due to the decrease in demand but would increase revenue from the increased water rate. The production costs for the utility would also decrease. The amount of the change in production costs will determine the overall effect on the utility. A shift from unmetered water rates, where any quantity can be used, to metered water supplies has also been shown to increase net benefits (Griffin, 2006).

Quantity rationing might be used when there is a temporary shortfall in the water supply. Certain water uses might be restricted, such as car washing and lawn watering. These changes are not likely to increase economic efficiency. Shifts in the demand curve are also possible as policy changes. One such change might be to recruit new industries into a community (Table 21.2). Generally, existing users would experience a loss in net benefits with a shift in the demand curve to the right, while new users would obtain gains. A shift (decrease) in the demand curve to the left due to conservation practices or education should result in users saving on water bills, and the utility should be able to supply water at a reduced price (Griffin, 2006). The supply of water can also be altered.

Table 21.2 Mechanisms influencing net benefits of a change in water policy.

Mechanism	Direction	Methods	Result to Consumer	Utility Revenue
Price rationing	Increase	Increase water rate	Loss	Increase & lower costs
Quantity rationing	Increase	Bar certain uses— e.g., lawn watering	Loss	Decrease
Demand shifting	Decrease	Education, conservation, plumbing codes	Gain	Can lower price
Demand shifting	Increase	Recruit new businesses, population growth	Loss to existing, gain to new	No change if costs = revenue
Supply shifting	Increase	Water project, lease/ purchase water rights	Gain	No change if costs = revenue
Supply shifting	Decrease	Reapportion water rights	Loss	No change if costs = revenue

Costs for the utility can be reduced by obtaining less expensive water supplies and by improving distribution efficiency (fewer leaks). Lowering costs would result in net benefits to users. Additional supplies can also be obtained to increase supply. Users that lose supplies, perhaps due to a loss of water rights, would lose net benefits.

Water Pricing

The price of water is a strong factor controlling the demand for water (Griffin, 2006). Therefore, when water is scarce, price can be used as a demand management strategy. To be economically efficient, the water price should equal the marginal cost (MC). Water prices are not determined by competition because water suppliers are typically monopolies. The term **water price** most often refers to a volumetric charge for metered water (Griffin, 2006). Water rate is often equal to water price, but it can include other charges that are fixed, such as connection fees or a meter charge. There are three common water rate structures: decreasing block, increasing block, and uniform. The term "block" refers to a range of water units for which the price per unit is constant. As metered use increases into the next block, the price per unit water would fall or increase. For example, a metered user might be charged $2.60/1,000 gallons for the first 2,000 gallons and $6.40/1,000 gallons for the next 2,000 gallons. Seasonal rates also are sometimes used, reflecting changes in demand during different periods of the year. A meter charge is like a minimum charge. For irrigators it is the charge per acre irrigated. Rates are also commonly regulated by governmental agencies.

There are both accounting and economic approaches to pricing. Accounting practice for determining water rates involves identifying revenue requirements, including depreciation and equipment replacements, the distribution of projected costs across clients, and designing a rate structure (Griffin, 2006). From an economic perspective, marginal costs (MC) should be incorporated into rates. This means that the marginal value of water should be included in determining the rate.

■ Cost–Benefit Analysis

Cost–benefit analysis (CBA) was largely developed during the period of large water development projects, primarily in the western United States. Economists use CBA to analyze major development proposals. This approach is similar to determining NPV. The basic approach is to determine all costs and benefits that would result from the water project. The federal government has developed "Principles and Guidelines" for federal investments in water resources (U.S. Water Resources Council, 1983; U.S. Council on Environmental Quality, 2013). It is difficult to quantify all of the benefits and all of the costs; usually there are certain benefits and costs that are included. The approach is to identify all the benefits and costs and discount them back to each year. A sample calculation using this approach is shown in Table 21.3. The first step is to determine the benefits (B_t) and costs (C_t) each year. The net benefits (NB_t) would be determined as the difference between total benefits and total costs. A discount rate is needed to determine the other columns. The NPV is the sum of discounted net benefits. The benefit–cost ratio can be determined from the present value (PV) of benefits divided by the present value of costs. Evaluation procedures have been developed for several obvious benefits, listed on the following page (U.S. Water Resources Council, 1983; U.S. Army Corps of Engineers, 2009).

Table 21.3 Table of cost–benefit analysis to determine the net present value (NPV).

Period	Benefit (B_t)	Cost (C_t)	Net Benefit (NB_t)	$\dfrac{B_t}{(1+d)^t}$	$\dfrac{C_t}{(1+d)^t}$	$\dfrac{NB_t}{(1+d)^t}$
0						
1						
2						
T						
				Σ = PV (Bs)	Σ = PV (Cs)	Σ = NPV

Source: Based on Griffin (2006).

- Municipal and industrial water supply
- Agriculture
- Urban flood damage
- Hydropower
- Navigation
- Recreation
- Commercial fishing
- Transportation—inland and deep draft navigation
- Hurricane and storm damage reduction

Nonmarket valuation techniques are needed for benefits such as biodiversity protection (Griffin, 2006). For example, what is the recreational benefit of a dam? The travel-cost approach has been used to determine the value of fishing and other recreation at a site. This method determines the benefit as the time and travel cost expenses incurred to visit a site. Another approach, the contingent valuation method, uses a survey of preferences of willingness to pay a certain amount for an activity, such as boating on a lake. Alternatively, the amount they might be compensated to give up an activity can be asked in a survey.

Direct and Indirect Economic Effects

Both direct and indirect (secondary) economic effects occur as a result of a change in production in an industry. For example, an increase in demand for the products of one industry will cause this industry to purchase more from other industries or other production sectors. The productivity of each sector can be expressed in terms of water used as part of the production. Water-use coefficients can be developed, which are the ratio of the water use for a given sector to the gross dollar output of that sector (Davis, 1969). Direct water-use coefficients can be expressed as gallons per dollar of output. Examples of such sectors include industry (mining, paper mills); hotel, motel, and commercial rental; households; education; agriculture; and government (O'Hayre et al., 1975). In the same sense as for purchases, there are direct plus indirect water-use coefficients for each sector (Lofting and Davis, 1968). An increase in demand for products from one industry will result in an increase in water use directly by that industry but will also result in an increase in water use indirectly by purchases from the other sectors. Economists use an approach called input-output analysis to evaluate these economic and water-use effects (Leontief, 1966). Input-output analysis also helps with solving water allocation problems. The basic approach involves matrix algebra, but it will not be presented here. The important idea here is that a change in the demand for water in one sector results in larger changes in the demand for water when indirect effects are considered. Input-output analysis has been used to assess impacts of water-supply restrictions (Gonzalez, 2011), water transfers between states (Mubako et al., 2013), and global life-cycle assessment of virtual water flows in products (Lenzen et al., 2013).

Problems

21.1 Determine whether it is worthwhile to install low-flow shower heads in your dorm based on the net present value. Assume the low-flow shower head will cost $50 and will be installed at no cost. A low-flow shower head delivers water at 2.5 gpm compared to an average of 5 gpm, or a 50% reduction. Assume that each shower head is guaranteed for years and saves the school $30 per person per year in water charges. Use a discount rate of 15%. There would be additional savings in energy costs as well.

21.2 What is the water rate structure for your municipality? If you live in a rural setting and your water is self-supplied, find the water rate structure for a large city near you. Is this rate structure decreasing block, increasing block, or uniform?

21.3 Using the point expansion method, determine the elasticity demand and the quantity of water demanded for a rate increase that is being proposed. Currently, the water use rate is $3.34 per 1,000 gallons. If the price were to increase to $3.50/1,000 gal, what would be the effect on demand using the point expansion method? The quantity of water is 2,281.6 MG per year. Assume the elasticity is −0.5.

21.4 Determine the BCR for Problem 21.1. Is it acceptable?

References

Brown, T. C. 2006. Trends in water market activity and price in the western United States. *Water Resources Research* 42:W09402. doi: 10.1029/2005WR004180.

Cech, T. V. 2010. *Principles of water resources: History, development, management and policy*. 3rd ed. New York: John Wiley & Sons.

Davis, H. C. 1969. Inter-regional production and water resource dependencies among western states. *Western Econ. J.* 7(1): 27–40.

Gonzalez, J. F., 2011. Assessing the macroeconomic impact of water supply restrictions through an input-output analysis. *Water Resources Management* 25:2335–2347.

Griffin, R. C. 2006. *Water resource economics: The analysis of scarcity, policies, and projects*. Cambridge, MA: MIT Press.

Lenzen, M., D. Moran, A. Bhaduri, K. Kanemoto, M. Bekchanov, and A. Geschke et al. 2013. International trade of scarce water. *Ecological Economics* 94:78–85.

Leontief, W. 1966. *Input-output economics*. New York: Oxford University Press.

Lofting, E. M., and H. C. Davis. 1968. The interindustry water content matrix: Applications on a multiregional basis. *Water Resources Research* 4: 689–695.

Mankiw, N. G. 2014. *Principles of microeconomics*. 7th ed. Mason, OH: Cengage Learning.

Mubako, S., S. Lahiri, and C. Lant. 2013. Input-output analysis of virtual water transfers: Case study of California and Illinois. *Ecological Economics* 93:230–238.

O'Hayre, A. P., J. C. Clausen, and A. C. Mace, Jr. 1975. *A hydronomic analysis of forest management alternatives for environmental quality: A case study of Itasca County*. Minneapolis: Minnesota Water Resources Research Center Bulletin 83.

Ribaudo, M., J. Savage, and J. Talberth. 2014. Encouraging reductions in nonpoint source pollution through point-nonpoint trading: The roles of baseline choice and practice subsidies. *Applied Economic Perspectives and Policy*. doi: 10.1093/aepp/ppu004.

U.S. Council on Environmental Quality. 2013. *Principles and requirements for federal investments in water resources*. Washington, DC: Author. https://www.whitehouse.gov/sites/default/files/final_principles_and_requirements_march_2013.pdf

U.S. Environmental Protection Agency (EPA). 2004. *Water quality trading assessment handbook*. EPA 841-B-04-001. Washington, DC: Author.

U.S. Water Resources Council. 1983. *Economic and environmental principles and guidelines for water and related land resources implementation studies*. Washington, DC: Author.

APPENDIX A
CONVERSION FACTORS

Length conversion factors

(Read as column units per row unit: e.g. 5,280 ft/mi)

	mm	cm	m	km	in	ft	yd	mi
mm	1	0.1	0.001	10^{-6}	0.03937	0.00328	0.00109	6.21×10^{-7}
cm	10	1	0.01	0.0001	0.3937	0.0328	0.0109	6.21×10^{-6}
m	1,000	100	1	0.001	39.37	3.281	1.094	6.21×10^{-4}
km	10^6	10^5	1,000	1	39,370	3,281	1,093.6	0.621
in	25.4	**2.54**	0.0254	2.54×10^{-5}	1	0.0833	0.0278	1.58×10^{-5}
ft	304.8	30.48	**0.3048**	3.05×10^{-4}	12	1	0.333	1.89×10^{-4}
yd	914.4	91.44	0.9144	9.14×10^{-4}	36	3	1	5.68×10^{-4}
mi	1.61×10^6	1.61×10^5	1.61×10^3	1.6093	63,360	**5,280**	1,760	1

Bold = important conversions

Area conversion factors

(Read as column units per row unit: e.g. 640 ac/mi²)

	cm²	m²	km²	ha	in²	ft²	yd²	mi²	ac
cm²	1	0.001	10^{-10}	10^{-8}	0.155	1.08×10^{-3}	1.2×10^{-4}	3.861×10^{-11}	2.471×10^{-8}
m²	10^4	1	10^{-6}	10^{-4}	1550	10.76	1.196	3.861×10^{-7}	2.471×10^{-4}
km²	10^{10}	10^6	1	100	1.55×10^9	10.76×10^6	1.196×10^6	0.3861	247.1
ha	10^8	10^4	0.01	1	1.55×10^7	10.76×10^4	1.196×10^4	3.861×10^{-3}	**2.471**
in²	6.452	6.4×10^{-4}	6.45×10^{-10}	6.45×10^{-8}	1	6.94×10^{-3}	7.7×10^{-4}	2.49×10^{-10}	1.574×10^{-7}
ft²	929	0.0929	9.29×10^{-8}	9.29×10^{-6}	144	1	0.1111	3.587×10^{-8}	2.3×10^{-5}
yd²	8361	0.8361	8.36×10^{-7}	8.36×10^{-5}	1296	9	1	3.23×10^{-7}	2.07×10^{-4}
mi²	40.4×10^6	2,589,998	2.59	259	—	27.87×10^6	3.089×10^6	1	**640**
ac	40.4×10^6	4,047	4.047×10^{-3}	0.4047	6.27×10^6	**43,560**	4,840	1.562×10^{-3}	1

Bold = important conversions

APPENDIX A Conversion Factors

Volume conversion factors

(Read as column units per row unit: e.g. 7.481 US gal/ft^3)

	cm	liters	m^3	in^3	ft^3	U.S. gal	ac-ft
cm^3	1	0.001	10^{-6}	0.06102	3.53 × 10^{-5}	2.64 × 10^{-4}	8.1 × 10^{-10}
liters	1,000	1	0.001	61.023	0.0353	0.26417	8.1 × 10^{-7}
m^3	10^6	1,000	1	61,024	35.314	264.17	8.107 × 10^{-4}
in^3	16.39	1.64 × 10^{-2}	1.64 × 10^{-5}	1	5.79 × 10^{-4}	4.33 × 10^{-3}	1.218 × 10^{-8}
ft^3	28,319	28.319	0.02832	1,728	1	**7.481**	2.296 × 10^{-5}
U.S. gal	3,785.4	3.785	3.785 × 10^{-3}	231	0.13368	1	3.069 × 10^{-6}
ac-ft	1.223 × 10^9	1.223 × 10^6	1,233.5	75.27 × 10^6	43,560	3.26 × 10^5	1

Bold = important conversions

Flow conversion factors

(Read as column units per row unit: e.g., 28.317 L/s/cfs)

	m^3/s	L/s	cfs	gpm	U.S. gpd	mgd	Imp. gpd
m^3/s	1	1,000	35.314	15,850	22.82 × 10^6	22.824	19.02 × 10^6
L/s	0.001	1	0.0353	15.85	22,824	2.28 × 10^{-2}	19,020
cfs	0.0283	**28.317**	1	448.83	646,323	0.6463	538.603
gpm	6.309 × 10^{-5}	0.0631	2.23 × 10^{-3}	1	1,440	1.44 × 10^{-3}	1,200
U.S. gpd	4.38 × 10^{-8}	4.382 × 10^{-5}	1.55 × 10^{-6}	6.94 × 10^{-4}	1	10^{-6}	0.833
mgd	4.38 × 10^{-2}	43.82	1.55	694	10^6	1	8.33 × 10^5
Imp. gpd	5.26 × 10^{-8}	5.26 × 10^{-5}	1.86 × 10^{-6}	8.33 × 10^{-4}	1.2	1.2 × 10^{-6}	1

Water quality conversion factors

(Read as column units per row unit: e.g., 1000 µg/L / 1 mg/L)

	% solution	ppm	ppb	mg/L	µg/L	ng/L	µg/g	mg/m³	mg/kg	kg/m³
% solution	1	10^4	10^7	10^4	10^7	10^{10}	10^4	10^7	10^4	10
ppm	10^{-4}	1	1000	1	1000	10^6	1	1000	1	0.001
ppb	10^{-7}	0.001	1	0.001	1	1000	0.001	1	0.001	10^{-6}
mg/L	10^{-4}	1	1000	1	1000	10^6	1	1000	1	0.001
µg/L	10^{-7}	0.001	1	0.001	1	1000	0.001	1	0.001	10^{-6}
ng/L	10^{-10}	10^{-6}	0.001	10^{-6}	0.001	1	10^{-6}	0.001	10^{-6}	10^{-9}
µg/g	10^{-4}	1	1000	1	1000	10^6	1	1000	1	0.001
mg/m³	10^{-7}	0.001	1	0.001	1	1000	0.001	1	0.001	10^{-6}
mg/kg	10^{-4}	1	1000	1	1000	10^6	1	1000	1	0.001
kg/m³	0.1	1000	10^6	1000	10^6	10^9	1000	10^6	1000	1

Appendix A Conversion Factors

Length

To convert

From:	To:	Multiply by:
foot	inch	12
foot	meter(m)	.3048
inch	centimeter	2.54
kilometer	mile	0.621
meter	yard	1.094
mile	kilometer	1.6093
millimeter	inch	3.94×10^{-2}
yard	inch	36
To:	**From:**	**Divide by:**

Area

To convert

From:	To:	Multiply by:
acre	ft^2	43560
acre	hectare	0.405
ft^2	m^2	0.0929
hectare	m^2	10^4
$mile^2$	$kilometer^2$	2.59
To:	**From:**	**Divide by:**

Volume

To convert

From:	To:	Multiply by:
ft^3	liter	28.317
ft^3	gallon	7.481
gallon	liter	3.785
m^3	ft^3	35.314
m^3	liter	1000
To:	**From:**	**Divide by:**

Discharge

To convert

From:	To:	Multiply by:
ft^3/s	gpm	448.83
ft^3/s	m^3/s	.0283
m^3/s	liter/s	1000
m^3/s	gpm	15850
To:	**From:**	**Divide by:**

Mass

To Convert

From:	To:	Multiply by:
pound	kilogram	0.4536
ton	pound	2,000
tonnes	pound	2,205
pound/ac	kg/ha	1.1208
ft³ – water	pound	62.4
To:	**From:**	**Divide by:**

Temperature

$$°C = \frac{5}{9}(°F - 32) \qquad °F = \frac{9}{5}(°C) + 32$$

Concentration

To convert

From:	To:	Multiply by:
mg/L	ppm	1.0
ppm	ppb	1,000
mg/L	mg/kg	1.0
µg/L	mg/m³	1.0
g/m³	mg/L	1.0
lb/ac	kg/ha	1.120851
% solution	mg/L	1×10^4
To:	**From:**	**Divide by:**

Metric

To convert SI prefixes

From:	To:	Multiply by:
Suffix	mega (M)	1×10^6
Suffix	kilo (k)	1,000
Suffix	hecto (c)	100
Suffix	deca	10
Suffix	Suffix	1
Suffix	deci	.1
Suffix	centi	.01
Suffix	milli	.001
Suffix	micro	.000001
Suffix	nano	1×10^{-9}
To:	**From:**	**Divide by:**

INDEX

acidic deposition, 132
acidity, 136, 142
acid precipitation, 133–134
adaptive management, 261
adsorption, 209
advection, 210, 211f
afforestation, 103
agricultural practices, BMPs
    confined animal facility operations (CAFOs), 227
    erosion and sediment control, 226–227
    grazing management, 230–231, 231t
    irrigation water management, 231–232, 232t
    Natural Resources Conservation Service (NRCS), 226
    nutrient management, 228–229, 229t
    pesticide management, 229–230, 230t
    silvicultural practices, 232–235, 233f–235f
albedo, 53, 103, 119
algal bloom, water quality, 7f
algicide, 202
alkalinity, 134–135
alternative courses of action, 257
alter shields, 30, 31f
Amphipoda, 154
Anabaena, 147f
annual precipitation, 28
annual water budget, 27–28
Aphanizomenon, 147–148, 147f
apparent color, 125
aquifer, 75
arithmetic approach, 32
arrowhead/duck-potato (*Sagittaria*), 159f
artesian aquifer, 75f
artificial circulation, 201
aspect, water yield, 102
Association of State and Interstate Water Pollution Control Administrators (ASIWPCA), 111–112
atomic absorption (AA) spectrometry, 142
Atrazine, 113, 210
available water, 71–72
average fixed cost, 273

average precipitation methods
    arithmetic approach, 32
    isohyetal approach, 33
    Thiessen polygon approach, 32–33
    watershed boundary/mapping, 33–34, 34f
average total cost, 273
average variable cost, 273

Bacillariophyceae, 148f
bacteria, 160–161
basal area, 41
baseflow, 83
basin lag, 85–86, 86f, 86t
basin transfers, 250–251
Beale ratio estimator, 18
Beck's Biotic Index, 154, 155b, 156t
bedload, 122, 123f
benefit–cost ratio (BCR), 274
best management practice (BMP), 217
    agricultural practices, 226–232
    silvicultural practices, 232–235
    urban stormwater, 217–225
bioassays, 161
biochemical oxygen demand (BOD), 136, 178
biological characteristics
    bioassays, 161
    macroinvertebrates, 154–156
    macrophytes, 156–159
    pathogens in water, 160–161
    plankton, 145–154
biological controls, lakes restoration, 202
biological degradation, 209
Blaney-Criddle method, evapotranspiration, 55
BMP. *See* best management practice (BMP)
BOD. *See* biochemical oxygen demand (BOD)
Bosmina, 152, 153f
buffering, 134
burlap bag, 65

cancelling, unit conversion, 13
capillary forces, 62–63, 63f
capillary potential, 70
Carlson Trophic State Index (TSI), 197t

Note: Page numbers followed by *b*, *f*, or *t* represent boxes, figures, and tables respectively.

catchment, 33
cattail *(Typha)*, 159f
censored values, 17
centroid lag, 85
centroid of precipitation, 85
Ceratium, 148, 149f
chemical characteristics
   acidity, 136
   alkalinity, 134–135
   biochemical oxygen demand (BOD), 136
   chemical composition, 130t
   classification of chemicals, 131t
   dissolved oxygen content, 136
   ground water, 130
   humans and human activities, 132
   methods of analysis, 142–143
   minor ionic species, 130t
   nitrogen, 136–139
   pH and carbonates, 132–134
   phosphorus, 139–141
chemical precipitation, 209
Chlorophyta, 146–147, 146f
chromatography, 142–143
Cipolletti weirs, 90f
Clean Water Act, 252
Clean Water Act Amendments of 1977
   (PL 95-217), 242t, 245
Clean Water Restoration Act of 1966
   (PL 89-753), 242t, 244
climate conditions, 102
closed lakes, 189
Coastal Water Quality Standards and Monitoring (PL 106-284), 246
Coastal Zone Act Reauthorization Amendments of 1990 (PL 101-508), 242t, 246
The Code of Federal Regulations (CFR), 242
cold fronts, 29–30, 30f
colony-forming units (CFU), 161
color, water, 125 126, 125f
Colorado River Compact of 1922, 251
colorimetric approach, chemical constituents in water, 142
common (base 10) logarithms, 18
compound weirs, 90f
concepts in water resources, 8–9, 9b
concrete frost, 65
conductivity, 126, 129
   detector, 143
   meter, 93
conjunctive use, 258
conservative pollutants, 205

consumptive use, 257–258
contaminants
   remediation, 214
   removal, 214
   sources of, 210t
   transport, 210–213
   treatment, 214
   velocities, 212
contingent valuation method, 278
continuous source, contaminant transport, 211–212
contour trenches, 104
convectional precipitation, 29
convection storms, 29
conversion factors, 281–284
coontail *(Ceratophyllum)*, 158–159, 158f
correlative rights, 248–249
cost–benefit analysis (CBA), 277–278, 277t
costs of production, 272–273
covariance, 51
criterion, 241
   water quality, 110
Crustacea, 152–154, 153f
cut-shoot method and evapotranspiration, 49
Cyanobacteria, 147–148, 147f
Cyclops, 152, 153f

Dacthal, 113, 210
Daphnia, 152, 153f
Darcy's law, 78, 78f
deep leakage, 27
delayed flow, 87
demand curve, 267
demand for water, 266–267, 267f, 268b
denitrification, 137
density, 8
deoxygenation, 179
Desmodesmus, 146f
Diaptomus, 152, 153f
dielectric constant, 8
diffusion, 210
dilution and flushing, 201
Dinoflagellates, 148, 149f
discharge of wastewater, 179
discharge zone, 76–78, 76f
dissociation constant of water, 132
dissolved oxygen (DO), 178–184
   biochemical oxygen demand (BOD), 178
   concentration, 195
   content, 136
   deoxygenation, 179

discharge of wastewater, 179
oxygen sag curve, 178
reoxygenation, 180
Streeter-Phelps model, 178
Streeter-Phelps oxygen sag equation, 180–184
double-ring infiltrometer, 65, 66f
drainage basin, 33
drainage law, 251
dry-weather flow, 83
dystrophic lakes, 196

earth's water balance, 26t
economic effects, 278
economic policy analysis, 274–276, 276t
eddy covariance, evapotranspiration, 50–51, 50f
efficiency, 266, 273, 274
elasticity, 269–271
Electric Consumers Protection Act of 1986, 252
EMC. See event mean concentration (EMC)
Endangered Species Act, 252
energy balance, evapotranspiration, 53
E notation, 14–15
environmental justice, 260–261
Environmental Protection Agency (EPA), 109
epilimnion, 190, 192f
equation of continuity, 88, 89f
equivalence units, 16t
erosion and sediment control, 221, 222t
errors in precipitation measurements, 37–38
eutrophication, 196t
eutrophic lakes, 196
evaporation, 47
  pan, 52, 53f
evapotranspiration, 47
  estimation of
    Blaney-Criddle method, 55
    energy balance, 53
    Hamon's method, 55
    lake evaporation, 56
    Penman equation, 55–56
    Thornthwaite equation, 54, 54t
    water balance, 52
  factors affecting, 47–48
  measurement of
    direct methods, 49–52
    indirect methods, 52
    rate of, 48f
    saturated vapor pressure and density for water, 49t
    stomata and vapor pressure gradient, 48f
  potential evapotranspiration vs., 56, 57f

evapotranspiration ratio (ETR), 56, 57f
event mean concentration (EMC), 15–16
event median concentration (EMC) of nitrogen, 138t
excludability, 265
Executive Order 11988–Floodplain Management, 252
executive orders, 241
experimental watersheds, 99, 100t
externalities, 271–272

federal regulations and rules, water quality
  stormwater regulations, 247
  total maximum daily loads (TMDL), 247–248
  water quality standards, 247
federal water quality legislation, 243–246
fetch, 51
field capacity (FC), 71
field checking, 34
filter strips, silvicultural activities, 235f
first-order reactions, 174–175, 174f
fixed costs, 273
fixed solids, 119
flame photometer, 142
Flood Disaster Protection Act of 1973 (PL 93-234), 252
flood frequency analysis, 93
floodplain management, 251–252
flow nets, 81, 82f
flumes, 89f
fluviatile, 188
fluxes, 50–51, 50f
food chain manipulation, 202
forest (vegetation) management, 103
Fragilaria, 148, 148f
frequency analysis
  probability of exceedance, 35
  recurrence interval, 35–36, 36f
frontal storms, 29

Gammarus, 154f
gas chromatography, 143
glaciers, 188
graded stream, 171
granula frost, 65
gravimetric measurement, 68
gravitational potential, 70
gravity, 62, 63f
Great Lakes Legacy Act (PL 107-333), 246
Green and Ampt infiltration equation, 66–67
gross precipitation, 39, 40

ground water, 113, 130
  aquifer, 75
  artesian aquifer, 75f
  contaminants, 214
    remediation, 214
    removal, 214
    sources of, 210t
    transport, 210–213
    treatment, 214
  discharge zone, 76–78, 76f
  flow, 78–80
  flow nets, 81f, 82f
  head, 76
  piezometric surface, 75–76
  recharge zone, 78
  water table aquifer, 75f
  well effect, 80, 81f

Hamon's method, evapotranspiration, 55
harvesting, lakes restoration, 202
head, ground water, 76
headwater streams, 170
heat capacity, 8
Helley-Smith bedload sampler, 122, 123f
herbicides, lakes restoration, 202
higher organisms and lakes, 188
honeycomb frost, 65
Horton equation, 66
Hortonian overland flow, 83–84
Hydrodictyon, 147f
hydrograph, 84f
  separation, 87f
hydrologic cycle, 23, 24f
  annual water budget, 27–28
  earth's water balance, 26t
  reverse, 23, 24f
  storages and fluxes, 25
  volume of water, 26t
  water balance, 26–27, 26f
hydrology
  definition, 4
  quantitative analysis, 4
  stochastic nature of, 9
hydrolysis, 209
hypolimnetic circulation, 201
hypolimnetic withdrawal, 201
hypolimnion, 190, 192f

IBWC. *See* International Boundary and Water Commission (IBWC)
idealized stream channel, 88, 88f

infiltration
  curve, 61, 62f
  definition, 61
  equations, 66–67
  factors affecting, 64–65
  forces involved in, 62–63, 63f
  infiltration capacity, 61
  infiltration rate, 61
  measurement of, 65–66
  percolation, 61
  soil water, 61, 67–72
infiltrometers, 65
input-output analysis, 278
instantaneous sources, contaminant transport, 212–213
instream flows, 252
insulosity, 189
interception
  gross precipitation, 39
  loss, factors affecting
    canopy structure, 44
    ecoregion, 43
    forest management, 44
    meteorological characteristics, 44t
    seasons, 44
    vegetation type, 42–43
  measurement of, 40–41, 41t, 42t
  net precipitation, 39
  process of, 39
  stemflow, 39–40, 40f
  storage capacity, 39–40
  throughfall, 39
  total interception, 39
intermediate flow systems, 80f
International Boundary and Water Commission (IBWC), 260
international watercourse, 260
international water policy, 260
international watershed, 260
ion chromatography (IC), 143
ion-selective electrodes, 142
isohyetal approach, 33

Jackson turbidity units (JTUs), 117

Kemmerer sampler, 149, 150f
kriging, 33

lag time, 85
lag-to-peak, 85

lakes
  area, 188–189
  breadth, 188
  depth, 188
  evaporation, evapotranspiration, 56
  length, 188
  physical origin of, 187–188
  volume, 189
lakes and reservoir water quality
  biological characteristics, 192–194
  chemical characteristics
    Carlson Trophic State Index (TSI), 197t
    eutrophication, 196t
    oxygen, 194, 195f
    prediction model, 197–201
    productivity, 195–196
  physical limnology, 187–193
  restoration and management techniques
    algae techniques, 201–202
    macrophyte techniques, 202
land management, 64
landslides, 187
latent heat, 8
law, defined, 241
law of demand, 267
law of supply and demand, 268, 269
Leadership in Energy and Environmental Design (LEED) rating system, 261–262
Lemna minor, 156f
Leptodora, 152, 153f
light, physical limnology, 189–190, 190f
light and lakes, 189–190, 189f, 190f
limnology, 187
littoral zone, 192
load allocations (LAs), 248, 272
local flow systems, 80f
logging, 102
log landings, silvicultural activities, 234
log rules
  common (base 10) logarithms, 18
  and computing stage-discharge rating curve, 18–19
  natural logarithms, 20
longitudinal dispersion coefficient, 168–170
long-wave radiation, 53
lysimeter, 49, 49f

macroinvertebrates, 155f
  Beck's Biotic Index of benthic, 155, 156t
  stream condition, 155, 156t

macrophytes
  emergent, 159f
  floating-leaved plants, 157–158, 157f
  free-floating plants, 156f
  growth forms, 156
  pondweeds, 158
  submerged plants, 158–159, 158f
management objectives, 257
marginal benefit, 267
marginal cost (MC), 273, 277
market
  equilibrium, 269
  failure, 266
  water economics, 266, 267t
mass export and loading, 17–18
matric potential, 70
maximum contaminant level (MCL), 131
meander scroll, 188
mean lake depth, 188
mercury, 132
mesotrophic lakes, 196
metalimnion, 190, 192f
meteorite, 188
Microcystis, 147–148, 147f
minor ionic species, water, 130, 130t
mixing, water quality, 168
molar solution, 17
moles/liter, 17
monopoly, water supplier, 266
municipal separate storm sewer systems (MS4s), 247
Municipal Wastewater Treatment Construction Grant Amendments of 1981 (PL 97-117), 242t, 245

National Estuary Program (PL 106-457 and PL 108-399), 246
National Eutrophication Survey, 138
National Flood Insurance Act of 1968 (PL 90-448), 251–252
National Flood Insurance program, 252
National Oceanic and Atmospheric Administration—National Weather Service (NOAA-NWS), 27
National Pollution Discharge Elimination System (NPDES), 247
National Primary Drinking Water Standards, 131t
National Secondary Drinking Water Standard, 126

Index

National Water-Quality Assessment Program (NAWQA), 119t
National Weather Service, 30
Nationwide Urban Runoff Program (NURP), 15
natural logarithms, 20
Navicula, 148f
nekton, 192
nephelometric turbidity units (NTUs), 117–118, 118f
net precipitation, 39
net present value (NPV), 274
neuston, 149, 192
neutral atmosphere, 51
nitrogen, 136–139
    export coefficients, 139, 139t
    mass balance, 114, 114t
nonconservative pollutants, 205
nonconsumptive use, 258
nonmarket valuation techniques, 278
nonpoint source (NPS) pollution, 111, 111t, 112t
normal depth analysis, 92
nutrient cycling, 170
nutrient spiraling, 170

odor, 123–124
oil-grit separators, 218
oligotrophic lakes, 196
open lakes, 189
opportunity cost, 272
organic accumulation, 188
orographic storms, 29
Oscillatoria, 147–148, 147f
osmotic potential, 70
Ostracod, 154f
oven-dry water content, 68
overland flow, 34, 83
oxygen, 194, 195f
    sag curve, 178

paleolimnology, 194
partial areas, watersheds, 84
particulate pollutant transport, 205–206
pathogens in water, 162f–163f
    bacteria, 160–161
    detection methods, 160
    protozoans, 161
    viruses, 161
    waterborne diseases, 160
Pediastrum, 146f
pelagic zone, 192
Penman equation, evapotranspiration, 55–56

percolation, 61
perimeter control, 220
periphyton (Aufwuchs), 149
permittivity, 8
pH and carbonates
    acidic deposition, 132
    acid precipitation, 133–134
    bicarbonate, 132
    buffering, 134
    determination, 134
    dissociation constant of water, 132
    photosynthesis, 134
pharmaceuticals, hormones, steroids, 113
phosphorus
    export coefficients, 141t
    forms of, 139, 140f
    mass balance, 114t
    mean phosphorus concentrations, 141t
    median phosphorus EMCs, 141t
    precipitation and inactivation, 201
    soil index, 208
    sources, 139
    total dissolved phosphate species, 140f
photosynthesis, 134
phragmites, 159f
physical characteristics
    color, 125–126
    conductivity, 126
    odor, 123–124
    solids (residue), 119–123
    temperature, 124–125
    turbidity, 117–119
physical limnology, 187–193
    characteristics, 188–189
    lakes, physical origin of, 187–188
    light, 189–190, 190f
    seiche, 192, 193f
    thermal stratification, 190–191, 191f, 192f
phytoplankton, 192–194
piezometric surface, 75–76
plankton, 192
    phytoplankton, 145–151
    zooplankton, 151–154
plant uptake, 209
plasma emission spectroscopy (ICP), 142
pneumatic potential, 70
point pollution, 110–111
policy formulation, 256–257, 257f
pollutants
    conservative, 205
    nonconservative, 205

nonpoint sources, 7
point sources, 7
soil water, 205
sources, surface water, 111–112, 111*t*, 112*t*
pollution
point, 110–111
prevention, 218
sources of, 110–111
treatment, 218
pondweeds (*Potamogeton spp.*), 157*f*
porosities and saturated hydraulic conductivities, 78*t*
porous concrete frost, 65
potency factor, 205–206
potential evapotranspiration (PET), 56, 57*f*
potted plants and evapotranspiration, 49
precipitation
average precipitation methods
arithmetic approach, 32
isohyetal approach, 33
Thiessen polygon approach, 32–33
watershed boundary/mapping, 33–34, 34*f*
errors in measurements, 37–38
frequency analysis
probability of exceedance, 35
recurrence interval, 35–36, 36*f*
measurement of, 30–31
storms types, 29–30, 30*f*
pressure potential, 70
price elasticity of supply, 270
prior appropriation, 249–250
probability of exceedance, 35, 37
production function, 272
productivity, 195–196, 272
profundal zone, 192
protozoans, 161
Public Health Service Act (1944) (PL 78-410), 242*t*, 243
Public Laws (PL), 241–242
Pyrrhophyta, 148, 149*f*

quick flow, 83, 87

rainfall simulators, 65
rain gage
value, 30, 31*f*
in watershed, 32, 32*f*
Rawson's nomogram, 137*f*
reaction kinetics, 172–173
reactions, contaminant transport, 211

reactors, 175–176
response to different inputs, 176–177, 177*f*
reaeration, 180
reasonable use concept, 248
recharge zone, 78
recommendations, 257
rectangular suppressed weirs, 90*f*
recurrence interval (return period), 35–36, 36*f*
regional flow systems, 80*f*
relative humidity, 48
Reorganization Plan No. 2 of 1966, 242*t*, 244
Reorganization Plan No. 3 of 1970, 242*t*, 244
reoxygenation, 180
reserved rights, 250
reservoir watershed management, 104
rest-dose management system, 139
reverse hydrologic cycle, 23, 24*f*
riparian, 248
river continuum concept, 171
Rivers and Harbors Appropriations Act (1899), 242*t*, 243
river water quality
biological characteristics of, 171–172
chemical characteristics of
first-order reactions, 174–175, 174*f*
reaction kinetics, 172–173
reactor response to different inputs, 176–177, 177*f*
reactors, 175–176
zero-order reactions, 173*f*
dissolved oxygen, 178–184
graded stream, 171
headwater streams, 170
nutrient spiraling, 170
physical processes in
longitudinal dispersion coefficient, 168–170
mixing, 168
river continuum concept, 171
road and highway BMPs, 224–225
rotifers, 151*f*
round-off rule, 15
runoff (discharge), 83
data, 28
prevention, 218

salt/dye dilution technique, 92
saturated-source area flow, 84
scarcity, 269
Secchi disk, 149, 150*f*
Sedgewick-Rafter cell, 150, 151*f*

sediment
  basin, 221
  oxidation, 202
  removal, 201
  removal and tilling, 202
seiche, 192, 193f
seston, 192
shading and sediment covers, 202
shore development, 189
shoreline lakes, 188
shortage, supply and demand, 269
significant digits, 14–15
silvicultural practices, 232–235
single-ring infiltrometer, 65
skid trails, silvicultural activities, 233f, 234
snow fences, 103
snowmelt runoff, 103
snowpack management, 103–104
soil
  bulk density, 68
  evaporation, 70
  freezing, 65
  mass balance, 208, 209t
  matric potential block, 71
  moisture, 64
  moisture loss, evapotranspiration, 52
  quality, 113–114, 114t
  structure, 64
  suction (tension) and moisture content, 72
  texture, 64, 64f
soil water, 61, 67–72
  adsorption of pollutants on soil particles, 206–208
  amount of water, 68
  available water, 71–72
  energy status of water, 69–71
  field capacity (FC), 71
  gravimetric measurement, 68
  particulate pollutant transport, 205–206
  phosphorus soil index, 208
  pollutants, 205
  potential, 70
  soil mass balance, 208, 209t
  soil suction (tension) and moisture content, 72
  time domain reflectometry (TDR), 68–69
  toxic metals in soils, 209
  unavailable water, 72
  wilting point (WP), 71
solids (residue), 119–123
solute potential, 70
solution lakes, 188

sources of pollution, 110–111
specific energy, 70
Spirogyra, 146, 146f
spring turnover, 190
SRO. *See* surface runoff (SRO)
stage-discharge rating curve, 18–19
standards, 110, 241, 247
statutes, 241
Staurastrum, 146f
stemflow, 39–41, 40f
  measurements, 43
  and throughfall, 43
stomata and vapor pressure gradient, 48f
storages
  capacity, 39–40
  and fluxes, 25
stormflow, 83
storms types, 29–30, 30f
stormwater regulations, 247
stream corridors, silvicultural activities, 235t
stream crossings, silvicultural activities, 234–235
streamflow
  basin lag, 85–86, 86f, 86t
  components of, 84f
  flood frequency analysis, 93
  hydrograph separation, 87f
  measurement
    flumes, 89f
    idealized stream channel, 88f
    stream gaging site, 93
    velocity, 89–93, 89f
    velocity-area method, 88
    weirs, 90
  pattern, 102
  runoff processes, 83–84, 83f
  time of concentration, 84–85
  uncertainties in discharge estimation, 94
stream gaging site, 93
stream restoration, 104
Streeter-Phelps model, 178
Streeter-Phelps oxygen sag equation, 180–184
submerged plants, 158–159, 158f
submergence potential, 70
subsurface
  runoff, 83
  stormflow or interflow, 83
supply analysis, 273
supply and demand, 269
  management, 261
supply curve, 268f
supply of water, 268–269

surface runoff (SRO), 65, 83
surface tension, 8
surface water, 111
    pollutants sources, 111–112, 111*t*, 112*t*
suspended solids concentration (SSC), 119, 122
sustainable water management, 261–262
sustainable water resources systems, 261
Synedra, 148*f*

Tabellaria, 148*f*
TDS. *See* total dissolved solids (TDS)
tectonic lakes, 187
temperature, 124–125
    and infiltration rate, 65
tensiometer, 71
tent (ET tent), 50*f*
terrestrial radiation, 53
thermal potential, 70
thermal stratification, 190–191, 191*f*, 192*f*
thermistor, 125
thermocline, 191
thermocouple, 125
Thiessen polygon approach, 32–33
Thornthwaite equation, evapotranspiration, 54*t*
threshold odor number (TON), 123–124
throughfall, 39
time domain reflectometry (TDR), 68–69
time of concentration, 84–85
titration, 142
TMDL. *See* total maximum daily loads (TMDL)
TON. *See* threshold odor number (TON)
total costs, 273, 273*f*
total dissolved solids (TDS), 126
total interception, 39
total Kjeldahl nitrogen (TKN), 138
total maximum daily loads (TMDL), 247–248, 272
total solids, 119
total suspended sample analysis, 119–120
toxic metals in soils, 209
transpiration, 47
truck roads, silvicultural activities, 232, 233*f*
turbidity
    definition, 117
    drinking water regulations, 118
    ecological implications, 119
    industrial water supplies, 119
    Jackson turbidity units (JTUs), 117
    measurement, 117, 118*f*
    National Water-Quality Assessment Program (NAWQA), 119*t*
    nephelometric turbidity units (NTUs), 117–118, 118*f*
    particles in water, 117, 118*f*
    turbid water, 119
    U.S. Geological Survey (USGS), 119*t*
turbid water, 119

Ulothrix, 146*f*
unavailable water, 72
uncertainties in discharge estimation, 94
units
    conversions, 13
    kinematic properties, 12
    length, mass and time, fundamental units, 12*f*
    log rules, 18–20
    physical quantity, 11–12
    significant digits, 14–15
    water quality, 15–18
    water quantity, 15
urban stormwater BMPs
    green infrastructure (GI), 218
    nonpoint source pollution, 218
    planning and construction period, 220–221
    post-construction period, 221–224
    principles, 218–220
    road and highway BMPs, 224–225
    stormwater management practices (SWM), 217–218
urban watershed management, 104
U.S. Agency for International Development (USAID), 260
U.S. Environmental Protection Agency (EPA), 15
U.S. Geological Survey (USGS), 119*t*
USGS Hydrologic Unit Codes watersheds, 34

Van Doran and Kemmerer bottles, 149–150, 150*f*
variable costs, 273
variable source area concept, 84
vegetation management, 103
velocity, 89–93, 89*f*
velocity-area method, 88
velocity—head rod, 92*f*
viruses, 161
viscosity, 8
V-notched weir, 90*f*
volatile solids, 119
volatilization, 209
volcanic lakes, 187
volume development, 189
volumetric water content, 68
Volvox, 146–147, 146*f*

warm fronts, 29–30, 30f
wasteload allocations (WLAs), 248
water
  availability and use, 257–259, 258f, 259f
  banking, 266
  and environmental justice, 260–261
  properties and their ecological significance, 7–8
  quality, 7
  quantity, 5
  resources problems, 5–7
  structure, 4f
  uses, 6f
  world population curve, 5f
water balance, 26–27, 26f
  components, 12
  evapotranspiration, 52
waterborne diseases, 160
waterborne pathogens, 162f–163f. *See also* pathogens in water
water economics
  cost–benefit analysis (CBA), 277–278, 277t
  costs of production, 272–273
  definition, 265
  demand for water, 266–267, 267f, 268b
  economic effects, 278
  economic policy analysis, 274–276, 276t
  efficiency, 274
  elasticity, 269–271
  excludability, 265
  market, 266, 267t
  pricing, 276–277
  rival, 265
  supply and demand, 269
  supply of water, 268–269
  water externalities, 271–272
water externalities, 271–272
water level drawdown, 202
waterlilies (*Nymphaea* and *Nuphar*), 157f
water management, 261
water-milfoil (*Myriophyllum*), 158f, 159
water policy
  factors influencing, 255f
  international, 260
  policy formulation, 256–257, 257f
  sustainable water management, 261–262
  water and environmental justice, 260–261
  water availability and use, 257–259, 258f, 259f
  water resources, governmental jurisdictions, 256t

Water Pollution Control Act Amendments of 1956 (PL 84-660), 242t, 243
Water Pollution Control Act Amendments of 1961 (PL 87-88), 242t, 243
Water Pollution Control Act Amendments of 1972 (PL 92-500), 111, 242t, 244–245
Water Pollution Control Act of 1948 (PL 80-845), 242t, 243
water pollution trading, 272
water pricing, 276–277
water quality, 7
  criterion, 110
  definitions, 65, 110
  federal regulations and rules, 246–248
  federal water quality legislation, 243–246
  magnitude, of the problem
    ground water, 113
    pharmaceuticals, hormones, steroids, 113
    surface water, 111
    surface water pollutants sources, 111–112, 111t, 112t
  management, 110
  pollution, 110
  soil quality, 113–114, 114t
  sources of pollution, 110–111
  standards, 110, 247
  total maximum daily load (TMDL) process, 242
  zones, 170–171
Water Quality Act of 1965 (PL 89-234), 242t, 244
Water Quality Act of 1987 (PL 100-4), 242t, 246
Water Quality Improvement Act of 1970 (PL 91-224), 242t, 244
water quantity, 5
  basin transfers, 250–251
  drainage law, 251
  floodplain management, 251–252
  instream flows, 252
  water rights (law), 248–250
water resources, governmental jurisdictions, 256t
watershed, 33–34, 34f
watershed management
  experimental watersheds, 99, 100t
  forest (vegetation) management, 103
  reservoir watershed management, 104
  snowpack management, 103–104
  streamflow pattern, 102
  urban watershed management, 104
  water yield, 100–102
water-shield (*Brasenia*), 157f
water table aquifer, 75f

waterweeds, 158*f*
water yield, 100–102
weirs, 90
well effect, ground water, 80, 81*f*
white waterlily *(Nymphaea)*, 157
wild rice, 159*f*
wilting point (WP), 71
winds, 188
Wisconsin plankton net, 149, 150*f*
withdrawal, 257–258
WLAs. *See* wasteload allocations (WLAs)
Wolffia, 156*f*
world population curve, 5*f*
world water balance, 26*f*

zero-order reactions, 173*f*
zooplankton, 192–194